FROM THE BOOKS OF

THE ROMANTIC REBELS

JOHN KEATS

A PORTRAIT BY WILLIAM HILTON

THE
ROMANTIC REBELS

By
FRANCES WINWAR, pseud,
Author of "Poor Splendid Wings"

With Illustrations

BOSTON
LITTLE, BROWN, AND COMPANY
1935

Copyright, 1935,

By Frances Winwar Grebanier

Published November, 1935

THE ATLANTIC MONTHLY PRESS BOOKS

ARE PUBLISHED BY

LITTLE, BROWN, AND COMPANY

IN ASSOCIATION WITH

THE ATLANTIC MONTHLY COMPANY

PRINTED IN THE UNITED STATES OF AMERICA

To

BORIS A. BABOCHKIN

With Admiration for the Artist
and Esteem for the Friend

CONTENTS

ILLUSTRATIONS

THE ROMANTIC REBELS

PROLOGUE

TOWARD THE NEW CENTURY

THE nineteenth century opened bright with promise over the civilized world. At Weimar, seat of a renaissance in music, literature, and philosophy, Haydn's *Creation* was sung, telling the war-racked nations that God had fashioned the world and that it was fair. At the Court Theatre the Duke's players gave a masque written by the Olympian Goethe. Schiller walked absently among the gay maskers, his prophet's eyes peering into the future. Six years back, when the wise and hopeful of mankind had looked to the French Revolution for the torch that should light the world, he uttered himself: The French Republic would pass away. Anarchy would follow, and the murder of innocents. And then a despot would arise, crushing in his fist the greater part of Europe. The prophecy had partly verified itself. The rest was to be.

In London, that first of January of the new century, the bells pealed joyously and the cannon roared as a changed imperial standard floated over the Tower. In Dublin the jubilation found echo. At last, through Pitt's efforts, Ireland and England were united. The clangor of the bells had scarcely died down when it sounded again, hollow with disappointed hopes. The first United Parliament met in London. Pitt would have placed the Irish Catholics on the same political footing with their English countrymen. George III opposed it and Pitt resigned. Harsher disappointments, disasters more dire, were to fill the remaining years of his life — the bitter defeats of Ulm and Austerlitz, the death of Nelson, the insidiously encroaching grasp of Napoleon over the whole of Europe. "Roll up the map," he commanded, turning away his darkening sight from the chart of Europe that hung on the wall. "It will be useless for ten years to come."

His were not the only eyes averted from the shame of Europe. In the last decade of the closed century ardent spirits had built their perfect states upon the outcome of the French uprising against tyranny. Man was perfectible, they said. Each century marked a rung higher on his ascension toward the supreme order. Now he broke the chains of ignorance, now the fetters of slavery, physical and moral. The time would come, hailed Godwin, intoxicated with his dream of perfection, when there should be no ignorance, no inequality, no distinctions of sex, no death! Condorcet before him had seen the bright vision. Godwin elaborated upon it for the good of his benighted countrymen. His *Political Justice* came out at a price that only members of a perfected society could have afforded. Men on the seat of power read the prophecies of the dreamer and, shaken, clamored for the suppression of such dangerous heresies. Pitt had smiled benignly. "A three guinea book," said he, "could never do much harm among those who had not three shillings to spare." He was mistaken. The ideas promulgated by Godwin's book were blowing as free in the intellectual air as thistledown on a summer breeze.

Wordsworth seethed with republican fervor and in his unpublished *Prelude* hoped that the French, representing the cause of man, might win over England, the oppressor. He was in earnest, what though, not many years later, when his hopes had been deceived, he was to shout: —

> No parleying now. In Britain is one breath.
> We are all with you now, from shore to shore.
> Ye men of Kent, 't is victory or death.

Coleridge too, and Southey, disciples of the doctrine of perfectibility, were shocked, but did not lose faith at the bloody example of the French revolutionists. Somewhere in the world there must be a place where they, youths scarcely out of their teens, might test the sublime principles with the purity of their idealistic hearts. Yearningly they looked toward the West. There they could still find some patch of virgin soil where they might establish their pantisocracy. Each man with his negro, whom he would buy on purpose to free and educate, would work his field, tend his flock, and weave his cloth, not for himself, but for the good of all. The rustic cabins would know the luxury of shelves filled with the noblest fruits of the mind. Inspired by their own innocent living, they, too, would produce imperishable works, and with the collaboration of the pure and mild helpmeets who would join lives with theirs, they would found a robust and glorious race — of the perfect man! Susquehanna. . . . They dreamed of the fertile valleys and limpid rivers of the West that should see the birth of their ideal society, far from degenerate empires whose very air was corruption. "O Chatterton," invoked Coleridge,

> ". . . that thou wert yet alive,
> Sure thou wouldst spread the canvas to the gale;
> And love with us the tinkling team to drive
> O'er peaceful Freedom's undivided dale."

Ah, woe! They could not be the New Adam in their American Eden without first purchasing their emancipation with the vile dross of decaying England. Two thousand pounds, said the American whom they consulted, was the very least the young men could have for their ideal colony. Two thousand pounds — and all were penniless. Southey had his epic *Joan of Arc* that might sell. Coleridge would gain adherents to the Susquehanna paradise by expounding its benefits and blessings in luminous English prose. But moon succeeded moon, year followed year, and each brought its changes. Susquehanna, the pantisocracy, were blotted out by the blackest ink of reality. The idealists themselves were smirched.

Instead of paradises founded in the wilderness, the wilderness itself grew rank with the vices of the Continent. The Corsican upstart, after successively becoming general and consul, finally assumed the imperial crown. Francis II of Austria followed suit. Not to be outdone in this skirmish for a title, Dessalines, a negro in Haiti, created himself, with satire as keen as it was ingenuous, Emperor Jean Jacques I.

Tragedy, comedy, dreams, and frustrations, noble ideals and crass self-seeking, sober madness and mad sanity, whirled the sphere in a dance of passions. Into this unstable world Byron, Shelley, and Keats were born.

I

A WIFE'S AE SON

Brig o' Balgownie, black 's your wa',
Wi' a wife's ae son on a mear's ae foal,
Down ye shall fa'.

LITTLE George Gordon Byron never crossed the Bridge of
Don near Aberdeen, but the dark words of the prophecy
brought him to a halt at its arch as he gazed fascinated into
the black waters below. For he was a wife's *ae son*, and
though he rode no mare's only foal, still the bridge might heave
and totter, flinging him into the waiting depths. *Black 's your
wa'* . . . To the mind of the nine-year-old the words were
charged with sinister meaning.

Already the boy had known what it was to live in want,
though he was the bearer of two noble names and had the expectation of a title and a fortune should luck favor him. His
granduncle, the sole heir besides himself, had died in 1794 in
Corsica during the siege of Calvi; and the fifth Lord Byron,
the Wicked Lord, could have in the course of nature but few
more years to live. In fact, he had fewer left than Catherine
Gordon of Gight, widow of Mad Jack Byron, had dared hope,
and it was with undisguised emotion that one day in 1798
she heard that the Wicked Lord was dead and her "Geordie"
the next lord of Newstead. The boy received the news with
becoming gravity, but to his childish fancy it seemed the new
dignity must come accompanied by some physical change.
Perhaps his clubfoot might be straightened. However it was,
he looked at himself long and earnestly in the mirror and then
turned to his mother, asking whether she saw any difference
in him since he had been made a lord. "I myself can see
none."

Prophecy had been the stranger, welcome or unwelcome, at the chief crossroads of the Byrons and Gordons, uttering its croaking warnings. Catherine Gordon, reared in the midst of dour superstition, had her ears ever on the alert and sometimes went out of her way to catch the sibylline sooth. Once, at least, the words had proved too true, as she bitterly realized when counting over the meagre seventy-four pounds remaining from the sale of her worldly goods before she started out for Newstead with her son and his nurse. Seventy-four pounds the whole riches, besides the linen and plate, of the once wealthy heiress of Gight! But prophecy had spoken, and the words had fulfilled themselves.

When the herons leave the tree
The Laird o' Gight will landless be . . .

and, in the present situation, nigh penniless to boot.

She well remembered the flight of the herons which, ever since she could recall, had made their home on the margin of the Loch of Gight. For centuries, it was said, they had come there, year after year, generation after generation. But she had hardly been married to John Byron when in one vast flock the birds flew over the water. The land followed soon after, purchased by Lord Haddo, whose side of the lake the herons now honored. Still, if there were ill prophecies there were also good, and since her son's birth she had jealously nursed the knowledge that he would not only be a great lord, but a great man. A fortune teller had made the prediction — and it would be verified. His lameness was one of the signs.

Ill blood, if noble, flowed in the veins of the two families now united in the sixth Lord Byron. On the Gordon side there was a royal strain from a Stuart princess, daughter of King James I of Scotland and mother of Sir William, the first laird of Gight. A curse pursued them from the beginning; none seemed capable of dying a natural death. What with drowning and murder and execution, the Scotch ballad makers had rich material for their minstrelsy. For centuries, to the last Gordon, Catherine's father, fatality had hounded them. Like his father before him, George Gordon was found drowned. Some called it accident, some suicide. It was the Gordon fate.

When Catherine Gordon came to her own, she might well have called herself wealthy, and not alone for thrifty Scotland. She was by no means beautiful. Not even the canny Scots who viewed her with an eye to her fortune could find it in their hearts not to wish her a few cubits taller, or at least a span or two less broad. But she had good hair and eyes that made up for her wide mouth and short neck. And, too, she had a freshness of complexion that drew the carping eye from the shortcomings of her figure. She was allowed to reach the ripe age of twenty still unclaimed. However, she was not discouraged. Prophecy had spoken and she waited for her Byron: she knew his name through a strange revelation.

She had gone to the Edinburgh theatre one night to see Mrs. Siddons as Isabella in *The Fatal Marriage* (woeful omen!). The house was packed close that June night and the heat unbearable. What with the weather and the Siddonic rending of her emotions, Catherine Gordon fell into hysterics in her box and had to be carried out. That in itself was nothing, for many were the cases of Siddons fever that had to be treated by the Edinburgh physicians. The name Catherine screamed, so loud that it was heard all over the house, was "Biron, my Biron!"

Captain Byron came to the summons. Whatever fairy godmothers had stood at the cradle of Catherine Gordon of Gight must have spread out their copes to keep out this weird, but a power beyond them let it come to pass.

John Byron was the elder son of the seafaring Byron whom his shipmates called Foulweather Jack. He had been a veritable Jonah on shipboard. The first vessel on which he was midshipman struck on a reef off the coast of Patagonia. He turned it to his uses by writing a narrative of the wreck, the mutiny, and the "great distresses." A few years later he made a trip around the world for purposes of discovery, charting nothing but barren seas for the glory of England. Then the American Revolution broke out. Raised to the post of vice-admiral, he was put in command of a fleet, only to head against a storm on the day of sailing and sink one of his ships. Warned, perhaps, by his father's mischances, young John

Byron became a soldier and distinguished himself chiefly by his mad recklessness and his conquests of women.

Mad Jack, however, did his part with the Guards in the American war, and when he returned to England he looked about for those fruits of peace that come accompanied by a wife and a fortune. That the wife was already another's and the fortune still to come daunted him not at all. He was only twenty; life could still wait for him. The Marchioness of Carmarthen, wife of the Lord Chamberlain, in the meantime gave him all she could and bided her time. Very opportunely her father died. Immediately the Marchioness, now become Baroness Conyers, with a yearly income of four thousand pounds for life, left her honorable lord and eloped with the handsome captain.

The four thousand pounds were as wind-blown chaff in the hands of the gallant John Byron, now husband of Lady Conyers through the courtesy of the Lord Chamberlain, who obtained a divorce and kept his three children. But England became impossible as a place of residence for the baroness and Mad Jack. In France, on the twenty-sixth of January, 1784, Augusta Mary Byron was born, endowed only with the beauty and frailty of her parents. Lady Conyers died a few days after the birth of her child; her income ceased with her.

Captain Byron, with no money and a child to provide for, lost no time in going a-wooing. The magic "Biron, my Biron" haled him to Scotland, where the heiress of Gight succumbed at once to his ravishing face. What though the Duffs, on her grandmother's side, railed against the Sassenach and bade the girl beware! What though the minstrels sang the fate of foolhardy heiresses who gave their hearts to strangers! Catherine Gordon had a mind of her own, and once she made it up there was no changing it. Her heart was more constant still. In its virgin soil her love of the gallant captain took root so deep that it possessed her whole being. Let the birds of ill omen croak. She had her Byron and she was happy. They were married at Bath on the thirteenth of May — an ill date. Lady Conyer's Augusta was fifteen months old.

If the bards had made their pibrochs wail before the wedding, they raised them to shrillness when they saw the heiress's

money and bank shares scattered like dead leaves in a squall.
The lands of Gight were going to rack and ruin. The deil
himself had made his home among them.

> O whare are ye gaen, bonny Miss Gordon,
> O whare are ye gaen, sae bonny and braw?
> Ye 've married, ye 've married wi' Johnny Byron,
> To squander the lands o' Gight awa'.

> The shooten' o' guns, an' rattlin' o' drums,
> The bugle in woods, the pipes i' the ha',
> The beagles a howlin', the hounds a growlin':
> These soundings will soon gar Gight gang awa'.

Whatever else the *soundings* may have done, they succeeded
in frightening away the herons of the Hagberry Pot. The
money from the sale of the lands of Gight took wing with
them, and the salmon fisheries on the Dee were parted with;
yet the proceeds scarcely satisfied a handful of the creditors
that Captain Byron had in a long train behind him. As once
before, he had to flee with his wife to France. Now that the
heiress of Gight had lost the gilding that had made her attractive, Captain Byron solaced himself with other charmers,
leaving her to take care of his child Augusta. The poor woman
struggled tight-lipped through it all, rearing the babe, living
in poverty, but in her brave Scots way making the best of the
weird she had to dree. She still loved her gallant captain
and could not deny him, though she knew of his chambermaids.
The most she could do was to vent upon him the violence of
her temper, — a match for his, — throwing about whatever
she had within reach and at last tearing her dresses to shreds.

If creditors had been importunate at home they were clamor-
ous and insistent abroad, what with the queue the gallant
captain had managed to annex through his gambling and
escapades. And now Catherine Gordon Byron found herself
pregnant.

It was a time of darkness and discouragement. The captain's ways, far from mending, took on more dangerous courses.
The forsaken heiress finally decided to return to England,
where at least she would have understanding ears for the long

tale of her complaints. On the twenty-second of January, 1788, her son was born in Holles Street, London. At his baptism the Duke of Gordon and Colonel Duff of Fetteresso stood godfathers. But the infant George Gordon Byron inherited nought but his high-sounding names. Before his birth his half-sister Augusta had been sent to live with Lady Holderness, Lady Conyer's mother.

Yet even London was not home to Catherine Byron. With her infant she was still alone in the midst of strangers. Captain Byron had pleasanter ways of spending his time in Paris and Chantilly than beside a dowdy wife and a squalling child. When debts became pressing he took passage to Dover — then a fleeting visit to London and the lean but nonresisting purse of his wife, and once again to his high-living friends and complaisant chambermaids. The rumblings of approaching social upheaval meant little to ears pricked up to the jingle of his few pleasure-giving louis. Catherine Byron went home to Scotland.

It was a sad return for the once-sought-after heiress. House and land, fisheries and bank shares, were gone — gone as at the wave of a magician's wand. All that remained for her and her child was a meagre pittance of one hundred and fifty pounds a year, and that thanks to the foresight of the lawyers who had seen the guineas as well as the pence streaming out to the ocean of debt. With May Gray, her Scotch maid, Catherine Byron took lodgings in Queen Street, Aberdeen, and awaited the coming of her laggard captain. He arrived in due time, handsomer, more irresistible, more exacting than ever. But now Catherine had her young son to think of and could steel herself against Mad Jack's demands for money. Life together became a continual storm, with the crash of china mimicking the larger explosions of nature. The captain found it inconvenient sharing the same apartment with his wife; she set up lodgings a little farther up the street. Certain afternoons the curious neighbors would watch the fine gentleman with the bonny face walk to the end of the street to visit his squat dame. After tea, he would return to his rooms. Sometimes he was seen talking to the nurse and his baby. Once the child was even allowed to spend the night

with him. But that was not again repeated. The captain
had had enough of young Geordie.

Then suddenly he left Aberdeen and was seen no more.
With the help of Catherine, who to the end could not resist
him, the captain crossed for the last time to France. Their
separation was complete. What need to follow the closing
year of this wayward moth? He plunged into the thick of
the French Revolution without knowing what was happening
about him, as in his boyhood he had fought in the American
war, heedless of anything but the adventure. While a Condorcet observed the bursting chaos and saw it big with the
dream of a sublime brotherhood of perfected man, Captain
Byron noted only the pretty ankles of the dancing women.
At the birth of a world he thought only of his own pleasures.
"Un clou chasse l'autre, and I believe I have had one third of
Valenciennes," he boasted, "particularly a Girl at L'Aigle
Rouge." [1]

He died in 1791 at the age of thirty-six. Catherine Byron
was not told by her sister-in-law, Mrs. Leigh, that there had
been indications of suicide. "Send me some of his hair,"
begged Mrs. Byron, faithful to the last. She felt the death
of her husband deeply and violently, and all of Queen Street
resounded to her grief.

But she had her son, in whom his father's features made the
captain live again. As ungovernable in her passions as she
was in her temper, she would now fondle the child, swearing
his eyes were as beautiful as his father's, and now waddle from
room to room after the limping boy to inflict punishment, calling him a "lame brat." The name seared itself forever in
the sensitive boy's mind, and he could never forgive the un-
couth, fat, ridiculous woman who was responsible for his lameness and then blamed him for it. Throughout his mature life
he accused her. Had she not been perversely modest at his
birth the doctor would not have injured him.

But more than Catherine Byron's modesty had been to
blame for the boy's lameness. When he was born he was a
perfect baby, both his little feet as beautiful and well-formed
as the rest of his body. As he began to toddle, however, it

[1] Quoted by Maurois in *Byron.*

was noticed that his left foot turned over from the heel; the Achilles' tendon was paralyzed.

The child took his deformity with unchildlike bitterness, aware, as he early became, of his otherwise extraordinary beauty. Whenever he walked with May Gray through the streets of Aberdeen, the good women would stop to admire the auburn-haired lad with the flashing eyes; but woe to them if they spoke pityingly of his lame foot. Then those eyes would shoot fire, and little Geordie would strike blindly with whatever he happened to have in his hand. Together with the Byron beauty he had inherited the Gordon temper.

Yet he could make fun of his deformity with a cool irony that would have been sad in a man but was tragic in a child. There was another lad at Aberdeen who limped as he did. "Come," Geordie Byron would say, laughing, "come and see the twa laddies with the twa clubfeet going up the Broad Street." That gift of laughing away the things that would else have been intolerable came to him early in life.

Mrs. Byron spent every penny she could spare consulting doctors to straighten the limb of her little "crookit deil." Ointments, massages, cruelly painful machines were prescribed. May Gray carefully tended her young master every night before bedtime, and to ease the pain she would distract him by singing the Psalms or telling in a hushed voice some legend whose wonder made him forget the anguish of the moment. And so, with Suffering, Comfort, and Faery at his bed head, the child was lulled to sleep.

Despite the torture, the limb was not straightened. Yet his disability did not prevent Geordie from joining in the sports of his playfellows and trying to outdo them. He had acquired the trick of standing on his toes without tiring, and in this position, like a bird half poised for flight, he would pummel and fully "pay off" some tyrannical aggressor.

When he was hardly breeched the lad was sent to Mr. Bowers's day school in Long Acre, Aberdeen, to learn reading at five shillings a quarter. There were some that said Mrs. Byron resorted to this expedient for keeping her "little deil" quiet because of its cheapness. Certain it was that, though Geordie's memory developed, he did not learn his letters.

"God made man. Let us love him." He repeated to admiration the first page of his reader. But alas, when he turned to the second page under the admiring eyes of Catherine Byron, and, deceiving rogue that he was, repeated what he had learned by rote, the failure of that first year was shamefully patent and his ears were soundly cuffed; "which they did not deserve," Byron would say in later years, "since it was by ear only that I had acquired my letters."

Under Mr. Ross, the clergyman, he learned that Aberdeen was not the whole world, that there had been fairer cities built thousands of years ago, and that in Rome stood great acres of ruins whose every fragment marked a memorable deed. And so the boy read avidly in Roman history, learning stories far more wonderful than any May Gray had told him at bedtime. Some day he would see those ruins with his own eyes. Mingled with these Roman tales were stories from the Scriptures to which the child listened with varying emotions. And there was the expounding of the true faith.

From May Gray he had learned, as well as his childish understanding could grasp them, the fearful teachings of a stern Presbyterianism. Mr. Ross, and later young Paterson, who taught him his Latin out of Ruddiman's grammar, made clearer to the infant mind that God is omniscient. And that, since God is omniscient, He knows all from the beginning to time without end. Not a leaf stirs but God knows of its every stirring and every motion. Not a sunbeam lights up a million motes of dust but the motion of every mote is known to God from the first. As with the mote, so with every man and woman and child. Each had a destined place in the scheme of eternity. There were the blessed who from their birth could do nothing to rob them of their garment of blessedness. And there were the others who, in God's mind, from the beginning, had been destined to eternal damnation. Do what they would, they could not escape their divine predestination.

But what if the blessed wrought evil and the damned good? Should not the doer of good deeds be saved and the other lost? . . . In God's mind there was no vengeance. It was not reward and punishment.

But why be good, then, if you are destined to be lost? . . . Man's finite mind does not know; act as if you were destined to be saved.

But what if a king is of the damned and his servant of the blessed? . . . This is the true teaching; this is the true equality: for all the seeming injustices of fortune, the servant may be blessed above the master.

What was he, George Gordon Byron? Where had he been in God's mind? When he thought of the father so dimly remembered, and of the stories he had learned of the Gordons and the Byrons from May Gray, he was afraid to answer, though he felt he knew.

Enchanted days of childhood that, like April's, cannot be long clouded — how much there was in their twenty-four hours to fill the light and dark with patterns of delight! There was that glorious summer passed in the Highlands when he was recovering from scarlet fever. For the first time the lowering Lachin-y-Gair reared itself before his eyes, and from then on the love of mountains and majestic solitudes possessed him. In their presence he felt at home, and dead voices rose and spoke to him.

Then came the visits to relations at Fetteresso, at Banff — Banff, whose name was always to be associated with his first love. He was nine years old; Mary Duff, who had been sent to live with her grandmother after her mother had been guilty of some sin the children could not understand — Mary Duff was slightly younger. Throughout his life the hazel eyes of the little girl haunted him, and the memory of those days at Aberdeen when Mary's baby sister Helen had played with her doll while he and his cousin sat "gravely making love." His was a mind that was touched more deeply than his heart. The image of Mary Duff was laid away as in a private gallery; it was something of his own that no one could take from him. He was sixteen when he learned that Mary had married, and the news brought on something like a fit. The lovely creature he had possessed in his imagination was no longer his; the private gallery had been rifled. He resented the loss with all the passion of his Byron blood, even though at the time he was in the throes of a far more significant upheaval.

Life was to change much for George Byron after his grave love-making with little Mary Duff. Sooner than he expected he was called upon to assume the responsibilities of his rank under the guardianship of the only near relation who could be found to take charge, and that reluctantly. Lord Carlisle, a nephew of the fifth Lord Byron, had neither love nor respect for the ungainly Scotswoman who came with her lame son to take possession of the Newstead estate. True, she was a descendant of the Stuarts; to Lord Carlisle she seemed more like the village charwoman. He took the boy in hand, therefore, with no enthusiasm, and accomplished his duty to the letter. But only to the letter.

An odd little farce, with Mrs. Byron as the stage director, marked the entrance of the new Lord Byron to his domain. Mother and son, and the faithful May Gray, had just reached the toll lodge. The ancient forest spread out before them; the abbey raised its gate spires in the distance. Approaching the tollhouse woman, "To whom does this place belong?" Mrs. Byron asked innocently. "To Lord Byron, ma'am, and he's been some months dead." "And who's the next heir?" again inquired Catherine Byron. "They say," said the woman, "they say it's a little boy who lives in Aberdeen." "And this is he, bless him!" cried May Gray, entering into the spirit of the skit. And triumphantly the three walked in.

What had Catherine Byron meant? Perhaps it was her way of telling the world that the heiress of Gight, who had not a square inch of land left in her native soil, was the mother of one of the noblest heirs in England. It was her proof that virtue at last had its reward.

The grand old abbey, alas, proved on closer view to be nothing but a magnificent ruin, but a ruin filled with how many associations for the expanding imagination of the boy! There were the ivied walls, more romantic, because his own, than the castles of legend. They said a White Lady haunted the gallery, and a Black Monk of the Augustinian order that had founded the abbey of *Sancta Maria Novi Loci* (New Stead), in propitiation of a Pope by a king, wandered through that pile from which his brethren had been cast out in the reign of a monarch who broke from another Pope's authority.

One holy Henry rear'd the Gothic walls,
And bade the pious inmates rest in peace;
Another Henry the kind gift recalls. . . .

That was when all over England the fair lands and gardens
tilled for the Church were seized by Henry VIII and given
over to reward his favorites. The second Henry's Augustinian
abbey went with them. What if the poor who lived on the
charity of the monks had the bread taken out of their mouths
and gnawed stones, and perished on the wayside? Lords and
barons found their estates enriched. Tithes that had gone for
the work of God served for the wars and costlier luxuries.
Sir John the Little with the Great Beard, a Byron, had no
reason to lament his king's feud with the Church of Rome.
Let Henry have all the wives he desired, with or against the
Pope's will. He, Sir John the Little, had acquired one of the
finest parcels in all England. There was his portrait on the
abbey walls for the boy lord to admire.

More ancient still was the nobility of the Byrons. In the
Doomsday Book, Ralph de Burun laid claim to his lands in
Nottinghamshire. During the Crusades Buruns and Byrons,
the same under different names, had fought against the infidel — witness those carvings in the panels of the huge, dark
bedrooms. The young sixth Lord Byron gazed at them in
awe. What ancestor of his had he been who in the armor of
a Christian soldier stands beside a dark Saracen? And who is
that fair lady beside the Moor? One whom that ancient
Byron had loved? There she is again, in another room,
guarded by two Saracens with great, staring eyes. Who was
she? Did her blood mingle with the varied strains in himself?
Or was she indeed, as some maintained, an allegory of the
Christian Church? A strange allegory. . . . He preferred
to think of her as one of the mothers of the race. Byron
women had played their part in history. There was one who
had been a king's mistress, to the profit, in lands and power,
of her husband — bless her! In the Civil Wars had they not
all, men and women, "been passionately the king's"? Under
the first Charles one of them had been made Baron Byron,
bringing to the estate the rich lands of Rochdale. From
Cressy, Bosworth, and Marston Moor, through Edgehill, where

seven Byrons shed their blood in the field, to the American war in which his own father had fought, the men of his race had been courageous adventurers. Perhaps he, too — But it was too early to think of that.

It was pleasanter for the moment to wander through the abbey and the grounds, the lord of the manor, though goodness knows, as Catherine Byron complained, he seemed only to have inherited a worthless pile. She could not get herself to forgive the wicked man who had destroyed the valuable timberland and let the place go to ruin. Indeed, like the people of the countryside, she was tempted to believe he had been the devil himself, worse than his two stone henchmen rearing their horns in the wilderness of the garden.

Indeed the old lord had left a savor of brimstone behind him. In his irascible middle age he had been tried for the death of his cousin and neighbor, Mr. Chaworth, in a trivial quarrel over the game in their preserves. After the testimony the court of peers decided that since Chaworth had died in a duel, Lord Byron had not been guilty of murder but of homicide. He returned to Newstead. Little by little the Byron was dropped and he came to be known only as the Wicked Lord.

The little boy from Aberdeen listened intently to the stories he gleaned from old Murray, the lord's remaining servant, and from May Gray, an expert at collecting tales. There, in the bedroom, hung the sword that had run Mr. Chaworth through. Were those marks of blood upon it? There was the brace of pistols the old man had always carried with him. What mysterious kinship had brought out that trait in the child Byron, whose cherished toys were the miniature pistols he had thrust into the pocket of his first boy's breeches?

He walked bravely through the gloomy vaulted halls, knowing of the Black Monk but hoping he might not show himself — not yet — not for a long time. His apparition was said to bring disaster to living Byrons. What grim retribution was it? Why had not the guilt died with the king who had stolen the possessions of the Church? The monks themselves had not always been men of God. There was that brass eagle that had been raised, not so many years back, from the bottom of the lake at Newstead. The monks had cast it in for safekeeping when they had been ordered out of their abbey by Henry VIII. In the body of the brazen bird the charters of Newstead were found, and a paper signed by still another Henry,— the Fifth, — granting the monks full pardon for crimes committed to a certain date — except *murdris*. Why should a ghostly monk whose brethren perhaps had murdered set himself up as a nemesis of the Byrons?

Round that same lake young Byron was shown the remains of small stone forts with which the Wicked Lord had been accustomed to amuse himself after his lady had left him for his cruelty and his favorite son had married against his will. The eccentric hermit, unable to wrestle against the powers of evil within himself, fought out his sham battles with old Murray to help him. He had ships of war built, small models of a private navy which he pitched one against the other in a warfare that held none knows what cryptic meaning! One of these ships had had to be transported on wheels from the shipyard to Newstead. The country people, mindful of Mother Shipton's prophecy that when a ship freighted with ling traveled dry across Sherwood forest the Byrons would lose Newstead, flung sheaves of heather upon the toy vessel as it passed by. The prediction had not yet come true; but predictions bide their time.

Yet it was a far cry from the Newstead of the past to the Newstead of the young lord's inheritance. In the days of James I, even when the family was not at the height of its prosperity, more than sixty servants had been in the great household. Now there was Joe Murray, with a helper or two, and before Catherine Byron came there had been "Lady Betty," the old lord's servant mistress. The fine wainscoted rooms had been allowed to house swarms of crickets that overran the place, the queer old man-hater taking them under his protection and allowing them to crawl and hop over his body. On the day of his death, "Lady Betty" recounted that they left the rooms in a cloud, thousands of them, for now there was none to feed them. Perhaps they were the only living things that regretted his dying.

It was soon apparent to Catherine Byron that she could not settle at Newstead with her young lord in its present state. She might as well have tried to make a home of Stonehenge.

Besides, there was no money but the hundred and fifty pounds a year that her lawyers had set aside. In her shrewdness, by pulling what strings nobody knows, she contrived to be placed on the civil list for a pension — was it perhaps in ironic recognition of Mad Jack's American adventures? However it was, by the king's command, and under the signatures of W. Pitt and S. Douglas, Catherine Byron was granted an annuity of three hundred pounds, a fortune in her thrifty hands.

Newstead was abandoned for the time, and mother and son again moved to lodgings with the reliable May Gray. But a young oak had been planted by the romantic boy in the garden of Newstead. It should be *his* oak. As it throve, so should he thrive. He already felt himself the hero of some extraordinary fate.

In Nottingham and London, where he followed his mother, a last attempt was made to straighten his wretched foot. New machines were applied, new agonies borne in vain. A shoe was devised at last that lessened the discomfort and made the foot appear like other people's — except when he walked.

Under the supervision of Lord Carlisle the boy's education was taken in hand, if anything so summary could be done under the tyranny of Mrs. Byron, at once doting and capricious. The boy was prepared for Harrow, but Lord Carlisle was estranged forever. Duty alone held him to his trust.

Again young Byron fell in love, this time with Margaret Parker, another cousin, a girl of thirteen. She was a beautiful being in whose pure features the boy's wordless dreams found expression. "She looked as if she had been made out of a rainbow — all beauty and peace." But she died. Finding common words too brutal for his loss, the grieved lad wrote his first groping verses.

> Hush'd are the winds, and still the evening gloom;
>   Not e'en a zephyr wanders through the grove,
> Whilst I return, to view my Margaret's tomb,
>   And scatter flowers on the dust I love. . . .

Dull they were, and unoriginal, but the colors of Margaret's rainbow beauty and its remembered peace soothed the vague longings of his heart.

II

THE YOUNG PHILOSOPHER

THE eminently respectable Mr. Hogg of York must have been not a little concerned at the full mailbag of his son Thomas Jefferson, returned home from University College, Oxford, for the Christmas festivities of 1811. Not a day passed but bundles of letters sped back and forth between Thomas and Percy Bysshe Shelley, son of the Tory Timothy Shelley, Member for New Shoreham, and grandson of the recently created baronet, Sir Bysshe Shelley of Castle Goring. It is well known that young men form emotional friendships during the impressionable years of adolescence spent at college, but never had there been anything like the epistolary plethora that accompanied the eternal brotherhood of Thomas Hogg and Shelley, two months his junior. Mr. Hogg and Mr. Timothy Shelley, the very pinnacle of conservatism, would have been more than alarmed had they been able to read a little of the correspondence that passed between their sons. Surely, never before had the postmen of the realm transmitted such inflammatory matter.

"O!" came from Field Place, the Shelley home in Sussex, "I burn with impatience for the moment of the dissolution of Intolerance . . ." a desire rendered not the less insurgent for the invocation to "Love! dearest sweetest power!" following close upon it. "How much superior are even thy miseries to the pleasures which arise from other sources!" A little farther the burning Shelley reverted to the hated theme with an icicle sharpness that boded ill for the state of his mind. "On one subject I am cool," he continued, "toleration; yet that coolness alone possesses me that I may with more certainty guide the spear to the breast of my adversary, with more certainty ensanguine it with the heart's blood of Intolerance,

—hated name! Adieu. Down with Bigotry! Down with Intolerance!"

Intolerance. More than a hated name, it was the too real monster of might over right, of the tyranny of strength over weakness, of parental injustice. It was the Goliath of society's imposed evils, to be slain by Shelley, a new David. How he was going to do it he had a clear idea. For a sling there was the power of the pen; for the stones, the just indignation of his mind, sent forth with the eloquence the eighteen-year-old author could command.

However, as in all abstract altruism, there was in this instance also a concrete, private motive which, like the snail in the cabbage patch, left its unmistakable track, for all it hid its horns. Young Shelley, unselfishness itself in all things, and so generous that he would take the coat off his back and his shoes off his feet for a needy stranger, felt not unjustified in expecting the world — in this case, his parents — to show him a tithe of that same generosity. It was not much he wanted, yet to the fervid mind of youth all that life held of happiness and beauty. He wanted his cousin Harriet Grove as his wife in the noblest, most idealistic sense. It was to be indeed "a marriage of true minds," such a marriage as needed no priest's mummery to make it holy. "I own it," he wrote months later to Hogg, "I desired, eagerly desired to see myself and her irrevocably united by the rites of the Church, but where the high priest would have been Love!"

However purely the guileless idealist looked upon the union, it is certain that Mr. Timothy Shelley and the Groves frowned so darkly upon such un-Christian notions that the platonic sky — at least for a month — was one vast cloud. Now all letters to Harriet from Bysshe, as the family called him, were intercepted by the Groves, and such heresy was found in them that they were relieved to have rescued their daughter from the toils of so dangerous a rebel. There had been enough to shock in the missives that came regularly from University College for Harriet. Bysshe would emancipate the child, would he? He would have her break the chains of convention and grow spiritual wings? He would demonstrate the fallacies of established religion and lead her to the true faith?

Let him go his heretical way. Harriet would go hers, as a proper wife to some worthy squire. Harriet herself made no grave objections.

Those had been pleasant days when she and Cousin Bysshe had worked together on his novel *Zastrozzi*. She had been fond of him, and both had considered themselves engaged. Under the spell of his great clear blue eyes that he brought close to one's face as he spoke, and that filled with a light as from an inner flame when he told of wonderful ideal worlds where there was no injustice, no Intolerance, she saw things as he saw them and reality was blotted out. The word *freedom* was ever on his lips, and to have had her soar on its wings would have afforded him his dearest bliss. But Harriet, though she had not feared to try a humbler flight, was dizzied and terrified when the solid earth she knew receded from her gaze, and, child that she was, she clutched at her parents for support. For them there was no flight. The good Sussex earth that had been their fathers' and was theirs should also suffice their children and their children's children. And so Harriet, with some relief, was married eventually to Squire Heylar.

Harriet's defection was a blow to Shelley. He had chosen her as the best of her kind; she had proved base metal. Like a female Atlas she had had laid upon her shoulders the structure of his new world, only to fall under its weight and shatter it. Worse, she herself became a clod beneath the ruins. "She is gone! She is lost to me for ever!" cried the grieved Platonist who believed in nothing less than eternities. "She married! Married to a clod of earth! She will become insensible herself; all those fine capabilities will moulder."

But if those capabilities were lost to him, there were others close at hand for him to develop. There was Elizabeth, the eldest of his four sisters, so like him that she might have been his twin. As she resembled him in feature, might she not have other, more important similarities? With the same ardor he had employed in awakening Harriet, he set about emancipating Elizabeth. She should be the New Woman, and his finished masterpiece he would lay at the feet of friendship. Hogg, his dearest friend, should fall in love with her, and Elizabeth with him. Thus, if he himself could not have the Myrrha of a regenerated race, Hogg would.

It was not long before the dream became reality in his mind, and Hogg was kept informed of the growing virtues of Elizabeth. The letters to York from Field Place now came fattened with enclosures composed by her. "I do not wish to awaken her intellect too powerfully," wrote the cautious preceptor, whose hopes were so high, however, that he, by anticipation, could hear "the expiring yell of Intolerance." "I wish you knew Elizabeth," he sighed. "She is a great consolation to me."

And the better to prove her worthy of joining that new brotherhood of mankind that he was eagerly awaiting, he enclosed a few stanzas of Elizabeth's written under his tutelage. Far different were they from the feverish ebullitions of Cazire, the pseudonym under which she had collaborated with him. The heat, though still there, was now expended on a nobler theme.

> All are brethren, and even the African bending
> To the stroke of the hard-hearted Englishman's rod,
> The courtier at Luxury's palace attending,
> The senator trembling at Tyranny's nod,
> Each nation which kneels at the footstool of God,
> All are brethren.

Ere this, however, Britannia stalks with Lion triumphant; Ocean echoes to shrieks of despair, and Earth is in a spasm of horror. The Andes in sympathy roar, and, not to be outdone, Ætna and Teneriffe, unmindful of latitude, stoop their brows. "The ice mountains echo, the Baltic, the Ocean," and even Spitzbergen, howbeit the author does not explain the cause of such geographic commotion. The gratified Shelley could not copy out all the verses, but promised to show Hogg "many more" at a future and more auspicious time.

Meanwhile Shelley's hurt still rankled, easing itself in vehement invective against the Monster. "I will crush Intolerance," he menaced. "I will, at least, attempt it," he amended wisely. Whatever solace writing to Hogg could not give him he endeavored to find in the accredited ways of Mrs. Radcliffe's heroes and those of "Monk" Lewis. For he was living a romance as sombre as any they had written. Should he commit suicide? He slept with poison and a loaded pistol under his pillow. "I did not die. . . . But can the dead feel; dawns any daybeam on the night of dissolution?" (The passage might well have figured in his wild *Zastrozzi,* the novel in the manner of Rose Matilda, for which he had received forty pounds from the publishers.) All of one January night he paced the churchyard, returning home so chilled that he could scarcely hold his pen for the daily screed to Hogg. "I will consider your argument against the Non-existence of a Deity," he announced ambitiously. A night in a churchyard gave ample scope for speculation. His writings and his friend's were duly shown to Elizabeth, the paragon in the making, who approved of Hogg's "little Essay." It coincided exactly with her "sentiments on the subject . . . indeed it has convinced her."

It was a harder task, however, to open her mind to that other theme on which the two reformers, rather, Shelley, never tired of writing — Anti-matrimonialism. Simply stated, it was Shelley's contention that a marriage is an agreement between two individuals allied in intellect and sympathy; it is not the decree that pronounces them man and wife. Matrimony needs neither legal nor religious sanction; it transcends both. As a true woman of the new era it followed that Elizabeth should be willing to take unto herself Hogg, — whom she had never seen, — without the conventional ceremony. Hogg, it is true, demurred and wrote many a defense of the established order. Happily for Elizabeth, she was spared the ordeal of committing herself. In the thick of the exalted romance she succumbed to scarlet fever.

Alas for human frailty! When Elizabeth convalesced from what had proved a siege of very serious illness, she so rejoiced in the life she had so nearly lost that she could not find the minutest flaw in her actual, recovered world. In vain her brother tried to lead her back to the vast expanse. The strait and narrow path pleased her mightily. Now no more poetic effusions on universal brotherhood; she was content with the prose of daily living. Worse, she forswore the sublime teachings, and whenever Shelley, with a tatter of hope still left, waved it before her as a flag of truce, she looked at him coldly and said, "This, then, is the honorable advice of a brother!" What scorn in those words, and what injustice! Such is the fate of the reformer. Such the reward of the idealist who would free woman from the indignity of Matrimonialism.

Mr. Timothy Shelley hardly knew what to make of his son, his first-born, heir to the considerable estate of the family when the miserly old Sir Bysshe died and he himself — God grant it might be many years hence — would be called to his Maker. He was forty years old when Percy was born that fourth of August, 1792, when the Continent was in a ferment of revolt and England overrun by *émigrés* — priests and nobles who were fleeing Paris, the seat of the mischief. Dangerous principles of equality were not only voiced abroad, but acted upon with the shedding of blood. England, so recently passed through an unpleasant experience with America, had reason to fear for the established order in this influx of revolutionary doctrines. There might not be a Field Place manor to be transmitted, in a state of greater prosperity, from father to son, what though, since the days of Edward I, the Shelley holding had grown richer and larger, like a snowball down the hill of time.

True, there had been foolish Shelleys, espousers of unpopular causes, like him who was executed by Elizabeth for an attempt to release Mary Queen of Scots. Of such Shelleys the less said the better. Now Sir William, Justice in the Court of Common Pleas, — a portly gentleman, painted, it was said, by Holbein, — Sir William had done credit to the name. You could see it at once in his ample, ermine-edged coat, in his shrewd, white-bearded face that looked down on his descendants from his canvas. He had known how to live well and wisely and his branch had flourished.

The family record became less illustrious as it traversed the centuries. There was Timothy Shelley, the present Timothy's great-grandfather, who had gone off to America to make his fortune in business, and had married a New York widow who made him the richer only by two children. He had been no great honor to the name. Bysshe, his son, Mr. Timothy's father, had done better in a practical way. He had at least married two heiresses, the second, Elizabeth Jane Sidney, a descendant of Sir Philip, the poet-soldier, bringing with her a substantial dower in land. Both wives, the one and then the other, had had the grace to precede their husband out of this vale of tears. The present Timothy Shelley, in expectation, long disappointed, of some day becoming heir to Sir Bysshe's title and estates, perused every morning the bulletin sent down by his father, and made some show of being happy at the old man's excellent health. Surely the Shelley fortune would prosper under Timothy's wise husbandry. Not only would he transmit it whole to his son, but he would add to it materially by wise investments. God grant him an heir worthy of his sacrifices.

Even as a child Percy Bysshe Shelley had puzzled his simple-minded, matter-of-fact father. He had been too beautiful for a boy, with his curling golden-brown hair, his wide blue eyes and sensitive mouth. As he had grown older that feminine loveliness had not left him, though there was nothing of girlish timorousness in the lad who used to wander out at night to pry into mysteries Timothy Shelley could never have conceived of when he sent a servant to follow the child. At Sion House, Dr. Greenlaw's academy at Brentford, which in its heyday, as the residence of the Bishop of London, had housed the Princess Pocahontas, the difference between his son and other men impressed Timothy Shelley still more forcibly. Fagged, tyrannized, tormented by the young bullies who easily detected an alien in their midst, he would bear patiently with their cruelty, seeking refuge from their roughness in solitude. When, however, their baiting became too brutal to be borne, he flew into such blind rages that he would seize anything, anyone, even some small boy, to hurl at his tormentors. Yet he was by nature a gentle lad who would step out of the way of the insect in his path rather than do it hurt. His pleasures he found in electrical experiments, in books, some of them the blue-covered thrillers at sixpence a copy that sent his imagination wandering over perilous regions, and in playing with water. Nothing, perhaps, gave him more pleasure than sailing some small craft, whether of driftwood or paper from the supply in his pockets, on any available stream or pond.

Some of his sports, however, were terrifying to his four young sisters, who adored him. He was a delightful companion except when he took out his chemical set or carried about in the dark a pot filled with blue flames that lighted his face and made him look like one of the ghostly creatures of whom he was ever telling them. That was after he had exhausted tales of the Great Tortoise in Warnham Pond, and the Great Old Snake that had lived hundreds of years in the garden, and of the Old Alchemist who had his abode in the garret, a presence the four little girls believed in, as they believed in everything Bysshe told them. Had not Bysshe's Great Old Snake had his venerable life shortened by goodness knows how many centuries through the careless scythe of the gardener? Those were magical days when their brother came home for the holidays.

The lad's preoccupation with strange, out-of-the-way things Timothy Shelley could not understand, nor could his wife, who shook her head and sympathized with the squire's consternation. A boy should be interested in wholesome sports like shooting and hunting. He should know the game in his preserves, and he should also relish eating it. The day he presented Bysshe with a loaded gun and sent him out to shoot with the gamekeeper, Mr. Shelley was horrified to learn that the youngster had kept his eyes glued on a book while he wandered docilely behind the servant, to whom he had left the business of filling the game bag. As for eating the game, the boy preferred a crust of bread and a pocketful of raisins to the most sumptuous pastry of the cook's art. No, it seemed hopeless to force this evanescent creature into the mould of a sturdy squire. It was with some relief that Timothy Shelley and his wife saw the advent of their sixth child, a boy whom they named John.

St. Leonard's forest on the outskirts of Horsham knew the footsteps of the youthful wanderer by day and by night, for was it not said that in those woods "the adders never stynge"? Not that Shelley feared them. Snakes and ghosts, fiends and hobgoblins, peopled his restless imagination, and when he did not weave them into tales for his sisters, he wrote them down for his own pleasure in the style of the terror novels then so much in vogue.   Gruesome phantasies they were, of betrayed love and eerie revenge.   When he was sent to Eton his urge for scribbling was at its height, and many were the pages he filled with prose and verse telling of how

> Her skeleton form the dead Nun rear'd
> Which dripp'd with the chill dew of hell.
> In her half-eaten eye-balls two pale flames appear'd,
> But triumphant their gleam on the dark Monk glar'd
> As he stood within his cell.

Ghosts of the blue books and *The Monk,* ghosts that were to reappear more gruesomely still in *St. Irvyne,* Shelly's second romance.

"Wolfstein has sped him into the château," he narrated grimly.   "He entered the vaults.   He fell on a body that appeared motionless and without life!   He raised it in his arms, and, taking it to the light, beheld, pallid in death, the features of Megalena.   The laugh of anguish which had convulsed her expiring frame, still played around her mouth, as a smile of horror and despair; her hair was loose and wild, seemingly gathered in knots by the convulsive grasp of dissolution. . . . He dashed the body convulsively upon the earth, and, wildered by the suscitated energies of his soul almost to madness, rushed into the vaults."

The dim world of the occult drew Shelley toward its shadows. His mind inflamed by his readings, he chafed it still more by attempts to raise spirits with the help of a handbook of magic. Even the charnel house of Warnham church held no terror for him as a scene for dark doings, and he contrived to spend a night within it to raise the mouldering bones of its grim tenants. Here indeed was a descendant of that legendary Sir Guyon de Shelley of the three magic conches, one of which had power over all enchantments; here too, though a trifle older, the curious boy who set fire to a faggot pile that he might enjoy "a little hell of his own."   Timothy Shelley had small influence over him; his submissive mother, still less.

What the boy could not find at home he sought elsewhere and fortunately found.   Dr. Lind, medical professor at Eton, became the guide to Shelley's tireless searchings.   A grand, benevolent old man was he, full of exciting tales of his early wanderings over the face of the earth, and generous with the accumulated store of his experiences. The light of his inquiring mind had not dimmed with the years, and received added fuel from the eager questionings of the lad at his feet, whose great, nearsighted eyes did not leave his own for a moment, whose hands ran through his long hair to calm the tumult of his thoughts. For hours at a time, before the hearth of Dr. Lind's room, age and youth strove to settle the problems of the universe, the old man resigned with the weight of life, the boy confident with budding power.

But besides the endless disquisitions there were practical experiments, when Dr. Lind, like the Old Alchemist of Field Place, caused many a wonder to come to pass. Here was magic, wrought with the captured lightning of heaven — a greater magic than that which Shelley sought "through many a listening chamber, cave and ruin," for where the other had failed, this worked before his infatuate eyes. From then on the boy's room was never without its electrical machine; retorts and alembics found place among his books and clothes, and there, on the sill of the brightest window, stood his beloved solar microscope.

More than guide the old man with the silvery hair became, in the boy's susceptible fancy a defender and a savior. Timothy Shelley by comparison was a despot who took advantage of his son's weakness to humiliate and crush him. The lack of sympathy that was all too apparent between them was magnified into hatred in the boy's imagination, and with the faculty he had had from his earliest consciousness of being carried away by his thoughts more than by actualities, he colored his father's actions in prevailing black. He told his friend Hogg later of a proposal so unnatural on Timothy Shelley's part that it were kinder to believe delirium had engendered it.

"Once, when I was very ill during the holidays . . . a servant overheard my father consult about sending me to a private madhouse."

The boy was in an agony of dread when the servant told him. He had three pounds in money put away. With the help of the man, he dispatched an express to Dr. Lind, who came to the rescue. "He dared my father to execute his purpose!" said Shelley with fire.

Yet in some things Timothy Shelley showed a certain appreciation of his son. A commonplace man himself, he was flattered that a boy of his should distinguish himself as an author, although he might have wished it were soldiering or some other manly sport. On the whole the Eton years were profitable. Timothy Shelley did not know, however, that Bysshe had acquired the title of "the Atheist," and that in the hours of recreation he would astound and delight his school fellows with an exhibition of cursing and anathema that would have put both Mr. Timothy and the hot-headed Sir Bysshe to shame.

Shelley's true development, however, came from his own chosen reading rather than from the instruction of the Eton masters. He reveled in the novels of the American Charles Brockden Brown. Lucretius and Pliny he read and read again, letting his speculative mind range over the book *De Deo*, where, for the first time, the gods of the ancients and the myths of their all too human frailties were soundly rated. Something in that criticism wakened a sympathetic response. Then there was Godwin's *Political Justice*, borrowed from Dr. Lind, which roused the young reformer to enthusiasm and hero worship. For him William Godwin became one of the world's benefactors, wresting Prometheus-like a measuring rod of lightning from the grasp of Tyranny. Alas that such men should die — for in his ignorance Shelley relegated the philosopher among the great shades, albeit at the moment Godwin was living in not silent obscurity behind his bookshop in Skinner Street within sound of Bow bell. Benjamin Franklin, too, Shelley read and admired, finding in him a confirmation of the power of man to subdue the forces of nature. Franklin, with Dr. Lind and William Godwin, was enthroned in his private pantheon, and under the stimulus of their ideas Shelley made a groping beginning in a poem that he was not to finish until several years later in the vision of *Queen Mab*.

Nevertheless the youth entered University College as a full-fledged author. Besides his published first novel and the

Victor and Cazire poems, he had the completed manuscript of his other romance, *St. Irvyne,* inspired indirectly by Godwin's *St. Leon,* and an additional poetic sheaf full of sound and political fury signifying a little less than met the eye.   Timothy Shelley accompanied his son to the college that had been his own Alma Mater, and on a visit to old familiar places introduced him, not without unction, as a lad "with a literary turn" to his friend Mr. Slater, who with his partner Munday kept a bookshop at Oxford.   "Do pray indulge him in his printing freaks," said he, unwilling to have it said of him that he withheld his part in encouraging the literary proclivities of his son.

It was a tall, stooping, delicate-looking youth, whose bushy locks stood out in an aureole, that joined the young blades of University College, all of them cropped to roundheads in the mode of the royal arbiter.   His clothes, well cut and of fine serge, were woefully rumpled about his spare person; one might have said he slept in them.   A well-shaped throat, feminine in its fullness, scorned both collar and stock and bared itself to the winds of heaven.   He had a cap, out of respect for some queer convention, but it was most often grasped in the hand, or stuffed in a pocket with a volume of the newly discovered Hume or Locke.

The Shelleyan paraphernalia were installed in his rooms on the first floor of the college in the corner looking out on the main quadrangle.   There the electrical bottles and wires, the chemicals in their phials, crucibles, and retorts, found their places with books and boots, as if "the young alchemist," said Hogg, "in order to analyze the mystery of creation, had endeavoured first to reconstruct the primeval chaos."   On the window ledge, receiving the fond attentions of the philosopher, stood the treasured microscope to which, countless times in the course of the day, an inquiring eye was affixed seeking to penetrate the secrets of invisible nature.

Before settling down to his studies Shelley went to London and sought out Stockdale the publisher, undaunted by the scruples his *Zastrozzi* had awakened in at least one sensitive breast.   "Not all his 'scintillated eyes,' his 'battling emotions' . . . ought to save him from infamy and his volume from the flames," anathematized the *Critical Review,* — so licentious did it find the romance, so lost the author to all sense of decency.

It was through Stockdale's offices that the *Original Poems by Victor and Cazire* — Shelley and his sister Elizabeth — had seen the light of print, and only of print, for hardly the light of any eyes save their authors' fell upon the pages. To Stockdale, too, was submitted the *Wandering Jew,* an epic collaboration of Shelley and his cousin Thomas Medwin, inspired by a tattered German fragment they had picked up at Lincoln's Inn Fields and destined to sink unpublished for many years into the Gothic darkness out of which it rose. Much had the authors hoped for it — fame, pocket money. Even Campbell of the *Pleasures of Hope* had been consulted about its publication; but not a jot of those pleasures had he to offer the aspiring poets. There were only two good lines in the whole poem, he said, and dismissed it at that.

St. Irvyne or the Rosicrucian had a happier fate. It came out, with due advertisement, under Stockdale's imprint, and to lend it weight it bore as the author "A Gentleman of the University of Oxford." That gentleman, now quaffing so fully of printer's ink and finding it good, promptly took out of his writing case the verses with which he had come laden and read them to Hogg, his newly acquired Saul.

Now Hogg, solid Yorkshireman that he was, greatly as he delighted in his friend's talents, could not fail to detect a certain falsetto in the revolutionary verses that jarred on his common sense as much as Shelley's excited declamation jarred on his delicate ear. He hesitated to make a harsh judgment, and instead offered a suggestion. Why not change the poems to burlesques?

There was a mad washerwoman, Peg Nicholson, who during the hot summer of 1786 had had some crazed notion of benefiting the country by attempting to assassinate George III. For her crime she had been imprisoned and was still living out her remaining years, no saner than before. But for the purposes of Shelley, who unconsciously thought all revolutionary virtue dead, she was made somewhat prematurely to join the departed. Shelley took on a kinship with her, and soon, through the courtesy of Mr. Munday, the bookseller, the *Posthumous Fragments of Mrs. Margaret Nicholson* appeared as an incongruously aristocratic quarto with an extravagance of margin and elegant type. The fragments were piously edited by her nephew, John Fitzvictor — son of the Victor who had made his first bow with Cazire.

The mad book, with its mingling of fire and smoke, sense and nonsense, became the vogue of a brief season at Oxford, whose sober gownsmen, Hogg was pleased to note, walked the quadrangles reading it, perplexed and amused.

The scholarly seclusion of college rooms pleased the young poet-philosopher. If he wanted privacy all he had to do was to "sport the oak" — in other words, to close the massive oaken outer door over the inner, which gave into the pell-mell of his sanctum. And sport the oak he did, against friend and intruder, when in the hours of study the youthful Faust raised a Mephistopheles of his own, whose fiery hoof marks were visible in charred holes on the carpets and the floor itself. A good part of the time, however, he spent in communion with the mighty spirits of the past, Euripides and Plutarch and Plato in Dacier's French translation, with nearer English philosophers, and in a correspondence so voluminous that it is remarkable he had leisure for anything else.

His was no mole-like seclusion, however. Though his mind delved into the wisdom of the past, he was fully aware of what was going on about him and, a Cato, he turned censor. A journalist and poet, Leigh Hunt, had got himself into the unfavorable notice of the ruling powers by his intransigent truthtelling in the pages of his four-year-old nursling, the *Examiner,* a Sunday paper which proposed to treat of politics, domestic economy, and the theatre. It tolerated no party leanings and offered no quarter to charlatanism. With his brother John, a high-principled publisher, Leigh had built up the paper until from a precarious beginning it had risen to a position of influence among the more liberal readers. The Tory forces watched it with an evil eye. At last Leigh Hunt was brought up on charges of libel, tried, and, wonderful to tell, acquitted. Shelley rejoiced as at a personal triumph. He must write to Hunt and congratulate him — more, he must devise some scheme whereby to guarantee the safety of free speakers, the illuminated ones of the world.

He took up his pen, therefore, and wrote to Hunt, expressing his pleasure at his acquittal and offering his scheme "of mutual safety and mutual indemnification for men of public spirit and principle. . . . Of the scheme, the enclosed is . . . the proposal for a meeting . . . of such enlightened, unprejudiced members of the community, whose independent principles expose them to evils which might thus become alleviated." Alas! How soon was he himself to stand in need of such a society "to resist the coalition of the enemies of liberty"!

With the whetstone of Hogg's mind on which to sharpen his own speculative wits, it was not long before Shelley was ready with views on religion and philosophy that demanded a wider audience than his friend and his correspondents afforded. He would write long demonstrations, therefore, in the approved way of Locke, and send them, under a pseudonym, to respectable clergymen with the implicit understanding that unless they disproved in writing the truths that met their astonished gaze, they were, Q. E. D., defeated. More than one honest dominus took pen in hand to confound the heretic or induce him to the ways of Christianity. The result was a treatise longer and more abstruse than the first, which silenced the poor clergyman forever.

Now there was one essay of Locke's on the *Human Understanding* that moved the disciple as not long before Pliny's *De Deo* had done. Shelley must write his demonstration of the nonexistence of an anthropomorphic Deity or die. He preferred to live, even though by now Harriet was lost to him forever. Accordingly, sporting the oak with a vengeance, he wrote an essay wherein he deduced with quotations in a plurality of tongues that since all faith rests on the perception of reason and the senses, and since their testimony is impracticable in proving the existence of a Deity, it is self-evident that under the circumstances atheism is justifiable. He called his treatise the *Necessity of Atheism,* and under that startling title it was announced in the *Oxford University and City Herald.*

No sooner was the pamphlet printed — Shelley himself,

perched on the compositor's stool, had helped to set the type —
than a supply of copies was left with Mr. Munday to sell to
fearless minds.   Indeed, like Æolus discharging all his winds
at once, in no time Shelley had strewn case and counters thick
with the tract while the bookseller looked on, not without misgiving.

Earlier than he expected the storm broke.   Irate dons con-
fiscated all the copies they could get hold of and made short
work of them in the back-shop stove.   But a goodly number
were wholly out of their reach, for the enterprising author had
decided to act thoroughly as his own distributor.   Many is
the *Necessity* that under an inoffensive wrapper carried worse
than the plague to England's churchmen.   Letters, arguments,
and proofs came for the elated philosopher whose teeming
mailbag turned the eye of suspicion upon him.

The morning of the twenty-fifth of March, 1811, the sported
oak was not respected, and a summons came for Percy Bysshe
Shelley to give an account of himself before a convention of the
University College authorities.   "Above all things, liberty!"
was the standard under which the rebel rode to the fray.

"Did you write this?" he was asked while the *Necessity* was
waved before his eyes.

With an inward glance at his invisible banner, and hugging
to himself Godwin's doctrines, Shelley answered neither yea nor
nay, incensed at being dealt with like a criminal for his efforts
to liberate the human mind.   But the judges had no lack of
proof.

Thomas Jefferson Hogg, who was held under suspicion for
being Shelley's friend, further incriminated himself on hearing
of the philosopher's predicament by offering to exonerate him
before the judges.   As often happens, the rescuer sank with
the drowning man.

The legal forms, however, were scrupulously respected by
the authorities, although their decision had been a foregone
conclusion.   The two miscreants were dismissed from the
august presences while they sat in solemn conclave in a
chamber facing the quadrangle.   Alas for the two shorn lambs!
Instead of hiding their shame in some dark cave, they sported
together on the green before the irate eyes of their henchmen,

who took their presence there, at that fateful moment, as an added sign of insubordination. The decision was pronounced. Later that day, a sealed document impressively signed by the hands of officialdom was posted on the hall oak, declaring by these presents that Percy Bysshe Shelley and Thomas Jefferson Hogg were thenceforth denied the benefits of University College.

They were expelled — "for refusing to answer questions."

III

ON THE PILGRIMAGE

WHEN the Lisbon packet left Falmouth in the summer of 1809, bearing Lord Byron on his first pilgrimage, he quitted the shores of England richer by three experiences. He had had his heart broken; he had published his poetical firstling; and he had taken his first revenge.

It was a nobly beautiful youth who, with the agility of a faun in spite of a slight limp, clambered into the boat. His hair, in clustering ringlets, framed a high forehead uncovered at the temples. His mouth, classically perfect, was only rivaled by the eyes, large, set wide apart. The grey-blue fire of the pupils smouldered more dangerously through the already famous Byron underlook, when the lashes half veiled but did not quench an expression that became dreamy passion, sensuality, mystic yearning — anything of perilous and magical that the susceptible read into it. His clothes were fashionable and well cut and moulded without a wrinkle a body trained, by what abstinence and exercise he alone knew, to the leanness of a greyhound's. Gone was the unattractive plumpness of adolescence. He dreaded fat as he abhorred ugliness, and goodness knows he had had both as living examples in his waddling, graceless, vile-tempered mother, whom he loved in his own way, and whom he despised. Besides giving him that cursed limb, she was responsible, too, for the tendency to fat that made him watch every morsel he ate. Beauty was not the only consideration; every pound of excess weight was so much more agony loaded upon his "little foot."

With Byron were a young page, old Murray, who was going with him as far as Gibraltar, William Fletcher, the valet, eager for the adventure yet loth to part from a newly wedded bride,

and John Cam Hobhouse, an "intellectual" friend from Cambridge who was to accompany him on his travels.   But the
spare, straight-haired, long-nosed, tightly-stocked, ascetic-look-
ing youth with the thoughtful, appraising eyes was going for
purposes of his own.   Adventure was a good thing, but the
fruits thereof were not to be neglected.   He fortified himself,
therefore, with dozens of quills, quarts of ink, and paper enough
to have lined the way from Falmouth to Lisbon itself, and set
down his impressions even on the gallant Captain Kidd's unruly packet. . . .

> Hobhouse muttering fearful curses,
>   As the hatchway down he rolls;
> Now his breakfast, now his verses
>   Vomits forth — and damns our souls.

Byron could afford to be merry.   He was a better sailor, and
as for wooing the muse, he did it as easily and propitiously as if
she were an earthly damsel; more easily indeed — he always
found her compliant.   Not that he ever intended courting her
again — at least he would try not to.   A young lord come of
age and into the possession of his family fortunes has manlier
sports to pursue.   Let Hobhouse drive his quills and utter himself on his shaky stilts.   In his heart of hearts Byron knew,
however, that he could no more keep away from her than could
Mad Jack from his "one third of Valenciennes" — and other
towns.

> 'T is done — and shivering in the gale
> The bark unfurls her snowy sail;
> And whistling o'er the bending mast,
> Loud sings on high the fresh'ning blast;
> And I must from this land be gone,
> Because I cannot love but one.

That one he carried in his secret gallery of affections, with
the empty frame of little Mary Duff and the phantom portrait
of Margaret Parker.   Mary Chaworth's, like an historical
panel in the style of the Italian primitives, stood out in aching
colors and vivid episodes.

It had all happened during a vacation from Harrow.   Unsuspecting, he left the passionate friendships of the youthful

nobles, Clare, Dorset, Delawarr, and Wingfield, the kindly guidance of Dr. Drury, and the seclusion of Peachey's tomb on the hilltop, where he would lie dreaming for hours, the wonder and admiration of less melancholic lads, to spend part of the summer at Newstead as guest of Lord Grey de Ruthven, who had leased the abbey for a short term.

Byron was ecstatic. He would now go, without his mother, to his beloved home. He would be free to wander through its gardens, to luxuriate in the gloom and mystery of the vaults, to be poetical in the cloisters, dreaming of vanished glories and glories to be. He would look at the little oak he had planted and clear the ground about it with his own hands. Lord Grey was young and had no care for trees, whose charmed significance he could never penetrate. For a few glorious weeks he would sleep under his ancestral roof. He need no longer gaze yearningly at its Gothic splendor from the little gatehouse where, to his mother's anger, he had several times spent the night.

The fifteen-year-old boy, all heated from the exciting but sterile attachments he had formed at Harrow, arrived eager and enthusiastic. Lord Grey showed himself a gracious host, if in the end a dubious influence upon a lad too quickly awaking to life.

In London Byron had come to know the Chaworths, tenants of Annesley Hall that bordered Newstead. Ties of blood had linked the Byrons with their neighbors, when the third lord had led his bride, a Chaworth, through the alley of oaks that connected the two houses. Blood had divided them when the Wicked Lord had too hastily drawn his sword upon another Chaworth.

Hardly had young Byron come to Newstead when he mounted his horse and bounded along the "bridal path" of oaks toward the ivied terrace of Annesley. Noble it was, though of a later and less storied elegance than Newstead. The double stair with its balustrade of stone, and the emphasis of massive spheres softened by leaf and tendril, ascended to a narrow walk. On one side, the formal garden; on the other a close weaving of ivy and climbing plants, following the arches of the wall; higher still, the massed tops of yews and gentler trees, floating like green clouds of sound and fragrance. This was the background of the first Chaworth episode; in the fore stood a slight bit of girlhood in a summery frock gently lifted with her light brown hair by the breeze that put the leafy clouds in motion. Mary Anne Chaworth, white and clear and calm, like a star at dawning — his morning star, the Morning Star of Annesley.

He breathed, he lived for the few hours passed in her company. She was seventeen, just two years older than he; this only added to her attractiveness. Through the grace of her girlhood one guessed at the grave beauty of woman. She was divinity itself to the lovelorn boy; heaven lay in the light of her eyes. He watched every curve of her lips, every stir of her bosom, for she sighed often. Sometimes she sat at her spinet and sang. Her sighs, her languor, her quavering sweet voice — were these all for him? Even the Chaworth portraits that he imagined had lowered ill-will upon him, the scion of the hereditary enemy, relaxed in the aura of such chaste rapture. Romance held nothing equal to this young love.

Next, — his blood always tingled at the memory, — next came that gay young party to the caverns of Derbyshire. Mary Chaworth of course was his chosen companion; he followed her as a shadow its body. The ferryman came with their little boat, slight and shallow and just wide enough for two. The grotto's roof overhung the water, so low that Mary and he had to lie stretched at the bottom, side by side, as the boatman, knee-deep in water, pushed the boat from the stern — "a sort of Charon," Byron thought. The skiff swayed; the bodies touched in the moment of tunneled darkness. . . . Charon? It was to no Lethe he led the boy, but to an inferno of emotions exalted to the pitch of anguish.

Mary Chaworth — wondrous name! She still sang her dreamy airs to the tinkling spinet; she still sighed prettily before the passionate schoolboy. But alas,

> Her sighs were not for him; to her he was
> Even as a brother,

and he wished to be so much more. All of man's potency was awake in him. When, or how, he made the discovery that

Mary loved another, it is not known.   In bitter jealousy he
learned that those soft looks had not been for him.   He had
basked in the beams of an orb lighted by the flame of another —
if the attribute of the divine Phœbus could have been given to
the rough-riding, prosy Jack Musters.   Disillusion came with
its dash of poison.

Late one night when the boy had accepted the hospitality
of the Chaworths that he might at least be under the same roof
with his lost one, — still so dear, — he overheard her voice and
another's.   The sense came distinct in the silence.   "Do you
think I could care anything for that lame boy?"   Mary had
spoken the words.   Those lips, upturned at the corners, must
have curled with a hint of scorn at the mention of his deformity.
A dagger's thrust had been more merciful.   Blinded with anger
and pain, hardly finding the way in the darkness, he left the
hateful Annesley and ran to the abbey.   But he could not remain long away.   Torturing though it was to be near Mary, it
was death to be parted from her.   The proud, high-spirited
Byron swallowed the insult in her presence; he spoke not one
word of the wrath within him when, with the unconscious
cruelty of happy love, she spared him nothing.   He went so
far as to defend her.   How could she, the Morning Star, love
a fat, awkward schoolboy who limped?

The vacation came to an end.   Byron did not return to
Harrow.   In vain Dr. Drury wrote; in vain Mrs. Byron expostulated with the truant.   He stayed on at Newstead, gal-
loping faithfully to Annesley for the daily flagellation and the
cup of pain.   He missed a whole term of school.   What was
school to a youth smarting under a hopeless love?

Another episode and the panel was finished.   Mary Chaworth had married Jack Musters.   She had borne him a child.
Perhaps in kindness, perhaps to gloat over an unsuccessful
rival, Jack Musters invited Byron to Annesley.   For the last
time he saw Mary, graver but more beautiful to his partial
eyes.   She turned her gaze upon him.   Did it waver at sight
of that slender young god, as different from the plump schoolboy as a moth is from the grub?   Time brings about miraculous
changes.   She too had changed, looking a little matronly perhaps as she held her child and Musters's for Byron to admire.

He drew back, jealous and resentful; but the child smiled and
called him to himself.

> I kiss'd it, — and repress'd my sighs,
>   Its father in its face to see;
> But then it had its mother's eyes,
>   And they were all to love and me.

The panel was finished, but Byron had not done with it.
Again and again he would return, laying before it in con-
scientious ritual the flowers and bitter fruit of passions loosely
sown. Mary lay at the root; hers was the harvest.

> Ah! since thy angel form is gone,
>   My heart no more can rest with any;
> But what it sought in thee alone,
>   Attempts, alas! to find in many, —

and in consolatory reading. Others had wooed and lost before. Woman at best was fickle; the sooner the lesson was
learned, the better: return fickleness with frailty, what though
the heart yearn for the anchored home it had never had.
As an infant his eyes had witnessed the storms between father
and mother. He knew Mad Jack had practised the lesson
well. That same inconstancy must run through his blood.
Surely there was no truth in that legend of the two Byrons
who had so dearly loved that even death could not part them.
Tales . . . tales.

Back again on Peachey's tombstone in Harrow churchyard,
he derived comfort for his hurt from the popular Little's [1]
amatory sophistries; and still another lesson impressed itself.
Death is the sole certainty. Live and deceive in those sweet
deceptions allowed humanity. Life is only a mournful jest.

Meanwhile relations with the "amiable Alecto," that "female
Tisiphone," Mrs. Byron, were strained to breaking. She felt
she had right on her side. For the caprice of her son she
moved her ponderous self from Nottingham to Bath, from
Bath to London, from London to Southwell during the long
vacations as Trinity College succeeded Harrow; but there
was no improvement in her son's life. He spent lavishly like

---

[1] Early pseudonym of Thomas Moore.

his father, as Hanson, the lawyer, could vouch, and when his allowance was exhausted he borrowed against his majority. The rooms he set up at Cambridge cost as much to furnish as would have enabled Mrs. Byron to live a year without stinting. He sported his grey horse,and rode it in a grey habit to match. He patronized the Southwell theatre, bought a carriage, ostensibly as a gift to Mrs. Byron, gave munificently to subscriptions, and kept his mistress dressed in boy's clothes to deceive her, his mother. But the masculine wool, however skillfully worn, was not pulled over the knowing Scotch eyes.

She ranted and fumed till all Southwell rang, "the higher notes being particularly musical." And when Byron said nothing, but spoke volumes with his contemptuous underlook, she resorted to action. The family crockery, as her son advanced in years and mischief, gave way to poker and tongs, which he avoided at the last moment by beating a nimble retreat. Words one could face, even from "Mrs. Byron *furiosa*," in one of her epical rages; iron warfare offered too many perils. It had to be admitted that "the old lady" and her son did not agree "like two lambs in a meadow." Mrs. Byron was sorely tried. Yet how could Byron guess, occupied as he was with the problems of his difficult young manhood, that the poor Dowager expressed in these outbursts her misunderstood love, and the fear that he, Mad Jack's son, was daily becoming irrevocably lost to her? Blood and the weird; there was nothing one could do against them.

College, Byron was aware on longer acquaintance, "improved in everything but learning." The midnight oil burned for purposes other than study; a dozen empty "dead men" under a table made easier company than heavy tomes. Not that Byron drank beyond two or three discreet glasses — he had to watch his weight. But it was the fashion to do as the Prince Regent did, and he was a conformist. Live high, drink hearty, wench and be merry, was the motto of the gay young bucks. There was time on the morrow to don the surplice and listen to homilies in the chapel.

Byron's studies were systematically ignored. "Nobody here seems to look into an Author, ancient or modern," and "the

Muses, poor Devils, are totally neglected" — except by himself. He saw to it that their ears found occupation listening to his outpourings in the manner of Tom Little and other elegant, if jingling, bards. In the intervals of his swimming, his lessons in boxing under the much-sought-after "Gentleman" Jackson, his fencing with Angelo, and the emotional bouts with his masqueraded mistress and his boy protégés at Trinity, he plied his quill with astounding facility over virgin sheets. As the gleanings increased to a goodly harvest, his yearning grew to feed the printer's devils, perhaps the public. It was no common thing for an ancient British peer, and a minor, to condescend to Grub Street — not that he, Byron, was condescending. He simply wished to know whether he could excel in the writing of verse as he did in swimming, riding, and boxing.

At Southwell he had friends, Elizabeth Pigot, who thought it an honor to act as his amanuensis, and her brother John, come from his medical studies in Edinburgh. And there was the learned Reverend John Becher, who watched his halting Pegasus and urged him to make it soar. As yet, however, its wings were unfledged. Byron's time for the flights had not yet come, however proficient he may have been on his earthly steed. The obliging Miss Pigot copied fair the young lord's verses. They were in turn handed to her brother, who, during a hasty flight of Byron's from his Alecto, brought them to Ridge, the printer.

Soon a handsome quarto made its appearance, its slimness of body a match for its author's. Copies were at once sent off to friends, including the Reverend Mr. Becher. No sooner did the eyes of age fall upon a luscious youthful description of woman's charms than the new-made poet was called to task. Such effusions might be expected of Little, the "young Catullus of his day." Lord Byron should aim higher. Let him read again his Shakespeare and Milton. Hark how the voice of the linnet was drowned in the mighty organ rush of heavenly Poesy! Byron listened and bowed his head. He did more. With a compliance of spirit that those who saw only the arrogant lordling could never divine in him, he recalled the quartos that had been sent out, and mercilessly destroyed them. Oddly, the Reverend Mr. Becher saved his copy from the general holocaust.

The poet could not rest easy. In his rooms in Piccadilly whither he had fled, leaving only his dogs to the mercy of "the Honorable Mrs. Byron," he dreamed of a praiseful public. He composed more verses and dispatched them to his amanuensis. A new volume shaped itself — the quarto amplified to pontifical dignity. *Hours of Idleness* he called it. Emboldened by the fame his juvenilia had won him at Southwell, not to mention the flattering words from no less an authority than the "Man of Feeling" Mackenzie, — a total stranger to him and therefore sincere, — he sent the *Hours* forth into the world as the works of George Gordon, Lord Byron, a Minor. But a jaded minor.

> Weary of love, and life, devoured with spleen,
> I rest, a perfect Timon, at nineteen.

A puzzling metamorphosis had come over the public version of the private volume. The offending poem was removed, as well as others which no longer found favor with their author, and all references to the *lowly,* where not excised, took on shapes so new that by a stroke of the pen a deceased young cottager became the last scion of "a failing line" whom his *sire* lamented. George Gordon, Lord Byron, had to be mindful of his rank. He was no leveler!

A romantic moodiness brooded over the *Hours,* casting her shadow over the noble minor who had already felt that too soon the *vale* follows the *ave* of life. He reviewed his past, his loves, the places endeared by association, and, poetically aware that he was a beloved of the gods, cast behind a look of farewell. Harrow, Newstead, Lachin-y-Gair, love and friendship — away, away! The noble minor has enjoyed you, but he is not long for this world. It is sad, yet it is also beautiful.

> "Shades of the dead, have I not heard your voices
> Rise on the night-rolling breath of the gale?"

At Eton, Percy Bysshe Shelley had devoured the *Hours* with his eager, myopic eyes. The two lines from *Lachin-y-Gair* worked powerfully upon him. Were they the noble

minor's?   Were they merely quoted?   No matter whose, their
spell roused his imagination and, seizing a ready quill, he had
composed in emulation a poetical paraphrase for his *St. Irvyne,*
then in progress.   The colors were deepened; the lines expanded to a canvas of whirlwind and violence.

> Ghosts of the dead! have I not heard your yelling
>   Rise on the night-rolling breath of the blast,
> When o'er the dark æther the tempest is swelling
>   And on eddying whirlwind the thunder-peal passed? . . .

Back at Cambridge, Byron resumed his old life, but with a
difference.   He was a poet.   Now John Cam Hobhouse, who
had disliked him as a feather-headed snob because of his white
hat and grey horse, sought his acquaintance because he had
appeared in print.   It was something to be publicly courted
by the founder of the Cambridge Whig Club, his senior, and
a man of weight in college life.   What though he had a vile
habit of punning on the names of Byron's youthful followers
and laughing brutally at such attachments?   He was a spirited
companion with whom one could rub wits till the sparks flew.
Then there was Charles Skinner Matthews, the erudite, who
looked like Pope and talked like him; and Scrope Davies, the
formidable gambler, the unanswerable humorist with his dandy
airs and endearing stammer.   Byron had come into his own.
Not to stint in her gifts, Fortune overturned her whole
cornucopia before her favorite.   He won through his lawyers
the Rochdale estate, which the Wicked Lord had illegally sold.
The profits meant sixty thousand pounds more upon Byron's
approaching majority.

Though Fortune may win cases and gain one friends, there
is one thing even she is powerless to do: to propitiate the
Critic.   Against his malice Satan alone is a match.   There
had been rumors that the noble minor was due for a slating
from the mighty of the press, — the lower ranks had published
their fawning reviews, — and Byron waited with evident uneasiness.   In the meantime he courted Venus in the higher
circles to which he was now admitted, and healed her hurts with
the art of Æsculapius, until between the two he was "harassed
to death."   But such harassment is nothing to what an im-

pending unfavorable criticism may cause. It was like having
the thread-suspended sword over one's head day and night.
Would five-foot Jeffrey, the Edinburgh executioner, take it
upon himself to do the bloody work, or would he delegate an
assistant? Would the technic of the hireling prove cruder
than the master's? Byron would wait and see.

And he saw, too plainly, from the opening sentence of the
January issue of the *Edinburgh Review* for 1808. "The poesy
of this young Lord belongs to the class which neither gods nor
men are said to permit. . . . His effusions are spread over
a dead flat, and can no more get above or below the level, than
if they were so much stagnant water. As an extenuation of
this offence, the noble author is peculiarly forward in pleading
minority. . . ." Ah, that luckless error of admitting to his
youth! But that was not all. The fellow wrote with a quill
dipped in verjuice. "He possibly means to say, 'See how a
minor can write! This poem was actually composed by a
young man of eighteen, and this by one of only sixteen!' . . .
His other plea of privilege our author rather brings forward in
order to waive it. He certainly, however, does allude frequently to his family and ancestors — sometimes in poetry,
sometimes in notes; and while giving up his claim on the score
of rank, he takes care to remember us of Dr. Johnson's saying, that when a nobleman appears as an author, his merit
should be handsomely acknowledged. In truth, it is this
consideration only, that induces us to give Lord Byron's poems
a place in our review, beside our desire to counsel him, that he
do forthwith abandon poetry. . . ."

The dastardly coward, hiding insult under the mantle of
his anonymity. Was it Jeffrey? Perhaps, though it was not
his style. So he, Lord Byron, was counseled to abandon
poetry! But had he not told them, to begin with, that "from
his situation and pursuits hereafter" it was not likely that
he should woo the Muses? Ay, the fellow had not missed
that from the preface. He pitched upon it as a snake on its
prey, swallowing it whole. "He is, at best, he says, but an
intruder into the groves of Parnassus; he never lived in a
garret, like thoroughbred poets. . . ." But it had been his
fault, entirely, for his humility. He should have offered no

apologies for youth and inexperience; he should have entered the poetical lists with banners flying — then the enemy would have been cowed. " 'It is highly improbable' . . . that he should again condescend to become an author. Therefore, let us take what we get, and be thankful. . . . We are well off to have got so much from a man of this Lord's station, who does not live in a garret, but 'has the sway' of Newstead Abbey. Again, we say, let us be thankful, and, with honest Sancho, bid God bless the giver, nor look the gift horse in the mouth." So, with a final lick of the fangs. . . .

But the snake was not long to bask in its triumph! It would see how a lord could sting it and its tribe. Mr. Anonymous would treat him as a schoolboy and condescendingly explain "that the mere rhyming of the final syllable, even when accompanied by a certain number of feet; nay, although (which does not always happen) those feet should scan regularly, and have been all counted accurately upon the fingers, — it is not the whole art of poetry." He, Lord Byron, would show him of what art a poet was capable; he should not soon forget it — he and his tribe. One word, twice used, must have hurt more than the whole vicious article, when the critic dismissed his "*hobbling* stanzas," his "*hobbling* verses." Like father, like offspring. His poetry, like himself, was lame. If the critic's choice of word was intentional, then no malice could have been more abominable.

Despite an assumed imperviousness to attack, Byron was sorely wounded. The heart he boasted of as being "as hard as a Highlander's heelpiece" in reality bled too easily. He was wretched after reading the review, and bursting with rage. At dinner with Scrope Davies that night he sat moodily drinking without pleasure three bottles of claret. Something had to be done to still that seething in his breast. As a child, in his "silent rages" he had found relief in ripping his pinafores and biting pieces out of saucers. He could not do that now. But he might cut up his enemy — Jeffrey, Brougham, whichever he proved to be. He would make a general slaughter of the pestilential race of critics and pretenders to the judgment seat of Parnassus. An unhappy generation was being corrupted by a parcel of literary panders and renegades. George

Gordon, Lord Byron, would learn their methods and beat them at their game. In a fury of revenge he trimmed his pens and, without diluting his ink, dashed off a few dozen verses. . . . No, that was childish. Anything done in a rage partook of its heat and chaos. He would have heat, but tempered to his needs. Slowly, deliberately, he set to work on a satire, witty as Pope, yet brilliant and scathing with the coruscations of his own genius.

He took his degree of Master of Arts in 1808 and set off for Newstead. He lacked six months to his twenty-first birthday — and freedom. At least, freedom from financial oppression. High life in Cambridge and London had cost him dear. What with the usurers and others, he was nearly ten thousand pounds in debt. That would soon be made good by his lawyers, and then the world was his. Meanwhile with his Cambridge cronies he would have a taste of a sybarite's paradise.

The noble abbey was more decayed than ever. Lord Grey de Ruthven had made the worst of his stay as a tenant. Moreover there had been a mysterious quarrel between him and his young landlord when the Star of Annesley had been in the ascendant. Since then they had not been in the same room together without heated words and fiery looks. But Lord Grey had gone at last, although his short reign had proved as disastrous as the long rule of the Wicked Lord.

Trembling with premonition, the Cambridge Master of Arts, become again the son of Catherine Gordon, a believer in fetches and forewarnings, ran to the garden. Everywhere dense nettles, harbingers of ruin. But there it was, his little oak, choked with weeds yet still alive. (Critics and enemies, they had not conquered him yet.) With his own hands Byron cleared the roots of his tree of fate and breathed more freely.

A wing of the abbey was made ready to receive him. The gardens were trimmed; the ivy, run wild, was cut and trained. The cellars were flooded and turned into bathing pools. A bear and a wolfhound guarded the gate. One day the gardener struck his spade against something that rang hollow. It was a skull, finely proportioned and well preserved. To whom had it belonged? To a monk of St. Augustine? Or to some

victim of the *murdris* mentioned in the kingly dispensation?
Lord Byron sent it to a Nottingham goldsmith to be polished
and mounted as a drinking cup.   And he who had loved to lie
on Peachey's grave, an acolyte of death, wrote upon it its
epitaph: —

> I lived, I loved, I quaff'd like thee;
>   I died: let earth my bones resign;
> Fill up — thou canst not injure me;
>   The worm hath fouler lips than thine.
>
> Better to hold the sparkling grape,
>   Than nurse the earthworm's slimy brood;
> And circle in the goblet's shape
>   The drink of Gods, than reptile's food.

To the laughter of Paphian girls — pretty servant wenches
from the neighborhood — the mottled skull went round a
curious company.   Hobhouse, Matthews, and Davies, attired
in black gowns which their host had obtained at a theatrical
costumer's, tasted with British qualms these pleasures of Satan,
feeling remarkably brave and delightfully wicked.   Byron,
self-styled the Abbot of the Skull, presided over the rites.

> Father of Light, on thee I call!
>   Thou see'st my soul is dark within;
> Thou who canst mark the sparrow's fall,
>   Avert from me the death of sin. . . .

From one extreme to the other the pendulum soul swung,
unable to find rest.   Now it invoked the Father of Light, now
it plunged itself in sin.   But his friends should never know
of the struggle.   Hobhouse the unbeliever would only laugh.
The Abbot of the Skull, therefore, a "votary of licentiousness
and the disciple of infidelity," drained the gruesome cup and
devoted himself to the mysteries.   Nothing mattered.   Was
not all predestined?

Meanwhile the "female Tisiphone" stormed from the distance.   Her son was twenty-one, ostensibly the master of a
large fortune, and yet to all worldly purposes as penniless
as a pauper.   Something was rotten in Rochdale; those
lawyers, all of them, were liars and cheats, looking after their

own interests. "Why is my son permitted to be plundered by you?" she asked with Scotch candor. She could not afford to mince words. Her son, bent on his verse making and less innocent pleasures, neglected his affairs. She had to speak for him, and she did, tactlessly but to the point. Soon, however, it had to be acknowledged that the sixth Lord Byron, installed at Newstead with the roasting of an ox and a ball for the tenants, had succeeded, at least for the present, to an empty title. As formerly, the moneylenders came to the rescue.

But something had to be done, and that soon. Lord Carlisle could not be counted upon to raise a finger for his erstwhile ward. The gracious dedication to him in the *Hours* he had scarcely deigned to acknowledge. Later, when as the nearest male relation he should have stood beside the young peer on his introduction to the House, Lord Carlisle, generous of advice, was sparing of his presence. Lord Byron had to front the woolsack alone and take the oath unescorted. His pride squirmed under the seeming affront. Was this the courtesy one peer showed to another? He learned his lesson.

> On one alone Apollo deigns to smile,
> And crowns a new Roscommon in Carlisle.

The pretty compliment in his satire, about to be published, the humiliated Byron at once canceled. Now that he was about it he might as well take a wholesale revenge and at one blow pay off all grudges.

> No muse will cheer with renovating smile
> The paralytic puling of Carlisle,

he substituted, together with still sharper verses. Carlisle might have fortune and power on his side; a Byron could sharpen his quill till it pricked like a dagger.

Literary vengeances, however clever, will not replenish one's coffers, especially if the author refuses remuneration. He might enter politics. For a time the idea tempted him. "I shall stand aloof," he dreamed, Napoleonic, "speak what I think, but not often, nor too soon. I will preserve my independence, if possible, but if involved with a party, I will take care not to be the *last* or least in the ranks." He found that

the late "underlings of Pitt," possessing his ill-fortune but not
his talents, as well as the malassorted "fragments of a worn-
out minority," could dispense with an inflation of their
ranks.   So could Mr. Windham, with his coat *"twice* turned,"
and my Lord Grenville.

Should he marry?   The Dowager had not only hinted at,
but encouraged, the possibility.   It must be a young lady
with a fortune, however.   No Southwell misalliances, no pretty
face but empty purse.   No more escapades like that with
the hussy who would have palmed off Lord Curzon's child
as Byron's.   Fortunately the poor mite was stillborn.   But
among Byron's papers there was a poem addressed *To My Son*
which surely the old Dowager had not seen.   Here the child
lived, but the mother had died.   Had it been an actual experience?   Or had Byron merely poetized?   The feeling throughout the poem was tender enough to give it the stamp of truth.

> Oh, 't will be sweet in thee to trace
> Ere age has wrinkled o'er my face,
> Ere half my glass of life is run
> At once a brother and a son . . .
>
> Although so young thy heedless sire,
> Youth will not damp parental fire.

A lowly grave had been its mother's lot; a stranger's breast
had suckled it; the world sneered upon its sinful birth.   The
complex of circumstances made a plausible argument for the
truth.   Mary Chaworth was married and had her child.   He,
too, had his son, though illegitimate.   Briefly the babe appears
in the one poem and then is heard of no more.   Better to
forget, when one has reached the years of discretion.   Mrs.
Byron wished him to marry.   Very well.   He would find his
Golden Dolly to set him on his feet and rebuild Newstead.
Heigho! . . .   The Abbot of the Skull thought of the gay
bachelor days at the abbey and lost all enthusiasm for
matrimony.

His satire at last appeared in print after the dull but devoted Charles Dallas, a distant connection and self-appointed
literary agent of his lordship, had shopped the manuscript

about among the publishers without success. It was clever, yes, but too violent and personal. Names of consequence were not spared; it meant great risk. One courageous soul, however, was found, and *English Bards and Scotch Reviewers* fell upon unsuspecting English heads in the middle of March of 1809. At the publisher's request it appeared anonymously. But there was no need for concealment. Everyone knew that the erstwhile noble minor had written it in answer to his critics. Everywhere it was asked for in Lord Byron's name.

The book captured the caprice of the literate. In a month the first edition was exhausted and a second appeared, much amplified, with the author's name on the title-page, a stinging preface, and a postscript that added seasoned fuel to the fire. Poets, critics, playwrights, were made to jump to the lordly ire. "A Bard may chant too often and too long," he warned Southey, the author of *Madoc*. And, Wordsworth, beware lest

> . . . all who view the "idiot in his glory"
> Conceive the Bard the hero of the story.

The sly lines were rolled upon the tongue of fashion. Byron's name resounded in the salons. All, especially the ladies, were curious to know more of one

> . . . least thinking of a thoughtless throng,
> Just skill'd to know the right and choose the wrong . . .
> Whom every path of pleasure's flowery way
> Has lured in turn and all have led astray.

Was that all true? Could the young poet peer be as he painted himself — so old in the ways of sin?

At twenty-one he felt weighed down with years. *Eheu, fugaces* . . . everything seemed slipping from him, his youth, his friends — some by death, some by estrangements crueler than death because they might have been avoided. Boatswain, his dog, — certainly the truest friend he had ever had, — was dead. He lay at Newstead, in a grave with a place set apart for himself and another for old Murray, the faithful. A cloud of misanthropy descended upon him that darkened for him the rest of mankind. He must leave everyone and everything, and go anywhere, away, out of the world he knew.

"I am like Adam," he reflected cynically, "the first convict sentenced to transportation, but I have no Eve, and have eaten no apple but what was sour as a crab; — and thus ends my first chapter."

IV

LIFE BEGINS

SHELLEY and Hogg had wandered out one day after a long session of reading Plato together. On Magdalen Bridge a woman was standing with her infant in her arms, a mite of a few weeks whose eyes peered out with wondering innocence upon the scene into which it had so newly arrived. Stopping abruptly, Shelley took the child in his arms, looking earnestly into its face.

"Will your baby tell us anything about preëxistence, madam?" he asked.

The woman, dumbfounded by the behavior of the youth with eyes as ingenuously earnest as her own babe's, stared and said nothing.

"Will your baby tell us anything about preëxistence, madam?" Shelley repeated with the solemnity of an angel.

"He cannot speak, sir," said the woman.

"But surely the babe can speak if he will, for he is only a few weeks old. . . . He cannot have forgotten in so short a time."

The questioner of graves, the seeker after the unknown, again was not answered.

Now the life of the inquiring scholar was closed to him, and also to his guiltless friend, by a conspiracy of the college bigwigs against a lover of truth. At eighteen and a half it is too early to fight the world single-handed. He was driven to it, and he would do it, and accordingly he turned his solemn eyes toward the enigma of life. Would it tell anything of what it held for an inexperienced philosopher, martyred for adhering to principles? Where should he go? What should he do? Field Place as a harbor of refuge was out of the question with the blustering of Timothy Shelley. York, Hogg's home, offered no better prospects of welcome. Packing their books, clothes, the electrical engines and the precious solar microscope, the two Galilei took the coach to London the morning after the expulsion from Oxford. They arrived that same day, sought out the Groves, who had nothing to offer but the gall and wormwood of practical advice, and then they knocked at Cousin Medwin's door, long after midnight. No consolation from that quarter, either. What should Thomas Medwin have to say to a cousin who had been expelled? Shelley and Hogg spent the few remaining hours in a Piccadilly coffeehouse, healing their hurts with sleep.

Next day they set out to look for lodgings where they could await in comparative safety the paternal thunders that must surely come after they had communicated the news of their glorious disgrace. Hither and yon they walked, along modest and likely streets, but here a huckster called too loud for Shelley's ear, there some other objection presented itself. Finally they found the perfect setting at number 15 Poland Street — a name well-augured for at least one rebel for freedom's sake.

From the sitting room decorated with wallpaper in designs of vine leaves and grapes, so tempting to Shelley's fancy that he forthwith determined to live there — an abstinent Bacchus — *for ever,* a letter was dispatched to Field Place, suggesting with no little tact that he and his friend in martyrdom should be taken into the bosom of the family — at least until Mr. Hogg of York should welcome back his son. Hopeful idealist!

A missive came from Field Place, as disconnected and vehement as Mr. Timothy Shelley himself in his ire. What! Bring that fellow to Field Place after he had got him, Shelley, into trouble? For to Mr. Shelley, Hogg's seniority was proof positive of greater guilt. Not only would Field Place refuse to shelter the miscreant, but Shelley himself would be shut out unless he promised to sever relations with Hogg at once. Mr. Whitton, the family lawyer, was engaged forthwith to take the disgraceful matter in hand.

Nothing Mr. Shelley might have suggested could have been better calculated to widen the chasm between him and his son. To Shelley, Hogg had become dearer still for having shared his punishment when he could easily have avoided it. Would he now, for the Field Place mess of pottage, abandon one to whom he owed the supremest loyalty? Never! And so, with the emphasis of righteous indignation, he answered his father. Very well, retorted Timothy Shelley through solicitor Whitton; but henceforth expect no help from me. And he tightened the purse strings viciously.

Had it not been for the aid of Captain Pilfold, his maternal uncle, and the small sums his sisters smuggled to him out of their allowances, Shelley might have thirsted and hungered unappeased in his luxuriant arbor. As it was he subsisted royally on warm loaves from the bakeshop and pocketfuls of raisins, satisfying substitutes for the unattainable clusters on his walls.

A week went by and Timothy Shelley pounced down upon the two rebels in London. Scolding, crying, swearing in Millar's Hotel, where he saw the two face to face and found Hogg less objectionable than he had expected, he sought between doses of ale and Paley to bring them to their senses. In vain. They were stiff-necked and obdurate. After the meeting he wrote to John Hogg, Esquire, at York. "Backed by the opinion of men of rank and influence . . . I have endeavoured to part them. . . ." Not content with that missive he sent another the following day. "Paley's *Natural Theology* I shall recommend my young man to read, it is extremely applicable. I shall read it with him. . . . I understand you have more children. God grant they may turn out well, and this young man see his error."

As for his son, he had little hope. How came he, the respectable Member for New Shoreham, to father this firebrand? He had to watch out; he owed it to himself, to his daughters and remaining son, to protect himself. He did nothing without Whitton's counsel.

Acting upon Mr. Timothy Shelley's letter, Mr. Hogg called his delinquent to York. Shelley remained alone among his grapes, in the street symbolic of liberty. The correspondence began anew. Shelley had more leisure now and a greater burden of trouble. Harriet Grove was lost to him; the university oak had closed as irretrievably upon him as the gates of Paradise upon the exiled Adam; Timothy Shelley, vengeful as the God he worshiped, had cast him, his son, out of Field Place. Thomas Jefferson Hogg, his friend, had been wrested from him by parental injustice. But he was not daunted. Intolerance stalked the earth; Shelley armed himself against it. "Nothing provokes him so much as civility," Mr. Shelley complained to his lawyer. "He wishes to become what he would term a martyr to his sentiments — nor do I believe he would feel the Horrors of being drawn upon the Hurdle, or the shame of being whirl'd in the Pillory."

Sooner than Shelley had anticipated he came upon a victim of the monster. True, he had met Harriet Westbrook when he had come down one day from Oxford as the bearer of a message from Elizabeth Shelley. He had seen her again at Miss Fenning's boarding school at Clapham Common when he went with Hogg to visit his sisters during those days when the two outcasts had found relief for their unsettled emotions in pedestrian exercise. He had not thought then, as he had looked at that beaming face, pink and white as a flower in sunlight, that it belonged to a victim of Intolerance. Besides, the name of Harriet had reminded him of another, too recently lost. How blind is man in his selfish grieving! There was he, nursing his misery, when before him stood a helpless sacrifice to the Minotaur!

Harriet Westbrook, though not of genteel birth like the young misses of the Clapham Common school, was so far above them in beauty that at a *fête champêtre* proposed by the teachers she was chosen to represent the goddess Venus. She was well-proportioned if not tall, light and graceful, with trim ankles and dainty feet that peeped from under her long starched skirts. Her fair hair — "quite like a poet's dream," said Shelley's sister Hellen — shone with golden tints, framing her face in brightness. Her complexion was ravishing, of that transparent bloom possessed only by healthy youth. She was just sixteen.

Miss Fenning pointed her out with pride. She read well, in a pleasant, even voice. She dressed with a simple elegance that might have been envied by a lady of fashion; she knew French and she danced. And she possessed a seriousness beyond her years, somewhat disconcerting at times, as when, in the midst of a gay gathering, she would suddenly ask, "What is your opinion of suicide?" She defended it as a legitimate way of quitting the world and its troubles, her voice stressing her arguments with cheerful gusto. The next moment she launched with the same airiness on the merits of Voltaire's *Dictionnaire philosophique*. Something drew Shelley to her against his will. Was it this talk of suicide — an enticing theme to a writer of Gothic romances who had himself tried it, as he told Hogg, fortunately without success? That had been before Oxford, when he had taken a dose of arsenic so strong that his stomach rejected it. Harriet Westbrook became more interesting. She was suffering, one could see; he soon learned from what cause.

The Minotaur was none other than Mr. Westbrook — Jew Westbrook, as he was commonly called by those who borrowed from him and found him exacting. He had kept a coffee-house near Grosvenor Square and his business had further prospered from his moneylending. Recently he had retired in comfortable circumstances. Like all fathers, he was a tyrant. He insisted on sending Harriet to school against her will — to that abhorred school at Clapham where the girls, seeing her interest in the disgraced Shelley, an atheist, and worse, made her life miserable by calling *her* names. "Abandoned wretch!" they flung at her, and assured her that she was wholly lost. Thus not only did she bear her father's cruelty, but she was suffering for his, Shelley's, sake. Here was a noble soul! Here was an elect spirit to be lifted from the mire of hateful circumstance! Inspiring epistles began flying from Poland Street to the distressed Harriet, and Shelley's writings were sent her that she might know him better. Godwin, political justice, the perfectibility of man, anti-matrimonialism — all were brought forward to rescue a struggling spirit from the tentacles of Intolerance. "She would be a divine little scion of infidelity if I could get hold of her," Shelley boasted to Hogg. And then, "I think my lessons have taken effect," he added with glee. He felt happier. He had made another proselyte. Two, perhaps.

There was hope for Eliza Westbrook, though she was nearly

twice her sister's age and therefore fixed in her views. She sided with Harriet, however, against Mr. Westbrook, which put her in the ranks of the libertarians. Shelley discoursed with her on his favorite themes, to which she condescended to listen. Anti-matrimonialism pleased her not at all. She inclined as little to his notions on religion and tried propagandizing on her own account. "I took the sacrament with her on Sunday," read the bewildered Hogg. But no, there was no danger in it for Shelley. Since the Misses Westbrook so graciously listened to him, he, on his side, did a little to please them.

The fair Eliza, more than the mother who kept in the dim back regions of the Westbrook household, secretly desired to make a capture of the young gentleman, heir to a title and a fortune. Though far from handsome, — the unprejudiced would have called her plain, — she had her own opinions of her charms, which she had managed to communicate to Harriet, who thought the world held no woman so wonderful as Eliza. In the generosity of her youth she praised the mature woman's fine long hair, which she spent hours in the day brushing, exalted her intelligence, her fine feelings, and paid tribute to her exquisite understanding. At first the solemn youth listened, acquiescent. She did have fine long hair, and she did talk intelligently; but privately to Hogg he confessed that Eliza was conceited and very condescending. And he did n't like the way she had of talking to him in dulcet tones about *l'Amour*. And why in French when there was just as good a word for it in English? Still he continued going to the Westbrooks', and soon Eliza perceived that her young sister's inferior intellect offered a greater temptation to the ardent proselytizer than her own solid qualities. Very well. She was a sensible woman; she would attain her end in another way. The important thing was to keep the young gentleman in the family.

"My poor little friend has been ill," Shelley informed the York correspondent. "Her sister sent for me the other night. I found her on a couch, pale; her father is civil to me, very strangely; the sister is too civil by half. She began talking about *l'Amour*. I philosophised, and the youngest said she had such a headache, that she could not bear conversation. Her sister then went away and I stayed until half-past twelve. Her father had a large party below, he invited me; I refused. Yes! the fiend, the wretch shall fall."

Here was an alarming pass. Shelley, so late in the shackles of love for Harriet Grove, was become the bedside comforter of another Harriet. The clear-sighted Hogg saw more in the scene than the guileless participant would ever have dreamed of suspecting. A pretty girl, lying with the attractive flush of suffering on her face; a scheming elder sister, endeavoring to suscitate the tender emotions; between them a very lamb of a Shelley, dangerous only to abstractions and chimeras. And below, the fiend incarnate, from whose clutch the ailing beauty was to be taken. A precarious situation for his friend. Thereupon Hogg tactfully led him into another literary discussion on the hateful, detestable institution of marriage.

The fervid anti-matrimonialist plunged into the fray, waving the Godwinian gonfalon. Ay, marriage was hateful and detestable slavery as it existed under the present social state. "A kind of ineffable, sickening disgust seizes my mind when I think of this most despotic, most unrequired fetter which prejudice has forged to confine its energies." He loathed it as only one piercingly aware of the bondage into which it too often cast heart and mind could loathe. And Shelley was passionately sincere. Hogg read, and for the moment his fears were allayed. Then other dangers menaced. "I spend most of my time at Miss Westbrook's. I was a great deal too hasty in criticising her character." Already he was throwing down the barricades he had set up to protect his heart. He had been too hasty. . . . The worst he had said of Harriet Westbrook was that she seemed "rather affected" and that she was young. In an effort to choose he placed the two sisters in the balance. "There is something in *her* more noble, yet not so cultivated as the elder, — a larger diamond, yet not so highly polished. . . ." The judgment came from Uncle Pilfold's at Cuckfield. The same day another letter was written. "Pray, which of the Miss Westbrooks do *you* like?" asked the philosopher, dazzled between the two diamonds. "They are both very amiable; I do not know which is favoured with your preference."

Happily at this point, through the efforts of Uncle Pilfold, whom Shelley by that time had successfully illuminated, and the persuasions of men of *rank* and *influence* who saw the youth battling bravely but unsuccessfully against the odds of life, Timothy Shelley allowed himself to be placated. The youth was invited to Field Place, though Elizabeth was kept far away from his baleful influence, and father and son drew up a treaty of peace under Mr. Whitton's supervision. Timothy Shelley would allow his son two hundred pounds a year, with the choice of living wherever he pleased. He was not, however, to pervert the minds of his sisters and he was forbidden to see Hogg, although he might correspond with him. The rebel swallowed his pride and made the best of the bargain. He had his freedom, after all; he might go where he chose and live as he pleased. No one could fetter his mind.

He saw little of his mother or of Elizabeth except when the Old Boy, or the Killjoy, as he dubbed the honorable Timothy, went down to London. Then the dangerous atheist sat meekly at his mother's feet, striving to open an intellect too closely bound by her lord and husband. It was a day of triumph for Shelley when she pronounced to his exactions: "I think prayer and thanksgiving are of no use. If a man is a good man, philosopher or Christian, he will do very well in whatever future state awaits us." If only her son had been a Christian, nevertheless, instead of a philosopher. . . .

Unrest laid hold of Shelley now that he had his freedom. Like a bird let out of a cage he fluttered here, there, resting no long time on any perch. From Cuckfield to Cwm Elan he darted, finding no more peace in rugged Radnorshire than in the gentle Sussex countryside. Significantly, he avoided London. He had to be away from the two Misses Westbrook to find himself. Perhaps the divine Elizabeth Hitchener of Hurstpierpoint would help him. He had met the tall, Roman-nosed school-teacher through Uncle Pilfold, and at once yielded to her superb intellect. Yet her other charms were far from inconsiderable. Her sharp black eyes spoke as readily as her tongue. Her dusky hair, if anything longer and finer than Eliza's, framed a face of masculine strength. A downy moustache and an incipient beard were not blemishes to repel

a seeker after the higher beauty.   Nor did a disparity in years
form a breach between the communication of one intellect and
another.   Miss Hitchener was twenty-nine.   Was not the other
Eliza as old?   Besides, mind has no age.

A noble soul was Miss Hitchener's.   With what feeling she
spoke of the suffering of the poor!   What sparks of hate
flashed from her eyes in her indictments against oppression!
She, too, was a standard-bearer against the unjust social
order.   A nineteenth-century Joan of Arc, she armed her
woman's body and found her place in the ranks of the re-
deemers.

So to Shelley's growing list was added another correspondent
who, with Hogg, shared the confessions of his perplexed spirit.
His dejection increased in his solitude, and the few events of
his life forced themselves into his thoughts.   He had loved,
and love had played him false.   Harriet Grove . . . Harriet
Westbrook. . . .   Had he truly loved his cousin, that radiant
being who for so long shone in the firmament of his dreams?
Was he now in love with the other Harriet?   What was it he
had loved in Harriet Grove?   Herself, as she was?   But he
could not have seen her as she had been, else now she would
have been his Harriet and not the squire's wife.   In his passion
for analysis he dissected his past emotions and brought them
face to face with the present.   Whom had he loved, if he had
truly loved?   What did he seek in woman?   With unusual
lucidity he set down his thoughts for Hogg.

"I loved a being, an idea in my own mind, which had no real
existence.   I concreted this abstract of perfection, I annexed
this fictitious quality to the idea presented by a name; the
being whom that name signified, was by no means worthy of
this. . . .   I regret when I find that she never existed but in
my mind."   Unhappy dreamer, rapt in his vision of the ideal
beauty. . . .   Unhappy the woman upon whose mortal shoulders the heavenly mantle should fall!

The visionary world was one thing, the actual another, and
one had to face it.   Two hundred pounds a year could not go
far; little good could be accomplished with it.   As it was,
Shelley had had no preparation for living with men.   Miss
Hitchener, noble soul, eked out her precious existence by

educating the girls of Hurstpierpoint and some little Americans, thus keeping her bodily flame alive while nurturing budding intellects. Shelley, too, might make himself useful to mankind. He would send forth his thoughts among them, but he would also minister to them in closer service. He would study medicine, so that, until the old order gave place to the glorious new, he might at least alleviate human pain. Godwin said there would be no more death in that wondrous era. Until then he, Shelley, would heal the ills to which unregenerate man was heir.

Meanwhile Harriet Westbrook wrote him of the persecution she had to suffer from that abominable wretch, her father. She opposed him, bravely. Had not Shelley counseled courageous resistance? But her weak forces were giving way under the oppression. She could bear no more. Let her guardian advise her; she would do anything he said.

Harriet's problems found their way to Hogg. Hogg read, and with sly humor cautioned Shelley against the wiles of woman. Nonsense, retorted the dreamer. "Your jokes on Harriet Westbrook amuse me. . . . If I know anything about love, I am *not* in love."

Hogg had his own opinion. Perhaps if he could get his artless friend to come to York, if he could talk to him, warn him against his simplicity . . . The invitation was accepted with a startling provision. "I shall certainly come to York, but *Harriet Westbrook* will decide whether now or in three weeks." What did Miss Westbrook have to say about a visit from friend to friend? He learned as he read on. "Her father has persecuted her in a most horrible way, by endeavouring to compel her to go to school. . . . She wrote to me to say that resistance was useless, but that she would fly with me, and threw herself upon my protection. . . . We shall have £200 a year: when we find it run short, we must live, I suppose, upon love!" O most innocent of idealists! "Gratitude and admiration, all demand, that I should love her *for ever!*"

There it was, and but a few days since he had disclaimed any such sentiment. But he, Hogg, should have been more discerning. Had not Shelley sent him a poem addressed to a sweet star gleaming o'er the darksome scene and lighting the hour of sacred love? Had he not put down in black and white for his dull friend to see, "I have been thinking of Death and Heaven for four days"? A man does not dwell on Death and Heaven unless something tangible on earth torments him. How myopic he himself had been! But now it was too late, too late to do anything but guide Shelley from the dangers of his idealism.

It was well to declaim against marriage. Shelley was living in no Utopia, and the gallant Englishman in Hogg rose up to the defense of female virtue. Accordingly he penned a long exordium pointing out the shame, the unendurable burden of obloquy that an unmarried wife must bear. Shelley must not think of subjecting Miss Westbrook to such indignity. Let him consider well.

Shelley considered, held fondly to his opinions, but — not without a struggle — relinquished them at last. He knew himself right in his beliefs, — he had Godwin to support him, — "yet the arguments of impracticability, and what is even worse, the disproportionate sacrifice which the female is called upon to make — these arguments which you have urged in a manner immediately irresistible, I cannot withstand."

In London, whither he had gone from Wales, he assured his afflicted one that she might count upon him as her protector. Eliza was informed, though not, perhaps, of the change in views that the anti-matrimonialist had suffered. She, too, as all who knew him, had heard enough of the abominable marriage service to which no man worthy of the name could subject "an amiable, beloved female" to look on him with dismay, and to caution prudence. Harriet, whatever the reason, now that the deliverer had come to fly with her from her prison house, showed an odd indecision, "not with respect to me," Shelley told Hogg, "but herself." What could have caused it? Was it coyness now that the victory was complete? Was she following the instructions of the fair Eliza, warning that one must not give oneself too cheaply, even if one is a tavern keeper's daughter and the recipient a future baronet? Eliza must have been told that at the end of the elopement the consummation of a legal marriage waited. Harriet came to a decision.

Shelley meanwhile was in a ferment of excitement. He was on the verge of flying with a charming girl who had generously thrown herself upon his protection. He was flattered and elated. He would no longer be alone in his battles against tyranny; his crusading ardor was shared by a creature of light, one whom he himself had raised from the pit of superstition and Intolerance. How eagerly she listened to his visions of the future world! With what earnestness she repeated the lessons she had learned on the true religion and that elevating love which was to make the beggar the equal of the emperor — not that such distinctions would exist in the ideal state.

Shelley was pleased with his handiwork. But he was not in love with Harriet. Too truthful to deceive, even for convenience, he made the admission to Hogg in letter after letter. There was no *inspired passion* in what he felt for the dainty, trim little creature who always looked as fresh and perfect as a newly opened bud. He admired, — if his bodily eye, full of an inner vision, could have been said to seize the physical impression, — he admired the orderliness and harmony, but his being did not thrill with desire. What he sought beyond the flesh-and-blood Harriet was, as he had admitted in an uncannily clear moment, the "abstract of perfection." At Eton, at Oxford, he had been as chaste as one vowing himself to celibacy. Never had an unclean word passed his lips. He had a horror of coarseness in any form. He was virginal in his nineteenth year, and in mind as pure as a seraph.

The abstract of perfection in Harriet had its corporeal entity. She saw no mere shadow in Shelley, but the beautiful, unkempt youth with his earnest ways and inspired speech. She revered him as a teacher, but she loved him, first and foremost, as a man — and a gentleman. The idealist took second place in her considerations. Whatever he taught her she learned to obtain his approbation, not out of love for lofty thinking. Intellectual flights made her tired. At sixteen she was a spirited girl, chafing under restraint and anxious to enter the unrestricted life of the adult. Marriage offered the way. She took it exultantly. Not in her wildest dreams had she hoped for such a marriage as fate — with Eliza's connivance — now brought to her.

The bridegroom, however, in spite of his brilliant prospects, found himself as much out of pocket while preparing for this momentous step in his career as the veriest bohemian. It was August. His allowance was nearly exhausted. He could not apply to the Old Boy, who would have scented something unusual and immediately fulfilled his function of killjoy. He wrote, therefore, to his Uncle Medwin — Uncle Pilfold having exercised his kindness on more than one occasion — for a loan of fifty-two pounds. Mr. Medwin, not knowing to what uses it was going to be put, sent it. All was in readiness for Harriet's flight.

Early one morning, perhaps the twenty-fourth of August, two youths walked down Mount Street in a state of intense excitement, and there entered a coffeehouse. They ordered breakfast, but it was obvious from their manner that it was only a pretext; Charles Grove and his cousin Shelley had little desire for food. They had not waited long when Harriet, flushed with the thrill of the adventure, but otherwise as neat and pretty as a doll out of a glass case, appeared with her traveling boxes. The two young men rose quickly, hailed a carriage, and, installing the little beauty and her cases within, entered after her and drove off. They descended at the Bull and Mouth, from where the mail left in the evening for Edinburgh, via York. What hours of anxious but delightful waiting! What fears that the dragons of authority might leap upon them before the coach bore them triumphantly away! However, Field Place was in ignorance of the escapade, and at the Westbrook precincts Eliza had seen that nothing leaked out until the fugitives were out of reach. Night came at last, and the Edinburgh mail. Harriet and Shelley clambered to the top of the coach, away from oppression, while Charles Grove, his duty done, took his sober way homeward.

Edinburgh. Why Edinburgh? Was it because the two adventurous minors hoped a legal marriage would more easily be performed there, or perhaps because it was to the Scottish capital Shelley was to have gone had he carried out his plan of studying medicine? Not so long ago he had told Miss Hitchener of it, and she had nobly assented. Now he was going there to get married instead, and to an inexperienced girl of whom his divinity might not approve. How was he to break the news to the "sister of his soul"? He had told Miss Hitchener that she was dear to him, very dear, and the Hurstpierpoint spinster, judging the ethereal philosopher by worldlier standards than he supposed, had given the words a meaning less platonic than they possessed. Shelley was somewhat dismayed. But with the bright Harriet beside him, he tried to forget.

At York, dear to Shelley for being the abode of Hogg, the coach stopped to change horses. London was nearly two days' journey behind. When Shelley looked into his finances he found that what with the expenses at the inns, and the traveling incidentals, all multiplied by two, there was scarcely anything left of Uncle Medwin's fifty-two pounds. A sad state for a bridegroom, whose next quarter's allowance was not due for yet a few days. How would he pay for the wedding, for the lodgings in Edinburgh? Harriet had come to him with little besides the clothes she wore. Pretty though they were, they added nothing materially. Hogg would come to the rescue. "Harriet is with me," Shelley wrote him. "We are in a slight pecuniary distress. We shall have seventy-five pounds on Sunday, until when can you send £10? Divide it in two." Hogg proved a real friend.

In Edinburgh the two runaway children were married, and the ceremony was duly recorded in the Register House. "August 28, 1811," read the entry. "Percy Bysshe Shelley, farmer, Sussex, and Miss Harriet Westbrook, St. Andrew Church Parish, daughter of Mr. John Westbrook, London."

Percy Bysshe Shelley, farmer. . . . A fantastic error, and not a little ironical. Who was responsible for it? Had the heir to a title sought to bring himself nearer to the humbly born Harriet? If so, it was a gracious gesture.

V

CHILDE HAROLD

When, two years after his departure, Byron returned to England, he brought with him, besides a shawl and attar of roses for his mother and a collection of Athenian skulls for himself, a few scribbled, discarded pages that held in them the runes of his fame. He had sailed as George Gordon, Lord Byron. He came back as Childe Harold, twenty-three years old, prouder of having matched Leander in swimming from Sestos to Abydos than of being the author of a "romaunt" which in less than a year was to make society a footstool for his pride.

Europe in the interim had suffered further changes through Napoleon. The French army in Italy had invaded Austria. The Pope excommunicated Napoleon, who, with breath-taking effrontery, imprisoned him. The Danube had been crossed; Wagram was won. Generals were made in one day, and the next unmade by death. In England, Wellesley, after winning the battle of Talavera, was created Viscount of Wellington. "He seems to be a man, that Wellesley," muttered Napoleon, swallowing his commandant's defeat. A game of battledore and shuttlecock sent duchies and principalities flying from one hand to another. From the remotest ice-covered fields of Russia to Sicily's golden vales the roar of the cannon echoed — all that a power-maddened Corsican might bestride the world.

Corporal, consul, general, king, emperor, he had advanced in the enchanted boots of fairy-tale, at each step encompassing a kingdom. The patriot of 1789 had become the tyrant of 1810. Josephine, risen to the glory of empress, no longer suited his ambition. She had borne him no heir, and therefore must suffer. After the peace of Schönbrunn and a visit to the court of Nymphenburg, he formed his plans. Unannounced, Napoleon arrived at Fontainebleau. Josephine was not there to receive him. That was the end. In a fury, the more raging because unjust, he ordered the doors barred between his rooms and hers. A divorce was decreed between them, and Josephine was sent to Malmaison. Maria Louisa of Austria, an eighteen-year-old girl, was chosen to supplant her, and so the little princess, who in her childhood had played at "burning the monster" in effigy in the Viennese court, married him. In the imperial carriage of crystal and gold Napoleon and his royal bride rode before the cheering populace, while in the various churches the six thousand French virgins who had chosen husbands from among the ranks of his army made sure of the dowry the Emperor had promised. Napoleon's power was at its height, but he had already taken the first step toward "the abyss covered with flowers."

From his voyages Byron watched the progress of his "little pagod," whose bust he had carried with him to Harrow, as a boy, with others of his homeless *lares*. It was not only because he had been brought up in the odor of Whig tradition by Catherine Byron. There was something challenging about the man's colossal daring. Yet he, Byron, was a match for any Napoleon. He was of ancient and noble blood; he was young. If an obscure Corsican of pygmy size could bring all Europe to his feet, why should not he, Lord Byron, dare to aspire? His lame foot, like Napoleon's lack of height, should not deter him, but only serve to show stepdame Nature that even her unkindnesses could be turned to godmother gifts by genius. In the darkness of the nights at sea, it seemed to him that his destiny was written in the stars. It was no common destiny. He did not speak of it to Hobhouse; Hobhouse would not have understood, nor would any man. Watching for signs and omens, the son of Catherine Byron wrote them down.

Prey to an unshakable melancholy, he journeyed in strange lands and places, on seas made deathless by the lines of poets, across mountains hardly known to man. First Portugal and Spain, their groves and churches desolated by war, but still cheerful in the brilliance of such sunlight as he had never seen;

Lisbon, Seville, Cádiz, where the saint-adorers tell the rosary before the Virgin, and the Spanish maid and the Spanish swain exchange sweet looks in the bloody thrill of the bullfight on the Sabbath; Cintra, with her mountain eminences crowned with convents and Moorish castles in ivied ruin, and at her feet the Atlantic glittering with silvery breakers; Mafra and Gibraltar — Lord Byron, now Childe Harold, noted them all, and on all of them made his comment. He did not begin the writing of his poem until he had arrived at Yanina, although the indefatigable Hobhouse had covered reams of foolscap with an account of their journey so meticulous that it would have done honor to a writer of parliamentary debates.

In Spain and Malta Byron's heart had suffered novel sensations. In the one place he had given it without love to a dusky beauty to whom he refused the ring he wore upon his finger; at Malta he had bestowed the ring, but withheld the heart in a sudden seizure of platonic coldness that left him more spent and shaken than excess. He had learned to withstand, unmoved, the lustre of a woman's gaze, and that woman one so fascinating that any other man would have committed madnesses for her. But little did Mrs. Spencer Smith know

> . . . that seeming marble-heart,
> Now mask'd in silence or withheld by pride,
> Was not unskilful in the spoiler's art.

How could she guess, poor lady, that Lord Byron, together with his scarlet cloak embroidered in gold, and his military epaulettes, had donned another disguise — that of the woman-weary Childe? A dangerous disguise, and irresistible, even to a woman whom Napoleon dreaded. "Sweet Florence," Byron called her, promising that could another (than Mary Chaworth) ever share that "wayward, loveless heart," it should be hers.

Prevesa, Zitza, Tepaleen, places whose very names spelled adventure, Childe Harold visited, thinking of home among the kilted Albanians with their gold-wrought cloaks, feeling a kinship with their savagery, their daggers and silver-mounted pistols. At last he was in his right milieu, that of romance, colorful, exciting, and perilous. Hobhouse took his voluminous notes and drew his sapient contrasts. With the Turks, Greeks, Albanians, and Moors in their many-hued array, he saw the soldiers in "most common dress, without shoes," and marked them down as worthy the notice of the erstwhile founder of the Radical Club at Cambridge. He was the intercepting smoked glass to Byron, mitigating the sun's too brilliant rays.

Fletcher the faithful was another trial to patience. In the sunlight he whined because of the heat; he complained in the mountain passes because of the cold. He sighed at the sight of coffee, after the heart-warming comfort of English tea; he yearned after British roast beef and his Sally, though in no long time, following the example of the Albanians in his lord's suite, he took unto himself a mistress. But still he lamented the fate that had brought him away from comfortable England, especially when he felt only the unsteady planks of a ship between himself and perdition.

At Tepaleen Byron was the guest of Ali Pacha, a vizier come to life from *The Arabian Nights*. The old gentleman, whom report affirmed to be the very opposite of the kindly patriarch he seemed, greeted Lord Byron standing, which flattered him exceedingly. The marble-paved hall surrounded by scarlet ottomans and cooled by tinkling fountains for once repelled comparison with England. Byron found himself in a world so different that he could take with true Oriental simplicity the compliments of the Pacha — that he, Byron, bore all the marks of noble birth in his curling hair, small ears, and little white hands. Immediately he retailed the flattering words to Catherine Byron, whose ears were far from small, whose hands were fat and puffy, whose noble birth, according to Oriental standards, nature literally made hang by a hair.

Across wild mountains made terrifying by a thunderstorm the Childe and his retinue wandered, deafened by thunder, blinded by lightning, while poor Fletcher wept for his Sally and repented him of his sins. They were nearly wrecked in a Turkish ship of war whose captain abandoned the tiller and left its guidance to Providence. "Could we get back to the mainland?" asked Hobhouse. "If God chooses," replied the quaking captain. "Could we make Corfù?" "If God chooses." The answer hardly reassured Hobhouse, the skeptic.

It looked, indeed, as if the last hour of the pilgrims had struck. Byron, whose lame foot prevented his being of service, wrapped himself up in his cloak and lay down on deck. When the confusion was over and the ship out of danger they found him — fast asleep.

To Fletcher's relief the journey was resumed by land, where such perils as attacks from banditti could at least be overcome by his lordship. Acarnania was crossed, and Missolonghi, exhaling its miasmic air, welcomed them to Greece. At Patras the travelers rested a fortnight; then onward to Vostizza and the hoary peak of Parnassus beyond the Gulf of Lepanto.

> Oh, thou Parnassus! whom I now survey,
> Not in the phrensy of a dreamer's eye,
> Not in the fabled landscape of a lay,
> But soaring snow-clad through thy native sky. . . .

At last he was there, beneath its shadow. His mortal eyes beheld the immortal mount toward which the gaze of vanished greatness had risen. Beneath its slope was nurtured eternal beauty, and liberty had chosen it as her throne. The past filed by before the Childe's memory; the names of poets and heroes sounded a pæan. He, too, might find a place among them. He had the passion; he might have the power.

> Yield me one leaf of Daphne's deathless plant,
> Nor let thy votary's hope be deemed an idle vaunt.

As if in answer to his unuttered prayer, a flight of eagles, birds of glory, circled in the air above him. There were twelve of them, a mystic number, and as he counted them he felt that Apollo had accepted his homage. He would dare and do. His name would be among the immortal. By that flight of birds he knew it — what though Hobhouse, that damper of sentiment, coolly assured him that they were vultures. But the two went on together, and like true British tourists they carved their names on a stone slab at Delphi, Hobhouse disdaining not this artless suing for immortality.

And them came Athens.

> Sweet are thy groves, and verdant are thy fields,
> Thine olive ripe as when Minerva smiled,
> And still his honied wealth Hymettus yields.

The bees on the flowering mount still sucked the honey from the yellow broom. But how was Athens's glory vanished! Like another Volney, the Childe lamented the majestic ruins where now the lizard held empire, and, worse, the antiquarian and the collector.

With mattock and spade Lord Elgin's men were plundering the Parthenon, razing its columns, hewing down its friezes — that, at any rate, is the way the Childe looked upon the Caledonian lord's activities, though there was one in London, a disciple of High Art, to whom the transported marbles were a godsend, to be copied on bended knees, with prayers of thanksgiving on the lips. Fourteen, sixteen hours at a stretch, without stopping for food, Benjamin Robert Haydon drew the "Ilyssus" in the damp, dirty penthouse in Park Lane where the Elgin Marbles were then lodged, copied the "Theseus," dreamed of glory when his own "Dentatus," painted on the principles of Greek art, should astonish the world — and starved. Fuseli, his teacher, was fired to view them, and David Wilkie, Haydon's fellow student. With him as escort, small parties tore down the Strand, avoiding collisions with coal carts and horses in the narrow lanes, waiting impatiently for flocks of sheep to get out of their path. The Park Lane barn, like the Parthenon, was a place of pilgrimage. High Art had come to England.

But the Childe was no collector — not of such carvings before which the wise Fletcher, learned in the school of his lordship, would exclaim: "La, what mantel pieces these would make, my lord!" To Byron they brought visions of the Mansion House. He preferred to survey the ruins, mourn over the glory that was dead, and feed his spirit on gloom. The acolyte of death still sang his threnody.

> Son of the morning, rise! approach you here!
> Come — but molest not yon defenseless urn:
> Look on this spot — a nation's sepulchre!

The son of the morning did not, but the Childe did molest the urn. The worshiper of decay brought away with him the bones and skulls of four Athenian heroes. Thenceforth the relics followed him in his journeys with the portraits of his friends which he had had painted before leaving England. The spoils of death, the shadows of the living . . . Byron felt at home among them.   Again, as at Newstead, he philosophized on the ruins of the human temple.   He had less now of the daring boy, intent to shock.   A manly courage possessed him in the face of the inescapable.   But the Childe, no less than Lord Byron, still postured with an eye to the audience that should find him infinitely interesting, alluringly romantic.

> Look on its broken arch, its ruin'd wall,
>   Its chambers desolate, and portals foul:
> Yes, this was once Ambition's airy hall,
>   The dome of Thought, the palace of the Soul.

For all that, life was not to be despised.   At Madame Theodora Macri's there were three excellent reasons for turning from the worship of death.   Even the marble-hearted Childe found the pose hard to sustain before the budding graces of Theresa, Catinco, and Mariana, daughters of the Consulina Macri, at present hostess to Byron and Hobhouse.   Whenever Byron looked out of his sitting-room window into the lemon-shaded court, his sight was charmed by one or another of the young girls, her pelisse flowing to the ankles, her muslin kerchief covering her bosom, her full, gayly striped skirt allowing a glimpse of bright yellow slippers.   Each wore a red Albanian skullcap tasseled with blue silk over a kerchief of many colors that left the hair free, falling over the shoulders.   Theresa and Catinco were both dark-eyed, black-haired beauties with delicate aquiline noses.   Mariana, a mere child, was very fair.   To each in turn Byron gave his homage, but it was for Theresa, not quite fifteen, that he tore open his shirt, and in the manner of the country made a gash with his dagger across his breast to show his love.   Theresa looked coolly on the procedure; the marble heart throbbed.

> Maid of Athens, ere we part,
> Give, oh, give me back my heart,

sang the Childe on resuming his wanderings.

Four months later, in unaffected prose, he closed the story of the romance in a letter to Hobhouse, already returned to

England. "Intrigue flourishes: the old woman, Theresa's mother, was mad enough to imagine I was going to marry the girl; but I have better amusement." He was again at Athens after having visited Smyrna and Constantinople. In the meantime he had concluded the second canto of his poem, swum from Sestos to Abydos, after an unsuccessful first trial, and narrowly escaped death from a malarial fever near Missolonghi.

He was so inordinately proud of his swimming feat that every letter crowed with his self-esteem. He and Leander had swum the Hellespont, Leander, less fortunate, — or more? — only to die.

> 'T were hard to say who fared the best:
> Sad mortals! thus the gods still plague you.
> He lost his labour, I my jest,
> For he was drown'd, and I 've the aigue.

He is a good laugher who can laugh at himself.

This time he did not lodge at the Consulina's, — relations were strained, — but with the Capuchin monks in their monastery facing Mount Hymettus and shadowed by the Acropolis. A half-dozen young monks-to-be in that period of boyhood that had always roused an inexplicable tenderness in Byron took a fancy to the handsome milord and drew him into their games, which had more to do with the world than with the church. He swam and boxed with them, in the midst of boyish clamor that brought out the good abbot with a threat to whip them. It reminded him of the Harrow years not so long past, and yet so long ago, and he felt an old man among those boys, at twenty-three.

Of Niccolo Giraud, a shy youth, he made a special pet. They walked arm in arm, they swam together, both wearing their lower garments, though the Greeks did not. But then, Byron never forgot his lame foot, and the youth was exceedingly modest: *"Questo giovane è vergognoso,"* he essayed in Italian. Once, while swimming in the Piræus with the boy, he met an English acquaintance and was reminded that soon he must return home. Home? He grew more attached to the land he was to leave, and to the boy who unaffectedly showed his devotion, calling him his master and friend and swearing that he would die with him. How often had Byron had to contrast the affection of these simple folk with that of the gentlemen he had called his friends! He still fumed at the remembrance that Lord Delawarr had refused to dine with him on the eve of his departure because he had had to attend some ladies to the milliner's! And here was a foreign boy, ready to die with him.

Notwithstanding the distractions of the young monks Byron wrote at the Capuchin monastery what he intended to be a sequel to his *English Bards,* and a short satirical piece, *The Curse of Minerva.* With him feeling had to find relief in expression. Day by day he came in contact with Lord Elgin's men, and his indignation rose. In his poetical dialogue between himself and the patron goddess of Athens the well-meaning Scotch lord was so cut up and hewn that his *disjecta membra* might have been gathered by his own assemblers of ruins.

Fletcher was shipped home, and the Childe reluctantly prepared to follow. Hanson was becoming importunate in complaints of the plaguy duns; there was no more money for protracted traveling. As it was, it would be some time before Byron could pay back Scrope Davies the loan he had advanced toward the pilgrimage. Davies, Hobhouse, dear old Matthews with his flashing mind and endearing eccentricities — they were the reasons for his returning to England. But there was his mother. How had she behaved herself as mistress of Newstead in his absence? Her *scenes* still echoed in his ears. Catherine Byron was too old to change, and he thought with misgiving of her disgracing herself before strangers by some inimitable outburst when nothing short of an act of Providence could quiet her. Cautiously he felt the way. "I trust you . . . agree with your neighbours; but you know *you* are a *vixen* — is not that a dutiful appellation?" It was the same playfully veiled reproof that had made Byron stand aside before his mother's oncoming furies, saying as he bowed profoundly, "Enter the Honourable Kitty Gordon." Affection, exasperation, irony, and dislike — he never could feel the one without an alloy of the others.

And yet he knew that she loved him and anxiously followed his success. In her maternal pride she filled her letters with so many excerpts from the magazines that in annoyance Byron had to tell her to spare him. "I have done with authorship," he said, "and if, in my last production I have convinced the critics or the world I was something more than they took me for, I am satisfied." She was a good soul, was Mrs. Byron, in spite of her faults, and an able manager. Certainly Newstead would be in better shape under her care than when he had left it. How was old Joe Murray, the last living relic of Newstead? And how were the dogs and the bear he had left in his mother's keeping? Had any improvements been made in the living quarters? According to Hanson, Messrs. Brothers, the Nottingham upholsterers, were executing for an unpaid bill. . . . No, life had not changed at home.

He sailed on the *Volage* frigate on the third of June, 1811, from Malta, where Niccolo Giraud took leave of him and received from his *padrone* and *amico* a large sum of money which Byron could ill afford. The skulls of the Athenians were stowed, a phial of Attic hemlock was secured against breakage, four live tortoises and a greyhound were accommodated as well as possible, while a cosmopolitan retinue followed the returning Childe in amazing and colorful array. The voyage proved too much for the greyhound, who found the "watery grave" that Fletcher, now safe at home, had so dreaded for himself.

By the middle of July Byron was in England. He did not go to Newstead, however — not yet. He could postpone his mother's welcome and have peace from the dreary duns. He stopped at Reddish's Hotel in St. James's Street, where Dallas was the first to call. Byron had changed. The handsome youth was become romantically beautiful, thin, and of transparent pallor. The malarial attack had left its traces, but only to spiritualize.

What had his lordship written during the two years abroad, wondered Dallas. Byron, who had "done with authorship," brought out his *Hints from Horace,* more Pope-like in their neat verses, he told his agent, and in all respects better than his first satire. He must find a publisher for it; it would create a sensation. Honest Dallas took the opus home and read it carefully. Was this all Lord Byron had produced in two years, this milk-and-water dilution of *English Bards?* A paraphrase of Horace, was it? It was rather a repetition of himself, at his feeblest. None of the vigor of his first satire enlivened it; the righteous anger of the original outburst had diminished to a pose. Nearly eight hundred lines of weak ranting against English *literati* — was this all, alas? His lordship might just as well have stuffed himself in a Grub Street garret; so much did the new satire smell of dust and the lamp.

Dallas could not tell Byron his disappointment. A publisher might be found to risk bringing out the *Hints;* Byron could only lose by it. Next morning when he called again, Dallas spoke with moderate praise of the *Hints* and tactfully asked whether his lordship had not written anything else. Why, yes, his lordship had — some Spenserian stanzas on his travels, but they were nothing, really. Satire was his special gift. Those stanzas were inferior by far. Someone whose opinion he valued had found them poor. . . . Dallas insisted on seeing them, and Byron was persuaded to bring them out of a little trunk, still speaking disparagingly of the work. Dallas could see, could he not, how severe were the marginal strictures of John Cam Hobhouse? Whatever one might say, Hobhouse was a just critic. Dallas hurried home with the manuscript before Byron could change his mind. He read it through the same night. He could not stop reading it.

More than a week passed, and Byron had not yet gone to Newstead. "My dear Madam," he wrote to his mother, "I am only detained by Mr. Hanson to sign some copyhold papers, and will give you timely notice of my approach. It is with great reluctance I remain in town. . . ." He subscribed himself "with great respect, yours ever, Byron." He might have been writing to an acquaintance with whom he was on cool, impersonal terms. Not a word of affection. She was *my dear Madam* to whom he would give notice of his approach so that neither the one nor the other should be embarrassed by the meeting. "You will consider Newstead as your house, not mine; and me only as a visiter [*sic*]." Catherine Byron's

son had been away from her for two years and he was now to
be considered only as a visitor. He meant the words graciously, that was certain; he did not wish to put her to any
inconvenience on his account. Yet how much rather would she
have turned Newstead topsy-turvy in arranging for his home-
coming, gathered his fantastic treasures in his room, — the
goblet skull, the bust of Napoleon, — summoned his dogs
from the farmers who were caring for them, dusted with her
own hands every trifle that belonged to him, that it might
glow its welcome! "If I should be dead before Byron comes
down . . ." she said to Mrs. By, her maid. It hardly seemed
possible that she should see again Mad Jack's son, the fruit
of a union the fates themselves had ordained for the heiress
of Gight. She had suffered through the father, — how brief
the happiness! — she had suffered through the son. She loved
them both and blessed the pain. Anxiously she awaited Lord
Byron's arrival. The days sped on, and still he did not come.
"If I should die . . ."

On the first of August Catherine Byron was dead.

The news sent Byron hastening to Newstead to behold for
the last time the still features of one whose last hours he might
have gladdened. He could have gone to her, and he knew it.
The thought stung his conscience. The poor old Dowager —
she was quiet now, as she had never been in her uneasy life.
How little had he thought when he had taken leave of her
that it had been forever! He had dreaded her temper as she
had dreaded his. After those storms at Southwell he would
go to the chemist's to warn him not to sell any poison to his
mother, unaware that but a few moments earlier she had been
there on a like errand. Each had feared that the other, in desperation, might commit suicide. How alike had they been,
for all their differences. Too late Byron discovered how much
he loved the poor, ungainly woman of whom he had been
ashamed.

At Newstead he learned that she had been ailing. It had
seemed nothing serious to the servants, accustomed as they
were to seeing her near apoplexy one moment and soothed the
next. Anything might bring on an outburst. The last time
it had been the upholsterer's bill — the one from Messrs.

Brothers, probably — that had precipitated the fit of rage that killed her. To her last breath she had fought for the interest of her son, whom everyone had been conspiring to cheat.

Her death, like the first bird of an evil flock, did not come alone. She was still lying, a corpse, at Newstead, when Byron received the intelligence that Matthews, the most promising of the Cambridge quadrumvirate, was dead — drowned among the weeds of the Cam. He had dived in where they had often swum. His delay in rising to the surface alarmed his friends who were on shore. When he came up at last his body was wrapped round in festoons of weeds out of which he struggled in vain to extricate himself. No one could help him where he was. When they reached him finally and got him to shore, he was past hope. Byron could hardly believe it possible. Only two days earlier he had received a letter, written on an ill-omened Friday. The next day the hand that had traced it was clutching hopelessly for life, a life which Byron would willingly have saved at the cost of his own, and he spoke truly. Some curse must hang over him and those he loved. He had hardly set foot in England, and he was shadowed by the wings of misfortune. How far was the shadow to spread? Must he always reside in the gloom of a charnel house? What wonder he set up its eyeless symbols as trophies! He was the high priest of a temple daily becoming desolate. Wingfield, one of the dearest companions of his boyhood, was gone with the rest, perished of a fever at Coimbra. Thousands of the Guards had been spared; he, one of the noblest and purest youths, had had to die. It seemed the roll call should never end. Who would be the next taken? Himself, perhaps, though that were no loss. In a sardonic moment he drew up his will.

He wished to be buried in the vault with his dog Boatswain. George Anson Brown should be his heir. His remaining friends should share his worldly goods among them. To Niccolo Giraud he bequeathed seven thousand pounds to be paid him on coming of age. With Niccolo might have been mentioned another lad whom he had loved almost as he had loved Mary Chaworth — Edleston, the chorister at Cambridge.

His name, however, closed for the present the list of the departed.

Theirs had been a sentimental attachment more akin to that of boy and girl than of male comrades. Edleston had sung for him, his tenderly beautiful voice stirring the youth as thrillingly as a woman's. They had exchanged love tokens, the boy giving Byron a cornelian heart which had had its place in the reliquary of Byron's passions and its garland of verses in the *Hours of Idleness*. Later, when Edleston had had to leave college to go to London, they had planned to set up house together — in the manner of Lady Butler and Miss Ponsonby, Byron had said roguishly, alluding to an ambiguous relation that had been scandalizing England.

A vague, romantic sweetness mingled with the loss of Edleston; it was a little as if Byron had lost, through death, another Mary Chaworth. Edleston's elegy became the lines *To Thyrza*, with whom no more he might share

> The smile none else might understand;
> The whisper'd thought of hearts allied,
> The pressure of the thrilling hand. . . .

VI

LOVE, FRIENDSHIP, AND HUMANITY

GEORGE STREET, in the newer section of Edinburgh built on a height, commanded a view of the mother city with the sea shimmering at its feet, bringing the outside world nearer, but not too near, in its commerce of ships. The chimney stacks of industrialism wafting their breath of smoke over the roof tops had not yet become a menace; in the distance the bright fishing sails showed through the smoke as through clouds in a fair sky. William Cumming, the ostler who let furnished lodgings at number 60, had never had so young and so inexperienced a married pair in his ground-floor parlor as the two who stopped with him that August: Mr. and Mrs. Shelley, the one aged nineteen, the other a mere bairn out of school. It was no wonder the jolly Cumming and his stout-drinking cronies should have wanted some good-humored sport at their expense, in a bluff heartiness that newly married folk could n't have taken amiss. But they were hardly prepared for the disheveled fury who barred their way to the parlor door, defying them to enter on peril of their lives. The shrillness of the voice and the flashing eyes drove back Cumming and his company more effectually than the pistol clenched in the young man's hand. There was no trifling with him, the sobered crew decided.

Shelley adjusted himself as best he could to his new situation. He was married; Harriet loved him; he was not unhappy with her, though the vision of another — but of her, no more. She was lost, lost to him forever. It was time he faced the present circumstances. Here he was, in the city of Edinburgh, with a wife and no money. Sunday passed, and the expected help had not arrived. Uncle Pilfold and Uncle Med-

win had been drawn upon; Hogg had been kind.   Taking his
courage in his hand, he wrote to Timothy Shelley to tell him
that the son who had troubled his peace was again in straits
and would appreciate the pecuniary blessing that was due
him.   "I know of no one to whom I can apply with greater
certainty of success when in distress than you," began the
naïf flatterer.   Not a word did he write of his marriage.

Blissful, high, but blind philosophy!   Certainty of success?
The household at Field Place cowered under the curses Timothy Shelley heaped upon his scapegrace of a son, the truth
of whose latest escapade had come to his knowledge.   He had
gone and married — he, Percy Bysshe Shelley, a gentleman,
married the daughter of a vulgar tavern keeper!   It was disgraceful enough that he had been expelled from college, caus-
ing the finger of respectability to point at the Member for
New Shoreham, the father of an atheist; bad enough that he
should have run off with a young female.   But to *marry* her!
How should his four sisters now be protected?   How could
one hope to make respectable matches for them with a brother
who brought ignominy first in one way, then in another, upon
them all?   How should the youngest child, the only boy now,
be kept from the knowledge of his brother's shame?   Timothy
Shelley tasted the very dregs of despair.   Not one penny
should that pariah have from him.   He sowed his wild oat;
let him eat in the ensuing famine the bitter and choking fruit
thereof.

Timothy Shelley must have someone to confide in or suffer
from a stroke.   Moreover, he had a duty to perform and
blame to lay at another's door.   "My son has withdrawn from
my protection," he wrote to Mr. John Hogg, "and has set off
for Scotland with a young female."   Let him look after that
thorn in *his* side, whose poisonous pricking had turned the
blood of his own son.   He wrote further.   Let Mr. Hogg
beware of that married scoundrel, and let not the two young
men get together, or, as sure as fate, Percy Bysshe Shelley,
once the novelty of matrimony had worn off, would leave his
wife on the junior Hogg's hands.   Timothy Shelley knew his
mad son's fickleness.

Perhaps Mr. John Hogg received the warning too late, for

little time had elapsed before, at Shelley's urgent invitation, Thomas Jefferson Hogg was installed in an upstairs room of number 60 George Street, gazing up sentimentally with the bride and groom at the comet that was the wonder of that clear, rainless autumn. Together they took pedestrian excursions to Arthur's Seat and the Pentland Hills. Together Shelley and Hogg listened to the lovely Harriet reading to them with much expression out of Volney's *Ruins of Empires*, which Bysshe loved, and out of Madame Cottin's *Claire d'Albe,* whose woeful lapse from connubialism lulled the bored husband of Harriet to sleep in his chair. Together they dined off biscuits from the bakeshop and drank cups and cups of tea made by Harriet's own fair but inexperienced hands. Together, gathering into a heap their portable property, they bade good-bye to the Scottish capital, where they had at first determined to establish themselves forever, and in fitting style took a comfortable chaise to York. Harriet promptly produced one of Holcroft's edifying but, alas, to Shelley, wearisome novels, and commenced her reading, pausing neither for yawns nor for protests. "Is it necessary to read all that, Harriet dear?" Shelley complained. It was necessary; a good book has to be read word for word to the, as it often proved, bitter end.

At York the young people found a suite of rooms for themselves, and Shelley's happiness was nearly complete. Now, with the lovely girl he was educating, he had also the "brother of his soul" — a Hitchener formula that brought the Hurst-pierpoint spinster before him. Time had passed, and he had not yet told her, his soul's *sister,* of the step he had taken. He had written for help to Uncle Pilfold, who had responded with his usual open hand. Perhaps Uncle Pilfold had told Miss Hitchener. He was somewhat uneasy. Moreover, since Hogg was with him, he felt the need of someone with whom to carry on a stimulating epistolary discussion. Miss Hitchener had always written at length and with a show of reading, if not at all like a philosopher in her rambling, and still less like a grammarian. But the sublime enthusiast could overlook such faults. He wrote to her, whose salutation had progressed from "Dear Sir" to "My dear Friend," and informed

her of the causes which had made the would-be student of
medicine become a practician in the theatre of life.

Elizabeth Hitchener outdid herself in the nobility of her
sentiments, like the superior woman she was. (Her Dear
Friend would not expect less of her, disappointed though she
was.) She magnanimously forgave him for the inconsistency
of his behavior. "Thus may a person do to-day what yesterday they had not thought of doing. . . . As to *marrying* that
was due to Mrs. Shelley; *with you* she might have borne 'the
world's dread laugh,' but I know you could not *risk* her being
depriv'd of your sympathy under it." How much more than
the world's dread laugh she, Elizabeth Hitchener, would have
borne had Shelley asked her to share his life. But *she* was
noble. "I hope to see realized such a Union as the children
of the world would tell me never existed but in my own imagination," she confided, ". . . but such marriages *are rare.*"

To the two happy children in York the ominous words meant
little. Shelley saw only the great-heartedness of the sister
of his soul and answered in kind. He was an heir, and on his
twenty-first birthday he would come into some share of his
fortune. He had Harriet, his disciple-wife; he had Hogg; he
had Miss Hitchener's luminous intellect. A combination of
such love, friendship, and brilliance should prove a power in the
world. He no longer scorned the wealth that was to be his,
because he now felt he knew the use of it. "It commands
labour; it gives leisure; and to give leisure to those who will
employ it in the forwarding of truth is the noblest present an
individual can make to the whole." Miss Hitchener, therefore,
should leave her school, and with Miss Adams, the friend of
her soul, with her little American charges, "nurslings of liberty," and perhaps with his sister Elizabeth and the fair Eliza
Westbrook, she should place herself in the vanguard of this
new battalion toward perfection.

The good schoolmistress widened her eyes at such unpar-
alleled magnanimity. That wonderful youth was actually
placing his fortune at her feet with manifestations of ardent
love — did he not write the very word? "*You,* who can contemn the world's prejudices, whose views are mine, I will dare
to say I *love* — Henceforth I will be yours — yours in truth,

sincerity and unreserve." He was married, and yet he could write to her in that loverlike strain! She did not know what to think, or how to take the offer. It might be nobler to reject it for the present, but she must do it in a way that reflected glory upon her. She confessed to him, therefore, that she had always wanted money because she, too, knew the use of it; thus, when he came into possession of his fortune, "I will tax your friendship for the Mother of my soul," she said, "the dear woman who educated me . . . but having *too much virtue* for her age has ever been an object of persecution." Yes, old Miss Adams, who nurtured the flower of her youthful mind, should join the battalion. Two important requirements she had: she was an enlightener, and she had suffered persecution, though how, Miss Hitchener did not say. One little scruple, however, which had no business in an emancipated intellect, Miss Hitchener expressed; after all, she had better be on the right side of everyone. She was not sure that Mrs. Shelley approved of the lengthy correspondence between her husband and the sister of his soul. "Can she generously permit . . . I long to see her and ask her this."

Perhaps the not yet sufficiently enlightened Harriet saw with the help of her feminine instinct more than met the idealist's eye in the divine Miss Hitchener's epistles; perhaps in consequence her permission came not so warmly as her husband might have wished. But Harriet was very young. She was still of the outer circle and but painfully making her way toward the orbit of perfection. She might arrive there. "If Harriet be not at sixteen," wrote Shelley, "all that you are at a more advanced age, assist me to mould a really noble soul into all that can make its nobleness useful and lovely." Oh, for a magic glass to have seen the expression of the divine preceptress before such sublime truthtelling! It was agreed, nevertheless, that at a later date Miss Hitchener should leave her school and go to live with the prospective heir and his family.

Nearly seven weeks had passed since Shelley's flight from London, and still his father averted his face; worse, he so tightened the purse strings that for all Uncle Pilfold's generosity and the Pythagorean teas, a shilling sometimes was

far to seek.   Uncle Pilfold had made overtures at Field Place
— in vain.   Driven by want, the young husband left Harriet
in the care of Hogg at York and started out intrepidly to face
the dragon.

The unconventionality of the situation, or perhaps that
same feminine intuition that had warned her with regard to
Miss Hitchener, prompted Harriet to write to Chapel Street.
However it was, soon after Shelley's departure the fair Eliza,
with hair glossier than ever, was found installed in the parlor
by the astonished Hogg.   He too had sent a filial communication to his father, little recking what consternation it was to
raise in that Tory breast.   The tale did not end there.   True
to an unwritten pact the two fathers had formed for mutual
protection against their dangerous sons, John Hogg wrote to
Shelley *père* with grave concern: "I received a letter from
York stating that your son left that place . . . about the
18th, leaving his lady to the protection of my son, saying he
should return in about a week or ten days.   Mrs. Hogg and I
were greatly alarmed, thinking it highly improper that they
should be left together, and remembering what you said in
a former letter, that you should not be surprised at your
son's leaving his lady on my son's hands."   Your son . . .
my son. . . .   Wretched are they who bring forth firebrands
into the world; they are the first to be scorched.

Unhappily for idealism, Hogg's parents knew him better
than did his trusting friend.   He had always been of exacting
passions, taking his pleasures when he wished them.   Moreover, Shelley's anti-matrimonialist arguments had converted
him, Hogg, as his own pleas for marriage, in Harriet's case,
had won over his friend.   Shelley was always maintaining
that the very essence of love is liberty, that "it is compatible
neither with obedience, jealousy, nor fear."   Surely, as a practising philosopher, Shelley would understand if his friend
put those teachings to the test.   Not that he was performing
an experiment.   Ever since he had joined the youthful menage
and had been allowed into its domestic intimacies, he had
wished the pretty Harriet had belonged to him rather than
to the abstracted Shelley, who, oftener than not, left her to
her own devices while he went chasing his chimeras.   At

Arthur's Seat Shelley had gone ahead and left them together.
A high wind was blowing, and on the great stone steps Harriet's skirts, in spite of her embarrassed efforts, had flapped
and risen, showing her dainty calves. She had then insisted
on Hogg's walking ahead; but that glimpse had roused his
blood. Harriet was too ingenuous to understand his advances,
and, if she did, she was too much in love with her poet-philosopher to be more than innocently flattered at finding herself
admired. With Shelley away, however, Hogg grew bolder.
One day, eluding Eliza's vigilance, he declared his passion to
Harriet with arguments grown too familiar, and begged that
she yield herself to him. Shelley would never know, he
pleaded inconsistently, as if love, so free in its essence, had
need of concealment.

Harriet drew back indignantly. How had she ever encouraged him that he should behave so shamefully toward
her and so dishonorably toward his friend? How could he
betray Shelley's trust? Was that friendship which could
take advantage of his absence to rob him of his honor? Harriet poured upon Hogg's guilty head the elevated moral sentiments she had gathered from her reading of *Claire d'Albe*.

Repulsed, and rudely awakened to the enormity of a crime
which no liberality could condone, Hogg sank into a state of
despair. How would he be able to justify himself before
Shelley? He could quote him his own defense of the freedom of love; but it was with Shelley's wife that he had wanted
to make free. How could he face his friend on his return?
Mortified and repentant, he would have written Shelley a full
confession, but Harriet forbade. Shelley was having a difficult enough time of it without being troubled with such
news as that. Let Hogg wait till Shelley came back, for of
course her husband must know. It would be easier and wiser
to tell him by word of mouth.

Disheartened by another futile encounter with his implacable
father, Shelley returned to an atmosphere of constraint and
mysterious looks. Hogg averted his gaze; Harriet seemed
nervous. Something had gone amiss. How amiss he learned
from Hogg later when they, he and Hogg, walked out together
in the meadows. Hogg, the brother of his soul, had proved

unworthy! That was all Shelley could grasp. He had taken a man to his heart, had admitted him like a dearer self to his home — and that man had betrayed him. What hope was there for mankind when the best of human creatures could fall so low? Hogg repeated Shelley's opinions to exculpate himself and to soften his friend toward him. Shelley could forgive, and did, but for the present he could not be toward Hogg as he had been. Their friendship must end.

Eliza, the moral censor, took matters in hand. Harriet's nerves could n't stand any more trials from that wretched Hogg; she must be taken away from the scene of the affront to her virtue. "Dear me, what would Miss Warne say?" . . . and Eliza shook her glossy head at the thought of what *her* arbiter, an innkeeper's daughter like herself, might have commented on the unpleasant business. Surely nothing flattering concerning Hogg — no, nor the husband who could leave his innocent, lovely young bride at the mercy of an unprincipled ruffian. Hogg was to blame, but Shelley was not wholly guiltless.

Shelley therefore took his wife and his sister-in-law, who seemed in no hurry to return to Chapel Street, and transported them to Keswick without taking leave of Hogg. He still had the sister of his soul, however, and to her he narrated the whole misadventure. "You can conjecture," he admitted naïvely, "that my letters to him will be neither infrequent nor short." Alas! From the heights to the depths. Hardly a month back he had been making plans for a perfect pantisocracy; now one of the solidest columns of the edifice had crumbled. "Oh, how could he be so blind to his own happiness!" exclaimed Miss Hitchener in horror. "What gratification could equal your esteem?" How understanding she was, and how devoted. And yet there were tongues that could speak ill of even their pure relation. "Before I close this, I hint a suspicion that our friends would willingly lessen us in each other's opinion." Those were her words. Their friendship was the theme of gossip. Miss Hitchener, the divine, the noble, was undergoing persecution for his sake. A less ingenuous Platonist than Shelley would have read the sequence aright and drawn the correct inference. Now that

Harriet, though exemplary in her conduct, was in a sense smutched, as is a flower when the slug leaves its trail upon it, Miss Hitchener could reveal her virtues, unjustly attacked, and more direfully. Mrs. Shelley had her husband to protect her. She, Miss Hitchener, was only his soul's sister, a relation open to misconstruction by the evil-minded world.

Keswick in the early winter offered a spectacle of calm beauty that fell healingly upon Shelley's torn spirit. His nerves, far more than Harriet's, had need of soothing. His health, never good, was rapidly breaking down, confirming the feeling he had always had that he was not destined for a long life. Painful spasms seized him whenever he was overwrought, and to obtain relief that should enable him to work he took to laudanum — apologetically for his weakness in resorting to it, but still grateful that such an opiate was at hand. Between his impassioned exchanges with Miss Hitchener and a Werther-like correspondence with Hogg, in which the culprit was taken once more to his soul as his brother, with many protestations of his own unworthiness, and then held again at arm's length, he read Southey's narrative poems and planned a long work of his own which had been maturing in his mind. Some beginnings had been made, but much was still to do.

The poetry-laden atmosphere of Cumberland worked beneficently upon him. Southey, whose *Thalaba* he read and reread with admiration, lived a short distance from Chestnut Hill, where he and Harriet and Eliza had settled — this time, perhaps, forever. Skiddaw, mighty and high, reared its mass above the huddled mountains. Dawn and sunset haloed its head in rainbows; the snows renewed it with constant changes of light and shade. On a cloudy day, in the sudden shafts of sunlight, the whole mountainside gleamed and glowed in patches of vivid chiaroscuro — a sight, once seen, never to be forgotten. Below the cottage at Chestnut Hill two lakes frozen in the grasp of winter shone smooth and dark as twin slabs of black marble. Shelley responded to the surrounding majesty, and in his solitary rambles shaped the visions that crowded into his mind. How beautiful was unspoiled nature! Would that man had been more perfect. Still he did not relinquish his hope. Somewhere, sometime, the fulfillment of his dream of perfection would come to be. As a lover of humanity he wished it; as a poet he would strive to give the message to mankind.

He went to Greta Hall to see Southey, not without a plan of attack. Years ago, when he was an infant, Southey and Coleridge had burned with that same love of humanity that consumed him. Their ardor had cooled with the years, and now, as the grey of age sprinkled their heads, the ashes of that spent fire were all that remained in their souls. His still unpublished *Wat Tyler*, his *Joan of Arc*, had given way to Oriental romances. Southey, a state pensioner, had become a pillar of things as they are; Coleridge, lost in his cloudy regions, fashioned his stately pleasure domes and had but abstract commiseration for the hovels of the poor. Shelley could not be silent before such faithlessness. Since Coleridge was not then accessible, he made his way to Southey, determined to "reproach him of [*sic*] his tergiversations," as he said to Miss Hitchener.

And reproach him he did in his shrillest excitement, in spite of the ingratiating flavor of Mrs. Southey's home-baked tea cakes and the bard's gentle patience. Yet once Bigotry, Tyranny, and Law — always gross personifications to Shelley — had been as hateful to that man before him, slowly sipping his tea, as they were now to him, Shelley. The iconoclast had become the votary of those hated idols — and why? As he and Harriet visited more often at Greta Hall he began to understand. "His writings solely support a numerous family. His sweet children are such amiable creatures that I almost forgive what I suspect." Shelley the reformer was becoming humanized. As he observed the doting affection of the *renegade* poet whenever his children, especially his favorite Herbert, a youngster of five, came into the room, he could not condemn. Passing strange were the ways of time; dolefully Shelley shook his head. Mrs. Southey he found very stupid, however, and he had nothing more to say to her, even though she attempted to initiate the impractical Harriet into the mysteries of housekeeping and lent her finest linens to the impecunious household.

Southey's library was Shelley's delight. Books, books everywhere along the walls, on the landing, in the halls; books in

calf and morocco, books in vellum, books in bright gingham
and calico in a sort of flourishing old age; for Southey's
Cottonian library, as he called it, consisted of those well-
thumbed veterans whose shabbiness Mrs. Southey and her
daughters clothed in the remnants of their sewing. Many a
time Shelley left the home of his host with an armful of books
extracted from their jealous owner with difficulty — the malicious Hogg said because Southey was afraid people would find
out where he drew the material for his poems. All the way
home Shelley would walk unmindful of the rainbowed Skiddaw,
blind to the sky's cloudy splendors, his eyes fixed to the last
ray of light upon that ever-renewable but never stale experience — a new book.

As for Southey, the appearance of the philadelphic Shelley
was like a vision of his own dead youth. That passionate love
of humanity had been his, that zeal for reform, in the falsely
hopeful days of the Revolution. Time had taught him better,
as it had others of his day. "The only difference between us,"
he would tell Shelley, "is that you are nineteen, and I am
thirty-seven." And he gave him Berkeley to read. The disturbing ghost gone, Southey would resume the routine of his
day, — so many hours for creative writing, so many hours for
reading, so many more for taking notes, so many for his
domestic duties, — an arrangement which had made a visiting
Quakeress ask the future laureate, "When dost thou think,
friend?" She did not know, the dear lady, that when ideals are
shattered and things of evil are seen crawling under the ruins,
it is sometimes better not to think. It is needless suffering, and
man must not unduly suffer who would give of his best to the
world. Shelley must be taught the lesson; he would then be
spared much avoidable pain. His calling himself an atheist
had already made trouble for him in a society that was frightened of labels it did not understand. Why did he not call himself a Pantheist, — a less terrifying name, — since he believed
"the Universe is God"? But Shelley had sooner avowed himself a Christian.

Unexpectedly Shelley heard from Uncle Pilfold, perhaps as
a result of his recent meeting with Timothy Shelley, that some
interesting plans were going forward at Field Place in con-

nection with the financial situation. There was hope that the black sheep would be admitted into the fold. Shelley was not averse to a peaceful settlement, and awaited developments. Timothy Shelley and Sir Bysshe, it appeared, had put their heads together and were ready with an offer which on the face of it promised complete freedom from future money cares. Shelley had only to agree to entail his estates on his male heir, if he should have any; otherwise, upon his young brother John. Two thousand pounds a year would be his for life if he signed the neat little document. Two thousand pounds a year — enough to maintain Harriet, Miss Hitchener, the mother of her soul, and Eliza in comfort, to pay for the publication of his political essays and of *Hubert Cauvin*,[1] the novel he was writing on the French Revolution, enough to buy food and clothing for the poor, and come to the help of some needy friend. All of that two thousand pounds could do.

So generous an offer, however, could not derive from Field Place without bearing the seal of the cloven hoof. Evidently Sir Bysshe and Timothy Shelley had abandoned all hope of ever making a conformist of Percy Bysshe; therefore, rather than let the valuable estate be thrown to the winds by the rebel's improvidence should he ever fall heir to it, they preferred to bribe him now that he was in need. Thus, by losing a little, they should in the end save all. But it was not this aspect that struck Shelley, ever alive to the higher motive. How could he with an honest conscience entail his "command over labour" on someone who might prove himself morally and ethically unfit for the responsibility? How could his father and grandfather so affront him as to imagine he would ever imperil the happiness of thousands for his own selfish gain? With fiery vehemence he rejected the proposal; better to starve than sell his birthright to benefit humanity.

The much needed help came unexpectedly from another quarter. Mr. Westbrook, relenting at length toward his daughter who had been guilty of the indiscretion of running off with a gentleman, yielded completely when he heard from Eliza that such notables as the Duke of Norfolk entertained them at Greystoke, and promised to win over the stubborn

---

[1] Not a trace of which has come down to us.

Mr. Timothy to a sense of his fatherly duty. He gave Harriet an allowance of two hundred pounds a year. Timothy Shelley, ashamed of the trick he would have played his elder son to advantage the younger, softened to the extent of resuming his quarterly grants of fifty pounds. But Field Place remained closed to the scapegrace and his wife — not that Shelley would have set foot there upon learning that his father had renewed the allowance "to prevent his cheating strangers!"

The year 1812 opened auspiciously. Although there was not sufficient money to establish the proposed Utopian phalanx *in toto,* the limited means still admitted of including the divine Miss Hitchener in the Shelley family. She must give up her school and come. "How Harriet and her sister long to see you! and how *I* long to see you, never to part with you again!" Shelley needed the strength of her mighty mind, her enthusiasm for freedom. "If two hearts, panting for the happiness and liberty of mankind, were joined by union and proximity as they are by friendship and sympathy, what might we not expect!" Ay, what might we not expect, the spirit of irony echoed.

The lady still demurred. Meanwhile a name had to be selected against the time when she should adorn the Shelley home with her presence. Elizabeth Hitchener, Elizabeth Westbrook, at some future date perhaps Elizabeth Shelley: they had to be distinguished. Would not Miss Hitchener rechristen herself to maintain her noble entity? *Call me Portia,* suggested the lady — Portia, Cato's daughter. This classical severity frightened Harriet. Would it not be better if Miss Hitchener came down to the level of mere mortals, at least in the matter of a name? It was left for the time in abeyance.

January had hardly begun when Shelley made a discovery that lifted him to the peak of ecstasy. Godwin, William Godwin, the author of *Political Justice,* was alive! Had anyone told him that Plato had left his urn and walked among mankind he could not have been more astounded. Since his first reading of Godwin he had taken it for granted that the philosopher had long joined the cycle of his peers, feeling in his adoration that such excellence could not then have existed in the mortal world without shedding the effulgence of a noonday sun. It is true Godwin, the individual, had outlived his earlier renown. With him his book had proved greater than the man, in contrast to his friend Thelwall, whose courageous uprightness in suffering for the same ideals, during the same tumultuous decade, had proved him of finer stuff. In his bookshop Godwin lived, a survivor of himself, closer to the dross of common life than his rose-spectacled worshiper could have seen.

It was at the dingy shop in Skinner Street that a pæan of such admiration arrived one day that William Godwin must have risen to the last inch of his squat height. Seldom, these many years, had such burning avowals come from a stranger and a self-confessed disciple. Ay, it was agreeable to receive tributes, but one must be wary. Acting with his usual circumspection, Godwin answered his admirer with moderated kindliness. Who was this P. B. Shelley? A young man, by his fervor, and anxious to do good. Godwin wished to know more of him. In his next letter Shelley wrote him of himself, omitting little, and, in the telling of his expulsion and his relations with his father, embroidering artistically upon the facts. But then, he was writing to the philosopher he revered, the guide of his youth, a sort of spiritual father. He had to make himself interesting to the august man. He must show that, though young, he too had fought for ideals and suffered for them.

William Godwin learned all that he wished to know and concluded it was worth his while to continue the correspondence. He felt interested in Shelley for three reasons, he wrote him. First, because Shelley was a pupil and a disciple; secondly, because he seemed to possess extraordinary powers, though still undisciplined; and thirdly, — did the philosopher mean the force to be cumulative? — "Thirdly, as a man of family born to a considerable fortune it is of the more importance how you conduct yourself, for money is one of the means a man may possess [sic] of being extremely useful to his species." And to William Godwin in particular, perhaps.

Spurred on indirectly by the knowledge of his master's living presence, and conscious of society's injustice, Shelley armed himself in earnest for the battle. Not so far away a people writhed under the heel of the oppressor. The whole Irish nation, ostensibly free, was subjected to the tyranny of a Protestant rule, bitterly opposing the movement for Catholic emancipation. Shelley the atheist had no concern whatever with the formalisms of religion; the political subjection of the weaker by the stronger brought him at once to the side of the Irish. His bundle of quills was got ready, and he proceeded immediately to write *An Address to the Irish People.* Keswick no longer held him. As if providentially, a robber came in the night to Chestnut Hill cottage and felled him with a blow on the head; he could no longer stay in a place where his life was in danger. He would go to Dublin, he informed his mentor. "We go principally *to forward as much as we can* the Catholic Emancipation." The unbeliever thus became a defender of the faith.

Godwin advised moderation. He must wait before he set himself up as a teacher. He was young and therefore liable to the errors of youth. He must not condemn wholesale. Almost every institution or form of society had been good in its place and in its time. "How many beautiful and admirable effects grew out of Popery and the monastic institutions!" But Shelley, with his family of two, was already settled in Dublin. He had a twinge of conscience when he read, "Your letter with its enclosures cost me, by post £1. 1s. 8d; and you say in it, that 'you send it this way to save expense.'" He must henceforth make his philosopher pay less dearly for those freights of knowledge.

Fifteen hundred copies of the *Address* were printed at Shelley's expense and set at the low price of a fivepenny bit. The paper was of the poorest, the printing worse, but the twenty-two-page pamphlet was a treasure of encouragement and hopefulness. The illiterate at the public houses where it was sown by the author and his helpers had it read to them and nodded soberly. Thinking men discovered far-reaching meanings. What if the young Englishman who addressed them at the Catholic meetings seemed too optimistic? Those things he prophesied might come to be, if not in their day, in their children's. Shelley thought he was setting himself a realizable task when he proposed to change the constitution of the British Empire, "to restore to Ireland its native Parliament . . . and to establish a philanthropic association for the amelioration of human society all over the world."

He and Harriet, now as zealous as himself for the good of humanity, would stand at the balcony of their window in Lower Sackville Street and angelically shower down their blessings in copies of the *Address, Proposals for an Association of Philanthropists,* the *Declaration of Rights,* and other emancipatory matter on the heads of indignant passers-by. In sublime strains Harriet wrote of herself to Miss Hitchener. "I looked with a fearful eye upon the vices of the great," reminisced this child of sixteen, "and thought to myself 't was better even to be a beggar, or to be obliged to gain my bread with my needle, than to be an inhabitant of those great houses, when misery and famine howl around."

In Dublin, however, skulking disillusion eventually showed its face. Protestants, Catholics — they were equally the sheep and the goats, striving only for self-advantage. Shelley confessed himself vanquished. Godwin had been right. He had attempted too big a task for his feeble powers and had looked for the harvest before the time of sowing. "I will look to events in which it will be impossible that I can share," he promised, "and make myself the cause of an effect which will take place ages after I have mouldered in the dust." As yet he thought only of the reformer rather than the poet in himself.

Restlessness again possessed him. Dublin, that was to have held him in the cause of humanity, saw a changed aspect in him before two months were over. With Harriet and Eliza he turned his back upon it, a wiser man, and a vegetarian whose letters now bore many an allusion to the slaughtered lamb and the "murdered fowl," victims of the appetite of bloodthirsty man. To North Wales the three Pythagoreans traveled, to Cwm Elan, revisited by Shelley in a happier spirit, to Chepstow and Lynmouth in Devon, to whose sea-girt seclusion and windy caverns he beckoned Godwin with his whole family, Miss Hitchener and Mother Adams. "You are to my fancy as a thunder-riven pinnacle of rock," he rhapsodized to Cato's daughter. ". . . Aye! stand forever firm, and, when our ship anchors close to thee, the crew will cover thee with flowers."

The philosopher of Skinner Street, expecting after the invitation that Shelley would have stayed awhile at Lynmouth with wings furled, left the bookshop and went alone to seek him out — a precautionary measure to assure himself of his reliability before introducing him into the bosom of his family. He was so improvident, however, as to set out with only sufficient funds to take him to his destination, relying on Shelley to send him prosperously back.   Arrived at Lynmouth, hollow of stomach and empty of pocket, what was his dismay on finding the golden gosling flown to Ilfracombe without leaving behind so much as a feather.   But Godwin did not waste the trip and visited the Valley of the Stones.

Miss Hitchener had no misadventure.   Her invitation had been of such long standing, and so often renewed, that she literally expected her thunder-riven majesty to be pelted with roses.   One, at least, of the crew welcomed her with an open heart.   Harriet was sweetly cordial.   Eliza looked her over. Portia did appear firm and rocklike, but no sister of Shelley's soul was going to take from her, the fair Eliza, the keys of household management or try to lord it over *her*.   With subtle equalization Portia soon became Bessie.

What with the freedom of his wandering life through changing scenes, and a sudden awakening to the full awareness of his manhood, Shelley enjoyed such happiness as he had never known.   Harriet had not disappointed his teachings; she loved him with all the fervor of her young heart striving upwards toward him.

> Ever as now with Love and Virtue glow,

he admonished her in verse.

> May thy unwithering soul not cease to burn,
> Still may thine heart with those pure thoughts o'erflow
> Which force from mine such quick and warm return.

The abstract of perfection had become concrete.   More, its life-warm presence ravished his senses, making him feel a bliss so keen that he could not distinguish what was earthly from what was eternal.   For the first time the poet sang of himself and the loved one with rapturous human joy that sought duration through eternity.

It is not blasphemy to hope that Heaven
More perfectly will give those nameless joys
Which throb within the pulses of the blood
And sweeten all the bitterness which Earth
Infuses in the heaven-born soul.   O thou
Whose dear love gleamed upon the gloomy path
Which this lone spirit travelled, drear and cold,
Yet swiftly leading to those awful limits
Which mark the bounds of Time and of the space
When Time shall be no more; wilt thou not turn
Those spirit-beaming eyes and look on me,
Until I be assured that Earth is Heaven,
And Heaven is earth? . . .
Harriet! Let death all mortal ties dissolve,
But ours shall not be mortal!

Yet now, when he saw most clearly in the poignancy of his
rapture, he was most blind.

VII

"THE LION AND THE LAMB"

"I AWOKE one morning and found myself famous." Byron underestimated his triumph.

It was March 1812, the peak of the London season. *Childe Harold's Pilgrimage* had hardly been out a fortnight when, to the delighted astonishment of John Murray, the aristocratical young publisher, his shop became more of a cynosure than the clock of St. Dunstan's opposite. Ladies of fashion drew up in their equipages, coming in person for their copy of Lord Byron's poem in the hope of catching a glimpse of the poet's face. At Holland House, at Lady Melbourne's, the topic of conversation at morning parties, at afternoon teas, at soirées, was Childe Harold, the poem and the poet. None would brook a schism between the romantic, marble-hearted, disillusioned scion of a "lineage long" and the noble young lord, the spokesman of his war-ridden generation, the living symbol of its blighted youth, seeking in forbidden ways sensations for its jadedness. Legends sprang up about him. He was a fiend, an incarnation of all things evil — but dangerously fascinating. He could corrupt the chastest virgin with an underlook of his deep, long-lashed eyes. What a life he must lead in the solitariness of his ruined abbey! What experiences, unwritten in those two cantos, but alluringly veiled, must he have had in the course of his meteoric youth! How learned in evil, how skilled in vice! Chaste Susannahs and Potiphar's wives were alike agog for a sight of the Childe.

The gay life went on apace, all England rejoicing at Wellington's exploits in Spain. Early in January, with Napier and Colborne, Wellington had assaulted the frontier fortress Ciudad Rodrigo, the French supply base, and had taken it, not with powder and shot, but with "the *could* iron." Craufurd,

Courtesy Boston Athenæum

GEORGE GORDON, LORD BYRON

FROM A SKETCH BY COUNT D'ORSAY

leader of the light division, fell in the fray; Mackinnon of the Highland Brigade was mortally wounded; Napier lost his right arm. Seven hundred men had given up their lives by that January midnight when beauty and elegance waltzed at Mayfair; but Ciudad Rodrigo had fallen, and with it the stability of the French Empire. One after another, as Napoleon was marching on toward disaster in Russia, the French fortresses at Cristobal, Saint-Roque, and Picarina fell into the hands of the English — at the cost of nearly three hundred lives a day. Wellington's men advanced toward Salamanca just as the Eagle was nearing Moscow.

It was a prodigious time for England. In Lancashire the cotton mills hummed with industry following upon the inventions of Watt and Arkwright. Wealth doubled itself, trebled, went on increasing with the rolling of the industrial snowball, as labor cheapened and houses were emptied of children to fill the mills with inexpensive hands. It was a time of prosperity; a time of glory. The Childe rose as a sun upon it.

At Melbourne House a young wife wrote tremblingly in her diary at first sight of his fateful beauty, "Mad, bad, and dangerous to know." Caroline Lamb read him better than she knew. From Melbourne House, too, where she had attended her cousin Caroline Lamb's waltzing party, Annabella Milbanke wrote to her mother after she had seen Lord Byron standing aloof from a pastime he could not enjoy: "It is said that he is an infidel. . . . His poem sufficiently proves that he *can* feel nobly, but he has discouraged his own goodness. . . . I did not seek an introduction to him, for all the women were absurdly courting him. I thought that inoffensiveness was the most secure conduct, as I am not desirous of a place in his lays. Besides, I cannot worship talents that are unconnected with the love of man, nor be captivated by that Genius which is barren in blessings." "Lady C. has of course seized on him," she had remarked earlier in her letter. "What a shining situation she will have in his next satire!"

Anna Isabella Milbanke, or Annabella, as she was called by her family, nineteen years old, fresh from the country for her second London season, painted her own portrait better than

Byron's. She would not meet him because all the other women "were absurdly courting him" — and she thought too highly of herself to follow their example. *Inoffensiveness*, in other words a demure modesty, would set her apart from the brazen females and keep her safe from Byron's satires, though not unmarked by his earnestly thoughtful eyes. Smitten in spite of herself by that beautiful face enhaloed by a deserved triumph, she would disparage the man and his work in self-defense. She loved the human and the good: Byron was neither. And she was jealous. Of course she would not admit it to herself. In all sincerity she ascribed her human jealousy to other causes — the affront to her sense of decorum, shame for her shameless sex. Most of all she resented Caroline Lamb for having seized on him, much against his will, as she could see. But she, Miss Milbanke, only daughter of her parents and a very desirable catch, could hold herself at her own worth. She was superior to Caroline Lamb, infinitely superior to those women who threw themselves at Byron. She had high standards and she loved God. Byron was an infidel. (Might she not convert him?) His poem showed that he was not past redemption. (Might she not be the redeemer?) The havoc wrought in the young girl's mind and emotions, the de-sires inspired by Lord Byron, were patent in her studiedly care-ful letter. Yet those grey-blue eyes had not yet spoken to her. Not one word from that too perfect mouth had as yet been addressed to her.

At the redoubtable Holland House the poet-peer found cordial reception, Lord Holland forgiving the barbs against him in *English Bards* once they became acquainted, and Byron heartily repenting of them as well as of others that had made him many unnecessary enemies. At the House of Lords he delivered his maiden speech on Lord Holland's side, as it hap-pened. During his stay at Newstead he had noticed with pain the miserable condition of the working population in the industrialism about Nottinghamshire. New machines were rapidly being adopted, among them power looms that threw six of seven men out of work. The weavers, doomed to poverty, looked upon the machine as an instrument of evil and started out in groups, destroying all they could lay hold of, thinking in this simple way to restore hand labor. The wretches who had the misfortune to be caught were severely punished. Capital sought redress for its broken property; the government was applied to, and a bill was presented before the House suggesting that frame breaking be made punishable by death. Byron was roused. What, those squalid creatures be put to death for opposing the system that brought them to their misery? Was it not enough that the cavalry and armed soldiers were sent to quell the defenseless wretches?

On the twenty-seventh of February, two days prior to the publication of *Childe Harold*, he stood before his peers and spoke with trembling eloquence a part that was not acted. Those men, he said, destroyed their looms only when they became useless in earning them their daily bread. They sought employment elsewhere, but found none. "They were not ashamed to beg, but there was none to relieve them." What remained for them to do? Their misery was abject. Not even in the poorest provinces of the East had he beheld such squalor as in the heart of a Christian country. And were these men, merely because they fought for their means of subsistence, to be punished by death? "Is there not blood enough upon your penal code that more must be poured forth to ascend to heaven and testify against you? . . . Can you commit a whole country to their own prisons?" The lawmakers must consider well before passing sentence of death upon their fellow men.

The speech was highly successful, though perhaps too dramatic. Lord Granville said that the construction of some of the periods was very much like Burke's — a remark that made the rounds in Byron's letters. Sir Francis Burdett declared it the best speech made by a lord "since the Lord knows when." Lord Holland brought Byron home to his celebrated lady, proud of thus being one of the first to exhibit the young lion.

Even the critics were mollified and gave unstinted praise. But then, had not the redoubtable Gifford succumbed — Gifford, of whom the gentle Southey said that his heart was full of kindness for all living things except authors, whom he regarded as Izaak Walton did the worm; Gifford, the Juvenal of criticism?   Since 1809, when the *Quarterly* was founded with the help of the enterprising John Murray, Gifford of the *Anti-Jacobin* had joined the publisher to parry with Jeffrey, the leader of the Edinburgh clans.   Conservatism was exalted under the Gifford rule.   The Church, the State, and John Bull had each an inviolable niche.   In this strange company Byron, the romantic iconoclast, found himself.   But he had no reason to grumble — for the present.   He listened with pleasure to the praises of the press, sent out his complimentary copies, and enjoyed his glory.

His sister Augusta received one of the earliest, inscribed to her "who has ever loved me much better than I deserved." He signed himself her *"father's* son, and most affectionate brother."

What of Augusta all these years?   After the death of her grandmother, Lady Holderness, — Augusta was then seventeen, — she lived with her noble relations on her mother's side under the guardianship of Lord Carlisle.   Byron had seen little of her, this earlier offspring of Mad Jack, but had always been curiously dazzled by the circles in which she moved — how different from the tawdry lodgings of "the Honourable Kitty"!   Mrs. Byron herself had often spoken with awe of these exalted family connections and would willingly have introduced herself and her son into their midst.   Lady Holderness had held aloof; Lord Carlisle always maintained an impenetrable reserve.   For a brief period Augusta had seen the Harrow schoolboy, and he had felt drawn to her at once. "Why should I not marry Augusta?" he once asked his mother after a delving into Roman history.

Later the girl had received his confidences, consoled him in the unfortunate Mary Chaworth affair, and acted as intermediary whenever intercourse was too strained between her Baby Byron and Lord Carlisle.   Then she had married a first cousin, Colonel George Leigh of the Dragoons.   Had it been love?   Byron did not believe it.   Had it been his dashing uniform, his way of riding a horse?   A reckless manner of life, always alluring to inexperienced girlhood?   Or had it been simply a desire in Augusta to have a home of her own? Whatever it was she had married her colonel, settled at Six

Mile Bottom, near Newmarket, spent her required hours at Carlton House, and did what she could with a home that in time became an untidy nursery, her husband only now and then deigning to put in an appearance from his pressing engagements with bookmakers, gamblers, and mistresses. Something, he could not say what, embittered Byron in all this. Though he was four years younger than Augusta, though she did call him Baby Byron, he felt for her a mature protectiveness that expressed itself in tenderness and meaningful banter. After all, was she not the only kin he could claim, the only one in whom was mingled the blood of *his* Byrons?

"I am losing my relatives and you are adding to the number of yours," he wrote her after his mother's death. And again, "So your Spouse likes children, *that* is lucky as he will have to bring them up." There was something not right in this marriage. Augusta was not happy and he could do nothing for her. As for himself, he didn't care for children, or for anybody — except the mastiff that had taken Boatswain's place, and the tortoises he had brought from Greece.

Suddenly everything had changed. The son of "the Honourable Kitty" had more invitations than he could accept; no circle was too dazzling for him to shine in. At a ball the Prince Regent had asked to meet him. They had talked of poetry and of Scott, whom the Prince admired, and of the *Pilgrimage*, which His Highness had read with pleasure. Would Lord Byron attend a levee at Carlton House? Lord Byron would, and one morning Dallas found him in full court dress and powdered hair, all ready to attend the levee, which was happily postponed. Byron's sense of humor did not fail him. Who knows but he might be "warbling truth at court" when Laureate Pye joined the celestial choir? He laughed at the thought, but it was pleasing, like the court disguise in which he might have strutted his hour upon the royal stage.

The *literati* of the day sought his acquaintance: Thomas Moore, whose delicate indecencies had fanned his blood in the Chaworth days; the admired Campbell and Samuel Rogers, the banker-poet of the *Pleasures of Memory*, who had written not a vulgar line in his life, and that a long one — a very Tithonus of poetry, as Byron was to call this seemingly immortal mortal.[1] Everyone worth knowing left his card at St. James's Street beside the crested invitations from titled ladies and the scented *billets-doux* from unknown fair ones. Now with Moore, the elegant *flâneur*, received in the best salons and clubs for all that he was the son of a Dublin grocer, Byron spent gay bachelor evenings at Stevens's in Bond Street, quaffing claret and now and then indulging in a lobster. From Lady Holland's he would go to Lady Melbourne's, thence to Lady Jersey's, and when elegance palled he sought ruder sensations.

On the dawn of the execution of Bellingham, who had as-sassinated the obstructionist Perceval in the House of Com-mons, bringing about a change of ministry, Byron hired a window opposite to see the prisoner "launched into eternity." He had not counted on the shock that preceded the execution. The night had not yet set. By the light of the paling lamps in a disreputable street he saw a woman huddled in a doorway. He walked up to her pityingly and would have given her a few shillings, but she rudely pushed away his hand and, starting up with a drunken laugh, she went before him imitating his hobbling gait with renewed yells of laughter. Byron was grimly silent, but against his friend's arm his own trembled violently. Ay, fame had come to him. He was the wonder of the season, but he remained Mrs. Byron's "crookit deil." Fate would not let him forget it.

No, nor that, for all his glory, he was as poor as he had ever been. The six hundred pounds that Murray had offered for the copyright of the *Pilgrimage* he had presented to Dallas with a generous gesture, saying that he would never think of accepting money for his writings. Besides, six hundred pounds would have been but a dead leaf in the stream of his ex-penditures. Hanson urged him repeatedly to sell Newstead. Why hold on to that pile of ruins when his client might realize enough from its sale to keep him in comparative ease? Byron regretfully consented to have it placed under the hammer as he looked about him for the Golden Dolly who should extricate him from his hounding embarrassments.

"Mad, bad, and dangerous to know." All golden and airy

---

[1] He lived long enough to give young Swinburne a poetical accolade.

as a sunbeam, Lady Caroline Lamb jotted down those words after her enormous eyes had gazed for one long silent moment into the Childe's that night at Lady Jersey's ball, while a circle of women were "throwing up their heads" at him in worship and coquetry. He did not speak; she did not wait to be introduced. Later, when those eyes were turned on her alone and his words had been only for her, she added after that first entry, "That beautiful pale face is my fate." She had felt it before she met him, even through Rogers's warning, "He has a club-foot and he bites his nails," as if he were speaking of his Satanic Majesty. "If he is as ugly as Æsop, I must see him," she had insisted. Then that face had shone upon her and, like the flower to which she likened herself, her whole being was irresistibly impelled toward him. In complete surrender she wrote to him that now the sunflower had gazed on the unclouded sun, it could not longer "think any lower object worthy of its worship and admiration." Her husband was included in that renunciation, William Lamb, the handsome, the accomplished — Byron's friend.

The Childe came at her bidding. She was not the Golden Dolly he sought, but she beckoned and he could not resist. The frail, fawn-haired will-o'-the-wisp, with her aureole of short curls about an alluringly fairylike face, had not the voluptuousness he admired. Daintily small, she seemed in the diaphanous gowns that floated about her more like the miniature of a woman than the solid flesh he looked for in his Paphians. Her voice, like the unreal music of a mechanical doll's, was further exaggerated by the quavering drawl affected by the Melbourne House set to which she belonged. "Lady Caroline baa-a-a-a's till she makes me sick," had commented the censorious Annabella Milbanke on her socially successful cousin. That bleating possessed a charm of its own, however, which captivated ear and sense more than the wise Annabella's ponderous periods. And she was bewitchingly pretty. Lady Caroline's childishness of manner, her nonsense mania, her harmless eccentricities, made her the Ariel of her circle, if at times, at some outburst of her abnormal sensitiveness, the Young Savage. She was so highly strung that the slightest vibration jangled her out of tune.

Even as a child, Lady Caroline, then Caroline Ponsonby, had been remarkable for her extreme sensibility, thrown too early into the forcing house of adult life. Lady Bessborough, her mother, had been a beautiful woman in her time, when her name had been linked more with Lord Granville's than with her lawful lord's. The child had sensed the relation. "I suppose Lord Granville would not deign to look at me if I am all pitted with the chicken-pox," she remarked to her mother while convalescing. Then had come Sheridan, who for many agonizing years had been keeping Lady Bessborough under a snakelike fascination. It was a torturing, indissoluble pact that held the two alternately attracted and repelled. "My eyes will be looking up through the coffin-lid" was to be his last warning to her.

When Caroline was ten years old, Lady Bessborough had had a stroke, and the little girl was promptly transferred to the house of her aunt, the Duchess of Devonshire. "Georgiana, the Lovely Duchess," Reynolds called the ravishing beauty with her flaming golden hair piled high in serried curls and topped with a wide hat billowing with preposterous pink ostrich plumes. During Fox's campaign in 1785 she had set out with her sister, Lady Bessborough, entering taverns and public houses with the offer of "a kiss for the vote." Fox had won.

The gayety of Devonshire House was notorious. Nightlong the windows gleamed with the lights of festivity, and when dawn dimmed them the Prince of Wales was seen staggering out to his coach, drunk. In this extravagant, helter-skelter life where the children received less attention than the hounds and horses, Caroline observed what went on about her, but grew up unschooled and woefully ignorant of those facts which mothers of that carefree era left to their daughters' husbands to impart. She was scarcely able to spell at the age of thirteen when she met William Lamb and loved him. The handsome, sophisticated youth, in whom everyone, including his father, found an astonishing resemblance to Lord Egremont, was his mother's darling. Lady Melbourne would have done any-thing for this, her younger son, and looked disapprovingly upon his interest in Lady Bessborough's little savage. He was twenty at the time, and much experienced in women and morals; he might outgrow his foolish fancy. But the discerning young roué saw something in Caroline Ponsonby that as yet others could not see. He waited while the young girl learned her Greek and Latin, when she suddenly blossomed out into a bluestocking, holding her own with the best of them and better than the best, for the words of wit and wisdom fell with charming piquancy from that pretty infantine mouth. Moreover, she had something that other women lacked, a pathetic innocence that drew William Lamb to her with the urgency of his jaded young manhood. Here was someone he could educate.

For years Caroline eluded him in spite of her love, afraid of him, frightened for herself. "I adored him, I knew I was a fury, and I would not marry him." He saw her possibilities more clearly still. She was twenty when she accepted him.

On her wedding night — she was married at eight o'clock in Cavendish Square — she flew into a rage during the ceremony, had a fit of hysteria, and fainted. Her costly gown of silk and lace was torn by her destructive little fingers. The bridegroom took her in his arms, bore her to the carriage, and drove off with her to the honeymoon: little Caroline promised better than he had imagined. For some months after her marriage she was languorous and ailing. William Lamb, the learned, the immoral, had begun her education.

"I cannot fancy Lady Caroline married . . ." wrote one of her admirers. "How changed she must be — the delicate Ariel, the little Fairy Queen. It is the first death of a woman." With Lady Caroline it was an awakening.

The bride and groom took up their residence on an upper floor of Melbourne House, where Lady Melbourne might have her darling near her and keep a vigilant eye upon her daughter-in-law. She too, like her son, though with the wisdom of experience, the vast experience of her sixty years, saw something that bore watching in the amazing little creature that had come to live under her roof. What made her say and do those inexplicable things that had already won her the reputation of being eccentric and unconventional? Extreme innocence? Inborn sophistication? She turned men's heads by the score — a valuable accomplishment, as Lady Melbourne knew, but it must be done discreetly. To the perplexity of the faded but still captivating beauty, she found that gallants came to Melbourne House as much for little Caro's sake as for her own. That season of 1812 Byron joined the ranks, his carriage one in the line that stretched from Whitehall to the Admiralty Arch.

His visits had a dual purpose. He came at the request of Lady Caroline, yet he was tangled into the subtler mesh of Lady Melbourne in the winter of her beauty. She could not give him love; she could induct him, however, into an ambiguous friendship that partook as much of love as was possible between her and a man nearly ten years younger than her son William. Byron surrendered to her; she became his confidante. What a mother she would have made him! He fell under her spell as later he was to fall under the more potent fascination of Lady Oxford, whose autumn, he averred, was preferable to other women's spring. He found something overpowering in a beautiful maturity, a charm he had looked for in vain in the mother of whom he had been ashamed.

Lady Caroline played with her lion and, a less guileless Una, had him follow her leading strings. He came to her one morning bearing a rose and a carnation, the first of that spring, offering them with a taunt. "Your ladyship, I am told, likes all that is new and rare — for a moment." Unhappily for him the constant sunflower answered, challenged by his mockery. She would show him that she could love, ardently and long.

She led him into her apartments; she allowed him to dandle on his lap her son and William's, a beautiful child to whom the Regent had stood godfather and to whom Sheridan had addressed lines of well-wishing. But the child did not develop like other children. His head hung heavily, and the large eyes were dull with an ageless misery he was never to outgrow, as he was never to outgrow his infantile mind. The sins of the fathers? William Lamb knew no such thing as sin. The child, however, was secondary in Lady Caroline's life. She was young, and now at last she had found the lover capable of appreciating such a mistress as she could be. She was only three years older than Byron, but looked still virginal with her slight figure and boyish breast. But how deceptive was her appearance. "Your heart, my dear Caro," wrote Byron, "what a little volcano! . . . And yet I cannot wish it a bit colder."

Appearances had indeed deceived him. Byron had thought to possess a sprite and found himself entangled with a wild, jealous, irresponsible vixen who threw discretion to the winds in the one desire that became the obsession of her life. Day or night, she wanted him with her — her acknowledged lover for whom she would have committed any indiscretion. William Lamb? He did not matter, though Byron, suddenly compunctious, bade her

> Deceive no more thyself and me,
> Deceive not better hearts than mine,

alluding to the man for whom he had an undisguised admiration.

But for Lady Caroline no one any longer had precedence over her lover. She was following her husband's teachings. He had shown no jealousy before. Why should he be jealous now?

William Lamb bore up with dignity before the fixed eyes and hissing tongues of scandal, showing himself a little more apathetic, a little more sophistical, than usual. They said his wife had been seen standing out in the rain at a ball where she had not been invited, waiting for Byron to come out. She had put on her page's costume and gone to her lover's apartment. She had thrust herself through the window of Byron's carriage as he was impatient to drive on. . . . Poor little Caro-Ariel could do no wrong.

Lady Melbourne saw her son's apathy deepening to gloom and spoke her heart out to Byron. He must do something . . . break off with Caroline, put an end to the gossip. What could he do, the much-harassed Childe? It was his first experience with a lady of quality; he heartily wished it had never been. Let them take the hussy somewhere out of his way. He desired nothing better than to be done with the whole mad business. Lady Bessborough was called in consultation. She was powerless, poor woman, against a sprite who had never been in her control. She sent for the sage Hobhouse. He excused himself from meddling; it was his friend's affair. The scandal reached such a pitch that the Regent, assuming the novel rôle of moralist, reproved Lady Bessborough for having allowed the affair to go so far. Lady Bessborough laughed in spite of herself.

Caroline's husband, her parents, all London, set themselves against her. Byron refused to see her. At last she admitted herself defeated. She would go with her mother to Ireland, but nothing in the world or out of it would keep her from loving Byron — not all his cruelty, not the condemnation of society. When she left London with Lady Bessborough, she was on the verge of a collapse, of insanity, the family feared. The buoyant Ariel had become a pallid phantom whose only life smouldered in the immense dark eyes, unnaturally saddened. She was rejected, despised by the man for whom she had incurred the censure of morality. But the world should not be allowed to gloat over her misery. She would show it how much Byron had loved, how much he still loved her. And she produced a letter, in Byron's hand, for everyone to see. He had parted with her only to save her. . . . Poor, unhappy Ariel, creating enchantments for her own deception! Her lover's hand was more easily mastered than her lover's heart.[1]

"My Dearest Caroline," the letter began, "If tears which you saw and know I am not apt to shed, — if the agitation in which I parted from you, — agitation which you must have perceived through the whole of this nervous affair, did not commence until the moment of leaving you approached, — if all I have said and done, and am still but too ready to say and do, have not sufficiently proved what my real feelings are, and must ever be towards you, my love, I have no other proof to offer. God knows, I wish you happy, and *when I quit you, or rather you, from a sense of duty to your husband and mother, quit me,* you shall acknowledge the truth of what I again

---

[1] Byron scholars have cast a doubt on the authenticity of this letter. Caroline Lamb, who could so skillfully forge Byron's hand as to deceive Murray, his publisher, exercised her talents, it seems to me beyond cavil, in this instance. (For specimen of Lady Caroline's forgery see a facsimile in *Lord Byron's Correspondence*, ed. John Murray, Vol. I, pages 130, 131.) The style of the composition is so different from Byron's, the sentiments are so appropriate to the exigency, that its presence among Byron's letters immediately strikes a false note. Only the parts pertinent to the present argument are here quoted. Italics mine.

promise and vow, *that no other in word or deed, shall ever hold the place in my affections, which is, and shall be, most sacred to you till I am nothing. . . . 'Promise not to love you!' ah, Caroline, it is past promising. . . . May God protect, forgive and bless you.* Ever, and even more than ever, Your most attached, Byron.''

Followed a postscript, emphatic by its isolation. "These taunts which have driven you to this, my dearest Caroline, were it not for your mother and the kindness of your connections, *is there anything on earth or heaven that would have made me so happy as to have made you mine long ago? . . . I care not who knows this, what use is made of it. . . . I was and am yours freely and most entirely, to obey, to honour, love, — and fly with you when, where, and how you yourself might and may determine.*"

It was a desperate gesture. She must make it if she would live and face society.

Meanwhile a pair of grave eyes had been watching the inception and wild progress of the affair, and a meticulous hand had been taking notes and writing soul reactions toward at least one party in it. Annabella Milbanke, who had by now both seen and spoken with Byron, found him, as the first time she saw him, wicked but worth saving. Nor had she escaped his notice. Before they had been introduced he had seen this simple, modestly dressed girl with her fresh cheeks and sedate looks, and had taken her for some lady's companion until Moore undeceived him to say she was the wealthiest heiress there. They had exchanged a few serious words on religion, on human beings, on friendship and other sober topics, and spoken, too, of the deceased cobbler-poet, Joseph Blackett, whom Miss Milbanke and her parents had encouraged. Byron had never liked him, but kept his feelings to himself on that occasion. He had seen some of her poems, too — shown him by Lady Caroline, then in her glory and fearless of rivalry. Besides, what could she have feared from Annabella Milbanke, unfashionable in her dress, serious in her manners? As well might the dandelion have competed with the sunflower.

Byron had read the poems and found them not devoid of

merit, especially one on the Irish poet Dermody, who had drunk himself to death, and whose elegiast Annabella had elected herself. "Degraded genius!" she invoked over his untimely grave,

> . . . thy dwelling here
> Is desolate, and speaks thee as thou wert,
> An outcast from mankind, *one whose hard fate*
> *Indignant virtue should forbid to weep.* . . .[1]

Did not Byron's heart warn him at such severity in a girl not yet twenty? It was at once admirable and frightening. He had no desire to be better acquainted with Miss Milbanke, he hastened to tell Lady Caroline, who must have read fate in the words that followed: "She is too good for a fallen spirit to know and I should like her better if she were less perfect." It would do him little good to know her, Lady Caroline had assured him; Annabella's heart was engaged . . . a harmless half truth that she had hoped would keep his fancy from wandering. Byron and Miss Milbanke met again after Lady Caroline's confidences to him and to her. They were both on their guard.

Annabella Milbanke might have proved Byron's Golden Dolly if he had not got into that sorry mess with Lady Caroline. Miss Milbanke was an only child, on whom would fall the wealth and title of the ancient barony of Wentworth — in not too long a time, as she had been born to Sir Ralph Milbanke and his wife Judith after fifteen years of sterile marriage. Nothing had been too precious for this, their "barley-sugar daughter," as they fondly called her. At Seaham by the ocean Annabella had spent her childhood, doted on by Sir Ralph, idolized, but with some show of severity, by her mother, who was ever conscious that her husband was the brother of Lady Melbourne, whose influence must be kept in check. Later, when Sir Ralph had come to his possessions, the family, with Mrs. Clermont, Annabella's nurse and governess, spent part of each year at Halnaby Hall in Yorkshire. The little girl had been brought up at home, learning her languages, practising dutifully her dancing and deportment, and, under

---

[1] Italics mine.

Clermont's direction, cobbling her own slippers like many another good little girl of the day. No children of her age were there to play with her. She disliked dolls. But she did love to read and make her own poems with her father, and laugh at his harmless jokes on lice and fleas and other undesirables of the world. Sir Ralph was her favorite, rather than her blustering, high-handed mother, who liked to have her husband as well as her child under her thumb.

Annabella grew up an austere, pedantic, very learned young lady who placed reason on a pedestal to be consulted and propitiated with every act of life. Humility was her watchword; goodness and morality stood with her at either hand. Whenever she met a new acquaintance or lived a new experience, reason was called to sit in judgment while goodness and morality testified — with all humility. The pronouncement was not always kind. Lady Melbourne, William Lamb, Lady Caroline, Mr. Walpole, Lydia White, the bluestocking, and Miss Elphinstone, Campbell, whose lectures she attended at the Royal Institution, Lady Wellington, the suitors who paid court — all were put on trial and none escaped judgment. Was she too exacting? Perhaps not. She put herself under the same ordeal.

The year of the "Byron fever" Annabella reappeared more self-possessed than in the previous season, when she had made her first curtsy before London society. She was not remarkable for beauty, though her fresh coloring drew the eye for its unusualness in the hothouse atmosphere of the salons. She was small but well made, and carried herself with dignity. Her dark hair, unlike Lady Caroline's, grew long and luxurious, and curled into short ringlets over too high a forehead. The brows, tapering toward the temples, shadowed the level eyes, deceptively placid. Her mouth was wide, the lower lip slightly full, the upper thin, compressed, and faintly arched to an expression between smiling and deprecation. A firm, broad chin marked the face with strength, somewhat at variance with the feminine grace of her small, perfect body. Annabella Milbanke would have been unique in any salon. The connoisseur of women was attracted by her very novelty. Too good for him to know? The fallen spirit, released for the nonce from his complication with Ariel, was tempted to try what such goodness could effect. But the girl, unlike the rest of her sex, kept her distance, responding with a clear, grave stare to his dangerous underlook. Byron was seriously interested, and turned over the possibilities in his mind.

Marriage now would be timely. Newstead might be saved. He would no longer need to think of entering politics, even if his second speech before the House, on the Catholic question, had been more successful than it was. Annabella Milbanke. . . . He saw her as Lady Byron, the mother of his children, whose paternity he could never doubt. There was still Caroline. Had he not wronged her? He presented his qualms to Lady Melbourne. The mother-in-law in her responded. Caroline was "no novice . . . and cannot be looked upon as the victim of a designing man." By all means let Byron marry. It was the best thing he could do. But marry whom? Annabella Milbanke, her brother's daughter, her niece. From the ridiculous to the sublime. . . . Lady Melbourne, for the first time, was taken aback by the idiosyncrasies of man's nature. She felt herself capable to cope with an Ariel — but with a saint? She confessed her bewilderment. Did he know his own mind, the fickle creature? Was he not going from one scrape into another? No, Byron was sure of himself. Annabella Milbanke was the wife for him, "pretty enough to be loved by her husband, without being so glaringly beautiful as to attract too many rivals. . . ." None of *that* in the Byronic scheme.

Annabella had already left London with her parents, disappointed. The season that had promised so well, with dozens of suitors and a great share of admiration, had fizzed down like a rocket to nothing. "Poor Annabella!" Even while Lady Melbourne wrote to her, communicating Lord Byron's offer of marriage, she pitied her niece for her triumph. Surely the unspoiled country girl would accept the hero of the season.

Annabella refused him. She had tried him before her private tribunal of reason, goodness, and morality, — how many times during those brief months! — and he stood condemned. She could not love a man like Byron. "Believing that he never will be the object of that strong affection which would make me happy in domestic life," she wrote, "I should wrong him by any measure that might . . . confirm his present impressions."

There was a touch of the ludicrous in this calm rejection of the man whom all women desired, and both Byron and Lady Melbourne felt it keenly. Byron's was a wry-mouthed laugh. He of the Paphian loves, who had felt "the fullness of satiety," turned down by a simple girl. . . . "My *heart* never had an opportunity of being much interested in the business," he solaced himself.

Hardly a month after Annabella's letter he was enjoying a Lucretian interlude with Lady Oxford at Eywood, tempering pagan excess with a love for her thirteen-year-old daughter.

VIII

THE WIT IN THE DUNGEON

At Nero's Hotel, more respectfully known as Carlton House, the Prince Regent led his riotous life, burning the inflated bank notes with as much zest as his namesake burned his Christians, and making of London another Rome. Crowds of hungry beggars were always by to gape at the royal celebrations and yell their meaningless cheers, but there were some who saw their wrongs in these dearly bought triumphs and spoke out unpleasing truths. It was a time of social unrest. The prosperity brought on by the war cost more in lives and suffering than those in power cared to compute. When, therefore, any voice was raised to reach the ears of the people, the door of a Newgate cell was promptly closed upon it. The British have always loved their monarch, with one notable exception; *lèse-majesté*, even when justified, was not to be countenanced.

Lord Byron in his few visits to Carlton House had seen enough of the flowering corruption to waken in him the lover of liberty. When he heard that the Princess Charlotte wept at the defeat of the liberal faction he penned a well-deserved, if tactless, address: —

> Weep, daughter of a royal line,
> A Sire's disgrace, a realm's decay;
> Ah! happy if each tear of thine
> Could wash a father's fault away.
>
> Weep — for thy tears are Virtue's tears —
> Auspicious to these suffering isles;
> And be each drop in future years
> Repaid thee by thy people's smiles.[1]

[1] Written March 7, 1812.

Others spoke as openly, but being of less favored birth suffered persecution with fines and, all too often, imprisonment. Majesty and the realm had to be protected.

Daniel Isaac Eaton, a radical printer, was sentenced in May of 1812 to one hour in the pillory and eighteen months at Newgate for the crime of having published the third part of Paine's *Age of Reason*. Eaton was an old man. For the full sixty minutes of the sentence he stood in the rack of infamy, his grey hair and solemn patience making the ruffians who had come to abuse him turn away in shame.

Paine's works had had a stormy history. In 1791, through Holcroft and Godwin, the *Rights of Man* had been published, making Holcroft invoke peace and eternal beatitude unto the soul of the author for the arguments that had won one revolution and bid fair to win another. But he did not hail the printing of the pamphlet without misgivings in his excited note to Godwin: "The pamphlet — from the row — But mum — we don't sell it — oh, no — Ears and Eggs — Verbatim. . . . Not a single castration . . . can I discover — Hey, for the New Jerusalem! The millennium!" Ears had been cut since then, and eggs thrown at pilloried victims in the cause of free speech and the rights of man. Neither the New Jerusalem nor the millennium had as yet shown the faintest ruddiness in the East, as its prophets, one by one, sailed the dismal waters to Botany Bay. In 1809 Paine, escaping with his life from England through the timely warning of William Blake, no visionary in his friendship, and later the guillotine in France by the carelessness of the prison keeper who put the death mark on the inside instead of the outside of his door — Paine, reviled and hated for his love of man, died unmourned in a land which he had helped to liberate. Hopeful spirits still believed in the rights of man and the age of reason, so that when Daniel Eaton was suffered to meet his punishment without a word of protest from the established press, at least one voice raised itself in "the perilous pleasure of becoming the champion of an innocent man."

Percy Bysshe Shelley wrote an open letter to Lord Ellenborough, who had passed the sentence. "By what right do you punish Mr. Eaton?" he asked boldly. And wherefore?

For having questioned established opinions. Ha, then, the mask is fallen off. Because the victim is a Deist and my Lord a Christian, Mr. Eaton is sentenced to prison and the pillory "in a nation that presumptuously calls itself the sanctuary of freedom." Courageously, with unanswerable logic, Shelley drove home the iniquity of the sentence that cast shame upon a whole nation, and in his defense of the victim himself advanced opinions that, had it not been for some beneficent dæmon guarding him, would have clapped him in worse than Newgate. "Suppose with the vulgar," he wrote, "that God is a venerable old man, seated on a throne of clouds . . . still goodness and justice are qualities seldom nominally denied him." Yet men, working in his name, worshiping a benevolent deity, imprison and torture the innocent. But, "I would have you to know, my Lord, that fetters of iron cannot bind or subdue the soul of virtue. . . . I warn you against festinating that period . . . when the seats of justice shall be the seats of venality and slavishness, and the cells of Newgate become the abode of all that is honourable and true."

That period, indeed, seemed to have come, when the brothers Leigh and John Hunt were tried for the fourth time for libel and, in this case, found guilty. Two years' imprisonment, in different prisons, and a fine of a thousand pounds, were imposed upon the hapless journalists for having dared to describe the Regent in the *Examiner* as "a corpulent man of fifty . . . a violator of his word, a libertine over head and ears in disgrace, a despiser of domestic ties, the companion of gamblers and demireps, a man who has just closed half a century without one single claim to the gratitude of his country, or the respect of posterity." Just as it was irrefutable that the Regent had passed his fiftieth birthday and that he was "a fat Adonis," it could not have been denied that he was guilty of everything else with which Leigh Hunt had charged him in his leader. The writer's fault lay in his having put down so explicitly what everybody knew. And for that, in his best suit and new gloves like a dandy going to a rout, Leigh Hunt was driven by hackney coach to Horsemonger Lane Gaol on the Surrey Side.

The enforced two years' stay in the palace of thieves and

criminals of varied dye soon proved to be far from the dreary sufferance it had promised. Sentiment was all for the prisoner. The elegant Tom Moore, forsaking for the moment the ladies' boudoirs, sent a message of cheer to the prisoner, reminding him that even in dungeons a poet could sing, as no bars could shut out thought free as the air of April — a comforting assurance to one whose greatest joy had been the welcoming of the Hampstead spring. In the little house Hunt had rented in West End Lane the busts of great men stood moveless on their pedestals. It mattered little to them that the laurel in the garden was in flower, or that the lilac was newly opening, filling the air with sweetness. Hunt would have done anything to be in their place — anything but unsay what he had said. At twenty-nine, however, life is not hopeless. A minor miracle might even be worked.

Because of his poor health the doctor had given him two rooms on the sunny side of the gaol leading to the prison yard. Perhaps Marianne and the children might share them with him. She might even be allowed to bring her clay and modeling tools and the cast of Apollo with the "good poetical head of hair" to copy. Hunt sent a petition to the authorities praying that he have his wife and family living with him, at least through the day. The request was granted, and the prison rooms were in short order converted into a miniature Hampstead cottage. The library of poets was transported: Milton, with flowing hair, took his stand above the classics, unperturbed by the changed surroundings as he gazed inwardly with his sightless orbs. The sitting room, scenically papered and rose-embowered, sheltered Hunt's pianoforte and lute. From other vantage points the busts of the immortals stared in meaningful placidity. Stone walls do not a prison make. . . . *His* poems were there on the shelves with Spenser's, Milton's, Dryden's. And there was the small writing table from where he, Leigh Hunt, could still edit the *Examiner* and, in more precious hours, write poetry. He could even go out into the prison yard, converted into a flower garden by virtue of his friends' persuasions of the gaoler.

Many were the visitors he received in a place become "the abode of all that is honourable and true." His dear friend

Charles Lamb came often with the capable Mary, whose presence was in itself a light, and the grumpy Hazlitt, and Bentham, and Maria Edgeworth. And Haydon too blustered in, choking with the injustice of the sentence, but soon fulminating against a nation that had little concern for historical painting in the grand style, and for High Art, and the immortal marbles of Greece that were being allowed to rot in a penthouse, uncherished — but for him — and unseen.

One day, that the prisoner might be as comforted as he was by Glorious Art, Haydon had his gigantic "Judgment of Solomon" transported to Horsemonger Lane for Hunt to see. Nearly thirteen feet by eleven it was — too huge to be shown in any room in the prison. Haydon had gazed on the Raphael cartoons that he might be imbued with the divine spirit; he had nearly blinded himself with application that he might make it a grand work; he had passed long, wakeful nights that heavenly guidance might help him in the task. "Thank God I am capable of enjoying the sensations Raffaele intended to excite," he wrote in his journal. "May they every hour interweave themselves with my being, and by mixing with the essence of the Elgin Marbles, produce such art as the world has not yet seen." He had sunk on his knees before his own work; his soul knew rapture. "I would not have exchanged my situation for Buonaparte's at Moscow," he exclaimed in a fervor of commendation. He breathed only for the monomania that was his art. Men and the world had no other reason for being. Once he had beheld a woman convulsed with agony at seeing her child killed by a horse. Haydon had drunk in her anguish from every fibre — the livid lips, the purple cheeks. "I heard her dreadful screams. . . . My heart beats at the recollection. I put her expression into the mother in 'Solomon.'" He starved himself, he got into debt to buy the materials for his painting. At last it was finished and, wonder of wonders, sold. Haydon bought Dante and Ariosto for Hunt.

Things other than colossal paintings were brought to Horsemonger Lane. Cowden Clarke, son of the Enfield schoolmaster, presented welcome baskets of fruit, vegetables, and eggs. Others brought books and music. Many came with gifts for the children. Little Thornton, who at the age of three knew his fifty words of Greek, had a tender singsong addressed to him by Lamb, whose pet he was.

> Gates that close with iron roar
> Have been to thee thy nursery door;
> Chains that chink in cheerless cells
> Have been thy rattles and thy bells. . . .

Aunt Bessie Kent, Marianne's sister, who had lived with them, came too sometimes, and helped to entertain the many visitors, though Mamma those days seemed out of temper. The truth was that Bessie Kent, a silent, bashful girl, had fallen in love with Leigh Hunt before her sister met him and turned his head. After the marriage she went on adoring in silence, doing for him the many things Marianne found no leisure to do, what with her art and the children, and feeling grateful for every attention from her straight, slender brother-in-law with his mass of dark wavy hair and the great, coal-black eyes sparkling with wit and intellect. She loved with no hope of requital, and but for Marianne's jealousy would have enjoyed a sufficing peace in ministering to him and listening to his poetry. Many thought, though they did not say, that she would have been the better wife for Hunt, and prevented many a difficulty that Marianne was too unthinking to avoid.

Hunt bore his fate with the cheerfulness of the household cricket, content to sing in return for a cozy nook and a little warmth — even in prison. He had never been familiar with luxury. Isaac Hunt of Barbados, fledged M.A. at an American university, had never had enough cash or held on to it sufficiently long to give his wife and numerous family a taste of anything but adventurous poverty. During the American Revolution he had been imprisoned for loyalty to the king, but, making his escape, he managed to reach London, while Mary, his wife, the daughter of a Philadelphia merchant, waited for a favorable opportunity to join him in his refuge. It was a long, hazardous voyage in normal times; it was a foolhardy venture during the war. The courageous woman and her brood at length reached London, where Isaac Hunt, advised to go on the stage because of his fine voice and effective delivery, had become a preacher. In the north suburbs of London the West Indian was soon known for his dramatic sermons that drew large crowds, chiefly of ladies. Whatever he made barely sufficed for his household. He was, moreover, self-indulgent and fond of costly elegances. Consequently he early became acquainted with His Majesty's prisons, made no whit more comfortable for his reception in spite of the loyalty that had indirectly brought him there. The child Leigh Hunt, born at Southgate, thus had an early initiation into the domicile he was so familiarly to know later.

There were other places he was to remember. With his mother he would often visit the gallery of the American painter Benjamin West. Mary Hunt, a sweet, unaffected woman, had a reverence of the arts amounting to worship. Holding Leigh by the hand, she would speak in hushed tones of the subjects — Agrippina with the ashes of Germanicus, Jesus healing the sick, Sir Philip Sidney, mortally wounded, giving his last drop of water to a dying soldier. She, too, though she would not have made the comparison, was capable of as noble generosity. On a cold winter's day, as she was walking in Blackfriars Road, a beggar woman asked her for help. Mrs. Hunt had no money to give, so she stepped into a doorway, took off her flannel petticoat, and gave it to her who needed it more. What if she did catch cold on the way home and became an invalid for the rest of her days? She did not regret her act.

At the age of seven Leigh was baptized according to the requirements and admitted as a Bluecoat boy to Christ's Hospital. The grim, low-buttressed building with its high arched windows for nearly two and a half centuries had been educating the sons of the poor. Although its founding under Edward VI had had for its chief purpose the sheltering of homeless waifs and the training of them to be skilled artisans, the church and the universities found that its excellent teaching provided them with distinguished recruits. At the time of Leigh Hunt's entrance Coleridge had already left for Cambridge. Charles Lamb, long since graduated to the school of life, still haunted Newgate Street near St. Paul's and the Tower, and sometimes turned into Christ's Hospital to see Dyer. Tradition hung over the school like a brooding presence.

Leigh Hunt sensed its indefinable prompting and early tried to express it in verse. He learned his classics, and Italian, which he loved, and for weeks after he discovered Metastasio the shocked echoes shivered with his piping invocation to Venus, bidding her, the delight of men and mortals, to come down, yea, even to Christ's Hospital.

Isaac Hunt read the lad's pretty verses and, pressed for money as he always was, decided, contrary to all poetical precedent, to make his son's muse swell his shrunken purse. He had a patron, the Duke of Chandos, whose nephew he tutored. He would help publish Leigh's poems by subscription. Quickly the lists went round; contributions came in, and at sixteen Leigh Hunt found himself the author of a pretty volume entitled *Juvenilia*. Young he certainly was. But a poet? The public evidently thought so. The light, effortless verses, easily read and easily forgotten, took their fancy. In two years a fourth edition was in the press.

It was a little while before the precocious Parnassan became the outspoken critic of the *Examiner*. The muse did not forsake him for the divided allegiance. Even in Horsemonger Lane she folded her mantle of peace round her lover and watched over the burning of the midnight lamps after the guests had left and Marianne and the children had gone to bed. The *Feast of the Poets*, an imaginative and sprightly satire, was nearly finished. Another work, harking back to the olden love of Italy, was shaping itself in his mind. His aims were high. He would free poetry from the shackles of a dead poetic diction and make Pegasus pasture in the blooming fields of daily speech that he might the more amply spread his wings in flight. For the present he wrote his weekly articles as fearlessly as ever, while his brother John, less sensationally serving his sentence at Clerkenwell, did his share of editing.

One day in the spring of 1813 there was a great to-do in the ground-floor rooms of the Horsemonger Lane Gaol, at a time when Marianne and the children had providentially gone to Brighton. Bessie Kent had taken charge of her brother-in-law in his wife's absence, and an extraordinary time it promised. Tom Moore was going to introduce to Hunt no less a personage than Lord Byron. His lordship, however, wished it to be a strictly private party, said Moore, solicitous, for Byron was uncomfortable before strangers. His foot, you see. . . . As for the dinner, no beef for the bard — it made him ferocious, Byron thought. Biscuits, vegetables, perhaps some fish. The preparations were under way. Bessie was all in a flutter, while Hunt donned his best suit the better to honor his guest.

Byron, for his part, was looking forward to the visit, and on the night of May 19, while dressing for Lady Heathcote's party, scribbled a versified reminder to Moore.

> To-morrow be with me, as soon as you can, sir,
> All ready and dress'd for proceeding to spunge on
> (According to compact) the wit in the dungeon —
> Pray Phœbus at length our political malice
> May not get us lodgings within the same palace! . . .

It was the season of the year when Hunt described the prison garden as covered with daisies, with the broom in a profusion of blossom and the Persian lilac hung with delicate bunches of blue. Perhaps out of curiosity for the visitor, the left-hand rhododendron, which had given promise, burst into staring flower. It is not recorded. The possessive Moore did say, however, that intruders, having got wind of the event, made their appearance, and destroyed the harmony of the gathering.

Byron liked the "wit in the dungeon." Besides the oddity of Hunt's situation, which he took in good part, there was a winning graciousness about him that immediately won him friends. His speech was vivacious and interesting. He knew literature and could criticize with sharpness and acumen. He played and sang at the rose-bowered piano; he knew painting as well as music. Lord Byron, whose taste in those arts was still to be developed, was amused by the caprice that had brought such talents under a prison roof.

A few days later he returned to see Hunt without the officious Moore, carrying a package under his arm. Hunt had told him of the poem he had begun on Francesca da Rimini; Byron brought him, therefore, some travel books on Italy, so that the mind at least, if not the body, might range over its beauties. The acquaintance ripened into friendship. With Marianne's arrival, however, it was discontinued. She *had heard* things about his lordship. Let Bessie admire as much as she pleased; as for *her*, she was not going to flatter anybody's vanity, lord or no lord.

Byron was not the only noble youth to sympathize with Hunt. Shortly after the sentence had been passed, Shelley, "boiling with indignation at the horrible injustice and tyranny" of it, wrote him a letter in which he made so generous an offer of his fortune that Hunt was moved to more than admiration of the idealist who once before had sent him words of encouragement. Needy as he was, and sunk in debt on account of the excessive fines, he declined the proffered help for the time. Nonetheless Shelley sent twenty pounds to Hookham, the publisher with whom he was then arranging for the printing of a volume of verse, suggesting a subscription for the "martyr of liberty." That too Hunt, in the *Examiner*, declined. He would not be a burden to his friends.

Meanwhile Shelley, with Harriet, Eliza Westbrook, and the sister of his soul, had been more than ever active, more than ever peripatetic. The Bristol Channel, besides carrying its heaving freight, bore flotillas of green bottles, each filled with the "heavenly medicine" of liberty in the form of one of Shelley's pamphlets. Wherever there was a navigable body of water he launched his fleets, Miss Hitchener, foreign-looking, and eyed with suspicion by the stragglers standing by, nodding approval. On dark nights bright balls of flame took their ethereal way, each bearing its weight of knowledge, where or whither Shelley did not know, though his heart beat with excitement at the pastime. Bottles, fire balloons, broadside ballads, political pamphlets, all served as awakeners of man's slumbering mind.

The autumn of 1812 had found him and his three Oceanides established at Tanyrallt, Carnarvonshire. Mr. Madocks, his landlord, had a wide-reaching scheme for reclaiming land from the surrounding sea. Homes would be built for workingmen, and an ideal colony would put humane principles into practice amid surroundings whose dales and hills and fells

would realize the earthly paradise. Shelley took fire. Whatever money he could raise would be at the service of Mr.
Madocks. More, he would gain adherents to the scheme.
October saw him in London with his following, one member
of which, by those gradual degrees of disillusionment, aided
and abetted by feminine subtleties, had by that time become
intolerable to him. Portia-Bessie must go back to Hurstpierpoint if Shelley would have peace. Eliza abhorred her
like a draught of poison. Harriet was convinced that, far
from having disinterested views, Miss Hitchener was a scheming, selfish woman, bent on separating her from her husband.
The artful creature had even gone so far as to say that Shelley
was really in love with *her* and not with his wife, who was
about to bear him a child.[1] And she had been worse than
the camel in the fable. Once she had found herself installed,
nothing availed to move her. Her situation was lost, Miss
Hitchener complained whenever they suggested her leaving,
her reputation gone, her health ruined by the barbarity of
those she had thought the brother and sisters of her soul.
How could she, deprived of her means of subsistence, go back
to Hurstpierpoint? She was a victim of their persecution,
penniless and despised.

Shelley, easily moved by every plea, now listened to Harriet
and her vehement ally, now fell into the trap of an intellectual
discussion with Portia-Bessie, thinking her not quite so black
as she was painted. At other times, when the wind blew
too strongly the other way, he found the erstwhile "embryon
of a mighty intellect" nothing but "a superficial, hermaph-
roditical beast of a woman," and blamed himself for the
bad taste that had so blinded him as to make her an inmate of
his house. "What would Hell be were such a woman in
Heaven!" exclaimed that compact of extremes. And in London, where once again he met Hogg and took him to his bosom,
he would quote him with mock sobriety some feminist verses
of Portia-Bessie, beginning with the amazing assertion, "All,
all are men, — women and all." At that point Miss Hitchener
had lost all designation in the family circle but that of the
Brown Demon. Still she made no move to go.

[1] Letter of Harriet to Catherine Nugent, Nov. 14, 1812.

The London visit extended Shelley's acquaintance. Thomas Love Peacock, a published but impecunious poet, became a frequent visitor and a recipient of Shelley's generosity. He was seven years older than Shelley. Already he had brought out three volumes, *Palmyra*, in 1806, strongly influenced by Volney, the *Genius of the Thames*, and his latest, the *Philosophy of Melancholy*, which, like the Holy Roman Empire of the wit, was neither the one nor the other. His poetry had had few readers and fewer admirers, so that it pleased him to find in Shelley an enthusiast as hyperbolic as he was sincere. It is flattering to be told of one's first work that its conclusion was "the finest piece of poetry I ever read." Secretly Peacock knew that his talent did not lie in verse, but he had still to find his true vein.

Like Shelley he loved to wander and had been in Wales, where the people, seeing his preoccupation with books, looked upon him with distrust as an atheist. No two youths could have been more foreign to each other temperamentally than Shelley and Peacock, the one passionately benevolent, aching with zeal to create a perfect world, the other absorbed in himself and his work, taking life as he found it and making the best of it with a philosophy that claimed to itself more of the pleasures than the pains of existence. He believed in savoring the grape while the bloom was yet upon it; Shelley mourned over the lees and would have remade them into the living vine. Together they talked of the work they had done and of what was still to do. Shelley told him of the volume he was projecting, and Peacock had suggested Thomas Hookham of Old Bond Street, his publisher, for the printing. Another friendship began.

Early in October the philosopher of Skinner Street at last met his mercurial correspondent. Youths had come to him, protégés and disciples, to whom he had been as a beacon in the tempests of their early manhood. Never had he found in them the depth of intellect that shone through the luminous eyes which rested on him as he talked, or witnessed such aching compassion for the sufferings of humanity as expressed itself in Shelley's mobile face. Those were no empty professions the youth made in his pamphlets. Here was one who would willingly die for his convictions. Yet there was a restiveness about him, undisciplined and undisciplinable. Godwin had in vain warned against it during the Irish activities.

Shelley was enchanted with his philosopher. The man had a majesty as he sat, his large head bent as by the weight of his rocky brow, his eyes cold as dark wells with the unaltering gaze of reason. He could have dominated any gathering so — but when he rose he seemed so insignificant by his lack of height that all majesty fell from him. His head was almost bald, showing the development of his bumpy cranium. The wisps of hair were grey and parched. He could never have been handsome. Southey, who had known him in his youth, found beauty in the fine eyes. The nose appalled him, "a most abominable nose. Language is not vituperatious enough to describe the effect of its downward elongation." At the age of fifty-six Godwin had not improved in beauty. The good Harriet, however, anxious to discover merit in those her husband admired, found a resemblance between the philosopher's head and the bust of Socrates, no great compliment on the score of beauty.

Certainly no family in England could have boasted the assortment of Mr. Godwin's. There was Mrs. Godwin the second, fat, comely, more than a trifle vulgar, who had captured her philosopher and friend in a weak moment by calling to him from her window in the Polygon as he was enjoying the cool of the evening on his balcony opposite: "Is it possible that I behold the immortal Godwin?" A widower with two little girls, wretchedly poor and baulked in his efforts to win the women he had wanted to marry, would have seized on less than that. Mrs. Clairmont that was, besides being an adept at flattery, knew still surer ways to a man's heart. They were married. On that point the second Mrs. Godwin insisted, whatever the immortal Godwin's notions might be on the subject, and she knew they were not orthodox. As playmates for Fanny Imlay Godwin and Mary Wollstonecraft Godwin she brought her son, Charles Clairmont, and her daughter Jane. In due course William Godwin, Junior, was added to them.

The new Mrs. Godwin, or M. J. as her laconic husband

styled his Mary Jane, did not join him to eat the bread of idleness. Under her capable supervision the Juvenile Library which she started as her own enterprise kept the young supplied with books of fables, histories of England, Rome, and Greece, and sometimes even of poetry, though on one occasion when Wordsworth was approached for the versification of a fairy tale he not very politely refused. However, Charles and Mary Lamb, more obliging, could accept a commission, and wrote moreover for the firm their *Tales from Shakespeare*. "M. J. Godwin and Company" thus justified its existence to generations still unborn.

Fanny, a grave, sweet girl of nineteen when the Shelleys met her, was a member of the family by sufferance. She was the daughter of Mary Wollstonecraft by her free-love union with Gilbert Imlay, an American who had been a captain in the army of the Revolution. The circumstances of her birth had been kept from her. How was a child to understand that the mother, who by her own acts had vindicated the women's rights she had defended, had been looked upon as an immoral woman, and that she, Fanny, had been born out of wedlock? Hence she had been made to understand by the prudent Godwin that she was the fruit of her mother's former marriage. How tenderly that mother had spoken of her in the *Letters from Norway* which she had written to Imlay while on business there for him! "I feel more than a mother's fondness and anxiety when I reflect upon the dependent and oppressed state of her sex. I dread lest she should be forced to sacrifice her heart to her principles, or principles to her heart — I dread to unfold her mind lest it should render her unfit for the world she is to inhabit." Mary Wollstonecraft had endeavored to save both her heart and her principles; the one had been trampled on by the man who should have cherished it, while her principles had been made into the mud that spattered her memory.

Mary Wollstonecraft Godwin and Jane Clairmont were nearly of the same age. Mary, born in August 1797, five months after Godwin's marriage to Mary Wollstonecraft, had been the innocent cause both of her parents' bowing to the laws of society and of her mother's death. Godwin and

Mary Wollstonecraft had met while the disillusioned woman
was still believed to be Mrs. Imlay. On her return from
Norway she found letters from Imlay telling her with cruel
bluntness that the end had come for them. She had not been
at fault. Imlay had failed to prize the woman to whom their
tacit union had been as binding as any legal marriage, since
it had been entered into freely and with a higher morality
than, alas, he was capable of understanding. In her absence
he had taken a mistress and would have freed himself by
offering a settlement to Mary for the child he relinquished.
She rejected the proposal with scornful pride. "I am not yet
sufficiently humbled to depend on your benevolence!"

Days of moral agony followed, days in which it seemed as if
the ideals for which she had lived had been a solemn mockery.
She tried to put an end to her pain by leaping off Putney
Bridge, but she lived. Then Godwin had come, his passionless calm soothing her storm-tossed soul. Here was a man
who could understand. Again, she entered into what both
believed the true marriage. They lived in separate apartments, he with his work, she with hers, meeting only during
their leisure. Whimsical little notes flew from house to house.
"Did I not see you, friend Godwin, at the theatre last night?
I thought I met a smile, but you went out without looking
round." A month later they were married at Old St. Pancras
Church that was soon to see her buried.

Like her elder half-sister, Mary inherited nothing from her
mother but an extreme sensitiveness verging on morbidity.
Physically she was like Godwin, short, though slim, with his
great tablet of a brow and cool, calm eyes shadowed by lashes
a trifle lighter than her reddish-brown hair. At the time of
the Shelley visits she was staying with friends in Scotland.

Jane Clairmont had her mother's handsomeness, some of
her unpleasant traits, and a few more of her own. She was as
dark as Mary Godwin was pale, with an intensity of expression
in her classically modeled face that might have belonged to an
Italian. Her soft black hair she wore parted, falling in coils
over her ears and gathered back in a simple knot. She played
and sang prettily, though not always accurately, and enjoyed
being admired. Her giddy little head, which was early turned

upon her entering into an environment of freedom that she was too young to evaluate, converted that freedom into license. Mary Wollstonecraft Godwin, the rights of the individual, M. J.'s whispered gossip of the two daughters who were not her own, all made their mark in the girl's mind. Ardent by nature, of an hysterical instability, she was already reaching out for adventure, the first phase of which translated itself into her soon changing her name to Clare. Clare Clairmont, the name of a heroine of romance. She wanted romance.

The two girls, Fanny and Jane, were enraptured with the philosopher's new friend. They did not take so readily to his wife in her rustling silks. Was she not too much the fine lady? Fanny was a little afraid of her. Shelley came gallantly to Harriet's defense. She was by no means a fine lady!

Harriet was not so comfortable as she might have desired in the philosophic circle. But she liked Fanny. "Very plain, but very sensible," was her comment. "The beauty of her mind fully overbalances the plainness of her countenance." She, the little beauty, could well afford to be magnanimous. Of Jane she had nothing to say, but she found the guest of the Godwins, Miss Curran, the daughter of the Irish patriot, "a coquette — the most abominable thing in the world." For Harriet, since the Hogg incident, had established herself as a matron of proved virtue.

With the moral support of William Godwin the Brown Demon was at long length got rid of — not, however, without the payment of an annuity of one hundred pounds to compensate for the many losses Miss Hitchener claimed to have sustained. Gone were her hopes of ever sharing the still-to-be-inherited fortune of the brother of her soul! The Hurstpierpoint schoolmistress returned to her desk a disillusioned but a wiser woman. Ideal societies, happy clans that would have provided for the needs of good old Miss Adams — all, all were vanished. Now the expectant Crœsus had his needy philosopher to take care of, for whose benefit, that winter, he borrowed the first large sum on a post-obit bond.

Back at Tanyrallt Shelley worked on the reclamation project and finished the long poem which was to embody his vision of the world. He did not wish to make it too strongly didactic, he wrote to Hookham, for "a poem very didactic, is, I think, very stupid." He would have two hundred and fifty copies printed "in a small neat quarto, on fine paper — so as to catch the aristocrats," who needed most of all to have their eyes opened. It was indeed a dainty volume that came out in March of the following year, fit to catch the most fastidious of aristocrats with its ivory-tinted paper and gracious type. A dedicatory poem to Harriet called her his purer mind, the inspiration of his song, the one beneath whose looks his reviving soul grew "riper in truth and virtuous daring." *Queen Mab,* he entitled the volume, issued from Mr. Westbrook's address, 23 Chapel Street. Never had gunpowder been disguised under a more innocuous label.

Setting out on a spirit-voyage, Queen Mab, no mere fairy, but an omniscient guide, leads the blue-eyed Ianthe through past and present, and vouchsafes her a vision of the future. History unfolds itself as a record of crimes and miseries. Like another Volney, Mab leads her heroine through the desolating pageant. "Behold," the fairy cries, "Palmyra's ruined palaces! — Behold! where grandeur frowned." Beside the eternal Nile the Pyramids too will crumble to dust. Where the Arab's tent flaps in the desert once reared the temples of Salem, cursed in the building by orphan and widow.

> There an inhuman and uncultured race
> Howled hideous praises to their Demon-God.

Where is the fame that vainglory would make eternal? All, all vanish, the emperor with the beggar. "There's not one atom of yon earth but once was living man." As in the past, so is it in the present. Power, poisonous institutions, religion, commerce, stultify the natural talents and keep man in oppression for the aggrandizement of the tyrannous few. "There is no God!" cries persecuted knowledge; and nature confirms the cry. Through the ages the worn concept of deity has kept the mind in subjection, has brought martyrs to the flame. "Necessity! Thou mother of the world!" Thou art the true divinity. "Unlike the God of human error, thou Requir'st no prayers or praises." Ahasuerus the Wandering Jew comes forth again to inveigh against the Biblical God of Vengeance. Alas! that reason should not yet have freed the mind from that error which has kept it in slavery. "O Happy Earth! reality of Heaven! . . . Genius has seen thee in her passionate dreams. . . ." In that transcendent vision man lives free and happy, no longer chained by institutions maintained in blood and death. Marriage prospers, unfettered by law; perfected man is unsullied by crime; innocently he lives his useful life, unstained by even the blood of the beast, and in the end sinks mildly into "the slow necessity of death." The spirit-voyage over, Ianthe is restored to her lover Henry, who had been kneeling by her bedside.

"Fear not, then, Spirit, Death's disrobing hand," comes Queen Mab's last message to Ianthe.

> Are there not hopes within thee, which this scene
> Of linked and gradual being has confirmed?
> Whose stingings bade thy heart look further still,
> When, to the moonlight walk by Henry led
> Sweetly and sadly thou didst talk of death?

Thus Harriet's frequent allusions to death and suicide found their place in the poem that held up to her a more hopeful view of life.

Shelley stood only half-revealed in this, his first sustained poetic effort. Echoes of his varied readings came insistently. Lucretius, Pliny, d'Holbach, Volney, Rousseau, and Godwin sometimes spoke independently of him; but they roused him to himself. Verbal magic was not yet his. Like Saint Augustine, he was content for the present that the spirit speak, however haltingly. He was still primarily the reformer, though here and there the poet drowned his voice. As he lived he wrote and thought. He was one with his work.

Again Shelley and his wife were in London, driven out of Tanyrallt by a felonious attempt on his life. Harriet gave his friends detailed accounts of a pistol thrust through the window, of shots in the dark. Shelley's nightshirt was pierced by a bullet; another was imbedded in the wainscoting. There had been a hand-to-hand tussle between Shelley and his unseen assailant, whose identity, but for vague suspicions, remained unknown. Some of the inhabitants of Tanyrallt

refused to believe a word of the affray.   Some threw the blame
on a shepherd of the neighboring hills, whose beasts, sick with
the scab, Shelley used to dispatch with his pistol in summary if
merciful fashion.[1]   Friends were skeptical.   The early part
of March Hookham received a letter reading: "Dear Sir, —
I have just escaped an atrocious assassination.   Oh, send
twenty pounds if you have it!   You will perhaps hear of me
no more!"

Had some enemy really tried to kill Shelley or had it been
a scene enacted in his imagination?   There were the bullet
marks.   Yet why should anyone have wished to murder a man
known throughout the district for his many charities?   Shelley
was firmly convinced he was a marked man.

Late in June Harriet was delivered of a little girl named
Ianthe, after Shelley's blue-eyed heroine.   It lacked two
months to his majority.

[1] See *Century Magazine* for October 1905.

IX

THE BRINK OF THE PRECIPICE

ARMIDA, Circe, Lady Oxford: she was the one and the same, the beautiful enchantress by whatever name Byron called her. After the first few weeks of classical delights in her company he marveled, but did not regret, that he was still unwearied. He would say that she resembled a landscape by Claude "with a setting sun, her beauties enhanced by the knowledge that they were shedding their last dying beams" — a pretty simile, but not wholly true. At twenty-four, forty may seem like the sunset time of beauty. He was to learn that Circe has no age. "A woman is only grateful for her *first* and *last* conquest." He flattered himself that his would be the crowning of Lady Oxford's achievement begun while he was yet a baby in his cradle. Again, he had much to learn. In the meantime the days and nights at Eywood passed with the timelessness that only gods enjoy, leaving no surfeit, yet nothing to desire. Lord Oxford — Potiphar, they called him — had been well schooled in the philosophy of discretion. What he had often done before he did again, and the Lucretians enjoyed their godhood unmolested.

Away in Ireland Lady Caroline tried to piece together her heart and mind pitifully shattered. Her mother nursed and humored her. William Lamb, annoyed by what had seemed too glaring a breach of propriety, put up a careless front and "laughed and ate like a trooper." A hollow-eyed, mournful Ariel was not at all to his taste. "When I laugh, play, ride and amuse him, he loves me," murmured Lady Caroline. "In sickness and sorrow he deserts me." Now if ever she needed sympathetic guidance; but William Lamb was preoccupied with his wounded vanity.

Lady Caroline had passed the crisis of her nervous collapse when she heard of Byron's sojourn at Eywood. So soon, so soon. . . . How could he go so quickly from her to another? And such another! Little did she know of his boasting that even during their love he had been false to her. But a year ago she and Lady Oxford had engaged in an exceedingly *blue* discussion on the subject of whether learning Greek purified or inflamed the passions. The Eywood Aspasia had more than Greek to teach a young voluptuary. Uncertain as yet of the progress of the new intrigue, Lady Caroline wrote to Byron, begging him to forgive her as she poured out her love and her unhappiness at knowing herself despised. She implored, — surely there was the faith of an angel in her, — she implored Lady Oxford to intercede for her.

In due time every detail of the insane affair found its way to Lady Melbourne, who read, judged, and tried to exert her influence in the right direction, if, poor lady, she could still distinguish the right in this tangle of wrongs. "I mean, *entre nous,* dear Machiavel, to play off Lady Oxford against her," Byron had confided to her on the eve of the new liaison. An unequal match, Circe against Ariel. For the sake of her son William, it seemed a good move to Lady Melbourne. Perhaps, too, for the sake of that miserable little daughter-in-law of hers. Little Mania, Byron now called her. A sinister threat lurked in one of his exasperated epistles: "Her worst enemy could not wish her such a fate as *now* to be thrown back upon me." Under his spiritual exterior slept a vengeful cruelty that were better let alone. Ariel had sensed it while there had still been time to pause on the edge of the chasm and fly away. She had plunged headlong down.

Her letters continued bolder and more exigent as she threatened to spread the scandal of the new amour. Maddened, she flung her mightiest thunderbolts, which fell, mere irritating squibs, in the Eywood Olympus. The two divinities frowned at this insistent interruption of their peace. Strange that a husband should be complacent and a cast-off mistress play the injured one. Circe could not understand. But then how could she when she had always been the first to tire? When the Ariel battery was no longer to be borne, Byron, at Circe's instance, hurled back a deadly bolt. "Lady Caroline, I am no longer your lover," began the letter, "and since you oblige me to confess it . . . learn that I am attached to another. . . . I shall ever remember with gratitude the many instances I have received of the predilection you have shown in my favour. I shall ever continue your friend . . . and as a first proof of my regard, I offer you this advice: correct your vanity, which is ridiculous; exert your absurd caprices on others; and leave me in peace."[1]

Never had a letter so coldly insulting been written to a woman guilty of loving too much. A sadic glitter heightened the cruelty of the cat-and-mouse play of the periods. The coronet and monogram of Lady Oxford were stamped on the seal.

The scorned mistress was beside herself with shame and anger. She knew who had framed that masterpiece and would rather have been slain by the hand that had written than that it should have set down that venomed dictation. No, Byron could not have been so cold and hard. Cruel he had been, but never so deliberately. Feeling that all was over, she tried to cut her throat with a razor. It was only Lady Bessborough's presence of mind in seizing the blade with her fingers and challenging her to draw her mother's blood that brought poor Lady Caroline to her senses.

She was removed at once to Brocket Hall, whose serene environment had always helped to calm her. In time her violence was gone, but she still brooded and indulged in vagaries that made Lady Bessborough fear for her reason. The foul fiend Flibbertigibbet possessed her, jeered Byron from his summit. It was a harmless possession, injurious to none but the bereft creature. A pitiful Simætha, Lady Caroline indulged in a naïve bit of witchcraft — not to hurt Byron, but to exorcise the spell that had blighted her life. Everything of his was potent with it — his poems, the trinkets he had given her, his letters and pictures, none of which had ever done justice to "that beautiful pale face" that had been her fate. "*Ma è la beltà della morte*" — ay, it was such beauty as

[1] The text of the letter may be found in Lady Caroline Lamb's *roman à clef*, *Glenarvon*.

death had, worse than death to her, knowing it another's.

One late autumn day she gathered about her the children of Welwyn and burned upon a bonfire the portrait of Byron, the books and love tokens he had given her, and *copies* of his letters. The originals she could not destroy. While girls in white danced in a ring round the flames, a page chanted lines she had composed for the ceremony, as she stood by, tense and pale. "Is this Guy Fawkes you burn in effigy?" the verses queried. Not Guy Fawkes who had proved a traitor to his country, but one who had been worse in guilt, in treason to her.

> Ah, look not thus on me, so grave, so sad,
> Shake not your heads, nor say the lady's mad.
> Judge not of others, for there is but one
> To whom the heart and feelings can be known . . .
> London, farewell; vain world, vain life, adieu!
> Take the last tears I e'er shall shed for you.

In vain she burned the links that had welded her to Byron. She could not dispel his power. *Ne crede Byron* she engraved on the buttons of her pages' livery. The admonition came too late.

February of 1813 still found Byron in *palatia Circes,* wondering, since he was no Ulysses, into what animal he would be converted. The interlude had lasted longer than either of the participants had expected. The gods of Olympus, however, had never been remarkable for fidelity. Lady Oxford proved no exception. Byron had been a charming, a most delightful lover. But now she desired change and told him. She had even chosen his successor for further classical adventuring. "Thou art not false, but thou art fickle," he sighed, in not wholly unpleasurable pain. In spite of the pang he could not but feel at the interruption of a blissful season which he had hoped would have a longer duration, he admired this woman whose *dying beams* left a more burning warmth than the noontide of others. "Too well thou lov'st — too soon thou leavest," was his sole reproach. They remained friends, and his invitations to Eywood were repeated. Charlotte, Lady Oxford's eldest daughter, was still too young. . . . He contented himself with writing for the girl a new dedication to

Childe Harold, and thinking of the summer, when he and the Oxfords were to set off for Sicily. Greece, Sicily — their blue skies were the same: the same gods had reigned over them.

June came, but the Oxfords traveled alone, Lord Oxford having been smitten with somewhat tardy scruples. Moreover, Augusta was temporarily breaking up home for financial reasons and would be living in rooms in St. James's Palace. As a brother, he would have to look after her.

Once again the Childe was seen in society, paler, more beautiful than ever. He met Madame de Staël and disliked her cordially, another prejudice he shared with his little pagod Napoleon, who had always looked upon her as a bird of ill omen whose arrival was the signal for trouble. For self-protection he exiled her who had been one of the pioneers of the French romantic movement in literature. Napoleon had writers he liked better. Staël the Epicene, as Byron called her, was not at all his ideal of woman; she was too masculine, too intellectual. In the years that had passed, her politics had undergone a radical change. Now she talked of nothing but devotion and the ministry, "And I presume," added the malicious wit, "expects that God and the government will help her to a pension." For her part the Baronne found the Childe affected, said he kept his eyes closed during dinner, and that he had no right to make love as he was "totally *in*sensible to *la belle* passion." He had used Lady Caroline barbarously, she told him.

Indeed, another scene had been enacted of the tragicomedy. Lady Caroline, after repeated efforts to meet Byron on her return to London, came face to face with him at Lady Heathcote's ball in July. Neither had expected the meeting. It was enough to unsettle her. Knowing the eyes of the world concentrated upon them, she seized the suggestion of Lady Heathcote that she should open the dance, and turning toward Byron, "I conclude I may waltz *now?*" she asked. They were the first words she had addressed to him since their parting. They meant more than met the ear. Now that Byron had rejected her and was no longer jealous, was she to take it that he released her of the promise never to waltz again? Byron understood. Unmindful of her nervousness, he said coldly: "With everybody in turn." . . . She danced. The shock of the meeting, the frigid insult of his voice, made the walls spin about her. She excused herself and went into the dining room for a glass of water. Lord Byron and Lady Rancliffe entered after her. "I have been admiring your dexterity," he needlessly flung at her. Lady Caroline felt herself growing faint, and in her agitation clasped a knife, not knowing what she did. "Do, my dear," said Byron. "But if you mean to act a Roman's part, mind which way you strike with your knife — be it at your own heart, not mine — you have struck there already." Childe Harold was at his best, superior and scornful. "Byron!" she cried, unable to say more, and ran off with the knife. Lady Rancliffe screamed, sending out the alarm that Lady Caroline would stab herself. The knife was pulled away from the hysterical woman, cutting her hand and covering her gown with blood. Immediately the cry rose that Lady Caroline had tried to kill herself because Byron had taken another mistress.[1]

Society mouthed the new scandal. The papers wrote it large. Byron stormed, especially since he had been thinking of making a proposal for the hand of Lady Adelaide Forbes, daughter of George, Earl of Granard, with the full approval of Thomas Moore, who had never countenanced the Milbanke suit. Lady Melbourne made her comment, a more urbane echoing of Byron's "One of her tricks!" Her poor son William — *he* was the one to be pitied.

As for Lady Caroline, she faded into the shadow of herself. Not even her cousin Annabella could now have called her Fair Foolishness, Beautiful Silliness. "The sunflower was punished for its temerity." Lady Caroline had long borne that in mind. Scorched but no wiser, she still believed its fate more to be envied than that of other flowers. She was impelled toward the sun, do what she might. Hardly had the Heathcote scandal died down than she went to Byron's rooms in St. James's. He was not at home. But she was too well known to Fletcher and old Mrs. Mule, the housekeeper, not to be let in. On the table lay a copy of Beckford's *Vathek,* that

---

[1] This account is based on Lady Caroline's version, with due deference to Byron's and Lady Melbourne's.

infernal admixture of fancy and strange luxuries. Did her eye fall on that final vision of Vathek and Nouronihar in hell, condemned to everlasting anguish, and knowing rage and despair instead of love? On a flyleaf she wrote the words, "Remember me," and left. Byron's answer she was not to know until after his death.

By midsummer of the year Byron had left behind a number of milestones. He had delivered his third and last speech in the House, surrendering all prospects of ever becoming an orator; he had published a poetical satire on waltzing so inferior in quality that its ill success made him disclaim authorship; he had brought out the *Giaour,* a wild, fragmentary Eastern tale of a girl drowned for adultery and avenged by her lover; and he had been graduated from the classical school of Lady Oxford. Life palled. He was restless, yet knew not the cure. Writing gave him little joy. Moreover, he had to recognize that since those first cantos of *Childe Harold* he had done nothing to equal even the parts where he had nodded. Intrigue and adultery — he had had enough of them; but still he found himself perpetually embroiled. Marriage might be his refuge if one would be willing to save him.

The season closed brilliantly with a ball, though there had been no lack of festivity since Wellington's triumph at Vitoria. The illuminations to celebrate it had caused a conflagration which only added to the fireworks. England was in a whirl of rejoicing. Though the war with the United States had not gone well for it, this last victory neutralized all defeats. Spain was rid of the invaders; France might be entered. . . . The Regent declared a national fête. The "four thousand" who did not sleep at night crowded to Vauxhall. Far away, too far for the merrymakers to be troubled, the fields of Vitoria were strewn thick with dead from the use of Shrapnel's new invention of explosive shells.

In the literary world other warfare was carried on. The *Giaour* was praised by Jeffrey in the *Edinburgh Review.* In the *Quarterly* Rogers was damned. Southey, newly succeeded to the money equivalent of Laureate Jonson's tierce of canary, embarked on his "ode-ous" job and went on producing his unsalables. "Is Southey magnanimous?" Byron asked Rogers on being offered an introduction. His sallies against *Joan of Arc* and *Thalaba* in *English Bards* pricked his conscience. Rogers put him at his ease and the two poets met. "His appearance is Epic; and he is the only existing man of letters," Byron wrote in his diary. Publicly, that is; to Moore he spoke with reservation. "To have that poet's head and shoulders, I would almost have written his *Sapphics*." In his private illustrative pyramid, Scott he placed at the apex, Rogers next below him, Moore and Campbell still lower, and Southey, Wordsworth, and Coleridge only above *hoi polloi*. Not even in that nondescript class had he thought of placing the author of *Queen Mab*, which had recently been sent to him with Shelley's compliments. As for him, Byron, where did he belong? High up, judging by popular acclaim.

He recked little for poetic fame, though he winced under criticism. What he wanted was a life of action. He champed like a steed at the bit; he grew morose and sullen, cursing fate for having lamed him. Happily there was still Newstead, which bid fair to return upon his hands after having been tentatively sold to a man who found in the end that he had not the means to pay for it. Newstead: he and the abbey would stand or fall together.

The artificial stimulation of the season abated, he fretted in his rooms. Oh, for something to rouse him to a full sense of the romances he could live! Augusta came.

They met almost as strangers, with all the vista of the possibilities in the situation. Both had changed. A sensation of rediscovery entered their relations as Augusta came and went like the veiled lady of mystery under the watchful eye of Mrs. Mule. What could the old dragon find wrong, however, in the visits of a sister to her brother, and she a respectable married lady, and a mother?

Augusta at twenty-eight had the figure of a young girl, not too slight or full, and well proportioned. She dressed with the sapient elegance of the court circle, only that a lock of hair in disorder, a ruffle out of place, gave her that appearance of disarray that lends more charm than the most faultless toilette. Something was always askew with Augusta, if not her frills, her thoughts, if not her thoughts her hopelessly muddled home life. Her large, dreamy eyes, far apart under level brows, had a trick of suddenly lighting with mirth. Then her face of pure oval, with its pert young Byron mouth, became irresistibly youthful. She laughed, and to his amazement the melancholy Childe found himself laughing with her. A bewitching creature, the Honourable Augusta Leigh, light-hearted and gay as a child. Never before had Byron been so much at ease in a woman's company. Perhaps because she was his sister. He did not have to pose before her, and if he did he was immediately called from the stage by some ridiculous sally. What slim, dainty hands she had! Ali Pacha would have had no doubt of her noble birth. Her hair, parted in the middle, flowed in wide, deep waves, lustrous in their darkness. One could not see her ears. Ali Pacha might have been assured that under those curls they were small and pearly as sea shells. A very attractive woman, Augusta. More than that, a Byron, with all that to which the name was heir.

Augusta, on her side, instead of her Baby Byron, found a singularly handsome man of the world, very much the master of himself. Gone was every vestige of the awkward school-boy. Out of her sight the chrysalis had been shed, and the transformation seemed therefore the more remarkable. A slight embarrassment interposed itself at first, owing to the estrangement there had been between them through Byron's criticisms of Lord Carlisle. It was soon overcome. No unpleasantness was long tolerated by Augusta, whose philosophy — if one could call philosophy the illogic of her actions — admitted of everything that gave one pleasure and made no one else unhappy. It was a far-reaching code, perilously bordering on no code at all. To one brought up in the dourness of Calvinism the license it admitted was no less than phenomenal. But then, Augusta had entered early into the life of the court, which had quite other teachings to impart. There she shone as that pearl of great price, a virtuous woman.

Colonel Leigh took the separation from his wife as a matter of course. Whether at Six Mile Bottom or in St. James's Palace, it was all one to him where she spent her time. He had his own friends; where they were, there was home.

Augusta had long accustomed herself to living a life of semi-widowhood, knowing that whenever her husband made his appearance it was for other reasons than affection for her or any care for the children.   Yet in her way she loved her un-practical, helpless colonel who was nothing but a charge, like another, more difficult child.   "Can't you drive this Cousin of ours out of your pretty little head (as for hearts I think they are out of the question)," the young Southwell rake had written to her before her marriage.   Byron did not know the real Augusta then.   She was all heart; emotion ruled her. Thought was to be used only in the calculation of Colonel Leigh's debts, and she had ample occasion to exercise it there.

Together Byron and Augusta attended the last festivities of the season.   Alone in the carriage, later, with her on his arm, he enjoyed a vicarious husbandliness.   He was old enough to have had a wife and children of his own.   Most of his friends whom death had spared had settled down.   Even Moore, the social butterfly, had married a young actress and offered him the naming of a child.   If Miss Milbanke had only said yes instead of no.   The rejection still rankled.   Yet would she have been the wife for him?   She was too serious and too good.   He needed someone like Augusta who talked nonsense and made him laugh.   Women with intellects, unless subservient to their femininity, as in the Eywood Circe, bored him, and he had need to be taken out of himself.

He saw Augusta every day.   "My sister is in town, which is a great comfort," he wrote Moore, "for, never having been much together, we are naturally more attached to each other." Lady Melbourne too was told, more in detail, of Augusta's stay.   Since he had not been permitted to go to Sicily with the Oxfords, he would go instead with his sister, he informed his confidante.   Lady Melbourne was aghast.   Clever though she was, a woman less worldly-wise than herself could have read between the nervous lines that extraordinary happenings, such as the most corrupt imagination dreaded to dwell on, had been taking place at number 4 Bennet Street, St. James's. Byron's was a rebellious daring, unafraid of god or man.   But there were things that even the boldest dare not attempt.   For them loomed the pain of everlasting death.   Lady Melbourne, never before a raven of disaster, sent him warning. "You are on the brink of a precipice; if you do not retreat, you are lost forever — it is a crime for which there is no salvation in this world, whatever there may be in the next." She pleaded for him, she pleaded for Augusta, whose peace he would be destroying forever.

He was cynically amused at this *volte-face* of his charming devil's advocate. "Lady Melbourne is a good woman after all, for there are things she will stop at," he commented. He obeyed her, however, in giving up the voyage to Sicily, but he still went on living with Augusta. Whatever stirrings of conscience he may have had found no place at first in his letters to Lady Melbourne. He was the same brilliant, perverse correspondent. "In this place we can only say what we are not doing," he wrote from Bennet Street. "I see no one; I say nothing; I do nothing; and I wish for nothing." He had eaten of the lotos and was lost to everything but the delight. Then came the reaction. The seeming peace gave way to restlessness. He was "miserably feverish." Augusta had returned to Newmarket; he could not bear her away from him. He was going to Cambridge, he said. Lady Melbourne knew he was on his way to his sister.

In the thick of the trouble, desire, and remorse, came a letter from Annabella Milbanke. They had met during the season, and had scarcely spoken, both equally embarrassed, both not knowing why. Suitors had come for Annabella's hand; she had accepted no one, seeing afar a beautiful, pale face which, though she had never said it, was her fate — darker still, as time was to show, than it had been for Caroline Lamb.

After her refusal of Lady Melbourne's suit for Byron, Annabella had sent at her request a list of the qualities she desired in a husband. The task was balm to the Princess of Parallelograms, as Byron labeled her. Very methodically she set down in concise form a modern Mirror for Husbands. Her ideal man must possess, among other virtues, "consistent principles of Duty, *generous* feelings. . . ." Genius, though desirable, was not in her opinion essential. She would have "an equal tenor of affection" from him rather than violent attachment. He must command sufficient fortune to keep her

as she had been accustomed to be kept, though rank was indifferent to her. And his family must have been free from
the taint of insanity.

How Lady Melbourne must have laughed at this man of
wax of her niece's moulding! Did Byron possess any of the
requirements? The principles of Duty were out. Genius?
He had it. Fortune? He commanded a larger share of the
less desirable rank. Had there been any strong tendency to
insanity in his family? Byron seemed hardly the man for
Annabella Milbanke. But fie on the girl's preposterous nonsense! In the face of Byron's present peril Lady Melbourne
played her card to save him. She wrote to Annabella with his
authority. What she said Byron had little desire to know.
He was seeking salvation in the expedient of another love.

Annabella's answer came, a sermon on Christian behavior
— longer than most sermons and but little to the point she
would have made. Briefly, she was interested in Byron —
how much she would not admit — and she would willingly
enter into correspondence with him. She had always been
concerned in his welfare. "I was interested by the strength
and generosity of your feelings, and I honoured you for that
pure sense of moral rectitude, which could not be perverted,
though perhaps tried by the practice of Vice." Did Byron
smile at the faith of his little mathematician? His moral
rectitude — bless the child! What would she say were she
to know — Spoiled darling that she was, always on her stilts,
looking down on sinful man! Here was indeed a sinner for
her to uplift.

In answering her he touched upon her rejection, assumed
the melancholy, and said he would probably never marry.
The more he wrote, the more he hypnotized himself into the
belief that he had loved her, and loved her still. He did not
know whether there could be friendship between them. "It is
a feeling towards you with which I cannot trust myself. I
doubt whether I could help loving you."

The effect of the words on Annabella was magical. She
had heard he would be leaving England and wrote him a
palpitant note of farewell. "I will not regret the friendship
which you deem impossible, for the loss is *mine*, as the comfort

would have been *mine.*" For Annabella it was a bold avowal of her love. What more could she have said to make him understand? Either Byron did not or, for the present, wished not to understand. "Your friendship I did not reject — though in speaking of mine I expressed some doubts on the subject of my own feelings. Whatever they may be, I shall merely repeat that if possible they shall be subdued — at all events, silent." He was marking time when, with but a little ardor, he might now have won her. Was it really true, as she seemed to imply, that she had long loved someone without hope? Was that someone himself, or that other of whom Lady Caroline had spoken? Women sometimes used such artifice to waken a slumbering heart. But surely not the moral little Saint Ursula. At any rate he would take her up on that later, and arrive at whatever hidden meaning she may have had.

Several more letters passed between them, leaving them exactly where they had started — Miss Milbanke still didactic and tedious, Byron wishing yet unwilling. He felt ashamed before her goodness; he pitied her for her all-sustaining faith. Tormented by his secret, he relieved himself by dangerous indirection. "The object of life is sensation — to feel that we exist, even though in pain," he wrote Annabella. "It is this 'craving void' which drives us to intemperate but keenly felt pursuits of any description. . . . I am but an awkward dissembler."

Annabella read, offered consolation and advice, and tried to clarify her sentiments toward this candid sinner by confessions to a girlhood friend. The spectacle of genius without heavenly grace roused her to missionary zeal. "Should it ever happen," she wrote, "that he and I offer up a heartfelt worship together . . . *my* worship will then be almost worthy of the spirit to whom it ascends. It will glow with all the devout and grateful joy which mortal breast can contain. . . . It is not the poet — it is the immortal soul lost or saved!" And she dwelt on him till her tears fell. Even then Byron was commenting in his diary, "What an odd situation and friendship is ours! — without one spark of love on either side." "When shall we meet in town?" he wrote to her. But she must not fear he would add to her "thousand and one pretendants. . . . I have taken exquisite care to prevent the possibility of that. . . ." Augusta, always Augusta.

"Dear sacred name, rest ever unreveal'd," he quoted in his journal, the night he finished writing the *Bride of Abydos*. Do what he would, — carry on a loveless correspondence with Annabella, discipline himself in platonics with Lady Frances Wedderburn Webster, write or be idle, — he could not rid himself of the thought of Augusta and of their sinful love. He had composed the new poem to wring his thoughts from her. It was for him "the lava of the imagination whose eruption prevents an earthquake." Yet, in spite of himself, his imaginings became tinged with reality. The thought still ran "through, through . . . yes, through." He became more overt in his allusions, to ease his overburdened conscience. Annabella was alarmed. "I fear he has done something rash from a romantic motive." How rash she was not to know, until too late for her, for him.

Meanwhile the serious Princess of Parallelograms was doing her best to make her unmathematical poet understand she loved him, whether his immortal soul were lost or saved. She had received more pleasure from his poetry, she told him naïvely, than from all the Q. E. D.'s in Euclid — a vast compliment. Byron had neither the will nor the inclination to think of her, however. The Seaham correspondence lagged. The genius, devoid of heavenly grace, was then discovering for himself that when it came, it had too well known a savor.

Lady Frances Webster, virtuous, still, fair, attached to God and "measured once a quarter for a new Bible," had held aloof from Byron, her husband's friend and guest at Aston Hall, Yorkshire, during his first visit there in September, although he had been willing to enter into a new love to drive out of his mind Augusta and the events of the past two months. Nothing compromising had happened on that first visit. In fact, all his desire had been for a poodle dog, which was given him. When he returned in October he looked at the young bride more attentively. Her husband boasted she was cold and chaste. The long looks she gave him out of her slowly lifted eyes, her susceptibility to tears, the trembling of her hand when it inadvertently touched his, told Byron otherwise. "She evidently expects to be attacked, and seems prepared for a brilliant defense," he told the Whitehall confidante, who looked indulgently on the new exploit. At least it would keep him from the fatal X (symbol of Augusta in their correspondence). Byron was right. With sighs, tears, and prayers, Lady Frances signalized too well the working of his power. There is nothing like a reputation for conquests to make women unbar their hearts to the conqueror.

But Lady Frances was a thorough devotee and therefore afraid of sin. Byron, on his part, had still too recent a taste of the forbidden fruit to find another love anything but flat. He kept the affair on a platonic height, Lady Frances tremblingly concurring. They exchanged ascetic *billets-doux* and flowers; they stole handclasps and now and then a kiss, Lady Frances, the while, looking as sinless as a painted angel. Byron, who could not be long with a woman without desiring to possess her, grew weary of platonics, which had more than once been in danger, and would have descended to facts. Lady Frances demurred. At Newstead, where he had invited her and her husband, there had been a moment of bittersweet yielding. Byron denied himself and spared her. He did not know why, nor could he explain to the very much interested Lady Melbourne. A white rose, shedding its lustre, meek and pale, that was Lady Frances: —

> So white — so faint — the slightest gale
> Might whirl the leaves on high;
> And yet, though storms and blight assail
> And hands more rude than wintry sky
> May wring it from stem — in vain —
> Tomorrow sees it bloom again!

With Augusta the white rose grew into Zuleika, the maiden of Abydos who loved her brother. Still, still, the thought ran through — He must tell his sin or perish, and so he avowed it in his verse. What if, for the sake of a shocked morality, Selim in the end is discovered to be no brother — still, still the rapturous kisses are there, the kisses of incestuous love.

To see thee, hear thee, near thee stay,
    And hate the night I know not why,
Save that we meet not but by day;
    With thee to live, with thee to die,
    I dare not to my hope deny;
Thy cheek, thine eyes, thy lips to kiss,
Like this — and this — no more than this:
    For, Alla! sure thy lips are flame . . .

How much truth there was in those lines would the world ever know?

The white rose of the unavailing surrender grew flushed with unplatonic passion. She besieged Byron with letters, placing herself and him in compromising situations. Her husband, jealous and hot-headed, might resort to violence. "C(aroline) would go wild that it *did not happen about her . . .*" scoffed Byron, weary of the unsatisfying experiment. "Do you know," he admitted to Lady Melbourne, who knew it only too well, "I am much afraid that the perverse passion was my deepest after all."

X

IN QUEST OF THE NEW IDEAL

THE mysterious Tanyrallt attempt had sent the Shelleys flying to London and Killarney, but not for long. Harriet's confinement brought them to London, with a temporary freedom from Eliza, who, in the absence of Portia-Bessie, was rapidly becoming odious to the inconstant enthusiast. The birth of Ianthe sped the reunited trio onward once more, though not far. High Elms, Bracknell, in Berkshire, was only thirty miles from London, within convenient reach of publishers and books, those treasures so jealously hoarded by Shelley — and so recklessly lost. A great pile of them, but recently acquired, had been left in Ireland in the keeping of Eliza, who, when the word came for her to join the birds in flight, finding her own wings encumbered, left the hoard behind, vainly awaiting some literary delver to bring it to light. They were not the first of Shelley's books to be so lost, nor were they to be the last.

At Bracknell Shelley found himself in the midst of a predominantly feminine intellectual coterie. He had met some members of the Boinville-Newton circle in London, through Godwin, when Mr. Newton's vegetarianism had so far impressed him, both in the Newton family's practice of it and in that gentleman's exposition of its benefits in his *Return to Nature*, that Shelley had enriched Queen Mab with a learned note in which Prometheus was made to appear as the cause of man's descent to the fleshpot by his gift of fire. He quoted from Mr. Newton's opus; he expatiated upon the glorious health of Mr. Newton's vegetable-fed children, all of whom had lived "for seven years on this diet without a death, and almost without the slightest illness." He did not mention there the cult of philosophical nakedness that had been imposed upon the young Newtons since their infancy. For several hours during the day they were stripped and made to *nakedize* that their bodies might receive the benison of nature's light and air. The parents, too, nakedized in the privacy of their rooms. Had not Dr. Franklin started the cult in America? And Blake, that most guileless of God's children, had he not been found in his garden arbor, playing at Adam and Eve with his wife? Nature, the mother of all, was innocent and beautiful. Her children could do no wrong in following her.

Thus Hogg, one day, gone to pay a visit with Shelley to these recently acquired friends, was startled, on the door's opening, to be confronted with the spectacle of five naked figures, from a boy of twelve to a little girl of five, hastily ascending the stairs at the sight of him, a stranger. It is not difficult to know who was the most embarrassed in that unconventional situation.

Hogg, however, was soon received by the Newtons and by Mrs. Newton's sister, Madame Boinville, though not with the welcome they accorded Shelley. Hogg was too matter-of-fact. His eyebrows perceptibly lifted during the *conversazioni* of the Boinville-Newton evenings. He went so far as to be jocular when they seriously discussed the locality of the Garden of Eden, or entered into sentimental disquisitions on the question: "What place would you choose to be buried in?" And he disgraced himself beyond forgiveness when, at a lecture in which a lady discoursed on the evil of stays, illustrating anatomy by means of a flayed rabbit, he pointed out that since it was a buck rabbit, it could not have been affected by the bane under discussion.

Thomas Love Peacock, too, joined the circle, again through the mediation of Shelley, but he was no favorite. His cool, analytical eyes disconcerted the ladies. He was too ready to laugh with a laughter so tempered, so urbane, that it offended more than downright mockery. Whereas the other doubting Thomas showed his scorn openly of the "two or three sentimental young butchers, an eminently philosophical tinker and several very unsophisticated medical practitioners" who were the satellites of the feminine orbs, and sneered at their clumsy attempts to enact the parts of adoring Petrarchs and melancholy Werthers, Peacock studied them with the coolness of a surgeon and noted their peculiarities. With Shelley he tempted Mr. Newton into lengthy expositions of his mystical system of the Zodiac whose two hemispheres were the provinces of Oromazes, the principle of good, and Ahrimanes, the principle of evil. It was the zodiac of Dendera, the ancient system that taught the use of the vegetable diet as the means of arriving at the golden age of purity and wisdom. The two young men listened intently: Shelley with his all-drinking eyes fixed upon this new fount of wisdom as he turned over in his mind the ways and means of dispensing its charities to thirsting humanity; Peacock, his tongue in his cheek, seeing Mr. Newton in caricature as a character in a satirical novel. It is to the credit of the Boinville-Newtons that of a good poet they made a better novelist; in their midst Peacock found himself.

Nothing could alter Shelley's rapt vision. Having looked at the sun of perfectibility, he saw it in everything else he beheld. Mr. Newton was a Godwinian; the ladies quoted the philosopher with approval. These facts alone sufficed for Shelley to convert a group of harmless faddists into saviors of humanity. In a sense it was a family trait, allowing for the exception of Timothy Shelley, to encourage the new. Old Sir Bysshe had patronized, indeed, at one time had collaborated, with the notorious Dr. Graham, famed for his *earth baths*, popular cures for rheumatism, nervous ills, even sterility. The good doctor took the earth baths himself, it seemed, though it is not on record whether he ever persuaded Sir Bysshe to try one. Up and down London Dr. Graham's purple curricle, paid for by Sir Bysshe, rattled away with dizzying speed, as he visited one patient after another, prescribing his never-failing remedy. Back in his garden at the Temple of Health, where Emma Hart, later Lady Hamilton, had assisted, he supervised the baths — watched the sufferer disrobe behind a screen, descend into a perpendicular grave in the ground, and allow himself to be covered to the neck with finely sifted mould like a giant mandragora. The screen removed, the patient found himself one of a fantastic bed of periwigged heads in animated conversation on their bodies' ills. Since the baths lasted from three to four hours, even that engrossing topic of conversation was in time exhausted and communion rose to higher planes, so that besides giving his patients health, Dr. Graham afforded them the advantage of a liberal education.

Harriet counted few friends in the Bracknell circle outside of Peacock and, discounting the grudge of the ancient rebuff, Hogg. Grown tedious with her half-hearted parroting of Shelley's ideas, she had not sufficient culture of the rarefied mediæval Italian or mystically German species to make up to the Boinville ladies for her too pretty face. Not that Madame Boinville and her daughter Cornelia were wanting in physical attractiveness. Madame Boinville, whose husband was fighting in the Russian campaign, had a winning vivacity of face and voice, besides personifying for the impressible Shelley Southey's white-haired yet youthful Maimuna. Cornelia, recently married to a Mr. Turner, possessed the romantic languor of the West Indian blood on her mother's side, and the elegance of her émigré father. She was versed in the Italian poets, quoted Dante, and every morning before breakfast memorized one of Petrarch's sonnets, that the rest of the day might be filled with its spiritual message. She herself seemed all calm spirituality, tinged with the poetic gloom that comes of too full a soul. Before such ethereal accomplishment Harriet's freshness had somewhat of the shoddy, a fact which the elevated ladies subtly underlined.

Nevertheless Harriet had changed. The long, ungainly months of motherhood seemed to have given her a new regard for her body. Once Ianthe was born, she would not suckle the child — Shelley thought on Eliza's advice — and spent more time on her toilette, with which she had always taken pains. Hogg, a visitor once more, was disappointed to find that "the good Harriet" no longer fell upon her edifying French books to read aloud, but inveigled him to go out with her, usually to some elegant bonnet shop, nothing astonishing in itself, but puzzling when coupled with humanitarian protestations.

She had insisted, too, most undemocratically, on owning a carriage, which Shelley ordered from one of the best makers in Bond Street, although he had no money to pay for it and consequently was obliged to avoid London when the bills became due. Because of that very carriage, Hogg, mistaken for Shelley, had had an execution served upon him and was in some trouble to escape being clapped in gaol for debt. Harriet rode about in it, however, forgetting in her sense of luxury that it ill became a good Godwinian, as she hoped against hope that her husband, now of age, would come into that fortune which he had been dispensing so liberally *a priori*. Surely it was not wicked of her to spend a little of it in advance, when Shelley was so generous of it in his philanthropies. There was Mr. Godwin — if Godwin might enjoy it, why not a Godwinian, the heir's wife in the bargain?

Shelley observed with pain the changes in Harriet. He had been happy at the prospect of being a father, of having a virgin mind to educate and love according to the precepts of perfectibility. As a boy he had dreamed of buying one of the gypsy tumbling girls that came to Field Place, that he might have something of his own to teach. He received his first shock when Harriet denied herself to the babe. In her awakened womanhood she took more interest in herself than in her child or, Shelley gradually realized, in her husband. Something had come over her with her first deep womanly experience. Eliza was not slow to aid and abet her. Little by little, as the golden promises failed to materialize through Timothy Shelley's obduracy and Shelley's own notions of honor, Eliza began to wonder whether she had not made a mistake in playing her best card against so impecunious a gambler. She undertook the care of Ianthe, therefore, and directed Harriet's motions from behind the scenes.

The rift between husband and wife did not come at once. At first neither was aware that even the slightest hairline of a cleavage was between them. Proud of having his own child in his arms, Shelley sang the unwitting Ianthe to sleep with a weird "Yáhmani, Yáhmani, Yáhmani, Yáhmani," putting into that lullaby in a magical language known only to poets and babes the love he felt for that

> . . . fair and fragile blossom;
> Dearest when most thy tender traits express
> The image of thy mother's loveliness.

He had written those lines in September of 1813 and he had meant them. A month later, when the unpaid carriage had taken him and Harriet and their friend Peacock on a pleasure trip to Edinburgh, Harriet could say with truth to Miss Nugent that the two years which she had spent with her husband had been "the happiest and longest" in her life. In the city that had been the scene of their runaway marriage, the year of the comet, they could afford to take stock of themselves. Perhaps to Harriet those happy years were but the prelude to a long life with Shelley. He might yet be reconciled to his father, even if the last visit to Field Place had again proved fruitless. Still, Shelley was young; they were both young. Mr. Timothy Shelley could not always remain stony-hearted.

Despite the poetical influence of the Bracknell ladies, Shelley could find nothing to engage his genius but a prose *Refutation of Deism*. The olden scenes in Edinburgh brought back the early activities. He was more revolutionary than ever, much to the distress of Eliza, who had hoped that his majority had at least given him wisdom of a safe, worldly brand. Relations between them grew insufferable. He hated to see her fondle Ianthe; he loathed the sight of the incubus that had settled itself into the very heart of his life and would not be shaken off. With horror of himself he watched growing within him "a terrible susceptibility to objects of disgust and hatred." He would have been unable to point to a definite cause. Was it that his long-suffering patience was rebelling at last against Eliza's ill-concealed tyranny over him and his? He had unconsciously been making comparisons between the Bracknell transcendentalism and his own hearth's worldliness — for in spite of Harriet's unchanging air he had heard the difference in her song. Had he not, Madame Boinville must have called it to his attention. Some day, some day, she would say, there would be a struggle between Shelley and Harriet. She, an authority on love and passion in their various æsthetic gradations, could see that, whatever the feeling between the two young people, it was not love. Neither was it passion — certainly not on Shelley's side. Friendship, perhaps.

Yet Harriet was lovely and attractive. So was Cornelia

Turner, with, besides, an indefinable something that Harriet had never possessed and could never have acquired — that something which would have prevented her, after two years with Shelley, from turning again into the coffeehouse keeper's daughter, with the aspirations of her class.   Not all of it could have been Eliza's doing, although much obviously sprang from her perverted spinster mind.   Harriet cooled toward her husband.   In London she gossiped about him with Mrs. Godwin, according to that impeccable lady.   She was afraid Shelley had fallen in love with Cornelia Turner, "and had paid her such marked attentions Mr. Turner the husband had carried off his wife to Devonshire."

However it might have been, whether out of jealousy of the Bracknell sirens, whom she felt to be no friends of hers, or out of obedience to Eliza's counsels, by the spring of the new year Harriet was oftener away from Shelley than with him. While he stayed at Windsor, at no great distance from the Boinvilles, Harriet went on excursions with her sister and the baby.   March found Shelley without his wife, a guest at Bracknell, where under the influence of Cornelia's pitying gaze he wrote: —

> Thy dewy looks sink in my breast,
> Thy gentle words find poison there. . . .

He saw, or was made to see, the pathos of his situation. "Subdued to Duty's hard control," he complained, "I could have borne my wayward lot."   Now its chains were crushing his soul.   Why had Harriet become so hard and cold?   Whose fault?   Whose fault?   She was not content with him.   She wanted life and society and freedom from that financial insecurity which even now was driving them into hiding from their creditors.   Shelley, too, wanted life, intensely, if still unsurely.   What had he done in his twenty-one years?   Nothing — nothing that mattered.   His efforts to help his fellow men had come to nought.   In Ireland, in Wales, fragments of his ideals were scattered, useless as the feathers fallen from a bird in flight.   He was too tired to fly.   To what goal?   "I have sunk into a premature old age of exhaustion which renders me dead to everything," he unbosomed himself to Hogg in a letter full of deep sadness. Yet that very death was necessary to usher in the new life that was before him.

His youth was dead. He was now a man, no longer pleased with boyish toys. There, at Bracknell, he had glimpses of a beauty other than Reason, where in the calm light of friendship the things of the soul could expand. What if Peacock saw the clay out of which such beauty grew and would have opened Shelley's eyes to it? He could see only the flower. Bracknell, after his own unfriendly fireside, presided over by the demon Eliza, became to him a paradise which had nothing of mortality but its transitoriness. The trees, the bridge, everything about it had become dear to him, and he thought almost with loathing of the time when he should have to leave it and return — to what? In the interim he studied Italian with Cornelia's help. "Did I not once tell you that I thought her cold and reserved?" he communicated to Hogg. "She is the reverse of this, as she is the reverse of everything bad. She inherits all the divinity of her mother." With the two goddesses, the white-haired Maimuna and the Petrarchan Cornelia, Shelley munched contentedly the bread and butter they gave him for breakfast, dinner, and tea, and in discourses on poetry forgot for the moment reality's prose. Sometimes he was still boy enough to indulge in his cherished sport of sailing, and, using the Boinville washing tubs in turn for a boat, floated blissfully on the shallow stream behind the house. The ladies looked on indulgently. They were not Elizas.

Hardly a week had passed since the happy days at Bracknell when, on the twenty-fourth of March, Shelley and Harriet were remarried at St. George's, Hanover Square. It was no added sacrament to seal a happy union. Shelley had seen Godwin, again in financial straits. Whether Shelley had told his mentor that Harriet was with child and Godwin hinted, should the infant prove a male heir, at possible claims for illegitimacy that might be made by Sir Bysshe and Mr. Timothy on account of that irregular marriage in Edinburgh, or whether Shelley sought by this means to call back the estranged Harriet, both he and the philosopher had gone to Doctors' Commons for a license. And so when Shelley and his wife were farthest apart, they were legally made fast.

A few days before that Shelley had made another attempt to resolve his affairs by applying to Grandfather Bysshe for help.   In spite of his hardness the old man had a certain affection for his rebel grandson, if only to annoy his own hypocritical Timothy, who, he knew, counted the days of his long life.   He proposed, therefore, to sell Castle Goring.   Timothy Shelley immediately sent a danger signal to lawyer Whitton. Sir Bysshe must do nothing of the sort.   Any such offer "wd be nutts for the un-christian and unfeeling-like spirit."   Writing himself thus Christianly, once more he made a wreck of his son's hopes.

April found Shelley and Harriet living under separate roofs. The situation was beginning to scandalize the Bracknell colony. "Shelley is again a widower," Madame Boinville informed Hogg. "His beauteous half went to town on Thursday with Miss Westbrook, who is gone to live, I believe, in Southampton." Shelley came to Bracknell for the consolation of Cornelia and the sympathy of her mother.   Yet what right had he there? He was as one under a spell of eternal restlessness.   Nowhere could his spirit find peace.

> Away! Away! to thy sad and silent home;
>   Pour bitter tears on its desolated hearth;
> Watch the dim shades as like ghosts they go and come,
>   And complicate strange webs of melancholy mirth. . . .

Yet what was he to do there, alone in the desolation?   Did he still love his wife?   Had she love left for him in her new and worldly living?   In May he addressed to Harriet a few touching verses to soften her heart toward him and forgive some unmentioned wrong.   In mercy, let her not drive him by her hardness to the misery of a *fatal cure*.

> Oh, trust for once no erring guide!
>   Bid the remorseless feeling flee;
> 'T is malice, 't is revenge, 't is pride,
>   'T is anything but thee.

She must pity him if she cannot love.   Harriet, however, still under the ægis of her erring guide, may have felt that alienation from Shelley would teach him a lesson and bring him back to her unconditionally. It was already too late — for him, even more than for her.

Recently there had come back to Skinner Street Mary Wollstonecraft Godwin, who had been staying with her friends the Baxters, in Scotland. It may be Shelley had seen Mary two years back; it may be he met her that spring of 1814 for the first time. However it was, he saw her with the fresh eye of an overwhelming passion.

Mary, just sixteen, was a quiet, serious girl whose feelings had been taught from childhood to be curbed by the power of Reason, her father's god. Reason above everything. And intellect. No child of Godwin's and Mary Wollstonecraft's was to go through life without leaving a golden mark upon her name. Mary, therefore, had early been encouraged to look upon herself as of a superior order, the enlighteners and pathfinders. She must prove herself worthy of her parentage if she would justify her right to live. Outwardly she presented a face of calm intelligence, the high forehead dominating the rest of her features. Her eyes looked thoughtfully on the world; her mouth had learned to repress the too impulsive word. She seemed at first to have hardly any kinship with her mother, whose portrait by Opie hung over the chimney-piece in the parlor, the gaze averted from the sometimes too painful scenes under the rule of the second Mrs. Godwin — the Bad Baby, as Lamb called her. Mary Wollstonecraft had been a handsomer woman than her daughter was ever to be. There had been more openness in her face; the full and generous mouth yearned after life in Reason's despite. Subtly the artist indicated that she had had it in its abundance and heartache.

Beneath her daughter's sedate exterior, life, too, made its claims. And life is stronger than reason, even Godwin's Reason. Her mother's impulsiveness, her love of personal independence, went hand in hand in the young girl with Godwin's reiterated precepts. She would walk with Reason, but her mother's unseen presence should be the guide. She pored over *A Vindication of the Rights of Woman*. Her mother had written it from her own hard experience. Mary Godwin would live to realize the dream of a free womanhood.

Many and various were the pilgrims who still sought out the shrine of the author of *Political Justice*. Friends, too, survivors of the ancient fight for freedom, came now and then for a meagre dinner, in spite of Mrs. Godwin's disapproving scrutiny behind her green spectacles. Mary used to sit respectfully before their learning, feeling a little pride, perhaps, at the homage her father received. Never before had anyone come who even remotely resembled Shelley. He was young, he was fervent, and though he bowed to divine Reason, he did not bend before Godwin, its votary on earth. It was all novel and exciting to the young girl whose imagination, had it needed such encouragement, had probably been inflamed by the reports of Fanny and Jane. Shelley was also beautiful — and he helped her father. Why should not her heart go out to so philanthropic a youth? He was a poet; she too had ambitions. Like her parents she would distinguish herself. For the present she made a cult of her dead mother, visiting almost daily her grave in Old St. Pancras's churchyard, and bowing reverently before the greatness of her father.

Shelley, chilled by the coldness of Harriet, could not live without the warmth of affection he required as much as the air he breathed. The Boinvilles had made the dreary weeks tolerable with their kindness and their Italian poetry. Cornelia had let in some beams of light on his darkened spirit. And now Mary burst upon his anguish like a sun of hope. She was womanly, though she looked like a child. She listened to the tale of his desolated hearth; she gave him comfort, such comfort as a serious girl could give, in tender looks and pitying sighs. She spoke to him of her mother, filling him with admiration of that liberated soul, that first champion for justice to her sex. She, Mary Godwin, had that woman's blood in her veins. The same fire animated her. Soon, by the side of the votary of Reason stood the monument of Mary Wollstonecraft in Shelley's worshipful mind. Between them Mary, the fruit of Reason and Emancipation, completed the perfect triune. Shelley became more than ever *helpful* to Godwin, and, having nothing of his own, proceeded to raise a large sum — nearly three thousand pounds — for him, on his own expectations.

Hogg met Shelley one day in Cheapside on his way to Skinner Street. The philosopher had gone out. Shelley and Hogg were waiting in the bookroom of the shop when softly a door was opened and a voice called "Shelley!" "Mary!" he answered, and, leaving his friend, darted out toward a small, pale girl dressed in tartan — probably a dress brought by Mary from Scotland. Shelley returned to Hogg in a minute or two, and they went away together.

"Who was that?" asked Hogg. "A daughter?"

"Yes."

"A daughter of William Godwin?"

"A daughter of Godwin and Mary."

The two names sealed his fate.

But Shelley did not submit without a struggle. According to the laws of society he was not a free man. That marriage, valid or no, performed in Edinburgh and contracted again but a short time since bound him to Harriet. Only legally. And for such legality Shelley had never had anything but contempt. No law in the world could normally shackle two individuals who no longer held anything in common. "A husband and wife," he had written in the notes to *Queen Mab* when he was not estranged from Harriet, "ought to continue so long united as they love each other: any law which should bind them to cohabitation for one moment after the decay of their affection would be a most intolerable tyranny, and the most unworthy of toleration."

Little had he known when he had dedicated to Harriet his "early wilding flowers" how soon they were to fade — how soon the arguments he set forth so generally were to have such personal application! Torn between remorse for Harriet and overwhelming desire for Mary, he seemed like one insane. Peacock, called by him to London that his cool judgment might help to make him, Shelley, see his way out of the murk, found him with eyes bloodshot and hair disheveled, "suffering like a little kingdom, the nature of an insurrection." He showed Peacock a bottle of laudanum, crying, "I never part from this." And then, to justify the passion that had seized him, powerful and irresistible for the first time in his life, he fell back upon poetry and philosophy. He had to have a partner who could share them with him. "Harriet is a noble animal, but she can do neither." Peacock reminded him that he had once been very fond of Harriet. "But you did not know how I hated her sister," he answered.

Peacock could make little of the violent contradictions of his friend. He felt sorry for Harriet and would have brought her and Shelley together. It could never be. The torrent had broken loose, carrying all with it, whether to a haven or to destruction only the gods knew, the gods of a calm and imperturbable Hellas. And Peacock might have queried: Who knows if they cared?

At Bath with her sister and Ianthe, Harriet was as yet ignorant of the progress of Shelley's love, intent as she was in teaching him gallantry by her indifference.

Thus far Shelley had kept his torment, at least the expression of it, from Mary. They would meet at her father's house and sometimes under the weeping willow of her mother's grave, where, in the undisturbed quiet of the churchyard, they read and talked together. Shelley had given her a copy of *Queen Mab* with, under the dedication to Harriet, the significant words: "Count Slobendorf [1] was about to marry a woman who, attracted solely by his fortune, proved her selfishness by deserting him in prison." A less mature girl than Mary would have understood the analogy. It required a woman of more experience to know it unjust. But Shelley had to convince himself, if only few others, that Harriet had sinned. Soon, together with the belief that she had married him for his money, he felt assured that she was unfaithful to him with a Major Ryan.

Torn by distracting emotions, further unbalanced by his use of laudanum, he yielded to these perverse imaginings. He had to see Harriet unlovely that he might condone his love for Mary, rendered a despairing agony because he could not speak it. But Mary found voice for him, as she admitted years later in thinly disguised biographical novels, as he declared in the verses addressed to her that June of 1814: —

> Mine eyes were dim with tears unshed;
> Yes, I was firm — thus wert not thou; —

[1] Shelley's version of the gentleman's name, Schlaberndorf.

Upon my heart thy accents sweet
Of peace and pity fell like dew
On flowers half dead; — thy lips did meet
Mine tremblingly.

Upon her, too, Harriet laid the guilt of the avowal, when, too late aware that Shelley was lost to her, she wrote to Miss Nugent in unadorned prose. "Mary was determined to secure him. She is to blame. She heated his imagination by talking of her mother, and going to her grave with him every day, till at last she told him she was dying in love for him. . . . He thought of me and my sufferings, and begged her to get the better of a passion as degrading to him as to herself. She then told him she would die —"

She then told him she would die. According to Harriet the illuminated Mary had used the arts she herself had employed to secure the romantic Shelley: the demonstration of her suffering and the threat of suicide. Perhaps Mary had sensed it was the only way of winning him from whatever loyalty he felt for his alienated wife. Harriet did not care for him; she, Mary, was ready to die for love of him. The declaration was a bold step. Mary Wollstonecraft, however, had she been alive, would have approved it. It was in keeping, too, with the young girl's character. "She is singularly bold," the dispassionate Godwin had written of her " . . . and her perseverance in everything she undertakes almost invincible." As yet he was ignorant to what extent that perseverance was exerting itself.

Every day through June Shelley went to dine at Skinner Street, a hospitality Mrs. Godwin did not begrudge, knowing what profits were to be gained thereby. Neither she nor Godwin suspected what it was that brought him there so regularly. Godwin attributed his assiduity to his own fascination. Harriet, at Bath, received desultory communications from her husband, so far without a hint of the struggles he was undergoing, and enjoyed the social life in that fashionable town. Mary lived in a romantic daze. The poet loved her. She was his. On the end leaves of *Queen Mab* she put down the overflowings of her heart, girlish, chaotic, and sentimental in spite of her rational upbringing, and straining after the literary: "July 1814.

This book is sacred to me, and as no other creature shall ever look into it I may write in it what I please — yet what shall I write — that I love the author beyond all the powers of expression, and that I am parted from him, dearest and only love — by that love we have promised to each other, although I may not be yours, I can never be another's. But I am thine, exclusively thine." Two stanzas from Byron were quoted to say what she could not express. "I have pledged myself to thee, and sacred is the gift," Mary's confession continued. "I remember your words — you are now Mary going to mix with many, and for a moment I shall depart, but in the solitude of your chamber I shall be with you. — yes you are ever with me sacred vision."

Ay, and with another as well. Jane Clairmont, soon definitely to be known as Clare, thought often of Percy Bysshe Shelley. She knew he was in love with Mary — but why should he not be her own liberator as well? She chafed under the discipline of her mother; she told him her troubles. She was dying, too, for freedom, for life. Something must be done for her, the caged songbird of Skinner Street. She had visions of a career on the stage, certain to be disapproved of by Godwin. She was destined to be a heroine and, whether in romance or in life, she was determined to be one.

Fanny knew nothing of what was happening. For some time she had been staying with her aunts, Everina Wollstonecraft and Mrs. Bishop, her mother's sisters, who kept a respectable girls' school in Ireland, both women as strait-laced — discounting early follies such as Mrs. Bishop's unfortunate marriage — as Mary Wollstonecraft had been free. They were considering whether or not to admit Fanny as an associate to their school; but first they must ascertain that the girl had not been infected with the virus of liberal ideas. She was serving her probation that eventful summer.

Shelley realized at length that the situation had to be brought to a head. He loved Mary and would not give her up, whatever the ties that bound him elsewhere. Harriet, suspecting by Shelley's silence of several days that something graver than she had thought was passing in London, wrote a distracted letter to Hookham for information. Shelley, on his part, had made an open breast of his relations with Mary to Godwin. Instead of receiving the sanction of Reason, as he had expected, he found his love branded as "licentious" and the door of the Skinner Street shop shut in his face. It was certainly unaccountable behavior in the high priest of the higher justice. Shelley had yet to learn that a philosopher may preach one thing abroad and practise another at home. However, since Godwin still accepted Shelley's help with the same openhandedness, if with stony demeanor, everything was not lost. Yet there were hours of spiritual darkness when it seemed better to make an end of it all.

Mrs. Godwin was alert for sensations. One day that hectic July, after Godwin had forbidden Shelley the house, the mad youth rushed into the shop looking wilder than ever, and went upstairs to Mary's room. Pushing aside Mrs. Godwin, he gave the trembling girl a bottle of laudanum. "By this you can escape from tyranny," he told her, "and this," he added, taking a pistol from his pocket, "this shall reunite me to you."

"Poor Mary turned as pale as a ghost," Mrs. Godwin elaborated pathetically as she recounted the incident. "With the tears streaming down her cheeks, she entreated him to calm himself and go home. . . ." Mary's voice, and the promise that she would remain forever his, seemed to quiet him, and he went away, leaving the laudanum behind.

Another scene succeeded after Shelley had an interview with Harriet on the fourteenth of July. With his customary sincerity he told her all. Mary was the true partner of his soul; he could not give her up. He described his struggles: "I loathed the very light of day, and looked upon my own being with deep and unutterable abhorrence." He spared his life only in the hope that, like the sympathetic friend he thought her, Harriet would understand and put no obstacles in the way of his union with Mary. He had never loved her, Harriet, he assured her. "Our connection was not one of passion and impulse." Friendship was its base. Had not Madame Boinville said so? Had she not foretold that the very contest they were undergoing would one day arrive? Surely Harriet did not love him, any more than he loved her. "Are you my lover whilst I am only your friend?" Harriet must understand. If she could only meet Mary. . . . "To the most indifferent eyes she would be interesting only from her sufferings, and the tyranny which is exercised upon her." Ah, the fatal word! Tyranny, with Mary the victim. Only three years since she herself had suffered from its oppression and Shelley had rescued her.

Then, as Harriet later told Miss Nugent, Shelley made a proposal. "Why should we not all live together? I as his sister, she as his wife?" Instead of the understanding he had deluded himself upon receiving, Shelley found himself turned into a faithless husband.

Her nerves shattered by his disclosures, Harriet was for days dangerously ill. Mary, played upon by Mrs. Godwin and her father, paid her a visit and promised to give up Shelley. He was beside himself. Without Mary life was not worth living, and he determined to die. He took laudanum. When the Godwins hurried to Hatton Garden they found the doctor walking Shelley up and down to sweat out the poison. He lived.

He lived, and he determined to act. Harriet would not listen to reason. Godwin, the very embodiment of it, behaved worse than a minister of Intolerance. Everything, everyone, conspired against him and Mary. He made a desperate shift for happiness.

By the light of the paling stars, on the twenty-eighth of July, 1814, as on another summer's dawn barely three years before, Shelley hired a post chaise for an elopement. This time two young girls accompanied him, Mary for love of him, Clare for love of adventure. At home Harriet, expecting a baby in a few months, comforted herself with the hope that, Shelley's passion spent, he would come back to her.

XI

THE FATAL YEAR

ON December 2, 1813, the *Bride of Abydos* was published. "It will for some reason *interest you* more than anybody," wrote Byron to Lady Melbourne. He was more explicit in his journal. "Whether it succeeds or not is no fault of the public. . . . But I am much more indebted to the tale than I can ever be to the most partial reader, as it wrung my thoughts from reality to imagination." The day of its publication he sent a copy to Leigh Hunt in the Surrey gaol.

Though the roses and Persian lilacs were withered in the prison garden, art, music, and poetry still flourished within. Every day, at his accustomed hour, Hunt, in his coat and kid gloves, as if dressed for a formal visit, took his exercise, back and forth, round and about the frozen ground of the yard, dreaming of his still unfinished tale of Rimini. In the tiny prison study, near the rose-bowered piano, he composed his *Feast of the Poets;* there, too, antithetically, his *Descent of Liberty.* All the poets of his day came figuratively to join his poetical banquet. Byron had some gracious tributes paid him. Wordsworth, working his slow, patient way, was dealt with unkindly; so, too, was Scott in this truthtelling session of the Horsemonger Lane satirist. The Edinburgh clans took note and saved their rancor, Wilson in defense of his friend Wordsworth, and Lockhart of his champion, Scott. Leigh Hunt was safer in gaol than he would henceforth be out of it.

He reminded Byron of the Pym and Hampden times. He had a fine independence of spirit and much talent. If he went on as he had begun, few men would deserve more praise. "I must go and see him again," thought Byron. He was a man worth knowing, though "a bigot of virtue." What would such a man think were he to read through the secret of the *Bride of Abydos?* What would anyone think? In the loneliness of his haunted rooms at night, in the salon of Lady Holland, before the garrulous de Staël, who had said of him that he was *"un démon,"* he could scarcely contain the burden of his crime. In his despite some allusion to an unmentionable sin would break through. Terrifying nightmares made even sleep a torture, so that he forced himself to wakefulness, smoking cigars and drinking bottles of soda water. In the passion of his anguish he sought relief in writing, covering sheets of paper with his disordered thoughts and burning them soon after. In January, while he was at Newstead, — with Augusta, — John Murray brought out the *Corsair.*

Byron had written it feverishly in ten days. Incapable of tearing himself away from Augusta or the scene of their sin, he escaped in imaginary adventures, seeking in them the relief whose denial would have meant madness. As Conrad the Corsair, — "that man of loneliness and mystery," — he wrenched himself from the thought and desire of Augusta, at least during the hours spent in writing. He engaged in perilous frays on land and sea, the leader of a band that trembled at the command of his eye. Like the Giaour, like Selim, he had his secret, a dark star that guided the bark of his life. Women loved him: the fierce Gulnare that murdered for his sake; Medora, his heart's beloved, who died for him. Their love was known only to themselves. Deep in her soul it flamed for him — in secret.

> There, in its centre, a sepulchral lamp
> Burns the slow flame, eternal — but unseen;
> Which not the darkness of despair can damp,
> Though vain its ray as it had never been.

Medora, Conrad: Augusta, himself. He could not forbear a hint at his own perverse love in that passionate, masculine tale. He must somehow keep from going mad.

So, when the poem was published, he told the story of his sinful passion not alone in hints but in forthright avowals. Not in his own words, however — that would have been too gross. He had Tasso and Dante, those two high priests of

the human heart, speak for him. Let him who knew the
language read the tale. *"I suoi pensieri in lui dormir non
ponno. . . . Nessun maggior dolore, che ricordarsi del tempo
felice nella miseria. . . . Conosceste i dubbiosi desiri? . . .
Come vedi — ancor non m'abbandona."* [1] The mottoes had
little reference to the cantos of the *Corsair,* yet how nearly
they touched the core of his own suffering! "His thoughts
cannot sleep within him. . . ." Sleeping and waking, he
could find no rest from the pricks of his conscience. Yet how
sweet had been the sin with Augusta, the embodiment of his
ideals in love: Mary Duff, the child; Margaret Parker, removed beyond his reach by death, a removal hardly more to
be bridged than that of the brother and sister relation; Mary
Chaworth, the perfection of womanhood. "There is no greater
sorrow than the remembrance of happy times in misery. . ."
as now, when he was recalling the brief, frenzied past of
Bennet Street in the present hell of his conscience. The
world, knowing, would condemn. "Have ye known those
dubious desires? . . ." Then only could you raise your
voices, or cast the stone of condemnation. You were not
born with the poison of the Byrons and Gordons in your veins.
Yours was not a father who begot children in the violence of
undisciplined passions and flung them, strangers to each other,
on the world. Your imagination, your young manhood, was not
stirred by illicit urges. He had met Augusta as if she had been
any strange woman in his life. She was beautiful, frail, like
the other women he had known, but, unlike all the rest, a
Byron. They clove to each other: the crime was society's.
They loved. Closer than those two lovers in Dante's hell
they clung, each to each. Like Francesca, Augusta could
well have said, "As thou seest, still he forsakes me not." Now
less than ever, when she was about to bear him a child.

In the middle of January, he and Augusta, with Colonel
Leigh's sanction, had started out for a few weeks at the abbey
in a coach "as large as the cabin of a '74." Augusta had never
seen Newstead. It was Byron's pretext to Leigh that he
would show it to her before it passed out of his hands. Young

---

[1] It is strange that no biographer or commentator should have read the
obvious meaning of these well-chosen verses.

Claughton, the would-be purchaser, was in vain trying to get together the money for the purchase, and a lawsuit was on, in the charge of Hanson. In the meantime Claughton remained in one wing of the abbey, while Byron and his sister occupied another, in a sensational domesticity.

Nothing was suffered to interrupt the three weeks of their life together. Mary Chaworth Musters, the Morning Star of Annesley, wrote to him after a silence of years. She was ill, unhappy, separated from her husband, who had treated her cruelly. Would he, Byron, come to see a *very old* and *sincere friend?* A trifling journey stood between him and her who had been the centre of his being but a few short years ago. Too bad . . . the snow shut him in. . . . The fire was warm. . . . A sick, pale, and gloomy woman could never be the Mary of his dreams. He did not go to her, though haunted by the thought of her, as by the memory of Margaret, and of Mary Duff, to whom, out of some inner region of desire, he had but recently written a poem, only to cast it into the flames. Ghosts, ghosts. . . . Better left alone. Besides, all that he had loved in them he held in Augusta. Who could have given him what she gave? "The kind of feeling which has lately absorbed me has a mixture of the terrible which renders all other, even passion (*pour les autres*), insipid to a degree," he avowed to Lady Melbourne, who in vain waved danger signals from Whitehall, reiterating, "A wife would be your salvation."

Ah, yes, a wife. Heigho! Byron yawned with the boredom of it all. "I must say that I never can quite get over the 'not' of last summer — no — though it were to become a 'yea' tomorrow," he wrote to her, hemmed in by the snows with Augusta in a desert island whose seclusion he could not but find pleasant for all its torment. Yet there was truth in what he wrote. He need never lie to Lady Melbourne. Miss Milbanke's rejection had wounded his pride, more vulnerable even than his heart. Again and again, in his journal, in his letters, a malignant *if* insinuated itself. If Annabella Milbanke had not refused him, perhaps he and Augusta would not have sinned. Lady Melbourne spared no words in her blame of Augusta. Byron reared at once to her defense. "Do not speak so harshly of her to me — the cause of it all. . . ." Still,

had he not been provoked to it? *If* Annabella had not said
no . . . In his journal he echoed, "A wife would be my salvation."

His birthday and Augusta's, four days later, they celebrated
together. He was twenty-six, entering upon that dangerous
year of which Mrs. Williams, the prophetess, had warned his
mother, long ago. "The twenty-seventh and the thirty-
seventh" — beware! Before the large fireplaces of Newstead,
with the chill world shut out and Augusta laughing her childish peals beside him, he had, for the moment, pleasanter
thoughts. How wonderful if he could but bar the door against
everyone — except Augusta — forever. Time honored him
with an added year, and yet, and yet — "Is there anything in
the future that can possibly console us for not being always
twenty-five?"

A few weeks before the joint visit to Newstead, Augusta
had sent Byron a lock of her hair, with her name on the paper
that wrapped it, and the message, *"Partager tous vos sentimens*
[sic] ne voir que par vos yeux n'agir que par vos conseils, ne
vivre que par vous, voila [sic] mes vœux, mes projets, et le seul
destin qui peut me rendre heureuse." She, too, could not trust
herself to say in English what could, with less embarrassment,
be written in French. "To share all your sentiments, to see
only through your eyes, to act only by your advice, to live
through you alone, such are my hopes, my projects and the
only destiny that can make me happy." Almost word for
word, hers were the feelings expressed by Zuleika to Selim.
More than ever Byron had run into reality, until he determined
to bring his publishing to an end. Accordingly, in the preface
to the *Corsair,* he assured the public he would not again
trespass upon its patience. Would he keep his promise?
Through the weeks at Newstead he held himself from pen
and ink, except for the writing of letters to Murray and Moore.
But then, Augusta was there to amuse him with her nonsense.
More important still, by enabling him to *live* the reality that
plagued his imaginings, she rendered that life not only bearable
but easeful.

From London came news of the *Corsair's* success. Murray
fairly burst into pæans of joy. Never before had a book of

poetry sold so well — thousands of copies in one day! Everyone read it to see what else its author had experienced, for as surely as Byron had been, and was still, the Childe, the wild Giaour, and Selim, he was also Conrad. The passion and energy of the verse struck home to the British heart, readily appreciative of the national qualities, even though the scenes were laid in foreign places. The static and pensive left the public cold except for the minority that ultimately builds enduring reputations. Wordsworth, and, even more, Coleridge, had one admiring reader to Byron's hundred. Young Shelley had so far disposed of a mere score of his *Queen Mab*. The name of William Blake was generally unknown.

There were yet other reasons for the *Corsair's* unprecedented sales, as Byron learned upon returning to London. Two years before, Perry, of the *Morning Chronicle*, had published anonymously Byron's eight lines "To a Lady Weeping." The just censure of the Regent had passed without comment. When, however, the lines reappeared in the *Corsair* volume as the acknowledged work of Byron, the peers and the press turned against him in abuse. The *Morning Post*, the *Sun*, the *Herald*, contained daily articles against the *lèse-majesté*. Byron, until then on a pinnacle, became the target of a thousand hands, hurling darts at what they could not reach. Murray, prudent man, would have omitted the offending lines — in fact, he did "shuffle" in a new edition; Byron had him immediately replace them. He would not be accused of cowardice. "My politics are to me like a young mistress to an old man, —" he boasted, concealing the smart, "the worse they grow, the fonder I become of them." His defiance did little to help him. Criticism that at first had been directed against the slight to royalty soon converted itself to personal abuse. Nothing was spared, neither his life nor his person. He was called an atheist, a rebel, a creature whose life was so black that it were better for morality not to penetrate its darkness. Augusta's name, first in whispers, then in shocked outcry, was joined with his as brother's and sister's had never been linked before, even under the Regency. Leila, Selim — again, and yet again. A nephew of Augusta's at Eton, where Byron was avidly read, was asked whether the lovers in the

Bride of Abydos were his aunt and Byron. The man was a fiend of hell, "deformed in mind as in body!"

Byron capped their insolence in bitter mirth. Ay, he was indeed "the devil — *boiteux,* I presume." To companion his misery he wrote to that other culprit, serving his sentence for a similar offense. To him also he repeated the pitiful jest of the limping devil. How keenly he felt the insult, that in itself revealed. No, he could not steel himself to criticism, try as he might. At the height of the storm John Hamilton Reynolds, a youth of eighteen, sent him an Oriental poem, *Safie,* published by Cawthorne and dedicated to Byron. "I wish *you* would take his production into dissection," Byron wrote to Hodgson, "and do it *gently.* . . . I know the misery, at his time of life, of untoward remarks upon his first appearance." Another youth, unknown to him, but destined to call forth his merciless abuse, was at the time reading him and adoring. "Byron! how sweetly sad thy melody," John Keats sighed in one of his trial sonnets. He, too, was moved by the myth of Byron, poet of romantic gloom.

> Still warble, dying swan! still tell the tale,
> The enchanting tale, the tale of pleasing woe.

Augusta was no consolation through the time of trial. She had her own troubles to bear. She was nearing her term, and Colonel Leigh was proving harder to mollify than she had expected.

And Annabella? She had written to Byron after weeks of indifferent silence on his part. She had been dangerously ill, but was now recovered. However, she would not be going to London for the season, and they would not meet. She had read the *Corsair.* Was not Conrad like Milton's Lucifer? Byron must read Locke, *On the Reasonableness of Christianity.* . . . He found time to answer her at great length in a sober, well-mannered letter in which he led her to understand that he would be pleased to renew the correspondence. "God bless you," the accused atheist closed his letter. Three days later he wrote again, informing her of the enormity the attacks on him had attained. The destruction of the customhouse by fire, while drawing general attention, had a little interfered with his undoing, he bantered, and Bonaparte's recent advantage had usurped the column generally devoted to abuse of himself. "My best respects to Lady Me. and Sir Ralph," he added in a dutiful postscript. Assuredly the rebel was amenable to the proprieties of life.

"I am told that I am *out of spirits*, —" he wrote Annabella within a few days, "which is attributed to the said paragraphs. He must however be a happy man who has nothing deeper to disturb him." How could he hint to this girl of his gnawing secret? "Pray how old are you?" he asked suddenly. "A few weeks ago I became six-and-twenty in summers — six hundred in heart."

"Had you humbly bowed before the Chastener, that fever of spirit would have been calmed," coolly responded the Princess of Parallelograms. "If the causes of those attacks of anguish ought to be secret, I will not seek to divine them." She was twenty-one last May, she informed him, adding that on the whole she believed herself formed for domestic ties, which, however, she could not seek "on the principle of Self-love and Expediency." Words, words, words. She could not unshackle herself from them.

A rumor had arisen — out of Byron's imagination? — that he had renewed his proposal to Annabella and had once more been rejected. She took the information he retailed in good part. Would he had really asked her again! There was something tantalizingly pleasant in this playing with fire. Byron was not the man to withdraw. "As for the *report* I mentioned," he returned to the charge, "*I* care not how often it is repeated. It would plague me much more to hear that I was *accepted* by anybody else than rejected by you." Was he sincere? He would have Annabella believe him so. He believed himself as he wrote, even though the truth of to-day were to become the denial of to-morrow. With pen and paper before him he turned, chameleon-like, to the emotional color demanded of him. The little mathematician expected him to be flattered by the rumor; he was flattered accordingly. She sent him reams of advice on the conduct of his soul. He discovered that he had one, guiltier than she supposed, and on paper he set about improving it. She ended her letters with

"God bless you," and he to whom Tom Moore sent the same benediction with apologies echoed the words which could not but look odd at the end of his letters. The chameleon could change color, but it did not always become him.

He had spoken truthfully to Gifford when he said that he was no bigot to infidelity, though he had early been "disgusted" with Calvinism.   Man was too insignificant an atom to aspire to immortality, therefore Byron placed small credence upon the life of the soul after death.   He did not, however, deny the existence of God.   That, at least, might comfort Annabella, although, if there were any truth in the "predestination" that had been impressed upon his infant mind, he had small reason to rejoice.   There was no salvation for him in this world, Lady Melbourne had said, whatever there might be in the next.   Better to deny the existence of that *next*.   "I want no paradise but rest," he cried with Conrad.

During Colonel Leigh's absence he paid repeated visits to Six Mile Bottom.   As the time of Augusta's labor drew near he felt an indefinable dread.   What would the child be like? Superstition had it that the fruit of incest was certain to be a monster.   Even Lady Melbourne hinted at "apes."   Augusta was as tender but as scatterbrained as ever.   Often, to dramatize their situation, as well as to give an outlet to his suffering, Byron tried to impress her with the gravity of their crime.   He would be seized with remorse; he grew morose and cruel.   Augusta could make nothing of his moods.   She had gone to him thinking no evil.   They had been alone together. He had desired her, and because she loved him she had yielded, not realizing her danger even when it was too late.   What had been the enormity in it?   *They made no one else unhappy.* Colonel Leigh?   He was going to father the child. . . .   Before such pagan innocence Byron bore a double burden.

The baby was born in April of 1814.   They called it Elizabeth Medora.   When he went to see it he wrote directly to Lady Melbourne.   "Oh! but it is 'worth while,' I can't tell you why, and it is not an 'ape.' . . .   But positively she and I will grow good and all that, and so we are *now*."   In spite of the fact that he could not avow his paternity openly, he had been making allusions in the salons to a woman who was

pregnant by him. *If a girl, it would be called Medora.*
That Colonel Leigh had to accept the child as his own added its
drop of gall to the already brimming cup. Byron's health
broke down.

Annabella, meanwhile, still sent her interminable letters
that fell like lumps of lead upon his restlessness. Sir Ralph,
her father, invited Byron to Seaham. Would he not accept?
"I *wish* to see you." The demure Saint Ursula was making
tremendous strides in the direction of her cousin Caroline.
Her insistence annoyed him. He was comfortable in his new
rooms at the Albany with his books and the companionship of
his old witch, Mrs. Mule, who sometimes made him laugh.
He had bought, too, a parrot and a macaw to cheer his
solitude. He had no desire to move unless it were out of
England, to the East, or perhaps to Italy. "To withdraw
myself from *myself*": it was neither woman nor travel that
accomplished it. And yet, perhaps he might accept that invitation to Seaham. He would consult his Whitehall guide.
Should he or should he not go? "I am not now in love
with her; but I can't at all foresee that I should not be so,
if it came 'a warm June' . . . and, seriously, I do admire
her as a very superior woman, a little encumbered with
virtue."

Really, he must come to a decision about marriage. Augusta
was strongly advising him, the more easily to break away
from her, for, Oh, dear! they could not go on like that forever.
People were saying such outrageous things. In his communications to Lady Melbourne he had been writing about so
many women and had undergone so many and such contrary
changes of heart that she was at a loss to understand him.
"If I pursued and succeeded in that quarter," he wrote, referring to Annabella, "of course I must give up all other pursuits. . . . My heart always alights on the nearest perch —
if it is withdrawn it goes God knows where." And yet he
answered not a word to Annabella's insistence. She wrote
again. No answer. She was becoming uneasy. "Please write
to me," she begged. He replied that he would go to Seaham
and subscribed himself hers "affectionately." He did not go
to Seaham, as Lady Milbanke was suddenly called away to

Kirkby Mallory. He went instead with Augusta to Hastings for a brief ten days.

The summer was nearly over and still no progress toward marriage had been made. Lady Caroline came again to the fore. They had seen each other at Watier's, at the masked ball celebrated on the first of July in honor of the Duke of Wellington and the peace between England and France. Byron had gone as a monk. Lady Caroline had worn a page's breeches under a domino. Byron, schooled in the Seaham homilies, was shocked, forgetting, at that moment, other and more strikingly costumed visitations in his rooms. "Not all I could say could prevent her from displaying her green pantaloon!" he exclaimed. His concern with her modesty encouraged Caroline, who began invading his privacy at the Albany. "The moment the door is open, in she walks," he cried in exasperation. "If there is one human being whom I do utterly *detest* and *abhor* it is she." Poor Caroline! She suffered infinitely by comparison with the slowly but surely rising star. "Do not marry yet," she had pleaded in the days of her own ascendency, "or if you do, let me know it first. I shall not suffer if she you choose be worthy of you, but she will never love you as I did." Did he confide in her, now that he was on the verge of choosing? Whether or no, he made no secret of that other and graver confidence. He showed her letters, he brought her proof, as if there had been such need. "Poor Caro, if every one hates me, you, I see, will never change." "Yes, I *am* changed," she answered, "and shall come near you no more." Not even the pressure of his lips on hers could mitigate the horror.

He was again driven to composition to prevent the earthquake he felt imminent. At the news of Napoleon's abdication he had written an ode, voicing his disappointment in his idol's fall. The Eagle, confined to his rocky eyrie in the middle of the sea, after his wings had cast their shadow over a world, was a sad spectacle. The little pagod over whose bust he had fought with the Harrow boys, Napoleon, in one fatal day had lost the crown of empire and become again the adventurer. Byron had no comfort in the writing; the shafts reached a nearer target. But he must write, write, in spite of his promises, if he would succeed in withdrawing himself from himself. In *Lara* he confronted Byron with his image as in a brilliantly polished mirror. He was writing pure auto-biography.

> Left by his sire, too young such loss to know,
> Lord of himself; — that heritage of woe —
> That fearful empire which the human breast
> But holds to rob the heart within of rest! —
> With none to check, and few to point in time
> The thousand paths that slope the way to crime;
> Then when he most required commandment, then
> Had Lara's daring boyhood govern'd men.

After mysterious wanderings he had returned to his "Gothic pile," bearing a secret — the recurring motif — that he revealed in his face alone.

> Chain'd to excess, the slave of each extreme,
> How woke he from the wildness of that dream?
> Alas! he told not — but he did awake
> To curse the wither'd heart that would not break.

People would read him for the story which they would find adventurous and stirring; he was only trying to find himself, the devil-whelp of an unhappy union, predestined to damnation. In this soul groping he strove to attain to some knowledge that would render life bearable. He reached it in one lucid line: "His madness was not of the head, but heart." Like the other, it was incurable.

By a publishing expedient *Lara* was brought out in the same volume with Rogers's faultless *Jacqueline,* a union no less ill-assorted than another that was shortly to follow. Ultimate separation was inevitable. The same season saw the publication of Wordsworth's *Excursion,* and, from prison, of Hunt's *Descent of Liberty.* *Lara* outsold them both.

It was a year of omens and portents. Joanna Southcott, at the age of sixty-four, declared herself with child by divine intervention and daily awaited the arrival of the prophet. Seals admitting one to salvation were sold at half a guinea a head, while Mrs. Southcott, ponderous with the spiritual burden, sat awaiting the day and the hour, amid a retinue of matrons who had all sworn to the undeniable fact of her pregnancy. Londoners, exalted from the aftermath of war, were all agog for the Shiloh's advent. Lace caps, embroidered bibs, silver cups, and a magnificent crib that cost with all its furnishings over two hundred pounds, arrived at the residence of the expectant mother. Paragraphs reported her minutest doings as if she were royalty. Nine months passed, ten, the while Mrs. Southcott increased in hope and faith. Her followers watched with hawks' eyes, lest the prophet come and they be unprepared. Another week, and another. At last the bulletins announced the pangs of labor. With prayers and groans Mrs. Southcott awaited her delivery as the midwives stood in a circle about her. Another hour, a day at the utmost, and Joanna would be delivered of the Shiloh. Not yet, not yet. William Sharp, her staunch supporter, who had got ready seals and engravings to usher in the arrival, waited uneasily. Two days, three, with everything in readiness, and yet no prophet came. A solemn bulletin announced at last that Joanna Southcott was dead. The world was still unripe for regeneration, and she "was only gone to heaven for a season," said Mr. Sharp, "to legitimate the embryo child."

Byron at Newstead showed more curiosity than any in the Southcott hysteria, begging Moore to keep him informed and writing him cynical commentaries. Anything, anything to cut through that Black Sea that had frozen over his passions. While in London he had again taken up boxing with Jackson, amusing himself at the same time with the man's liberties in the use of the aspirate as well as in domestic arrangements. Yet while sparring tempered his body, it did not benefit his mind, and it was his mind that needed help. Augusta still reigned first and foremost in it, a Persephone in a murky hell. Moore had asked him for some verses to set to music. Full of the thought and the torment of her, he composed five stanzas, each a dagger in his living heart, each bleeding with the wounds he must perforce conceal.

> I speak not, I trace not, I breathe not thy name,
> There is grief in the sound, there is guilt in the fame:
> But the tear which now burns on my cheek may impart
> The deep thoughts that dwell in that silence of heart.

Too brief for our passion, too long for our peace
Were those hours — can their joy or their bitterness cease?
We repent — we abjure — we will break from our chain —
We will part, — we will fly to — unite it again! . . .

And stern to the haughty, but humble to thee,
This soul, in its bitterest blackness, shall be;
And our days seem as swift, and our moments more sweet,
With thee by my side, than with worlds at our feet. . . .

Never had he shown himself more the poet than in this heart-wrung avowal. Moore was to write pretty music for it, and sing it to his admiring ladies. How could one find the adequate sounds for the cries of the damned?

"And stern to the haughty, but humble to thee . . ." By that time he had got out of patience with Annabella on her pillar of righteousness, and had made unflattering remarks about her to her aunt. "That eternal Liturgy," he called her. No, he was not in love with her; he had never been in love except for that *perverse passion* that coursed through his being in the blood of his life. It was Augusta he had loved — and he had destroyed her. The world was equally guilty with him in that destruction. Annabella, too. If she had not refused him they might have been married and Augusta — his love, his sister — would have been spared. Stern, ay, stern in its bitterest blackness would his soul be.

His suit to Lady Adelaide Forbes, that alpha and omega of beauty whom Moore had set up for him, received no encouragement. Byron dropped it even before it was begun. He had no energy for playing the sighing swain. It bored him, as did everything he did not feel. "Obstacles, the slightest even, *stop* me. . . . If a straw were in my way, I could not stoop to pick it up." Therein lay one of Augusta's strongest holds over him. She was the leaf to his tempest, driven as he willed. There was nothing he could ask which she had not already yielded. He dominated her, yet, by the inexplicable strength of weakness, she ruled him wholly. Her very womanly frailties forged his strongest chain. "I hate an esprit in petticoats." The poor muddled brain of Augusta had all it could do holding together the scattered strands of her household without laying claim to learning or wit. Hers was the innate Byron charm, the Byron cleverness whose sparks blinded one to grave defects of character.

Colonel Leigh bore his new paternity heavily, even after Byron had made Augusta a handsome gift of three thousand pounds at the birth of Medora. "You must marry, my dearest Byron." Her voice joined Lady Melbourne's. But whom? Augusta was much attached to Lady Charlotte Leveson, not a pretty girl in the strictest sense. "But there is an air of *soul* about her," Byron discovered after the Augustan persuasions, "— and her colour changes — and there is that shyness of the antelope." Shyness, that was it. The antelope linked her to those soft, large-eyed women of the East, subdued yet passionate, whom he had loved. Annabella Milbanke had always been cold and reserved. Augusta was intimidated before her many perfections. Yes, he would woo Lady Charlotte. But for a long time he did nothing, though there seemed to be no straw in the way. Augusta undertook to do the wooing for him. He let her, after he had sent a tentative declaration to Seaham, only to be told that Annabella feared he might not be the right partner, after all, to accompany her on earth "with a view to Immortality." The capital letter was hers, a column too arduous to scale in his present state of indifference. Very well, then.

Augusta wrote a proposal of marriage for her brother to Lady Charlotte and both waited for an answer, Augusta anxiously, Byron deep in his chill Black Sea. A month had elapsed since his overtures to Annabella, who, in the meantime, had sent him propitiatory letters. He would try again, this time without wasting words. Augusta still demurred. Her dearest Byron must remember that Miss Milbanke had as yet no fortune of her own, and in the present tangle of his affairs he must have money. Besides, Miss Milbanke was a learned lady, and he ought to know she would never suit him.

Even while they were discussing the matter a letter arrived from Lady Charlotte's parents courteously rejecting the proposal. "You see that after all Miss Milbanke is to be the person," said Catherine Byron's son, seizing the omen. "I will write to her." What matter if the Black Monk had been seen of late, prowling about the abbey in cowl and beads, walking with grave and noiseless tread, to warn by his ghostly presence that danger threatened the Lord of Newstead? One omen nullifies another. Byron wrote while Augusta still made her objections. The letter finished, he gave it to her to read. "Well, really, this is a very pretty letter. It is a pity it should not go." "Then it shall go," decided Byron. The letter was sent.

"It is not without a struggle that I address you once more on this subject," read Annabella after the preliminary paragraph. "If I offend, it is better at a distance. With the rest of my sentiments you are already acquainted. If I do not repeat them it is to avoid — or at least not increase — your displeasure." Nothing farther from the pretty or the loverlike could have been conceived. The offer was made with sufficient directness, however, and Annabella, who had long been awaiting it in its proper form, answered at once.

Released at last of her reserve before this man whom she had loved from the time she had set eyes on him, she spoke out from her soul. She had pledged to make his happiness the first object of her life, she wrote him. "I will *trust* to you for all I should look up to — all I can love. . . . This is a moment of joy which I have too much despaired of ever experiencing — I *dared* not believe it possible." It was the fourteenth of September, 1814, a memorable day for her and Byron. Later she informed her girlhood friend that she had at last fixed with mature judgment "on the person most calculated to support [her] in the journey to Immortality." Calvary would have been the right word.

At Newstead, Byron, Augusta, and the apothecary who was there to observe his lordship's nerves were seated at dinner when the gardener came in with a ring he had found while digging under the window of Mrs. Byron's room. Byron recognized it as the wedding ring his mother had lost many years ago. While he was still holding it, the letter carrier arrived with Annabella's reply. "If it contains a consent," cried Byron, "I will be married with this very ring." He tore open the letter and read it silently. The *not* had become a *yea*, and in her anxiety that he should know it at once Annabella had sent still another letter to his rooms at the Albany. "It never rains but it pours," he remarked cynically, giving the letter to Augusta, who perused the outpouring of the girl who was to be her brother's wife. "It is the best and prettiest I ever read!" she said.

Nothing but those words. Did she feel any pang that now she and her dearest Byron had to be *good*, and that in their future intercourse a third party, one with a lawful right, had to be admitted? Augusta showed no jealousy then or ever, conscious in her own vague way that her place could never be usurped by wife or mistress.

Of course Seaham had to be visited, that he might see Annabella, after nearly a year, and meet his future parents-in-law. Letters had to be written announcing the engagement, and the Claughton-Newstead affair brought to a head. In the meantime he put on the lover, feeling the part genuinely the while, as he wrote to Annabella two, and sometimes three, letters a day. She and Augusta must be friends. He told her of "that least selfish and gentlest creature in being — and more attached to me than any one in existence can be. . . . She is now nursing" . . . his own child Medora. Augusta too wrote to Annabella, letters full of her dearest Byron, and of the old abbey and of how much she loved it. Byron's love-making, however, through the speeding weeks, remained epistolary. There were matters of business he had to clear with Hanson, other affairs to settle. Annabella at Seaham tried not to show her heartache.

His fiancée's patent virtues, strangely, formed Byron's chief boast in his communications. He relished the triumph of having won a chaste virgin to be his "mother of the Gracchi," the naming of one of whom he already offered his friend Moore. Yet through his boasts uneasiness sounded a warning note. This jewel invested with golden opinions, who had no fault except that of being a great deal too good for him, weighed upon his spirit, making him feel too strongly by contrast his own unworthiness. However, for one great crime she had been partly to blame. "The truth is," he wrote to Annabella herself, "that could I have foreseen that your life was to be linked to mine . . . I would have been a different and a better being. As it is I have sometimes doubts . . . whether the past ought not to make you still regret me — even that portion of it with which you are not acquainted."

When finally he left for Seaham he stopped on the way to stay with Augusta at Six Mile Bottom. The visit left him spent and desponding. For one mad moment he was tempted to give up the Seaham visit and Annabella, and with difficulty overcame the lassitude that oppressed him. "I am proceeding very slowly," he informed Lady Melbourne — as slowly and unwillingly as a prisoner to the block.

He and Annabella met again at last. She went to him with the eagerness of her pent-up longing; he remained immobile. During his stay he was so moody and unaccountable that An- nabella had to admit with a pang that he did not love her. He could not have behaved so if he had loved. Had he been dis- appointed in her, the dowdy little body in her prim high dress and her country-girl face? There were long sessions of un- endurable silence. "Annabella is the most silent woman I ever encountered," he complained to Lady Melbourne. With Augusta it was always chatter, chatter, chatter, and gay peals of laughter that drowned all unpleasantness. "I fear she won't govern me; and if she don't, it won't do at all." Lady Melbourne at Whitehall held her breath. Would this marriage ever come to be? She was beginning to lose faith in it.

When Byron left Seaham to arrange for the wedding and to get himself a blue suit, — they had made him understand it would never do to be married in a black one, — he carried away very troubling impressions of Annabella. For some hidden reason she would be ill every two or three days, he knew not why, as she looked the picture of health. She would brood and make scenes very much like her cousin Caroline, compensating for her former taciturnity in long disquisitions on fine feeling or the lack of it, until Byron felt his senses reeling. A word carelessly uttered by him, an inflection of voice, would call for mathematical analysis. "Sometimes we are too much alike, and then again too unlike."

He went back to London with a heavy and resentful heart. For this he would be giving up his freedom, the gay nights at the Cocoa Tree with the claret and champagne and the boon companions who, at any rate, had the merit of making one merry. For this he would have to sacrifice Augusta. It was all the fault of his "bitch of a star."

Hurt feelings and disappointments, however poignant, may be soothed by distance and the virtues of ink. Letters on both sides did their work valiantly. Byron wrote his delightful chitchat; Annabella essayed to respond in kind. *Mam* was confecting a perfect mountain of a wedding cake, and good old Sir Ralph, that kindly "red-faced spirit," was overworking his Muse, composing, if you please, an epithalamium for his daughter and her bard. "Dearest — you and happiness will come together," came her veiled reproach from Seaham at his protracted absence. Again the delay on his part, again the prisoner-to-the-block pace of the previous journey, with its inevitable stop at the place of consolation for a last — surely the last — farewell to Augusta before the end. He spent Christmas with her. Her letters came to him like echoes of herself. "La Dame did talk so — oh my stars! but at least it saved me a world of trouble — oh! but she found out a likeness in your picture to Mignonne. . . ." Medora, who was not an ape. "I want to know dearest BX your plans — when you come X when you go — umph! when the writings travel — when ye Cake is to be cut — when the Bells are to ring."

He and Annabella were married on the second of January, 1815, with Hobhouse, returned from his tour of Napoleon's battlefields, acting as best man. Byron, very pale in his wedding suit, kneeled on a mat in the drawing-room; Annabella, in a white embroidered muslin gown, kneeled beside him. She wore no bridal veil. While the service was being read by the Reverend Thomas Noël — an illegitimate son of Lord Wentworth's — she held her eyes steadily on Byron, while he looked blankly before him and thought, — O tyranny of the mind! — and thought not of her, but of Mary Chaworth, whose unhappy life was now clouded with insanity.

"Miss Milbanke, are you ready?" he asked after she had changed her wedding gown for a traveling dress and pelisse. Her companion murmured of bad omens as Annabella entered the carriage that was to take her and Byron to Halnaby for

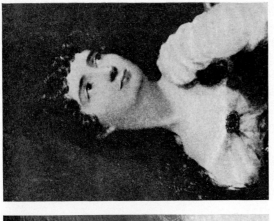

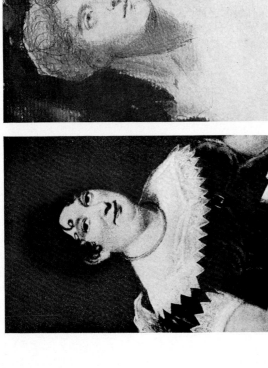

Mrs. Byron

Augusta Leigh

Annabella Milbanke

A PORTRAIT BY THOMAS
STEWARDSON [1]

FROM A DRAWING BY SIR GEORGE
HAYTER

FROM A MINIATURE BY SIR
GEORGE HAYTER

([1] *Reproduced, by special permission, from André Maurois's "Byron," D. Appleton-Century Co.*)

the honeymoon. Byron went in after her. Hobhouse offered his congratulations. "I wish you every happiness."

"If I am not happy, it will be my own fault," Annabella answered bravely.

Byron held his friend's hand, loth to part with him. He was still clasping it fast through the carriage window when they drove off. There was a long silence as the carriage left Seaham behind and came upon the road. Neither the one nor the other could find the words to dispel it.

Suddenly, in the still morning, Byron broke out into a strange, wild, defiant singing.

XII

AN ELOPEMENT IN BLACK SATIN

AT the corner of Hatton Garden, where Mary and Clare met Shelley with the post chaise, the two lovers flew into each other's arms. There was no time to lose, even for endearments. At any moment Mrs. Godwin might enter the girls' room and find them flown, and then— A few last-minute arrangements remained still to be made, however, and Mary left her lover for a brief space during which it seemed to him they were trifling with life and hope. In a few minutes she was safe beside him, on the road to Dover.

The excitement was too much for the high-strung girl. It had been a struggle for her to leave her father, who loved her dearly, she knew, in his self-centred fashion. Although he had made no definite plans for her future, a good marriage entered into them. Women should marry, even the most intellectual of them. In spite of the fact that William Godwin had denounced the institution and looked forward to the day when it should be abolished, he had twice submitted to it himself. Until that perfect time when men and women would be equals in all things, it was best for the marriage law to be respected. Now she, Mary, was eloping with a married man. Even if she were willing to descend to her father's practical expediency, she could not marry Shelley. Lawfully he belonged to Harriet.

Clare liked to believe that she had not run away from home with the lovers, but that they had, in a pleasant way, kidnaped her. She knew French. They did not. In order to have her as interpreter in a foreign country, Mary, she pretended, had persuaded her to join her in a morning walk — when, behold, there was Shelley with a chaise all ready for a romantic flight. What could she do under the circumstances? She could not let Mary go alone, though that was the time-honored procedure in elopements. She joined them, to be obliging. There were more holes than threads in the tissue of her defense, still, it served to cover her scruples. If questions should be asked, as they surely would be, she had her answers ready.

Between four and five of a late July morning was an unconventional hour for young girls to go out walking. Black satin gowns, their best, did too much honor to the occasion. How opportune that Shelley should have been at Hatton Garden, waiting with the vehicle that brought freedom and adventure! Something near obliquity marked Clare, even as a young girl.

As the sun rose higher that hot day, and the roads grew sultry with the heat, Mary felt so faint that they had to stop at every stage for her to rest. Clare bore her kidnaping with great equanimity. Shelley was too anxious about Mary's health and too nervous about pursuers at every stop to give much thought to the enormity of the adventure. He, Harriet's husband, was running away with Godwin's daughter — indeed, with his two daughters, for in the face of the law he was responsible for Clare as well as for Mary. The girls were both minors, Mary at the time within a month of her seventeenth birthday, and Clare three months past sixteen. If Godwin should come to claim them, he would have to give them up. Once again he, Shelley, might have to resort to the laudanum bottle. If Mary and he could not be united in life, there was death. As they went from Dartford to Dover, taking four horses to make up for lost time, and the evening fell, inspiring them with a sense of security that daylight had not given them, the two lovers felt more closely united. At Dover, however, they learned they could not take the packet until the following day. There was not a moment to lose while they were on British soil. Hiring a small boat, they engaged some sailors to take them to Calais. The crossing could be made in two hours, the seamen assured them. As a bright moon had risen and a gentle breeze flapped the sails, the three young fugitives set out to sea. Mary, exhausted from the journey, was prostrated by the boat's rocking and lay, hardly moving, in Shelley's arms. The moon that had risen so auspiciously sank, hours later, in a ruddy sky. They were still far from the Continent.

The breeze increased to a storm wind and the frail boat with
its occupants found itself at the mercy of the waves. The
sailors watched with set faces the surge rushing into the frail
skiff. Shelley knew they were in danger. In the roar of the
storm, their faces lighted by gleams of lightning, the lovers
neither spoke nor looked at each other; but they felt their
nearness with a strange happiness. "I had time in that
moment to reflect and even to reason upon death," Shelley
wrote later of that night. He felt no horror of dying, only a
vague regret that "in death we might not know and feel our
union as now."

Toward morning, while the lightning flashed palely in the
sky, the boat struck shore. Mary was asleep. Shelley called
to her. "Look, the sun rises over France." And both watched
the dawn of their first day together.

At the inn in Calais they took a room and waited for the
Dover packet to bring their boxes. Toward evening, the boat,
delayed by the storm, arrived, bearing not only their boxes but
a "fat lady" who declared to all and sundry that a man had
run away with her daughter. Shelley and Mary had no difficulty in applying the description to Mrs. Godwin, whose
excursion, in their pursuit, had been duly noted down by her
methodical husband in his daybook. "M. J. for Dover."
Why or wherefore, he would not incriminate himself to write.
Yet in those notebooks, written in his precise hand in a laconic
jumble of language all his own, were recorded, as on funeral
tablets, the joys and sorrows of his life. They meant little to
the reader, these jottings of the days that had passed. But
here vague words told that he had known love; there, that the
cruelest heartbreak in his life had come to him; here again
that he had himself risen as from the dead to go on with an
existence that must perforce have meaning. Those initials,
these meticulous figures, designated creditors and debts. All
had their commemorative inches. On the twenty-eighth of
July at five o'clock in the morning, it was simply *M. J. for
Dover*. Yet to him it meant that his daughter by the only
being he had ever dearly loved had left his home to be the
mistress of a man she could not marry. That man had helped
him, Godwin, out of admiration for his work. He had, only

three weeks since, arranged to obtain a large loan for him. But he had run off with his daughter, and the Clairmont girl. Godwin would not go in pursuit of them — it was unbecoming a philosopher. So M. J. had left for Dover to take the unpleasant matter off his hands. He had his books to write. Under no circumstances must his work be interrupted, though the old leathern heart bled, as if it were of flesh.

Mary would not have been loth to see Clare Clairmont follow her mother back to the packet and leave her — without a French interpreter — alone with her lover in France. It was not to be. M. J.'s arguments fell on deaf ears. In her black satin dress, and with the feel of a foreign land under her little boot, Jane felt more of a Clare than ever. Skinner Street with its dusty shop and the too few rooms for their many occupants seemed unattractive enough to a young heroine who had experienced her first elopement, vicarious though it was. Dutifully, out of consideration for the many acts of favoritism Mrs. Godwin had shown her in the past, Clare spent the night with her. The following day she bade her good-bye. Vexed and weary, Mrs. Godwin returned home, full of resentment for the man who had made havoc of her household. How could she hold up her head before her neighbors?

Hardly a week had passed when William Godwin, Junior, only eleven at the time, began lusting for freedom and decamped from Skinner Street. The poor philosopher felt the universe tumbling about his ears with this new calamity. All day and all night, with growing anxiety, he searched everywhere for the lad. Had he run away? Had he met with some accident? In the midst of his wretchedness he received word that Patrickson, a youth he had befriended and helped send to college, had committed suicide. He was like a man accursed. Everything, everyone connected with him seemed doomed. After two weary days, the truant was found out and brought home. But having tasted of liberty he yearned after it the more. From now on he began a series of escapades.

Fanny Imlay, still absent from home, was informed of the various visitations by Charles Clairmont, the only one who had the heart to retail them. Mrs. Godwin was sure Fanny would "never get over" the elopement. Somehow, she had

settled in her mind that the unhappy girl had fallen in love
with Shelley and was wearing out her heart for love of him.
Those who knew Mrs. Godwin better found a reason nearer
home for Fanny's melancholy. Except for the tie of blood
between her and Mary, she was unrelated to the other members
of the family. Godwin had always been fond of her for her
mother's sake, but he was too far removed from mundane affairs
to cast more than a passing glance in the girl's direction. With
Mary gone, Fanny would now be wholly among strangers, a
useless burden upon their charity. What would Aunt Everina
and Mrs. Bishop say to Mary's elopement? They had been
among the first to be shocked and indignant at their sister's
writings, and the earliest to cast a stone when the unfortunate
woman had found herself abandoned by Gilbert Imlay. After
her death, as if to atone for her independent life, they had taken
shelter in the strictest conventions and watched with dubious
eyes over the two daughters she had left in Godwin's trust.
They had shown some kindness to Fanny because she was plain
and knew her place. What would they do now that Mary had
followed in her mother's footsteps? Would they refuse to
have anything to do with Fanny, too? "I dread lest she should
be forced to sacrifice her heart to her principles. . . ." Poor
Fanny had no such principles as her mother thought of to
sacrifice. She was tired — tired of being unwanted, tired of
living, almost. If only her aunts would give her a place in
their school she might supply her own wants instead of being
reminded by Mrs. Godwin that she was only another mouth to
feed.

On the Continent the fugitives continued their honeymoon
trip à trois. From Calais they went to Boulogne, thence to
Paris in a cabriolet drawn by three horses running abreast.
At the Hôtel de Vienne the lovers unpacked Mary's box and
together looked over the papers she had brought — her own
writings, letters from her father, Shelley's treasured notes.
There were her mother's books, and Byron's poems to be read,
some night other than their first in Paris. That August evening they spent walking in the Tuileries, a young Adam and
Eve cast out from their homeland, but happier than they had
ever been, even if the new-found gardens were formal and with-

out grass.   Back at the hotel, they were "too happy to sleep."
Like Harriet, Mary liked to read aloud.   The following
evening she read to Shelley out of Lord Byron, who, all unwitting, had been a Galeotto to their love.   "I was not before
so clearly aware," said Shelley, "how much of the colouring
our own feelings throw upon the liveliest delineations of other
minds."   Innocently he was admitting that life had thrown a
light upon the prism of his emotions, and for the first time his
whole being was aglow with color.   In the fullness of his happiness he saw realized in Mary all that he had been seeking —
vainly in Harriet, imperfectly in Cornelia Turner and her
mother.   Ecstatic and gratified, he set up Mary above all
womankind — overlooking, or idealizing, the little sharpnesses
that even so early began to find their way in their joint diary,
as he declared himself hers to shape.   Clare, not to remain too
much in the shade of the romantic relation, sought to make herself interesting in Shelley's eyes.   She fell unaccountably into
moods varying from hilarity to depression; Shelley alone could
get her out of them.   She was physically much stronger than
Mary, however, so that in all excursions that required walking
and exercise she joined Shelley, while Mary remained at home.

In Paris the little money which Shelley had had in reserve
was soon exhausted, and he found himself obliged to sell his
watch and chain.   Eight napoleons would not go far, but
Tavernier, the French agent, promised money from England.
In the meantime they visited the Louvre and Notre-Dame,
finding, in the self-confidence of their youth, nothing remarkable except a picture of the Deluge.   "Terribly impressive,"
Shelley called it, harking back to the Gothic horror chills of
his boyhood.   Days passed and no remittances came from
London.   The walks through the streets and gardens of Paris
began to pall.   They felt what they were, virtually prisoners
for lack of the funds to take them to the Swiss mountains,
whose air they gasped for in the sweltering French capital.   At
last sixty pounds arrived from England, whence heretofore had
come only "cold and stupid letters" from Hookham, who had
befriended Harriet; Peacock too looked after her affairs.   He
had not liked Mary and felt that Shelley had not made a change
for the better.

Early next morning Shelley and the inevitable Clare set off for the animal fair to buy Mary an ass. He and Clare, both good walkers, would go to Uri on foot. They came back to the hotel leading a wretched little beast that through either native stubbornness or laziness seemed to find it an effort to place one hoof before the other. A *fiacre* was engaged to take the trio — Shelley in his loose coat and the ladies in their black satin — as far as the barrier, the ass trotting behind. When the time came for Mary to mount him, they discovered to their consternation that the creature found it burden enough to carry his own carcass. And so, all the way to Charenton that evening, the three carried the ass instead of being carried.

Scenes of havoc and desolation met them on their journey. Napoleon, exiled at Elba, had left a distraught and demoralized army that terrorized the hamlets and stopped at nothing in its recklessness. Whole villages were left in ruins by the disbanded soldiery, the homeless inhabitants forced to forage for food like beasts. Violence and murder threatened in the unprotected roads. "The ladies would surely be stolen," the hostess at the hotel had warned the young wayfarers. However, they reached Troyes without mishap. At Charenton the burdensome donkey had been exchanged for a serviceable mule which carried the two girls in turn, and, toward the end, Shelley, footsore and with a sprained ankle.

Yet despite the discomforts of the journey and the wretched accommodation they were forced to put up with in garrets, where the rats, Clare swore, put their cold paws on her face at night, they were happy and would have been light-hearted had not thoughts of England damped their spirits. Sometimes a shadow of sadness flitted across Mary's face when she thought of her father. He was cold and undemonstrative, but she knew he loved her more than anyone else in that cheerless household, more than anyone in the world. And there was Harriet. Mary did not like her. With strange illogicality she thought her selfish. From the lovers' point of view an enlightened Harriet should have surrendered her husband with noble generosity to her successful rival, — nay, not rival, that was not the word, — to the wife of his soul, while she herself would have felt honored to remain the sister and friend. Harriet had not received the proposal with grace.   She had, indeed, been vulgarly shocked.

Shelley made another overture from Troyes, addressing his wife, "My dearest Harriet," and urging her to come to Switzerland, where she would find "one firm and constant friend, to whom your interests will be always dear."   She need not live with him and Mary; if she would come he would welcome her "to some sweet retreat . . . among the mountains."   In other words, he would take care of her and cherish her as a friend. "But what shall be done about the books?" he asked suddenly, thinking that another library was perhaps to suffer the fate of the one he had left in Ireland with Eliza.

Harriet made no move toward the sweet mountain retreat. The rôle of platonic friend to her husband did not suit her at all.   Hopefully she listened to Eliza and to other equally perspicacious counselors who told her to possess her soul in patience, for Shelley would return, a docile and repentant husband.   In the meantime, since Shelley had told her she might help herself to funds at the bankers', she drew upon them generously.

The Swiss tour, far from lasting *for ever*, was abruptly cut short by homesickness and bad weather.   At Brunnen, it is true, inspired by the landscape, they engaged two rooms at a guinea a month in a château as large as a cathedral, with the intention of staying there at least half a year.   A few pieces of furniture were with difficulty obtained and moved into the apartment; a fire was lighted in the stove.   They received the neighborly visit of the Abbé and the town doctor, anxious to make the tourists feel at home.

That they might find their holiday useful as well as enjoyable, the three now solid citizens began writing romances. Shelley's "The Assassins" achieved a few pages, dictated to Mary while the rain poured down on vale and mountain.   In the new story once again the Wandering Jew made his appearance; again he had to withdraw to the limbo of the unpublished.   Mary's "Hate" — they gloried in startling titles — made a beginning and ended there.   As for Clare's "Idiot," though she set herself the task of showing that her titular hero was as clever as any other man, and was called a bad name only because the vulgar did not understand him, he left nothing but that name to immortalize him through the ages.

With only a few pounds to take them to England, and with the experience of the walking and donkey-carrying tour to discourage their returning the way they had come, the weary wanderers made the voyage by water. Down rushing rivers, past green islands and castled banks, they arrived at Bâle, Shelley in the meantime having chivalrously defended his ladies against the jostling of a group of noisy men by knocking one of the bullies down. The rest of the journey was made in peace, if not in comfort. Quietly they celebrated Mary's seventeenth birthday. "We expect to be not happier but more at our ease before the year passes," they recorded optimistically. In the meantime Shelley delighted in the landscape, eager and bright-eyed. He was on a boat, under the open sky, with a realm of enchantment on every hand. Along the Rhine mediæval towers alternated with vine-covered hills; the water, now calm, now swift, changed with the colors of the sky and the day, sunrise and sunset each making it a new wonder to admire and re-member. The scenes etched themselves in Shelley's mind. Some day he would recall them in the magic glass of imagina-tion.

Far different was the journey up the Thames — and home. No dear friend came to meet them; no friendly voices hailed them. They had arrived without a farthing and had to argue long with the captain before he trusted them for the passage to Blackwell. They took a coach and called on Hookham, whose letters had been unduly cold. He was not at home. Money must be obtained at any cost. They called at the bank. All the funds had been drawn. Shelley found himself obliged to leave Mary and Clare in the coach while he went to see Harriet. An hour passed, and Shelley had not returned. Impatient, hungry, tired, and uncomfortable, the girls waited, wondering what Harriet could have found to say that kept Shelley there so long. At last, after two hours, he returned, with twenty pounds and his head full of Harriet's reproaches. He must see her again next day.

He went there, accordingly, to arrive at some understanding about their relations, now that the Channel no longer divided them. He pleaded with her again to be his friend and Mary's. Harriet would hear nothing of it. While he was abroad, the hope had thrived that he would miss her and yearn to be with her. When he returned, however, not only unanxious to assume his marital responsibility, but more than ever attached to Mary, Harriet for the first time saw her position in its true light. Naturally her resentment rose against Mary. It is possible that she did not curb her tongue in speaking of the Maie, as Shelley now called her. In her journal for that day Mary recorded that Shelley had seen Harriet, "who," she commented, somewhat out of patience, "is a very odd creature." From Mary's point of view it made Harriet *odd* for wishing to thrust herself upon a husband who no longer loved her. From the point of view of the world it would have been *odd* had Harriet not endeavored to win him back, and Harriet, with all her brave imitations of freedom, had never lost her respect for public opinion.

Although this second time she and her husband remained once more long in conference, all was not said between them, for immediately afterwards Shelley sat down to write her a letter in which he attempted to clarify points that had remained obscure. He wished to remain her affectionate friend — the price of that friendship was confidence and truth. (Eliza still pulled the strings of her sister's actions.) "You think that I have injured you," he wrote. "Since I first beheld you almost, my chief study has been to overwhelm you with benefits. Even now when a violent and lasting passion for another leads me to prefer her society to yours, I am perpetually employed in devising how I can be permanently and truly useful to you. . . . It would be generous, nay even just to consider with kindness that woman whom my judgment and my heart have selected as the noblest and the most excellent of human beings. . . . Are you above the world, and to what extent?"

Poor Harriet was so little above the world upon reading this amazing epistle, in which she was told with great explicitness that her husband preferred a far superior woman to herself, that she left his query unanswered. But Shelley would not let her off so easily. He demanded truth and frankness from his former proselyte. "I am deeply solicitous to know the

real state of your feelings toward myself and Mary," he
stressed, though had he known, he would not have been pleased.

More than once Harriet had intimated how she felt about
Mary. She was the woman who through unforgivable arts, as
she thought, had seduced her husband. She could have nothing
but recrimination for Godwin's daughter. This, in her despair,
she now voiced loud and long to all who would lend an ear.
Not content with accusing Mary, she implicated Godwin in a
plot to secure the heir to the Shelley fortune. He had connived
in the abominable intrigue. Indeed, he had sold his daughter
Mary to Shelley before the elopement for eight hundred pounds,
and Clare Clairmont for seven hundred.

Rendered cunning by her bitterness, Harriet spread the
rumor to gain sympathy and charged Godwin with it, to hear
whether he would deny it. She, of course, did not believe a
word of it, but — The philosopher was stung out of his usual
calm. How was the fair sun of speculation clouded by the
exhalations of sordid reality! Sunk deep in poverty and distress, with M. J. adding her comments to the scandalous business, with his ideals turned against him, and his daughter, in
the view of the world, nothing better than an adventuress,
Godwin had need of his utmost impassibility to face each
wretched day. Fanny, returned from her aunts, tried to cheer
him with gentle attentions. She had her own secret burden
of grief.

If Harriet had chosen this means to recall Shelley, she could
have done nothing to alienate him more completely. Everything said against Mary only made her the dearer for the onus
she bore for his, Shelley's, sake. Dreadful weeks, weeks of
hardship and unfriendliness, followed their arrival. Hookham,
Hogg, and Peacock came to see them, but they were no longer
the same. Though, unlike the rest of the world, they did not
think him and Mary criminals to be ostracized, they were
nevertheless reserved and cool. Peacock was annoying in his
insistence that justice be done to Harriet, as if Shelley were
not anxious to do that and more. Had he not asked her to
sign the terms of a settlement and present them to their lawyer?
She would do nothing of the sort, deluded as she was by her
counselors that the longer she delayed, the better the prospects

of her ultimate gain. He had been mistaken in her. The liberal principles she had echoed had served only for display. In her heart she remained the slave to the vilest superstitions. She was lost.

Out of patience at last with her behavior, he wrote her his mind. "You are plainly lost to me," he repeated, "lost to me forever," the words making a strange echo of the selfsame sentiments expressed of another Harriet. *She* had been lost to him for having bowed to the wishes of society and forsaken him for another; Harriet Shelley was "plainly lost" because, in obedience to the dictates of convention, she would *not* give him up. Irony was holding festival. Harriet made another desperate attempt to take him from Mary. Through Mr. Westbrook and Eliza, Shelley was threatened with having the case brought to court. For the moment nothing came of it but a more painful estrangement between him and Harriet.

Ever since he had set foot in London, Shelley had been hounded by his creditors. Charters, the coachmaker, who had not yet been paid for the elegant carriage, sent out bailiffs to serve his client with an execution. Like Charters, others dogged Shelley's steps. To avoid arrest he had found lodgings in an obscure section of London, but through Harriet's carelessness his address had been discovered. Four pounds a week had to suffice him and Mary and Clare for food and shelter, yet even that small sum proved difficult to salvage from the flood of debts. The dreary lodging on Margaret Street had to be abandoned for a cheaper and safer one in the sordidness of Somers Town. Shelley did not dare stay home in the "execution" hours, but wandered about the London streets, sometimes with Clare, oftener alone. Mr. Timothy behaved as if he had never had a son. Godwin had forbidden all communication between the runaways and Skinner Street. Fanny, however, understanding Shelley's danger, made herself acquainted with his lodgings and kept a sharp lookout for suspicious-looking characters. At the approach of a bailiff she quickly sent a word of warning.

The time came when there was not a shilling in the house, and, one by one, pieces of furniture and books had to be sold to buy food. Perhaps with the rest Wordsworth's *Excursion* found its way to the bookseller's shop.   It had not given Mary pleasure.   "He is a slave," she had condemned.   It may be from the sale of the slave's work a loaf was bought to sustain their painful freedom.   Shelley found it no longer safe to live with Mary, as she and Clare were known to the bailiffs. They were forced to separate.   In Peacock's rooms in Chancery Lane he found temporary shelter but no peace. Now added to debt and poverty was the torment of being away from his love.   His health suffered.   An old weakness of the lungs, aggravated by want and worry, kept him in constant pain.   The only cheer in his misery was Mary's devotion. Notes full of tenderness passed cautiously from one to the other, notes crying with longing for each other and impatience for the days to pass until Sunday, when bailiffs declared a holiday and debtors had a breathing spell.   In out-of-the-way lodging houses they met clandestinely on weekdays whenever possible; on Sundays he returned home.   "Talk to Shelley," Mary marked one of these red-letter days.   "Talk to him all evening; this is a day devoted to Love in idleness."

Of Harriet for some time there had been no news.   At Shelley's urgent request she had let him have thirty pounds to keep him out of prison, and with childlike earnestness had begged him to abstain from washing his head during his illness, and to remember to wear his flannels.   She would not let him see her, however.

As the period of her confinement neared, she sank into despondency.   Her previous labor had been a painful one; she dreaded the second.   At nineteen she had had the experience of a too full life — love, motherhood, disillusion, despair.   Now, when she most needed the fond care of a husband, she was forsaken.

Mary had little sympathy with Harriet's suffering, and pettish outbursts found their way into her diary.   After all, think what she might, and in the loftiest of terms, the fact remained that Harriet was Shelley's wife, and she, Mary, in an ambiguous position.   The situation was not pleasant.   Soon a child would be born to her and Shelley, an innocent being who would have no place in the existing scheme of society. It was therefore with undisguised annoyance that she heard of

Harriet's confinement and noticed Shelley's rejoicing. Under December 6, 1814, she marked: "A letter from Hookham to say that Harriet has been brought to bed of a son and heir. Shelley writes a number of circular letters of this event which ought to be ushered in with ringing of bells, etc., for it is the son of his *wife*. A letter from Harriet confirming the news, in a letter from a *deserted wife!!* and telling us he has been born a week."

The birth of a son brought little joy to Harriet, though her father and Eliza lost no time in pointing out the advantages that would be hers if she played her cards well. Shelley visited her at once, elated at this unexpected brightening of his prospects. Harriet was shocked to hear him talk of money. "He came to see me as soon as he knew of the event," she wrote to Miss Nugent, "but as to his tenderness to me, none remains. He said he was glad it was a boy, because he would make money cheaper. You see how the noble soul is debased. Money now, not philosophy, is the grand spring of his actions." It was Mary's fault, she knew, none other's.

No sooner was 1815 rung in than Sir Bysshe yielded up his tough old soul, an event so long awaited by Mr. Timothy that he had despaired of its happening in his own lifetime. Shelley's lawyer duly received the information from Mr. Whitton, who begged that "the young gentleman" be kept from seeing both his father and his mother, as his presence in their bereavement would be most painful to them. Nevertheless, with the ubiquitous Clare to relieve the tedium of the journey, and with Mary's copy of Milton to keep his mind occupied, Shelley betook himself to Sussex. Mr., now Sir Timothy, Shelley would not have his afflicted heart further grieved by a sight of his son, who was therefore compelled to sit on the doorstep during the opening of the will, and beguile his thoughts with *Comus*.

The new year augured well. The Westbrooks, too, were of the same opinion, as they charged Harriet on no account to sign a deed of separation from the father of her boy.

XIII

MARRIAGE FOR VENGEANCE

The fire had not died down in the hearth of the Halnaby wedding chamber that night in January, and through the crimson hangings of the bed the light filled the enclosed darkness with lurid flickers. Byron, suddenly awake, cried out with terror, as nightmare and reality merged confusedly in his mind. "Good God! I am surely in Hell!" Beside him Annabella, the bride of a few hours, heard the terrible words that found an echo in her heart. Here was no jest. Byron, startled from his sleep, could not so quickly adopt the Byronic pose. He shrieked in cruel earnest, and the young girl trembled at the revelation, as she had done all of that day which should have been the happiest in her life and which already was assuming the hazy incredibility of an evil dream.[1]

It was no man but a fiend with whom she had found herself shut up in the bridal carriage; it was a creature of black looks and boding silences who glared before him in sullen hatred. She had not known how to break the spell and, frightened, waited for him to speak. As the carriage rode through Durham, for which Sir Ralph had been a Member, the bells were set ringing for the jubilant occasion. "Ringing for our happiness, I suppose?" Byron sneered. And then followed outbursts of accusations and half confessions, threats and vows of vengeance.[2] She, Annabella, was to blame for the sort of marriage theirs was going to be. Why had she not married him years ago when he had first asked her? Then she might have saved him; now it was too late. He did not say what it

[1] The only detailed account of the honeymoon is Lady Byron's.
[2] Both Miss Mayne and M. Maurois incline to treat Byron's honeymoon behavior as a pose. "A fine theme for a Byronic frenzy," M. Maurois calls the vengeance motif. It is the author's conviction that vengeance was indeed one of the reasons for Byron's marriage, as evidence shows.

was from which she might have saved him. Like one fascinated by the depths as he stands on the edge of an abyss, he seemed impelled downward, but stopped at the plunge. His grim defiance, his spasms of remorse, hinted at some dark and unspeakable crime. In his letters during his courtship meaningful sentences had met her too innocent eye. Hints had been there, too, of that sin which so tormented him now, but Annabella, accustomed to think of him as essentially a noble spirit who had discouraged his own goodness, comforted herself that he was painting himself blacker than he was. What had he done? How had she contributed to his perdition by refusing him the first time? And how, in reason's name, how was that refusal linked with his threats of vengeance? "I will be even with you yet," he promised sinisterly, after he had softened, in a moment of weakness, before her Griselda-like submissiveness.

Resentment against Annabella had long been rankling in his mind, and letters to his intimate friends after her acceptance had borne ominous repinings. "It might have been *two* years ago, and if it had, would have saved me a world of trouble." *Two* years ago. Reasoning oversimply, he charged Annabella with culpability of the crime which had occurred in the interval. *Because* of her refusal, he had seduced Augusta. If Annabella had accepted him then, he would have been safely married when temptation came his way. Perhaps there would have been no temptation. Now, because of that *not* which had too late become a *yea*, he was damned and the being he loved best in the world sacrificed to society and a God of vengeance. The guilt for it all lay at Annabella's door and she must suffer. What he had said of Lady Caroline, he might have repeated, and did repeat more terribly on that direful wedding journey: "Her worst enemy could not wish her such a fate as *now* to be thrown back upon me."

Annabella had listened to his ravings, hardly believing what she heard. How was the man changed! He was hardly the same person she had seen fall into a faint during one of her courtship "scenes" at Seaham, when by dint of interminable analyzing she had sought to convince herself that he loved her. Now he had the mastery, and a fiendish tyranny it promised to

be. Not a tender word did he utter. No gesture betrayed
that he was in the least moved by the pale quiet girl who had
left doting parents — to reform *him*. "Oh, what a dupe you
have been to your imagination!" he mocked. Reform him!
Sooner might one try to bring back Lucifer to his original glory.
Byron seriously believed himself to be like Lucifer, a fallen
angel. And here was a mere mortal girl, yoked to his un-
mortal wickedness. "You might have saved me once. Now
it is too late." Once? Who could have saved Lucifer from
a fall predestined since the dawn of time in the consciousness
of God?

Halnaby Hall was like a palace in the power of an evil genius.
Annabella had never liked it. Even as a child she had taken
no pleasure in her parents' sojourn there. The large, many-
windowed house in the purest seventeenth-century style had
always seemed cold and forbidding. It looked magnificent in
the dark of the winter's night that brought her there as the
bride of Byron. No heroine of his romances had ever found
herself in such a situation as Annabella's; none ever bore a
lover's hardness with such humility. She could not take
Byron's behavior seriously. Rather, she did not think it possible that even a Byron could carry his pose so far — if pose
it was. She did not know what to think. Gossip, rife in
London, had not reached her at Seaham. Even if it had, in the
romantic glamour of her engagement she would have thought
it one of the many myths that were always being woven about
Byron's name.

The following morning found him in a vicious humor. He
met her like an enemy. Succeeding days showed no improvement in temper or affection. Sometimes her frightened face,
a look of pitying tenderness, dispelled his viciousness. But
only for a moment. Then, as if ashamed of revealing human
weakness, he became harsher and more cruel. His nights were
waking nightmares. Like his own Lara, who prowled among
the portrait galleries and the vaults of his ancestors, he spent
uneasy hours in the corridors of Halnaby Hall. His dagger
and pistols never left him. When he went to bed he laid
them beside him on a table — with the Bible. What enemy
did he fear? "A sound — a voice — a shriek — a fearful

call!" Would that be his tale some dread midnight? One's conscience does not meet one face to face: the sight would be too terrible. The mortal hand would fall powerless against such horror, the living frame turn to stone. Nevertheless, he still wore the dagger in his belt; night and day he looked to meet the enemy. Once he caught its shadow.

Annabella was reading Dryden's *Don Sebastian*. She turned to Byron with a question on incest. "Where did you hear that?" he asked in a rage, holding his dagger over her. "Oh, only from this book," she answered, innocently. He put his dagger down, cowed by the purity of her expression.

And yet, since the beginning of their life together, as previously in their correspondence, he had attempted to unburden himself of his secret. He spoke with a lover's passion of Augusta, as if, for some perverse pleasure, to rouse Annabella's jealousy. The morning after their wedding a letter had come from his sister to the "dearest, first, and best of human beings." He gloated over it and flaunted it before his wife's eyes. What did she think of it, he asked, as he read over certain phrases exultantly. "As the sea trembles when the earth quakes . . ." So had Augusta felt when she knew that her Baby Byron was getting married. Before his unloved wife he was in a transport for that other, his sister. She was indeed his sea, and he the earth that embraced her. Any convulsion that shook him found its response in her. It may be Augusta had wasted no thought in the penning of her letter, jotted off between one household duty and another; but it brought her bodily before her brother — and made him turn his impotent rage against that little country bluestocking, that eternal Liturgy who had married him, an old English baron, him, a portent of the age, to thrust him into the mould of petty virtue. She was welcome to break her heart at the task.

The snow fell incessantly the first days of their Halnaby honeymoon. Only one short year ago, on that other January, snow had covered the roads and roofs of Newstead. Before the huge fireplace he had felt contentedly at home, knowing Augusta with him. "Snow-bound and thaw-bound," they had been removed from the world, even as they were removed from their fellows by the icy barrier of their crime. And yet they had been happy. Never had he known such tranquillity. Even his conscience had left him in peace. Now that snowfall shut him in with a stranger whom he hated, tormented, feared, and pitied.

Annabella's goodness agonized him, as a sight of the cross is said to throw the devil into the only pain he can know. He took an evil pleasure in seeking to sully that innocence, ever present as a living reproach. If only he could initiate Annabella into his secrets. . . . Then if her devotion were as great as she said, she would love him even in his crimes. He pried cunningly into her mind and heart with accounts of all his wickednesses, real and imagined — except one. "There is *no* vice with which he has not endeavoured to familiarise me," she confessed many years later. His assaults were powerless against her innocence. The probity of her nature as well as a fanatical inflexibility guarded her against complicity. Of that other sin he never spoke directly, though it was the one he wished most to dash against her unassailable purity. He had made the public his confessor. That was not enough. Scandal had bandied it about, a glowing coal that warmed chill nights and dull gatherings. No salvation for him there. Annabella alone offered absolution, if not peace.

He used his secret as a sword and shield against her, to thrust at her complacency and cover himself. She thought she had made a fine marriage; well, she had been yoked to a monster — let her make what she would of that. There had been insanity on both sides of his family, and all his ancestors had been known for strange crimes. He was one of the damned, as impregnable in his evil as she in her goodness. One thing alone would have saved him, came the refrain — if she had accepted him that first time. Now it was too late, too late. She was to blame. Some day she would know, and she would be made miserable as long as she lived. "I will be another Falkland to you," he exulted. He used so many wiles to bring low Annabella's integrity that his assaults became at last a form of spiritual rape. The body she had dutifully yielded; mind and soul remained her own. He used all his ruses to horrify her. The half-revelations that brought

blood to her cheek spurred him on to directer truths for the
pleasure he had in seeing her suffer.   Always his sister Augusta
was brought in to play a part, until suspicion preyed on Annabella.   Perhaps what Byron was trying to confess was some
affair he had had with one of his father's illegitimate daughters,
and he had discovered the truth too late.   Not once during
the Halnaby weeks did she link Augusta with her imaginings.
Impossible!

After the first few terrible days there were times when Byron
relented enough toward the girl on whom he had vowed vengeance to show her kindness.   Then, when he succeeded in dispelling the black mood, he prattled and jested like a child, as
he used to do with Augusta in outbursts of nonsense that, like
bubbles, released the pressure on his volcanic spirit.   Gratefully Annabella humored him in her stilted way, remembering
that he only wanted a woman to laugh, as she knew Augusta
laughed, and foolish Caroline Lamb, until that laughter was
choked in her throat by Byron's insults.   Those moments Annabella's face flushed and her cheeks rounded with mirth, and
she became the pretty child of Seaham who indulged in coarse
little jokes with good old Sir Ralph.   Pippin, Byron nicknamed
her for her red apple cheeks, while he, the tragic hero, became
Duck.   And comedy entered briefly in the otherwise un-
relieved tragedy.

In spite of scenes of regret and remorse, Byron took his
marriage seriously, and any trifle that threatened it upset
him.   Mrs. Byron's ring, with which he had married Annabella, was too large for her finger, and she had tied a black
ribbon round it to secure it.   Byron had her remove the
ribbon in superstitious horror.   A moment later the ring
slipped off Annabella's finger into the fireplace, and the accident plunged him into gloomy revery.   The occurrences,
following one upon the other, boded no good.   As his mother's
marriage had proved an evil one, so would his be, and he
watched for other signs, creating them where they did not
exist.

The "treacle-moon" over, as he called those three weeks at
Halnaby, he and Annabella returned to Seaham, where Sir
Ralph and Mam were waiting with open arms for their "barley-

sugar daughter." How had the dear child stood the ordeal of the change in her life? Was she happy? Was her husband good to her? Of course — who could be cruel to their darling? Her letters had all been reassuring, for Annabella had not dared write the truth to her parents. They would have been needlessly hurt. Besides, who knew whether in time Byron might not change and become the real companion with whom she would joyously accomplish the journey to immortality? He showed himself an ingratiating son-in-law to Sir Ralph. He cajoled the rather formidable Mam, whose wig, one night, in the hilarity of a "dressed-up" party, he had the boldness to snatch off! And to Tom Moore, who had not yet ceased shaking a disapproving head over the marriage, he wrote, — after what extraordinary pleasure? — "I still think one ought to marry upon *lease;* but I am very sure I should renew mine at the expiration, though next term were for ninety and nine years."

But Seaham soon wearied him, and the company of Sir Ralph, with the same joke over the mutton and his speech for the Durham tax meeting delivered to him whether he would listen or no, bored Byron to a frenzy. Under his in-laws' roof, however, he had to guard his actions. Neither Sir Ralph nor his wife Judy would have stood for any ill-behavior to themselves or to their daughter. Byron thought back on his bachelor days, become his happiest in retrospect, and settled into his sullen silences. He would walk by himself along the dreary coast, watching the sea, in a ferment like his own spirit, tossing the jetsam of decaying wreckage from billow to billow. It brought back to his memory the Bay of Biscay in a tumult of surf and foam; it reminded him of the squalls in the Archipelago, and he wrestled with the net of convention that had caught and threatened to kill him. "I must return to the East, I must return to the East to die," he moaned to Annabella.

At Halnaby he had written some of his *Hebrew Melodies* for the Jewish composer, Nathan, to set to music. At Seaham he wrote another poem which he sent to Moore. Ostensibly the death of his schoolfellow, the Duke of Dorset, set him to the writing of the lines. In reality he mourned not his once dear friend, but his own dead self and the peace he could know no more.

"There's not a joy the world can give like that it takes away," flowed the long elegiac line, broken only by a rest, like a sob,

When the glow of early thought declines in feeling's dull decay;
'T is not on youth's smooth cheek the blush alone, which fades so fast,
But the tender bloom of heart is gone, ere youth itself be past. . . .
Then the mortal coldness of the soul like death itself comes down;
It cannot feel for others' woes, it dare not dream its own;
That heavy chill has frozen o'er the fountain of our tears,
And though the eye may sparkle still, 't is where the ice appears. . . .
Oh could I feel as I have felt, — or be what I have been,
Or weep as I could once have wept, o'er many a vanish'd scene;
As springs in deserts found seem sweet, all brackish though they be,
So midst the wither'd waste of life, those tears would flow to me.

Byron, writing of things past, felt he was also crying out on the future in this lament sprung from his soul's misery. "Do you remember the lines I sent you early last year?" he asked Moore when the words reëchoed in his mind. "I don't wish . . . to claim the character of 'Vates' — but were they not a little prophetic?" Echoes from them filled the later years of the lonely Annabella. "As springs in deserts found" she spoke of the brief moments of tenderness that Byron had shown her, and to the last she recalled the tears of pity for her suffering which had filled his eyes and, "freezing there, gave the appearance of more icy hardness." It was almost a paraphrase of those verses which she had copied out for him during those comparatively peaceful days at Seaham.

Frequent letters came from Six Mile Bottom, first for the groom alone, then for both bride and groom — affectionate, confused, charming letters that threw Byron into fits of restlessness. His sister's influence was necessary to quiet him, thought Annabella, and she wooed the older woman. Would she ever teach her the secret of calming Byron? She wrote to Augusta from Halnaby, inviting her to spend a little time with them. Byron was so pleased that he showed his wife some grateful attention. But Augusta could not accept the invitation. Later, perhaps — and she went on with her pretty trivialities which Byron pondered as if they were oracular. Often, however, the seemingly offhand words did have hidden meanings for him, even when written to Annabella. Between them the poor girl was a mouse tumbled about in the padded claws of two self-absorbed cats. Annabella could see only half her danger. "Augusta," she implored, "will you be my *only* friend?" It was a touching, a childlike request. Yet instinctively she knew that if Augusta were on her side, Byron would follow. What if the victory meant subsequent defeat? At present she was fighting for the peace, at least, if not the happiness she had dreamed of, in her inexperience.

At Seaham amid the tedium of elderly married folk Byron thought again of Augusta. He would go and pay her a visit by himself, he proposed. Annabella demurred. If he went, she would go with him. He raged and stormed, and then unwillingly assented. Augusta was thrown into a fluster. She did want to receive them, but the house was, Oh, so small, and she was expecting old Aunt Sophia. The Colonel might or might not consent to be absent . . . the children . . . the fuss. . . . In reality she dreaded her brother's visit after their final leave-taking and their vows to be *good,* and as usual she floundered about in search of any excuse but the one which would have served — a trait that had become a habit in her life of expediency. The horizon cleared with the Colonel's departing on a shooting trip, and Augusta put everything in readiness to receive dear *Baby* and his wife.

Byron set out in ill-humor, with Annabella prim as a governess by his side. She was *de trop* and he saw to it that she felt it. A man could not go out even to see his sister without a chaperon! He was exasperated with her and furious with her parents for spoiling her and letting her have her way. She would go with him, would she? Well, she would pay for it. The big vengeance, like a Chinese ball, contained within it a nest of smaller ones.

At Six Mile Bottom the two women met without effusion. Strangely, Augusta did not kiss her sister-in-law, a fact remarked with vicious pleasure by Byron. Was Augusta jealous? He liked a touch of jealousy in the women who loved him. In the bedroom, while removing her wraps, Annabella meekly kissed Guss, as she had learned from Byron to call her in her letters. Guss returned the kiss and promptly informed Byron of the touching scene. It was a promising beginning.

But not for Annabella. Too soon she discovered that now Byron had Augusta, his wife counted for less than nothing, except as an object for suffering his displeasure, and that was often in the jangled state of his nerves. A word sent him into a rage, when even Augusta was not spared. An insidious unrest seemed to possess the untidy house on the arrival of the bridal pair. Augusta waited, expectant and uneasy; Byron fumed; Annabella stood fearfully by, knowing herself on the brink of a disclosure yet, like one in a dream, keeping her eyes tight shut against the looming horror.

The first night she spent at Six Mile Bottom Byron came into her room wild and disordered and flung at her, "Now I have *her*, you will find that I can do without *you* — in all ways." The same insinuations as at Halnaby, only now scarcely veiled. Was it possible? Could Byron and Augusta have been guilty of such abomination — and still be suffered to live by a righteous God? Annabella cast the suspicion from her, — it was still a suspicion, — with loathing of herself for having harbored it. Never. Byron in a mad moment might have approached his sister, but she could not have consented, never. She seemed such a simple woman, and so kind, taking her part even against Byron.

But Annabella was not suffered to remain long in doubt. Each day in Augusta's house marked a station of her Calvary, with, at the end, the death of her heart. In the evening, when the three were together, Byron contrived to send her away so that he might remain alone with Augusta. Sometimes, in spite of his taunts, she forced herself to stay, but he assailed her so brutally that she had to rush to her room, if only to cry out her bitterness. Soon after their arrival the London jewelers sent two brooches that he had ordered made, containing his hair and Augusta's plaited together, and the symbol of three crosses. "If she knew what these mean!" he said to Augusta. Annabella did not know, but she conjectured when she saw the two wearing them constantly like the brands of their sin — for, no, there could be no doubt that what she had not dared think of had really been. But was it *now,* in Augusta's house, under her very eyes?

In her sleep one night Annabella brushed against her husband's body. "Don't touch me!" he cried in loathing. Humiliated and broken, she rose and spent the remaining hours sobbing in another room. Was it, *even now?* Augusta seemed to shrink from him in fear and drew closer to Annabella, more as if to seek, than to give, protection, while Byron roamed the house like a maddened beast, brutalizing them both. Was it the working of his conscience, making him turn against a compliant Augusta, or was it fury at her resistance? Annabella could no longer bear to be in a house the air of which breathed madness and corruption. A little before their departure, Byron, pointing to the baby Medora, said, exulting, "You know that is my child." She had seen how tenderly he had looked at the little girl, and had remarked innocently how beautiful was his expression as he fondled the child. He had said nothing at the time, but Augusta had nearly sunk down in confusion. Was it the truth she was hearing now? Now, when she was beginning to feel the first stirrings of another life within her?

She refused to believe it. Byron, she argued to herself, exaggerated his weakness into fault, his error into sinfulness. Just as to himself he was no man, but a fallen angel, he tried to appear to her no mere sinner, but the blackest of monsters. In his darkened state of mind every glimmering brought forth from the shadows shapes of horror enacting inconceivable crime, and always he was the chief actor. The laudanum he began taking to quiet his febrile activity only served to cast a deeper dye over his imaginings. Annabella thought she understood, and looked hopefully toward London, where, under their own roof, they would begin life anew. All his talk of vengeance, his behavior to Augusta, his ravings and cruelties — they would all vanish under her patient and devoted care. For still she loved him, more than ever now because he was under that cloud of evil. Besides, Annabella had something of the Christian saint about her; Byron was perhaps the cross of her martyrdom, through whom she would attain her supreme election.

Poor Augusta had no regret at seeing her guests go. She had liked Annabella in her superficial way and would have had her happy. But she could not long withstand that "dearest, first and best of human beings" who had chosen her for his inconvenient passion. Everything, honor, duty, loyalty, and that religion which she had made so much of, had been swept aside to please him, with no rewards but shame and remorse — so far as she could feel them. Now that for *her* sake, to spare *her* further suffering, he had married "a perfect being in mortal mould," as she described Annabella, she *must* endeavor to keep him "good." The two dreadful weeks just past had been the most trying in her life, with Byron exacting and she, out of her new sense of honor, denying. Never had she had such a contest, she, the easy-going Augusta who stopped at nothing if it made nobody unhappy. How long her endurance would have lasted was difficult to tell, for unlike Annabella she grew not stronger but more weak when sorely tried.

At 13 Piccadilly Terrace, in a small mansion rented from the Duchess of Devonshire, the young pair set up their town home. Byron's books and dogs were transferred from the Albany, and Mrs. Mule, the terrifying beldame who had frightened away importunate visitors, established herself as housekeeper. In the midst of familiar things, Byron seemed quieter. Kinnaird, his banker, had bought him some shares at Drury Lane, and he became a member of the Subcommittee of Management. Again, with Hobhouse and Kinnaird, he began to enjoy a little of the freedom he had had before marriage. Through Murray he met Scott, who sent him a handsome Turkish dagger; in exchange, he presented him with a silver urn filled with Athenian bones. Life was becoming a trifle less boring.

Annabella drank in hope with a full heart. Byron wanted an heir. Perhaps with the coming of the child he would forget his fantastic vengeances and turn to her. From the first he began writing to his friends about her "gestatory symptoms." Leigh Hunt, out of prison at last, received an invitation to a box at Drury Lane and the news that Lady Byron was "in a fair way of going through the whole process of beginning a family." It was phrased awkwardly for a man of his fluency, but then he was experiencing what he would never have admitted, a normal, if embarrassed, pride at the thought of becoming a father. Moore, too, was sent bulletins concerning Annabella's health. "I wish to keep her quiet in her present situation," he said. With gloomy satisfaction he watched her growing "prosperous and ponderous."

Alas for Annabella's hopes. The period of quiet too soon gave way to lowering looks and scenes of violence. The very child she was bearing was turned into another subject for his cruelty. As soon as he had an heir, he said, he would leave her — he would end his existence. In the meantime he had nothing for her but disgust and hatred, intensified to madness. Annabella, after endeavoring in all ways to placate him, had to admit she was powerless. There was Augusta, her *only* friend. She must come to her now to help bring him back to sanity, for surely, — and she clung to the thought as the last straw in his defense, — surely he must be insane. In no other way could she account for his savagery toward her. He hated her and everything connected with her. He abhorred her mother and Mrs. Clermont, her governess. When Lord Wentworth died and left his estates to Lady Milbanke, his ferocity knew no bounds, for he had expected Annabella, a favorite niece, to be remembered with a legacy instead of having to wait until her mother's death for her inheritance. Even harmless Sir Ralph, who had changed his name in accordance with the provisions of the will, got his share of malevolence. "Sir Ralph Noël *late* Milbanke — he don't promise to be *late* Noël in a hurry." . . . Bailiffs began knocking at the door of 13 Piccadilly Terrace with bills and executions, and there came a time when one of them installed himself in the house. In vain Annabella tried to raise funds for her husband. Her parents, left without ready money by the expenses involved in maintaining their new estate, had to watch every pound for their own needs. No help from that quarter. Interpreting as miserliness their inability to produce the very much needed cash, Byron inveighed against them and called their daughter a beggar. Yes, that was the sort of heiress he had married, fool that he was!

All this Annabella could have borne. Once more, however, he took to enacting the Halnaby scenes, in and out of season, adding to the recitals of his past crimes lurid accounts of present exploits with actresses at Drury Lane. And again the theme of vengeance reappeared. She was paying for it now, and that would not be all. He would strangle their child when it was born, and then he would kill himself. No, she could never reform him. Never. He was lost. He had been doomed to damnation by an unreasoning God whom he could not respect. Well, he would deserve his damnation. The dagger and pistols reappeared, and the sleepless nights when he would lie wide-eyed on his pillow, listening for the approach of the unseen persecutor. However, the two long poems he wrote between July and September had less in them of the Byronic hero and more of a quiet, though uninspired, energy. The *Siege of Corinth* he dedicated to Hobhouse; *Parisina* to Scrope Davies. Annabella dutifully copied them out for him. . . . So far he had dedicated nothing, written nothing — to her.

Augusta had come and gone on a visit to Piccadilly Terrace, doing Byron no good. With her near he seemed to exercise his most perverse powers to see which of the two he could hurt more, his wife or his sister. When they could bear no more, he changed his tactics like a Gilles de Rais with his victims, as if to give them a renewed space of hope, and then again resumed the torture. But not with any pleasure, for he bore as much suffering as he inflicted. Then, at the sight of the haggard eye and the convulsed face, Annabella in an access of pity blamed Augusta as the sole cause of it all. *She* had tempted Byron, — for now she no longer doubted their incestuous relations, — Augusta alone was blameworthy. Once, when what had been presented itself with blinding vividness before her eyes, Annabella, seizing a weapon lying by, would have plunged it into Augusta's heart. Horror of herself prevented her dealing the blow.

With wisdom too bitter for her young years, she realized that those two could not be kept apart. She had not wanted to believe their sin; she had willfully blinded herself to its existence.   Too late she had to admit that it had been, and that brother and sister were united by a bond closer than blood — their very guilt.

> We repent — we abjure — we will break from our chain, —
> We will part — we will fly to — unite it again! —

"I wrote that to you, Guss," he had boasted in Annabella's presence.   He had written more truly than he knew.

Once Annabella arrived at her conclusion she had a morbid satisfaction in keeping them together under her vigilance — for, she was to admit, though she knew it hopeless to keep them apart, it might not be hopeless to keep them innocent.   She set herself up as the guardian of these two extraordinary portents of nature, and, more than ever infallible, saintly in her suffering, she formed vague hopes of bringing them both back to God.

XIV

WATERLOO — AND ANOTHER'S

WHILE the diplomats of the allies were rearranging the map of Europe in Vienna, a voice like the wind scattered their charts with the news that the Eagle had flown his cage at Elba. Immediately bickerings over the changing ownership of the square miles were forgotten, and all the nations joined in a common interest. How had Napoleon escaped from his prison island? Conflicting rumors built up the legend. It was known, however, that from the beginning of his exile he had gathered together his most loyal veterans as a bodyguard. Then, with the three million francs he had been permitted to keep, he had bought four small coasting ships, ostensibly for his pleasure. Early in the new year (1815) Fleury de Chaboulon was seen to land at Porto Ferrajo. But the ears of the spies did not catch the purport of the words which he earnestly addressed to the fallen emperor. "Come back," he urged. France swayed as a ship without a rudder. The Congress of Vienna was on the verge of dissolution. "Set forth for Naples," Napoleon commanded, while in the same breath he ordered a grand ball at court. His mother, who was with him, and his sisters, made the necessary preparations. To his mother alone he confided his plan. While the guests were assembled in the ballroom and the music played, Napoleon withdrew, unobserved, galloped to the quay where nearly a thousand of his soldiers were already embarked, and set out on his last attempt to reconquer the world.

The morning of March the first saw him and his men landed near Antibes; they bought guns, horses, and provisions. They slept the night in the olive groves of Provence, and the day after, leaving the guns behind on the ships, and heartened by Napoleon's promises, they made for the hills toward Grenoble.

Through thawing roads and snow-covered ravines they marched for days, until, within a few miles of their destination, they found the royal soldiery blocked against them. Napoleon recognized the faces of his men among them. Boldly, he rode forward. "Soldiers!" he cried. "I am your Little Corporal. Who among you would fire against me? Let him shoot!" *"Vive l'Empereur!"* came their united cheer, and tossing their white cockades to the ground they trampled them into the mud, deserting one and all to their former leader. "To-night we shall be in Grenoble," Napoleon promised, "and in ten days, in Paris!" One by one, the royal regiments surrendered to him, reforging their allegiance. Enthusiasm for the Little Corporal reached the peak of frenzy. "Soldiers! In my exile I heard your voices!" Napoleon exercised his old hypnotic spell. . . . "Your General, raised upon your shields, is now come back to you! Tear down those colors behind which France's foes have hidden! Then will you be the liberators of your country." Thirty thousand men posted to keep the returning emperor out of Lyons deserted to him. A few days later the town was his.

At the Tuileries fat Louis XVIII quaked on his tottering throne. "Sire," Marshal Ney comforted him, "I shall bring you back the Eagle in an iron cage." Face to face with Napoleon, however, he could not carry out his boast; they embraced as brothers. In a day the whole army was in Napoleon's hands. At this juncture Louis thought it time to rise up and go, before he was unceremoniously shoved off the throne, and on the night of the nineteenth, while Napoleon had already proceeded as far as Fontainebleau, Louis and his family fled to Beauvais, changed horses for Lisle, and hurried off to Ghent and safety. The following night Napoleon's carriage stopped at the palace gates amid throngs in a transport of enthusiasm. He had scarcely set foot on the carriage step when he was seized bodily by his friends and carried aloft on their arms. A brilliant court welcomed him in the reception hall, lighted by triumphant tapers and the jewels of the waiting women. He was once more Emperor.

But not for long. The royalists in the Vendée stirred up ominous uprisings. Internal dissension disorganized the still unstable government. The great powers, in solidarity against the renewed menace, met again at the Vienna Congress and set springes to ensnare the escaped Eagle. Now when, after many years of war, peace seemed on its way, Napoleon again swooped, a black shadow over the dovecote. He must be destroyed — at any rate, recaptured. Each nation pledged itself to provide one hundred and eighty thousand men in this final aggression; England, as the wealthiest, financed the enterprise. There was to be no respite till the Eagle was once more in chains.

Napoleon cocked an eye, studying his position. There was no time to be lost on civil warfare — that should come later, when the greater danger of the allied powers had been passed. Three vast armies were being turned loose against him, one under Schwarzenberg, on the Upper Rhine, a smaller on the lower Rhine under Blücher, and the third under Wellington, for whom Parliament had voted additional supplies of men and money. Again war raged. "It began and ended in a single battle," said Lamartine. Waterloo.

The flower of British manhood had been sent to increase the forces of Wellington in Belgium, and with them went sisters, wives, and mistresses, to cheer their hearts and to heal their wounds. Death was not thought of: it was too near. Meanwhile at the British Embassy the Duchess of Richmond gave a grand ball. Suddenly, at its height, the sound of the music was drowned by the blare of the trumpet calling the men to their ranks. Napoleon was advancing. With brief farewells the British officers took their leave, the strains of the waltz still ringing in their ears, the kisses of their dear ones warm on their lips.

Waterloo. Two miles of fertile valley, high with the faint green spears of grain and brightened with patches of clover, stretched in the sunlight of a fair June morning after a wet night. The hamlet of Hougoumont on the right wakened to a Sunday of fearful preparations; on the left La Haye Sainte glistened in all its branches with the gathered drops of the night's rain. Behind it, on a range of low hills, the British army lay waiting; beyond, on the other side of the valley, the French held their position on another line of hills enclosing

the village of La Belle Alliance.   Hope ran high in Napoleon's
army.   Now that the Little Corporal had returned to them,
the same sun that had shone on Austerlitz ten years before
would light him again to victory.   From their station opposite,
the British could hear the shouts of command, the echoes of
the "*Marseillaise*" and the deafening cheer of the army shout-
ing, "*Vive l'Empereur!*"   The Dutch and Hanoverian auxiliaries moved uneasily.   " 'T is the worst army that ever was
gotten together," grumbled Wellington, surveying his forces.
"The mere name of Napoleon has beaten them before they
have fired a shot."

Wellington had arrived late that morning, it was rumored
on account of Lady Frances Webster, Byron's White Rose,
who, loth to unfold before the poet, had come to full blossom
in the heat of the battlefield.

The French opened fire a little before noon.   By two the
British batteries had come near the end of their strength and
d'Erlon was at once dispatched to attack them on their weak
left.   The Dutch brigade turned tail in a body before the
enemy onslaught, and rushed madly through the British ranks.
Wellington groaned.   Four o'clock saw a squadron of French
cuirassiers, a living wall of flashing swords and breastplates,
advancing solidly against the British squares.   Until nightfall the fighting continued.   The farmhouse at La Haye behind which the British held their ground was in a blaze; opposite, the château of Hougoumont was a burning shell filled
with dead and dying Frenchmen.   Still the fighting raged,
lighted by the conflagrations and the sharp flash of the guns.
The British were gaining, but they needed reënforcements.
At last the Prussians came upon the field, and with the hosts
of the English they bore forward upon the remnants of the
French army.   Wellington spurred his men forward.   Of Napoleon's Old Guard, ten thousand strong at sunrise, only one
hundred and fifty remained.   "Surrender!" shouted the British.   "The Guard does not surrender," came the answer.
"It dies."   And with them died Napoleon's glory.

The Eagle's defeat was complete and decisive; with Waterloo he knew his career ended.   He would have plunged desperately into the field to die, but Marshal Soult turned his

white Persian charger by the bridle. "Is not the enemy too fortunate as it is?" he asked, and urged him to escape. At Genappe the carriage was overtaken, and Napoleon forced to leave it and flee. His sword, the sword of many victories, and his hat that had covered the most powerful head in Europe, he left behind him in his haste. Uncovered, unarmed, he ended as he had started, a Corsican adventurer who did not know what the future might bring. Death? Final victory? It was too late to hope. "Three million Frenchmen have perished for one man," cried Lafayette when, once more in Paris, Napoleon gathered up his strength for another act of defiance against Europe. "We have done enough for Napoleon. Let us now save our country."

The news of Waterloo quickly reached England, which went into a tumult of rejoicing at the victory, forgetting, in the elation, its dreadful cost. Wellington was as usual explicit. "Such a desperate action," he wrote in his dispatch, "could not be fought, and such advantages could not be gained, without great loss; and I am sorry to add that ours have [sic] been immense." Waterloo alone cost England fifteen thousand dead and wounded.

Lord Byron, from the depths of his private despondency, heard of Napoleon's defeat with singular petulance. "Well, I'm damned sorry for it," he snapped at his astonished informer. He and his little pagod — strange how their destinies followed the same courses!

Annabella kept her husband vigilantly under her eye and, when he would listen, she spoke to him of Duty. Most times he flew into a passion and restrained himself with difficulty from striking her. Once, in his fury, he seized a clock, dashed it to the ground, and began stamping on it until not a part of it remained whole. Fearing for herself and the child within her, Annabella begged Augusta to come and live with her. Better to have Augusta there, in spite of everything, than encourage Byron to drive himself to insanity, as he was surely doing. The two women observed the fixed stare with which he glared before him in a concentration of loathing, and quaked to see his eyes suddenly start up in a threatening look under his lowered lids. That was the way the king had behaved before he went mad, Annabella would say in a whisper. One night while they were all together at the theatre he began talking to himself. George Byron, who had been invited to stay at Piccadilly Terrace for Annabella's safety, warned her of her danger. There could be no doubt — his noble cousin was not in his right senses.

Still he behaved rationally enough with everyone but Annabella and Augusta. Only while they were by did he give way to his savagery. It was as if their presence touched some sensitive stop that set his whole being jangling. Augusta succeeded sometimes in calming him. Annabella invariably brought on a crisis of nerves. His dislike for her was becoming so intense that he could not bear her physical nearness. At this juncture she decided to consult the doctors.

One day while Byron was in his room writing, two men forced their way in, a doctor and a lawyer sent by Annabella. They asked him a number of questions which Byron thought "singular, frivolous and somewhat importunate, if not impertinent," but though he protested, he answered them, not knowing at the time the purport of their visit.

The examiners did not think him insane, and Annabella's hope that her husband's loathing of her might have been explained by something outside herself had to be abandoned. She could ignore the truth no longer. Byron, possessed of his faculties, fully aware of his actions, hated her because innocently she had been the cause of the sin that preyed on his mind. "If you had married me two years ago, you would have spared me what I can never get over. . . ." Again and again he made her feel his blame. His was twisted reasoning, but then, what could one expect from a man who did not fit into the simple category of mankind? He was a being outside all categories. So was his sister, who fascinated Annabella almost as much as did her brother. Before the two she was as a dove under the hypnotism of a pair of snakes, brilliant and deadly. That she might not herself be lost, she clung closer to God.

It was the unwisest procedure she could have adopted, this display of her saintliness before Byron. He had always stood in awe of it. "She is too good a person. . . ." "A great deal too good for me. . . ." The words had recurred in an uneasy burden whenever he had spoken of her before their marriage. And to her he had written from some inner prompting, "I did not believe such a woman existed — at least for me — and I sometimes fear I ought to wish that she had not." The Gordon fetches had warned and no one had heeded, and the union of the blessed and the damned had taken place.

Outwardly, however, their life made a show of order. Sometimes they would go out together in their carriage to Edgware Road, where Byron would descend to chat with the freed Leigh Hunt on the now completed *Story of Rimini,* while Annabella, perhaps fearful of betraying her sorrow, waited outside. Marianne, never fond of his lordship, transferred her dislike to her ladyship, who, she was certain, thought herself too elegant to enter their humble home. A fine lady indeed! Marianne had her own opinions as she cast a look at the aristocratic equipage outside, and then at his lordship in the tiny garden, rocking away on little Thornton's hobbyhorse until her ladyship had to send up the footman to remind Byron that she was waiting.

How was it that Byron, of a deeply affectionate nature, who could mourn over the death of a dog, had only cruelty for the woman who married him? He claimed he liked none but those who amused him and made him laugh. Annabella had learned to put aside her natural gravity and with the help of Augusta had gained some proficiency in their coterie nonsense. But it was only an acquired art and struck false. She was most herself when in her prim, old-maidenly way she seized on her black sheep and lectured him for as long as he would put up with it. In consequence he resented her the more. Her very goodness was a reason for him to hate her. Satan, yoked to a Saint Cecilia, could not have been more uncomfortable. Thus as day followed day, in a life grown increasingly difficult through financial pressure and incompatibility, Byron found himself on the brink of desperation. He could not in honor escape from the marriage; nor could he think without horror of continuing in it. The motive of vengeance played strongly upon his emotions; but no vengeance can endure forever. Besides, Annabella bore it all so meekly that, instead of his obtaining the insane satisfaction he sought, he succeeded only in despising himself. Then, with Byron thus lowered before Byron, he turned with redoubled fury upon the cause of his abasement.

By the eve of Annabella's confinement his hatred of her had reached such violence that he screamed at her that he wished she would die, and the child with her. Mrs. Clermont, her governess, had been installed in the house for her protection, and Fletcher, reading too well his master's brooding, would lock the doors at night for Lady Byron's safety. Augusta, herself on the point of losing her scattered wits, was torn between her love of her brother and her duty to Annabella. There was no more question of a secret between them. Though avowed only in half words, in the trembling of her hands, in the frightened look of her eyes, she had little to withhold from Annabella. On her part Annabella, coldly analytical before that hopeless situation, studied the poor woman's behavior before Byron — noting her embarrassment, her too transparent ruses to do in all innocence what had else emphasized her guilt. She knew that in spite of her love for her husband she could no longer live with him, for her salvation as well as for his — if there was still time to save him. She would have left his home before the child was born, but that she hoped death would prevent her taking the step.

On December 10, 1815, Lady Byron gave birth to a daughter. Even here destiny had proved unkind. Byron had hoped for a son — "the tenth wonder of the world," as he had been able to jest with Moore, a month before, "Gil Blas being the eighth, and he (my son's father) the ninth." With an amazing defiance of what one name, at least, implied, the baby was put down on the baptismal register as Augusta Ada.

Annabella's parents invited the young family to Kirkby Mallory, the Wentworth estate. When on January 15 of the following year Annabella, with her child in her arms, entered her carriage, she left her home forever. Before her husband's room she had experienced a moment of weakness. There was a mat in front of the door, where his Newfoundland dog used to lie. She would have flung herself down and waited until the door opened, but she steeled herself and went on. There was no good-bye.

Twice she wrote to him, first midway on her journey, at Woburn, praying him to be *good*, and not to give himself up "to the abominable trade of versifying — nor to brandy — nor to anything or anybody that is not *lawful and right*," and then from Kirkby Mallory, addressing him as "Dearest Duck," and sending love "to the good Goose" who had remained at Piccadilly Terrace to try her calming processes upon him. They were unwise letters from a wife who was deserting her husband; but Annabella always strove to temper her justice with mercy. Moreover, even now that she had left him, — ostensibly only to pay her parents a visit, — she hoped that something, she scarcely knew what, would intervene to prevent a separation. The case was definitely decided when Sir Ralph and Lady Judith saw her haggard face and hollow eyes, and when, almost in spite of herself, words escaped her that told too clearly what she had suffered. Though she might waver, they would not.

At first her parents inclined to believe their son-in-law mad, for surely none but a madman could have behaved heartlessly to their darling. (As yet they had no conception of the magnitude of his crimes.) Why should Byron not join his wife and babe at Kirkby Mallory? The change would do him good. But Dr. Le Mann, who had been studying his patient, had to admit that he was not insane, though he found him excessively unstable, and communicated his latest findings to Annabella. She had not expected any other report. Dr. Baillie had already confirmed it — the best for Byron, the worst for her. And to her parents she was obliged to confess all. "My dearest Augusta," she wrote ten days after arriving at Kirkby, when she could no longer remain undecided, "shall I still be your sister? . . . I must resign my *rights* to be so considered. . . . I follow my Duty and look to the peace which it alone can ensure — here or hereafter. . . ."

Augusta, as she read the letter, must have realized that here at last was the thing she had been dreading. When Annabella spoke of Duty and the hereafter, it was time to give up all hope. "There is too much probability of a *separation* between him and his Wife . . ." she wrote frantically to Byron's friend, Hodgson. "Alas! I see only *ruin* and *destruction* in every shape to one most dear to me." Her lack of caution and her underlining plainly betrayed her agitation. What would happen if her brother and his wife really separated? Scandal would stop at nothing . . . her name again would be dragged to the fore. . . . There would be more lies to tell, other deceptions to carry through. Once more she would be at the mercy of her brother — more than brother. Desperately she struck out everywhere for help, sending her incoherent notes to all his friends. They must come to Byron's rescue. The separation must be prevented at any cost. She pleaded with Annabella. She must think of her happiness, of the love she bore her husband. But Annabella, her mind now fixed, answered, cold and implacable: "*Happiness* no longer enters into my views, it can never be restored, and the greater or less degree of misery I must endure will depend on the *principles* of my conduct, not on its *consequences*. Now, independent of any advice whatever, I deem it *my duty to God* to act as I am acting, and I am resigned to the misfortunes that may flow from that source, since by any other conduct I should forfeit my peace of conscience, the only good that remains to me." No, no, Augusta could do nothing against such terrible goodness.

Sir Ralph had written Byron a letter informing him of his daughter's decision. Fearful of its effect, and hoping to retard the blow, Augusta had sent the letter back to Sir Ralph, who came to town in person and saw that his proposal reached Byron's attorney. "I recommend it to you in the strongest terms," Hanson warned the prostrate Byron, "not to acquiesce to the Measure proposed to Sir Ralph Noël: you would repent it all your life." Lady Judith, who had preceded Sir Ralph to London, had already seen Sir Samuel Romilly about the separation, bringing for his perusal a statement from Annabella. On Sir Samuel's advice she had consulted Dr. Lushington, and it was at his suggestion that Sir Ralph had written to Byron. Henceforth the matter was to be handled solely by the lawyers.

Byron was aghast. Little had he thought when Annabella had submitted with such meekness and patience to the outbreaks of his "state of mind" that she would in the end turn against him. Not Annabella. It was all the doing of Lady Judith, whom he had never liked, and of that witch of a Mrs. Clermont. He would not believe it when Augusta broke the news to him; he was incredulous even when he held Sir Ralph's letter in his hands. It could not have been sent with Annabella's sanction. . . . He begged Augusta to write her and find out whether *she* had concurred. Annabella answered succinctly that she had. Then Byron wrote. He must have the words from *herself*. If it were all true, he would in the end abide by her decision; but let her weigh well the probable consequences. Annabella was forbidden by Lushington to answer, and again Byron wrote, calling her "Dearest Bell." . . . "The whole of my errors — or what harsher name you choose to give them — you know; but I loved you, and will not part from you without your *own* most express and *expressed* refusal to return or to receive me."

His words reawakened the yearning she had tried to still, but memory gave her the strength she would else have lacked. How often had he shown tenderness, to cancel it a moment later with cruelty? If she weakened now, she would only be preparing future woes for herself and him. She answered coldly. Once more he wrote, pleading with her, calling up those moments of happiness that had been theirs. "I still cling to the wreck of my hopes, before they sink for ever." She rolled on the floor in paroxysms of grief, struggling against the impulse to forget the past and return to him, but in agony of heart she dominated herself. Her answer was brittle with the chill she had to assume. "I cannot attribute your 'state of mind' to any cause so much as the *total* dereliction of principle which, since our marriage, you have professed and gloried in. . . . I have *consistently* fulfilled my duty as your wife. It was too dear to be resigned till it became hopeless. Now my resolution cannot be changed."

It was the end. Augusta, Byron's officious friends, the persuasions of his lawyers, all broke ineffectually against the rock of Annabella's resolve. There could be no condoning the actions of a man judged sane enough to assume moral responsibility for them. In her decision Lady Byron became as inflexible as she had been submissive.

At first Dr. Lushington, whom the susceptible Lady Noël found the "most *gentlemanlike* clear-headed and clever man" she had ever met, had considered the possibility of a reconciliation between his noble client and her husband. However, when Lady Byron came to London and disclosed to him in person as much as she could of certainties of guilt before marriage between Lord Byron and his sister, and "suspicions" of a resumption of incest after marriage, he no longer hesitated to declare himself for separation. Rumors were spreading, hinting clearly at the true cause. Lady Melbourne, Caroline Lamb, friends and enemies of husband and wife, besieged them with letters. Was it true they were separating? And could there be any foundation in fact in the dreadful things that were being noised about? Lady Melbourne and her daughter-in-law had no need to inquire, for both had received Byron's confidences. Most considerately, Lady Caroline, herself on the verge of being cast off by William Lamb, offered Byron an expedient that had always worked between her and her husband. "See your wife and she cannot have the heart to betray you — if she has, she is a devil," she added, subtly hinting that *she* had always stood by him, even after he had injured her.

Hobhouse, believing the gossip a lie, nevertheless sought substantiation for his belief in his methodical way. He drew up a document for Lady Byron to sign, disclaiming "for herself and her family any participation or belief in the several [*sic*] scandalous and calumnious rumours tending to the total destruction of his Lordship's character." What these rumors were, he could not put down in writing for the eye of virtue to see, nor could he trust himself to write them in his diary. Incest was one; the other he stigmatized as "a crime more enormous" — sodomy.

Lady Byron was advised not to sign the document. Instead she wrote a simple disavowal stating that the two reports "do not form any part of the charges which in the event of a

Separation by agreement not taking place, she should have been compelled to make against Lord Byron."

Mrs. Villiers, a friend and partisan of Mrs. Leigh, also wrote to her, begging her for Augusta's sake to put an end to insinuations by an open declaration of their falseness. Again Annabella declared nothing of the sort. ". . . As I can *positively* assert that *not one* of the many reports now current have been sanctioned and encouraged by me, my family, or my friends, I cannot consider myself in any degree responsible for them." It was a skillful evasion of the truth, neither denying nor affirming. She could not, indeed would not, publicly exculpate Augusta. There was too much at stake. If the separation proceedings were taken to the courts, a thing which the lawyers for both parties wished to avoid, and if then Augusta and Byron, through lack of evidence, were judged innocent, Ada, her child, might be taken from her and given to Augusta's keeping. In reality there was little probability of it, but the thought nearly drove her mad. Night and day she had visions of Ada with Augusta, and of herself alone, without a home of her own, deprived of husband and daughter. No! Augusta had taken too much from her. She must not have all. Dr. Lushington reassured her. She could never be deprived of the child, however strong its father's pleas, in the face of such written evidence as he had in his possession — for future use, should it ever be necessary to present it. In the meantime, Lady Byron was to preserve an austere silence against friends and enemies alike.

She obeyed. Rumor increased in force and virulence. The press attacked Byron, printing possible and impossible surmises. He was hissed at Drury Lane and cut in public. Throughout, Lady Byron said nothing, making of her silence the deadliest instrument against him. How heinous must his crimes have been, judged society, if Lady Byron could not even make them public!

Byron, seeing that all was lost, worked out a comforting drama in his mind. *He* was the injured party, but he would act nobly. He had never willfully wronged his wife. Whatever had been, had taken place before his marriage. Ill-health — he was still suffering — had been the cause of his irritability. Lady Byron should not have forsaken a sick and helpless man. Nevertheless, he would speak no word against her. "I do not believe," he wrote magnanimously to Moore, who was prepared to cast stones, "I do not believe . . . that there ever was a better, or even a brighter, a kinder, a more amiable and agreeable being than Lady Byron. I never had, nor can have, any reproach to make her, while with me." And he believed it, both because it was true, and because she was now lost to him. Annabella had seen rightly into his mind. "It is unhappily your disposition to consider what you *have* as worthless — what you have *lost* as invaluable." Lost or not, however, she was not invaluable. There were things more precious still: Byron and freedom. If he had humbled himself to plead for her return, it was because the habit of her had become part of his life and he had learned to be happy in his unhappiness. In the loneliness of Piccadilly Terrace he could even induce himself to shed tears over a sentimentalized past and call up blisses that had never been. They had loved, romantically loved, in his imaginary life drama, until serpents entered his Eden and poisoned Annabella's mind against him. Lady Judith and Mrs. Clermont: they were the evil counselors responsible for a young wife's desertion of her husband's hearth; and upon them he heaped the reproaches he did not dare as yet to make, except indirectly, against her.

"Born in the garret, in the kitchen bred," he began a sketch of Mrs. Clermont that seemed limned of vitriol and flame, "an only infant's earliest governess," she had sought ever to pervert a mind

> Which flattery fool'd not, baseness could not blind,
> Deceit infect not, nor contagion soil,
> Indulgence weaken, nor example spoil. . . .
> Nor fortune change, pride raise, nor passion bow,
> Nor virtue teach austerity — till now.

And now only because that vile mask of Gorgon prompted. He was beside himself with loathing of his present victim, which he had to expend or bring on "an effusion" against which the doctors had warned him.

Mark how the channels of her yellow blood
Ooze to her skin and stagnate there to mud,
Cased like the centipede in saffron mail,
Or darker greeness of the scorpion's scale,
(For drawn from reptiles only may we trace
Congenial colours in that soul or face). . . .

It was the horrible evocation of a disordered fancy, but the writing of it gave Byron relief.

To his wife he addressed farewell stanzas colored by the imaginary drama, sobbing with heartbreak. The manuscript of them that was handed round by sympathizing friends was blotted with his tears. What wonder that when they were published sympathy for Lady Byron was turned to blame in certain quarters, and Madame de Staël sighed, "How gladly would I have been unhappy in Lady Byron's place!" Other verses, to Augusta, were wisely kept from the public.

The notoriety of the separation, however, made living in England impossible for Byron. None but his intimate friends received him, and everywhere he was spoken of with abhorrence. At distant Newstead the family portents had rumbled warning in an earthquake that shook the abbey. Ay, Byron had come to his fall. Like his little pagod, fretting in exile on a rocky island lost between two continents, he too must forsake the land of his triumphs. London; 1812, his *annus mirabilis!* How long ago it seemed. And now for him as for that other, with whom for a brief season he had been on every man's lip — the bitterness of exile.

While he was deep in the separation proceedings and with the bailiffs quartered in the house, he received a letter signed *E. Trefusis.*

XV

CLARE IN SEARCH OF ROMANCE

ONE of the first to reach out a lean hand toward the money left by Sir Bysshe to his heirs was none other than the author of *Political Justice*. The old baronet had done his duty by everyone, not omitting his bastards, honorably mentioned in his will; but he made no provision for meritorious charity. Thus, he left no reference to William Godwin, whose book he probably had never read and would have anathematized as immoral if he had. He was not, moreover, of those who believed that the superfluities of wealth should be put at the disposal of indigent genius according to the creed of the same Mr. Godwin. However, Sir Bysshe did specify his grandson Percy Bysshe Shelley as one of his beneficiaries, and here is where William Godwin entered his claim. Though still unreconciled to his disciple for having too literally put his theories into practice, he did not scruple to make his wants known in arrogant letters that insulted while they begged. But such procedure was not unphilosophical. He condemned the giver, though he respected the gifts that kept the firm of Godwin and Company on its feet for yet a while and gave to William Godwin the leisure for sublime speculation. From those heights he could stoop to exclaim: "How beautiful is Shelley, — what a pity he is so wicked!"

Sir Bysshe had left a large fortune both in lands and in money, amassed during a long life of miserliness. Besides the ready cash accounted for, nearly thirteen thousand pounds in bank notes were found sewed in the lining of his dressing gown, stuffed in his couch, and concealed in the bindings of his books, otherwise unmolested. According to his will, on the death of his son Timothy, his grandson Percy Bysshe Shelley should succeed to fortune and estates. But Shelley was too hard pressed for the want of a shilling to lay plans for the future, a future which to him, obsessed by the thought of early death, meant at the utmost some ten years of life. He renounced his interest under Sir Bysshe's will, therefore, and agreed to sell his claims in favor of his young brother John for the immediate sum of £7400 with which to discharge pressing obligations, and an income of a thousand pounds a year for as long as he and his father lived. Shelley's agreement was "nutts" to Sir Timothy, who had long been endeavoring to make such terms with the scapegoat of the family for the benefit of his favorite John. Whitton gladly gave his approval and the deed was done.

A thousand pounds a year was little enough when compared with Sir Timothy's income, but it meant wealth and freedom to Shelley and Mary after the poverty and persecution of that bailiff-haunted winter. They might even be welcomed at Skinner Street instead of having to depend for news on stealthy messages delivered by Fanny and the fence-straddling kindnessess of Charles Clairmont. Shelley would not have to undergo again the humiliation of borrowing from his "deserted wife," while listening to her increasingly bitter reproaches.

Harriet, with Godwin, was among the first to be thought of by Shelley. Besides two hundred pounds which he gave her for present needs, he arranged that she receive two hundred pounds annually from his income. With the like sum provided by Mr. Westbrook, she had enough for her support. As yet she had not signed the separation papers, nor did she seem disposed to do so. Eliza, standing craftily by, withheld the pen.

In spite of overtures, the door of Skinner Street remained obstinately shut to Shelley and Mary, Mr. Godwin considering his honor not yet sufficiently medicined. The young pair, with other concerns on their minds besides the sensitiveness of Mr. Godwin, hoped that time would help to make him see what the pure light of philosophy had not effected. As the months passed, they found their love for each other increasing under the world's censure. Compelled as they were by the ostracism of erstwhile friends to depend almost solely upon themselves, they were all-sufficient and found in each other

treasures inexhaustible.   Never had Shelley enjoyed such happiness in communion with another being.   It was something he
had sought and never found in Harriet, not even during those
days in Wales when, in his first experience of physical rapture,
he had deceived himself into spiritual ecstasy.   Mary was
everything to him — wife, companion, guide.   He saw in her
the incarnation of the Ideal.

Mary, for her part, kept up with him bravely.   Though well
read and of a scholarly mind, she had neither his learning nor
his imagination; neither had she his patient sympathy with
all weak and suffering things.   She could not enter into his
humoring of Clare when, a prey to nerves, she saw ghosts and
had to be sat up with and comforted for hours before she
could be made to go to bed.   When anything weighed upon
her mind she would go to her mother's square tombstone in
St. Pancras's churchyard, and under the weeping willow read
her father's *Essay on Sepulchres*.   She could not understand,
nor perhaps did Shelley, that Clare, her ardent temper excited by their love, was in her way groping for life.

In February of 1815 Mary gave birth to a seven-months
girl child so weak and puny that it was not expected to live.
It clung to life, however, and Mary and Shelley began to build
dreams of its future.   Mary nursed it, happy in her motherhood.   Clare and Shelley went out to buy a cradle and find
new lodgings.   Hogg came to pay his compliments and talked
so much that Mary was obliged to go to bed at six.   The frail
babe gained strength, almost miraculously; but one morning,
hardly two weeks after it had come into the world, it quietly
slipped out of it in its sleep, and Mary awoke to find the little
body cold beside her.   Hogg, the comforter, was sent for at
once; again his sprightliness brought no solace.   "Talk.   A
miserable day," Mary recorded with Godwinian terseness.
But she felt the loss of Shelley's child, the more, perhaps, because the other, his *wife*, had borne him two children, one of
them an heir.   "I was a mother and am so no longer" — the
thought shadowed her every act for days while she worked at
her netting or tried to find refuge in study.   The morbid self-
absorption that she had inherited from her Irish mother was
stronger in her than her father's calm detachment.   "Dream

that my little baby came to life again; that it had only been cold, and that we rubbed it before the fire and it lived. Awake and find no baby."

During these moods even Shelley was neglected, and he pined at finding himself shut out. There had been other times when the completeness of their happiness was marred by imperfect understanding, but those were shifting clouds that only for a moment hid the face of the sun. Mary was the body of his ideal; he could not find such another elsewhere. "Content yourself with one great affection . . ." he admonished himself in moments of doubt, "let the rest of mankind be the subject of your benevolence."

With financial worries in abeyance, Shelley and Mary began to look for a more permanent home. London, associated with creditors and bailiffs, had become intolerable. Besides, summer was approaching, and Shelley, who had been ailing throughout the winter, decided to remove to the country. He had been visiting the hospitals with his cousin Grove to gain practical experience in his work with the poor and needy, and the suffering he witnessed affected his impressible nature. By the time he set out with Mary — and without Clare, to her relief — for the Devonshire countryside, he was certain he was dying of consumption. Spasmś and a constant pain in his lungs convinced him that he would not live a year, and it was in a deep depression of spirit that he reflected on his state — not because he did not wish to die, for the thought of death had never ceased to shadow him, but because he had done so little with his life. Everything he had touched had crumbled in his hand. Now, even his present happiness, diminished by uneasiness for Harriet and his children, was further menaced by ill-health.

He and Mary did not stay long in Devon. Peacock had settled for the summer in Marlow, whereupon Shelley took a house at Bishopsgate, east of Windsor Park, at no great distance from him. In spite of fluctuations of sentiment toward Peacock, Shelley enjoyed his company, rich in all manner of classical association. He admired the scholar and the poet, mistrusted his pleasure-loving habits, and resented his partisanship of Harriet. Peacock did not like Mary, while he admitted her "intellectual attractions"; he felt that Shelley had made a mistake in forsaking Harriet for her, and he implied, though he did not express, his feelings.   His attitude did not endear him to Mary, who thought him calculating and cold, but she would not allow her personal prejudices to make any difference in the companionship of the two men.

Through the summer, autumn, and winter of 1815 Shelley and Peacock were almost constantly together, reading or sailing paper boats in the near-by river.   Under his friend's hedonistic régime, Shelley abandoned his diet of bread, tea, and lemonade, and for the first time in his life, perhaps, was wholesomely fed.   "Three mutton chops, well peppered," Peacock maintained, would have rid Shelley of his morbid preoccupations.   They were his own favorite food, and no one could have said of him that he suffered from melancholy.   He took life as he found it, poetized when the muse smiled, and laid by a store of sardonic notes when he saw that mortals were such fools indeed as Puck thought them.   The Bracknell experiences, his friends' emotional tangles, their eccentricities, were all finding new life in *Headlong Hall,* the satirical novel in which he was then engaged.

Shelley too felt a resurgence of creativeness.   He was never so happy as when he could be close to nature, and the bordering woodland of Windsor Park saw him often with his tattered notebook — alone then, for he found himself only in solitude.   Here his first perfect poetic work was conceived and written.   No discordance now, no frantic "yells" against Intolerance were suffered to jar upon the pure music of his verse.   It soared, assured and unimpeded, in the autumnal calm that was its inspiration.   The life of the deepening year had entered him; he was one with it in a magic of empathy in which self was transformed into the thing that possessed him. There was no objective writing for him.   He felt, he breathed, he was his poetry.

Like a prelude to *Alastor, A Summer-Evening Church-Yard* set the mood.   Shelley, Peacock, Mary, and Charles Clairmont had taken a boating excursion up the Thames, along the alder- and willow-bordered reaches, to Lechlade.   In the hush of a September sunset the church, with its small city of the dead, stirred the chords of Shelley's death-haunted soul; he sang, and his song was an elegy. The languid day, the silence and the twilight, the moveless strings of the church-tower ivy, are held in the deathlike spell, wherein nothing lives but death itself. Only there where the dead sleep in their sepulchres,

> . . . a thrilling sound,
> Half sense, half thought, among the darkness stirs,
>   Breathed from their wormy beds all living things around,
> And mingling with the still night and mute sky
> Its awful hush is felt inaudibly.

Terror is not in this vision of death. It is solemnized, and made as serene as the night.

> Here could I hope, like some inquiring child
>   Sporting on graves, that death did hide from human sight
> Sweet secrets, or beside its breathless sleep
> That loveliest dreams perpetual watch did keep.

He returned to Bishopsgate to find Windsor Forest in sombre autumn leaf, as if to harmonize with his mood. His life so brief, and, as he thought, so soon to end, came to him with the sequence of a dream. The allegory at once became reality, and as the last leaves of the oak and elm crackled under his tread, he saw his own life spent with the dying year. It was no grim death, but a gentle euthanasia, the closing of a life day, under the shadow of Alastor, the spirit of solitude. The poem was a spiritual biography.

A young and pure idealist set out in quest of beauty, and wandered far, through the enchanted east to Cashmire, where

> . . . a vision on his sleep
> There came, a dream of hopes that never yet
> Had flushed his cheek. He dreamed a veilèd maid
> Sate near him, talking in low solemn tones.
> Her voice was like the voice of his own soul
> Heard in the calm of thought. . . .
> Knowledge and truth and virtue were her theme,
> And lofty hopes of divine liberty,
> Thoughts the most dear to him, and poesy,
> Herself a poet.

Moved by her rapturous message, the body of the vision kindled, and its flame enveloped the poet with love. Then night engulfed her and roused him to the shock of his loss and the sense that now he could not live without the ideal.

> . . . As an eagle grasped
> In folds of the green serpent, feels her breast
> Burn with the poison, and precipitates
> Through night and day, tempest, and calm and cloud.
> . . . Thus driven
> By the bright shadow of that lovely dream,

the poet sped through the desolate darkness. Now hopeful, now despairing, "his scattered hair sered by the autumn of strange suffering," singing dirges in the wind, his body worn and life "burning secretly from his dark eyes alone," he paused at length upon the lone Chorasmian shore, where he embarked on a shallop "to meet lone Death on the drear ocean's waste." Through weirdly beautiful countries he journeyed, amid winding caverns, down rushing cataracts, the frail boat bearing him onward as he cried out his longing for that ideal beatitude that was ever before, and ever unattained. In a golden dell, he would have paused to deck his withered hair with flowers, "but on his heart its solitude returned," and on he went, in ever more hopeless pursuit. In a Dantean forest, where

> The children of the autumnal whirlwind bore,
> In wanton sport, those bright leaves, whose decay,
> Red, yellow, or ethereally pale,
> Rivals the pride of summer,

he died, prematurely old, without having found the vision that in his dream had captured him.

Alastor was but the first stanza of a poem which he was to continue in the *Hymn to Intellectual Beauty,* and *Epipsychidion,* even as *Queen Mab* had sounded a theme later to go through grander variations in *The Revolt of Islam* and *Prometheus Unbound.*

With *Alastor,* Shelley, while writing the Poet's death, emerged to poetic life. A new voice sounded over the land, and the universe, under its word, put on garments of wonder, though England would not hear and her eyes remained obstinately blind to the renascence taking place about her. Byron's Murray, who was sent a copy of the poem for publication, rejected it, perhaps without even consulting his back-shop synod. Discouraged, Shelley published it at his own expense with a few shorter pieces, limiting the issue to two hundred and fifty copies, most of which remained as dead stock on his hands for years. The mighty critics did not deign to notice the poem, but so devious are the ways of literary chance that a copy reached none other than Sir Timothy Shelley, who "reviewed" it for his faithful Whitton. "P. B. has published a poem with some fragments," he wrote, "somewhat in his usual style, not altogether free from former sentiments, and wants to find out one person on earth the Prototype of himself." Unlike the rest of the world he had at least read the poem, though it fell without meaning on his never-powerful mind.

By a stranger chance still, *Alastor* descended upon the persecuted and prosecuted misanthrope at 13 Piccadilly Terrace, introduced by no less a sponsor than Clare Clairmont. How did Byron meet her during the storm of his separation, and how came Shelley's poetry to be discussed by them? The key lay in the letter signed "E. Trefusis" that had come to Byron among bills and other unpleasant correspondence. "I tremble with fear at the fate of this letter . . ." began E. Trefusis. "There are cases where virtue may stoop to the garb of folly; it is for the piercing eye of genius to discover her disguise. . . . Mine is a delicate case; my feet are on the edge of a precipice; Hope flying on forward wings beckons me to follow her, and rather than resign this cherished creature, I jump through at the peril of my life." Who was this E. Trefusis, eager to break her neck in following a winged hope? And what insane hope was it? Byron did not have long to ponder. "It may seem a strange assertion, but it is not the less true that I place my happiness in your hands. . . . If a woman, whose reputation has as yet remained unstained, if without either guardian or husband to control she should throw herself upon your mercy, if with a beating heart she should confess the love she had borne you many years, if she should secure you secresy [*sic*] and safety, if she should return your kindness with fond affection and unbounded devotion, could you betray her, or would you be silent as the grave?" The case was clear. Another fair incognita was throwing herself at Byron. By her writing she was young, innocent, — else she could never have been so bold, — inflamed by the reading of romances whose style she had captured to perfection, and reckless to admiration. "I am not given to many words [!]" the lengthy offer concluded. "Either you will or you will not. Do not decide hastily, and yet I must entreat your letter without delay."

The situation was intriguing, yet dangerous. Perhaps, too, Byron, as in the case of Caroline Lamb, despised a mistress who took the initiative — and such an initiative. The offer could not have been more brutal had the woman come to his door as they did in the French romances, naked under a cloak. He decided to be *silent as the grave*, trusting the fair one would pursue her winged hope elsewhere.

Not long afterwards another letter, this time bearing the initials "G. C. B.," requested Lord Byron to state whether seven o'clock of a Sunday evening would be convenient for him to receive a lady who had business of peculiar importance to impart. She desired to be admitted alone and with the utmost privacy. Though the initials differed from the name in the first letter, the hand was the hand of E. Trefusis. This time, Byron, caught perhaps when he was weary of conjugating the verb *ennuyer* in the present tense, answered his unknown correspondent. "Lord Byron is not aware of any 'importance' which can be attached by any person to an interview, etc. . . ." He would, however, be at home at the hour mentioned.

The mysterious lady presented herself at Piccadilly Terrace, but the servants would not admit her. Lord Byron was out of town, they said. Undeterred, she called again, and again was turned away. "Perhaps the kindest favour I can confer on you is to make my letter short and my demands slight," she wrote him once more, launching inconsistently upon an interminable epistle. She wished to go on the stage and desired Lord Byron, as a member of Drury Lane, to obtain advice for her on what course to follow. "My style is harsh and my sentiments ungracious," she rambled on. "Will you attribute this to my little intercourse with the world; to the entire seclusion of my life, and to the ill-humour I feel for everything by which I am surrounded? Remember how many live and die blamed and despised, whose meed should have been praise? . . . It is not the sparkling cup which should tempt you but the silent and capacious bowl. . . . My actions are not the result of momentary temptation, the impulses of passion. . . ." This time "E. Trefusis G. C. B." signed her name, Clare Clairmont; she had entered into her life of the heroine of romance.

Byron, for once the cautious Scot in affairs of the heart, passed the silent and capacious bowl to his friend Kinnaird, contenting himself with the sparkling cup the "left-handed *Mrs.*" Kinnaird sent round at their brandy parties. He was weary of everything and had no heart for adventure. Out of patience with the young hussy who flung herself at his neck, he would gladly have been rid of her epistolary persecution, and told Kinnaird everything in the hope of his releasing him. It was not to be. Miss Clairmont was too tender of her name, and since she could not use another pseudonym for fear of what Kinnaird might think, she preferred not to see him at all. Besides, she did not now know whether she should adopt a theatrical career or a literary life. Would Byron help her decide? She had written half a novel which she wished to submit to him for criticism. "Shelley used frequently to express a good opinion of my literary talents; but his affection might blind him, or perhaps he was afraid to say rude things."

Somehow the correspondence had taken a literary turn. Shelley, who had evidently been mentioned previously, though he as well as Mary was innocent of the slightest suspicion of what was going on between Clare and Lord Byron, suddenly appeared prominently in the letters, a blameless go-between in the girl's intrigue. She wrote patronizingly of him and of his work, from such heights of infallibility as would have done credit to the Edinburgh reviewers. "The 'Demon of the World' is an extract from the poem entitled *Queen Mab*. The latter was composed at the early age of twenty; although it bears marks of genius, yet the style is so unpoetical and unpolished that I could never admire it. . . . *Alastor* is a most evident proof of improvement; but I think his merit lies in translation. . . . If you think ill of his compositions I hope you will speak; he may improve by your remarks." Then suddenly, as if stricken by her own inadequacy, "Do you know," she said, "from the fear I entertain of your believing me mad, I endeavour to write as short and laconic sentences as I can. . . ."

She was indeed mad, with the madness of her exigent youth. Since the summer when Mary and Shelley had left London for the country, she had been living away from them, now at Skinner Street, until the shrewish tongue of her mother drove her away, now as governess with some private family. Her knowledge of foreign languages easily fitted her for her position; her impatience with any form of confinement made her occupation a torture. At the time of her correspondence with Byron she gave as her address 13 Arabella Row, Pimlico.

Ever since she had left home on the morning of Shelley's elopement, Clare had been a prey to the suggestions of her imagination. She was very fond of Shelley. From the first she had labored to make herself interesting to him, much to the annoyance of Mary, who, though striving with Godwinian equableness to be sympathetic, found her patience exhausted by the trying girl. Many a night when she had had to retire early for her health, Clare stayed up late with Shelley, who made matters worse by keying up the girl's overwrought nerves with ghost stories or trying on her the hypnotic power of his eyes. There would be shrieks and fainting spells, and then Clare would be conducted to rest. No sooner would Shelley be settled in his bed than cries from Clare's room would bring him to his feet as he dashed to the girl's help. Now her pillow had unaccountably flown from her bed and settled itself on a chair; now she was certain there was a ghost in the room; again she could not sleep because the look in Shelley's eyes came back to her and filled her with terror. After doing his best to soothe her he would bring her to Mary, whose common sense would prove more potent than his sympathy. The innocent Shelley would then leave the two women together and snatch a few hours of sleep. Clare's cries always came at night after Shelley had gone to bed. She would then groan and sob so loud that, after listening for an hour or two, he would be forced to get up to comfort her. Such behavior would have taught a less simple student of the human mind that what Clare desired, consciously or unconsciously, was to separate Shelley from Mary for the night. No such suspicion entered Shelley's head, though Mary, better acquainted with Clare's ways, thought her own thoughts, as her diary sometimes hinted.

The proximity of two young people very much in love, and living in a relation condemned by society, worked disastrously on Clare's undisciplined mind. To her they were not so much a man and woman practising their ideas of what constitutes true marriage, and practising them with well-nigh religious fervor, as two characters in a novel, living their thrilling experiences in the centre of a social storm. They were interesting and they were to be emulated. Although like every weaker mind that came in contact with Shelley's hers was colored by his opinions, she reflected them only as in a mirror. Her words were echoes of his own, stressing, like all echoes, the final utterance. She became an ardent anti-matrimonialist. Unlike Mary, however, she did not become so through conviction of what, under the circumstances, was right. Neither was she like Harriet, who had adopted Shelley's opinions through love. Clare saw in them a means toward an end. She wanted freedom and excitement. Since no one had so far offered himself as the guide to the great adventure, she took the helm of her own career. Too much in love with the adventure itself, she cared not whether she rode toward happiness or destruction.

Like everyone else in London she heard of the Byron separation. As it was, her fancy, like every other young girl's, had been inflamed by the Byronic myth. Even the little invalid Elizabeth Barrett had thought for a time to disguise herself as a page and follow him secretly, like the heroine of *Lara*. Clare's was a more practical nature — she had not lived her most impressionable years near Godwin for nothing. Now that Byron was in disfavor with the world and his wife, now when, of all times, he needed someone to cheer him, she must approach him. And she did, although she could have chosen no surer way of rousing the contempt of the libertine, who liked his women chaste. Her name, too, when she gave it at last, must have come as an unpleasant shock to one so ridden

as Byron with belief in omens. Clairmont . . . Clermont.
. . . "One thing I am afraid of," Clare wrote to him. "You
rather dislike me." She was undeterred, however. Even if
his lordship delayed in accepting her offer, he had not said
no. He must be informed at once that she did not believe in
the ties of marriage, or those of any other kind. Quoting a
sonnet of Dante's in which the poet speaks of the happy state
when familiarity rouses a keener desire for the loved one's
company, the canny minx wished that God had bestowed that
desire upon married people, "since he has imposed such an evil
on the world. . . . Do you remember his inscription over
the gate of Hell — *Lasciate ogni speranza voi ch'entrate?* I
think it a most admirable description of marriage. The subject makes me prolix. I can never resist the temptation of
throwing a pebble at it as I pass by." Certainly the moment
for throwing pebbles was well chosen.

Byron, the quick to yield, whose heart always alighted on
the nearest perch, still wavered before Clare's assaults. She
did not desist, however, for Hope on forward wings beckoned,
in spite of everything, with greater promise than before. A
man who hesitates is lost: so much she had learned of homely
wisdom. She envisioned Byron's fall. Again she wrote, but
with becoming impersonality and chiefly about her "production," a piece of propaganda literature which "to a common
reader . . . would appear to be written as a warning to young
people against extraordinary opinions . . . but Atheists might
see and understand my meaning." The droll gravity of the
situation must have brought a smile to Byron's face. Here
was a mad young girl turning heaven and earth, descending
to Dante's hell, even trotting out atheism, that *bête-noir* of all
good Englishmen, for his sake. This time he answered her,
bidding her "write short" and to consider well whether it were
not fancy that made her cherish the illusion that she loved him.
On the whole it was an encouraging letter, and Clare took the
leap. "I do not expect you to love me," she put him at his
ease. "I am not worthy of your love. . . . I may appear to
you imprudent, vicious; my opinions detestable, my theory
depraved; but one thing, at least, time shall show you that I
love gently and with affection, that I am incapable of anything

approaching to the feeling of revenge or malice. I do assure you your future will shall be mine, and every thing you shall do or say I shall not question."

She would have him know by implication that she was unlike a certain cold, unrelenting, revengeful woman who was now making him suffer. She was willing to give herself up to him, and whatever his future actions, she would be a model of generosity and patience. Let him take her and leave her: never would she seek to hold him against his will. And then, with a brazenness that would have given a harlot pause, the eighteen-year-old girl in the rashness of her innocence made an assignation. "Have you then any objection to the following plan? On Thursday Evening we may go out of town together by some stage or mail about the distance of ten or twelve miles. There we shall be free and unknown; we can return early the following morning. I have arranged everything here so that the slightest suspicion may not be excited."

She had returned to live with Mary and Shelley, but fearing that they would have advised against the step she was about to take, she kept it secret from them. As it was, they had a new interest in life, for in January Mary had given birth to a son whom they named William in honor of Godwin. The pretty little blue-eyed babe made up to Mary for the infant daughter she had lost, and to Shelley for his two children reared under the loathsome guidance of Eliza. He had asked to keep Ianthe after Harriet demanded an increased allowance for her and the boy, but she had refused. She did not approve of Shelley's religious opinions, she said, and would not have Ianthe brought up under his pernicious doctrines. The Westbrooks had again threatened to bring a case at court, this time for the maintenance of the two infants, and they went so far as to draw Sir Timothy into the conflict. Mr. Whitton sent warnings from his legal sanctum, "It is not the money but the Company in which you may be placed . . ." warnings which the friend of the Duke of Norfolk took very much to heart. The matter was for the moment at ebb tide.

The proposed assignation between Clare and Byron was postponed at his request to Saturday, when he suggested that she come to him at Piccadilly Terrace. The thought of giving herself to him in his own home frightened her, and she told him why. "Now pray read this letter entirely," she pleaded, as she prepared to cover every inch of the paper. "You have already been extremely kind . . . it will cost you little to complete my wishes which are decidedly averse to the appointment being kept at your house." The servants might come upon them, unexpected visitors arrive. "Besides, however you might assure me to the contrary . . . yet I could not help feeling that we were liable to interruption, a feeling which would entirely destroy my happiness, since there is no pleasure in love without security. . . ." A Ninon, aged in intrigue, could not have generalized so positively as this young girl about to surrender to her first lover. "Do not delay our meeting after Saturday — I cannot endure the suspense. . . . On Saturday a few moments may tell you more than you yet know. Till then I am content that you should believe me vicious and depraved. . . . May I request you to bring my letters . . . that they may be committed to the flames?"

Before that Saturday Clare had gazed upon "the wild originality" of the countenance that had been lighting her nights of rash dreaming. She had sung to him in the wilderness of his life. That night, however, came the consummation of her dearest wishes. Besides the hearth, together, they may have made a holocaust of her letters, as she had requested; after Byron's death, however, copies of them were found, carefully preserved. He took her, without love. Before Annabella's implacability he needed someone to assure him that the Byron spell was not gone, that there were women, generous and loving, who found him no monster of iniquity, but a man. The following day, the twenty-first of April, he signed the papers that parted him forever from his wife. It was Sunday. She was probably attending her devotions; there were sins she had to expiate, oaths forgotten, vows unkept. On the margin of the document he wrote a message for her eyes: —

> A year ago you swore, fond she!
> "To love, to honour," and so forth:
> Such was the vow you pledged to me,
> And here 's exactly what 't is worth.

Annabella endorsed the document the subsequent day. Back with her parents, she tried to find comfort in Byron's child; it was not enough. Heart-hungry, she needed someone other than a helpless baby to fill the void left by its father. Annabella was not essentially a maternal woman. As a child she had despised dolls and turned to books; now, at the age of twenty-three, she found herself with an infant by a man she still loved, but never could forgive. The youth of her life lay at her feet, a garment briefly worn, to be laid aside as unbecoming the withering old age that had come upon her. What was she without Byron, that storm that had come over her youth and blighted everything in its way — love, laughter, the ability to feel? All that was left her of him, Ada, she almost hated. He had called the infant "an implement of torture" the first time he had seen her. An implement of torture it was to her, reminding her hourly of Byron, of their one dreadful year together, and of his past — a past more alive than the present in the nearness of Augusta, whom she had not been able to dismiss from her life. Like another creature of his blood, Byron had left his sister to her care. Annabella felt for her poor, weak charge the maternal devotion which Ada failed to inspire. It was as if Augusta had been engendered by Byron on her soul, as Ada on her body. In a complexity of emotions unusual with her, in other things so cold, Annabella, loved, hated, pitied, despised, and envied the flighty being who had yet possessed herself forever of Byron's heart and soul. The letter he sent her, Annabella, from Mivart's Hotel on Easter Sunday, after Augusta had come to take leave of him, was a series of heart-wrung cries of love for her and sorrow at the parting the scandal had forced upon them. He had no word of kindness for Annabella — only reproach and the reiterated cry, "Be kind to her. . . . Be kind to her and hers . . . be kind to her . . ." like the rhythmic surging of blood from an open wound. It was his own blood pulsing from the emptiness the severing of Augusta from his life had left. The letter was all disjointed phrases and dashes; he wrote in a fever.

" 'More last words' — not many — and such as you will attend to — answer I do not expect — nor does it import —

but you will hear me. — I have just parted from Augusta — almost the last being you had left me to part with — and the only unshattered tie of my existence — wherever I may go — and I am going far — you and I can never meet again in this world —   Let this content or atone. — If any accident occurs to me — be kind to *her*. . . . I say therefore — be kind to her and hers — for never has she acted or spoken otherwise towards you — she has ever been your friend — this may seem valueless to one who has now so many: — be kind to her — however — and recollect that though it may be advantage to you to have lost your husband — it is sorrow to her to have the waters now — or the earth hereafter — between her and her brother. . . ."

In Piccadilly Terrace the house was dismantled and the furniture ready to go under the auctioneer's hammer. Byron was leaving England — forever, bankrupt in honor and fortune. But friends came to cheer his last days in London: Hobhouse, and Scrope Davies; old Rogers, who had not believed in any sinful relation between Lady Caroline and Byron, and was too pure in mind to lend credence to the current scandal; Kinnaird, with brandy and champagne and his left-handed spouse.

And Hunt called, fresh from the bursting-bubble popularity that came to him with the publication of his *Story of Rimini*. He arrived once soon after Coleridge, white-haired and dark-browed, with his great inward-gazing eyes, had been reciting *Kubla Khan* to him who had found the honey-dew of love as gall, and poison the milk of Paradise. Coleridge, after long years during which he had thought himself, the poet, dead, was having a volume published by Murray, through Byron's influence. The poems were chiefly the works of his youth. As long ago as 1801 he had written himself down as spent. "My imagination lies like a cold snuff on the circular rim of a brass candlestick, without even a stink of tallow to remind you that it was once clothed and mitred in flame. . . ." If he died, he had said to Godwin, let him write in his biography: "Wordsworth . . . by showing him what true poetry was . . . made him know that he himself was no Poet." By Wordsworth the candle, mitred in flame, had been quenched, leaving only the smoke of metaphysics over the glowing core.

On the twenty-third of April, 1816, Byron, with Hobhouse, Davies, and Polidori, his young physician whom the jealous Hob had nicknamed "Polly-Dolly," left for Dover. The carriage that had borne him and Annabella to Halnaby on their honeymoon, and which had later taken her alone to Kirkby, he left with her. In its place he, bankrupt though he was, bought a sumptuous vehicle, copied from Napoleon's. If he was going into exile, he would go in state. Among his traveling provisions, besides Kinnaird's champagne, he had a packet of Jewish Passover biscuits given to him by Nathan the musician. The unleavened bread of exile. . . . He would not moisten it with tears. Though he had lost Augusta and everything that would have made England dear, memory and freedom remained to him.

Since the boat at Dover was not leaving till the following day, he insisted on visiting the tomb of Charles Churchill, a poet who, like him, had "blazed the comet of a season." Hobhouse and Polidori accompanied him. In the old cemetery of St. Martin's Church, they came upon the grave being returfed by the diggers after years of neglect. On the headstone the epitaph, taken from one of Churchill's poems, was barely legible. "Life to the last enjoy'd, here Churchill lies." He had had thirty-three years of life. He had loved and hated and sung his hatreds in stinging satires, exalting independence of spirit and loathing hypocrisy. He had fought battles and won and lost, making, like Byron, many enemies and few friends. In the last battle, against death, in a foreign land, he was beaten. Pious friends bore the corpse across the Channel to Dover. Now he lay a handful of dust, under a grave sodded with new grass — a name, nay, not even a name to those who had the tending of his bones. "So soon, and so successless?" Without a word Byron stretched himself out upon the grass of the grave.

And Hobhouse made a note in his journal.

XVI

KEATS, LIBERTAS, AND HAYDON

On the second of February, 1815, while Charles Cowden Clarke was walking toward London to see his friend Leigh Hunt, recently out of the Horsemonger Lane Gaol, he was met on the road by John Keats, one of his father's former pupils, on the way to see him at Enfield. Glad of the meeting, the young man retraced his steps and walked toward the city with his friend. As they parted at the last field gate he shyly slipped into his hand a sonnet "Written on the Day that Mr. Leigh Hunt left Prison." It was the first indication Cowden Clarke had ever had that John Keats wrote poetry, though he had known him from the time when, as a child in petticoats, he had entered the seventeenth-century doorway of the Clarke school.

John Keats, the first-born of a love match, came into the world prematurely toward the end of October, 1795, in lodgings over his grandfather's livery stable, the Swan and the Hoop at Finsbury. His mother, Frances Jennings, a lively, coquettish, pretty, and very ardent woman, fell in love with Thomas Keats, her father's head ostler, and after a short courtship they were married, not at the little church of the parish, but at St. George's, Hanover Square, the prosperous Mr. Jennings wishing to show himself a fond and indulgent father before the little world of Finsbury Pavement. Mr. Richard Abbey, a tea merchant, staid, prosy, and not lacking in malice, although an amateur phrenologist was to describe him as possessing "a great piece of benevolence" sticking up on top of his forehead, wryly watched the grand doings. He had known Frances Jennings since her childhood. He had watched her growing into a pretty lass who did not scruple to show her uncommonly

handsome legs in foul weather, and he had been overly concerned about her chastity. With brother gossips he had been
both relieved and disappointed when the stocky Thomas
Keats carried off the prize. The birth of the first Keats child
after a full year of marriage put the Abbey mind at ease on a
certain score, though the fact that it was a seven-months
babe made him lay the cause to Mrs. Keats's imprudence.
But what could one expect of a young woman who was the
slave of her appetites?

For some unexplained reason Mr. Abbey had no love for
Thomas Keats. He was an honest young man, it is true, who
worked hard to advance himself, but after he married his
master's daughter he set himself up too ostentatiously as a
man of consequence. He kept a fine horse of his own which
he would ride on Sundays, he dressed well, and he had friends
of means with whom he would go to town for his liquor. That
was no way, thought Mr. Abbey, for a groom, even a head
groom, to behave. It was some satisfaction to his moral sense,
therefore, when one spring dawn Thomas Keats was found
dying opposite the Methodist Chapel in the City Road. He
had been dining out at Southgate with some friends and was
riding home in the dark when his horse threw him against the
iron railings near the church. He died the following day, leaving his wife with four children — three sons, the eldest of
whom, John, was not yet ten, and an infant daughter of nine
months.

Mrs. Keats married again before the year was out. The
boy John was then at Mr. Clarke's school learning his Latin
with the sons of small merchants and tradesmen in the red
brick schoolhouse, once the residence of a wealthy West India
trader with a taste for fine architecture. The child felt keenly
the domestic tragedy. He had been accustomed to his father's
visits; he loved him, and knew that Mr. Clarke thought well
of him. His stepfather, Mr. Rawlings, a clerk at Smith
Payson and Company's, made little impression upon him.
Perhaps he never met him, for shortly after her marriage his
wife left him. Mr. Abbey spoke sinisterly of drink and
degradation as the portion of the once comely Frances Jennings. He whispered of her having lived at Enfield as the wife

of a Jew called Abraham before she returned to her mother's house to die. Mr. Abbey's talk, fortunately, never reached the boy's ear. He had been devoted to his mother. It was told of him that as a small child he armed himself with a sword as she lay ill in bed and with a threatening face dared anyone to disturb her. He was fourteen when she died of consumption, and the world seemed suddenly empty. In grief and loneliness he crawled under the master's desk at school to hide himself with his sorrow. He was an orphan. George and Tom, his brothers, little Fanny, his sister, and he himself had no one in the world to care for them but their grandmother, and she was seventy-four years old. But the children were not left without provision. On Mr. Jennings's death, not long after his son-in-law's, his will disposed of a fortune of thirteen thousand pounds, a good part of which had been left in trust to his grandchildren.

Old Mrs. Jennings was now the only prop of the family. How was she to take care of four young children, one of whom, Tom, was weak and delicate? She knew too much of the disease that had killed her daughter not to watch with dread every ailment in the children. She felt the weight of her responsibility, and, knowing she had not long to live, called on her friend Richard Abbey and on Rowland Sandell, a merchant in whom she had confidence, to execute a deed in which she named them guardians of her grandchildren.

The first thing Mr. Abbey did was to take John Keats out of school within a year. He wished the boy to become a clerk at his wholesale tea house in Pancras Lane, but since he declared himself unfit, Mr. Abbey bound him apprentice to Mr. Hammond, a surgeon at Edmonton. Thus at fifteen John Keats was rudely shifted from the pleasant schoolhouse and its smiling countryside, and thrown upon the world to fend for himself. He was not cut off from the schoolmaster's son, however. Edmonton was only two miles from Enfield, so that four or five times a month, his work in the surgeon's office done, young Keats would walk, book in hand, to see Charles Cowden Clarke.

The young man had early been attracted to the winning, bright-faced boy who had left the nursery to be educated at his father's school. Except for the last year Keats had been an indifferent student, relishing a fight with boys bigger than himself better than his studies. Many 's the time he had been extricated from a scrape provoked usually by his unruly temper. Perhaps his lowly birth, which made even attendance at Mr. Clarke's school a great stride forward, rankled in his child's mind and fostered a pride inordinate in one so young. He never spoke of his family. When he lost his parents he let few guess his grief. Toward his two younger brothers, who followed him into the Enfield school, he had a devoted protectiveness, though both were taller than himself, and in and out of season he saw fit to lend them the aid of his fists. When adversaries failed he engaged in fisticuffs with George. During the last months at Enfield he went through his studies at top speed, to the amazement of his fellow students, who saw him carrying off the prizes, one, fit to make Mr. Abbey's heart leap, no less a treasure than a *Dictionary of Merchandise*.

At night when the other boys in the dormitory were asleep, he would lie awake listening to the dimmed strains of music coming from the parlor where Charles played Mozart and Haydn on the pianoforte. In the daytime he read during every moment of leisure, and when the school library was exhausted, Clarke lent him books out of his private shelves. Robertson's histories, Miss Edgeworth's works, books of travel and discovery — he read them all with equal zeal. Tooke's *Pantheon* and Lemprière's *Classical Dictionary*, once he discovered them, were seldom out of his hands. Greek mythology opened up a world of wonder and beauty which from those early days he longed to make his own. The pagan gods were not dead. Beings so real to him could not have vanished from the earth. Into the surgeon's room, and later the medical school, he carried his visions.

Young Clarke encouraged Keats's taste for books. He read aloud for him Spenser's *Epithalamion*, watching the expressive face light up at every happy phrase. One night he lent him the *Faerie Queene*, which the enchanted youth went through, Clarke would say, "as a young horse would go through a spring meadow — ramping!" What Clarke did not know was that the *Faerie Queene* had cast a charm over Keats, setting him

apart from other men.   For the first time he took up his pen
to write a poem.   Shyly and secretly, as if performing a
mystery, with the echoes of Spenser chiming in his head, he
wrote the things he heard.   It was wonderful to him that
words could be turned to music and that he should have the
power, feeble as yet, and imitative, but his nonetheless.   George
and Tom were shown the verses and they beamed with pride.
Now they could understand why the strange boy would vary
in his moods from gay to sad and sometimes hide away for
hours in what had seemed unreasonable melancholy.   He was
a poet.   There were those lines which he read in a voice
husky with emotion: —

> Now Morning from her orient chamber came,
> And her first footsteps touch'd a verdant hill;
> Crowning its lawny crest with amber flame,
> Silv'ring the untainted gushes of its rill. . . .

Those, and the verses that followed, were to them a miracle.
   A year before the expiration of his term with Hammond
Keats quarreled with him and went to London.   He was not
quite nineteen.   Mrs. Jennings had died, and Mr. Abbey,
sole guardian of the Keats children after Sandell had surrendered his interest, turned his thoughts to providing for
their future.   Fanny was still a child.   He took her into his
own home at Walthamstow.   George and Tom, both in their
teens, could be made useful in the countinghouse.   He called
them to London, therefore, and placed them in his office as
clerks.   So far, so good.   If John could be made to fit his
mould, Mr. Abbey's problem would be smoothly solved.
But John refused to fit either Mr. Abbey's or any other mould.
He had nearly completed his apprenticeship with the respectable surgeon of Edmonton, his premium had been paid
regularly, and here he was in London, still without a profession.
Was it so hard to pound powders and make plasters and hold
his master's horse?   Why had he quarreled with him, indeed,
raised his hand against Mr. Hammond?   Abbey disliked John
and would have broken his independent spirit.   There was no
occasion for it this time, however, for John quite docilely consented to continue his medical studies, and was entered at St.

Thomas's and Guy's hospitals as a student. Within a month he became a dresser.

Life was not unbearable, although after Edmonton he stifled in the dense London air and the crowded lodgings at Dean Street in the Borough. He was lonely. The urge to write poetry tormented him, the more because he knew his whole being was dedicated to it. He had to force himself to study. "The other day," he said to Clarke, who had come to live in London, "the other day . . . during the lecture, there came a sunbeam into the room and with it a whole troop of creatures floating in the ray; and I was off with them to Oberon and Fairyland." The spell of the *Faerie Queene* bound him forever. At night, in the hours after study, he wrote the thoughts of his teeming mind. Would he ever be among the great poets? George and Tom had faith in him. At times he almost believed in himself.

Soon he left Dean Street to live with three fellow students above a tallow chandler's shop in St. Thomas's. It was a large apartment, made possible by a union of their four purses. Besides the bedrooms it had a common sitting room provided with a window seat which soon became known as Keats's place. Whether reading, dreaming, or peering out of the windows, Keats was sure to be found there. One of the students divined his poetic ambitions. As he wrote verse himself, he showed some of it for criticism. Keats found nothing to praise and held his peace, but Stephens — later to make a fortune on a new ink — readily forgave him. He knew he could never aspire to the heights Keats reared before him, even though at times that creature of moods could stoop to fun and scribble light verse in other people's notebooks.

> Give me women, wine and snuff
> Until I cry out "hold, enough!"
> You may do so sans objection
> Till the day of resurrection;
> For bless my beard they aye shall be
> My beloved Trinity.

Stephens had found it one day, in Keats's hand, on the cover of his chemistry syllabus.

Keats at nineteen was hardly the gay rake his doggerel would have had one believe him. It is doubtful that he had had more than a bowing acquaintance with the women of whom he spoke so cavalierly, and as for wines, though he did enjoy a glass of claret, his duties, which required a level head and a steady hand, kept him from emulating Bacchus. Like the young blades of his day he took snuff. Occasionally he smoked a cigar.[1] Always he had before him the path he was to follow — not medicine, a course which life had somehow imposed upon him, but that other, the true road, leading to magic horizons.

He was no recluse, either, nor did he believe with the ascetic that one should shut one's eyes to the beauty that blossomed on the wayside. He enjoyed everything that was strong and healthy. He witnessed boxing matches. Once he attended a bearbaiting. Occasionally he went to the theatre, which he loved, watching the stage from the noisy gallery, the only accommodation his student's purse permitted. Lust for life intoxicated him. He would have thrown himself headlong into it, like his mother, whom he resembled. He would have loved with consuming intensity — a word and state of being that even so early obsessed him. Something which he felt to be a physical handicap checked him. Who could have loved John Keats, five feet high? For nature had played one of her capricious jokes. To a head which was to be likened to a study after the Greek masters, a face mobile and sensitive, and a fine, broad-shouldered torso, she had added the short legs of a dwarf. Women turned to look again at the striking youth who passed them in Cheapside, and wished him taller.

Had I a man's fair form,

he wrote in a moment of pain — then might he whisper love into a woman's ear. But who would listen to the declarations of "little John Keats"?

In Vauxhall Gardens he had seen a girl whose face lighted his nights like a moon. They had exchanged neither word nor sign, but their eyes had met, and the memory of that look

---

[1] Miss Lowell declares roundly in her *Keats* that the poet never smoked. In his letters, however, there is at least one definite statement, "Smoked a segar."

had disquieted his life. He could not keep his mind on his work; he could not sleep. No wonder he exhorted part in jest, but more in earnest,

> Fill for me a brimming bowl
> And let me in it drown my soul:
> But put therein some drug, designed
> To Banish Women from my mind.

It was not poetry, but one of those confessions that had to be made if only to oneself. Still indefinitely he sensed that for him to love was to destroy himself. There was the root of his fatal *intensity*. In the meantime, to appease the hunger of his body, for lack of a real woman's "honied roses" he sought those of the imagination.

> And when the moon her pallid face discloses,
> I'll gather some by spells and incantation.

They were poor substitutes, at best, but for his present peace they had to do.

George, tall and good-looking, had no such compromises to make. He easily made friends in London, the most assiduously visited of whom were the widow and children of a naval officer, the Wylies. Georgiana Wylie was only eleven when George saw her; nevertheless he knew that she was to be his wife. John was taken to meet the Wylies and he too fell under the witchery of that "Nymph of the downward smile and side-long glance" who so fascinated his brother. She was indeed a charming girl, pretty and fairylike and completely unspoiled. John Keats rejoiced in this "glorious human creature," for his brother's sake.

He soon made his own friends, however. Charles Cowden Clarke, the day he went to see Hunt, showed him the poetical tribute of his young friend. Hunt was delighted. It was pleasant to be greeted back into the world by the admiration of the aspiring young who looked upon one as a hero and a martyr.

> What though, for showing truth to flatter'd state
> Kind Hunt was shut in prison, yet has he
> In his immortal spirit, been as free
> As the sky-searching lark. . . .

Kind Hunt, immortal spirit. . . .   His years in prison almost
seemed well spent in the face of such praise.   When, a few
months later, Clarke brought him a handful of Keats's verses,
Hunt read them with pleasure, selected a sonnet, to Solitude,
for publication, and invited Clarke to bring the poet to Hampstead.

The fifth of May, 1816, was memorable to Keats.   His
sonnet appeared in print in the *Examiner* over his initials,
"J. K."   Leigh Hunt had found it worthy to come out with
his own work — Leigh Hunt, who, besides being a poet, was a
powerful critic.   Before so happy a triumph how could Keats
feel satisfaction in his study of medicine?   What wonder that
during the anatomy lectures he drew flowers in his notebooks,
as if he needed those unconscious signposts to point his true
way, the way to poetry!   Unhappily Mr. Abbey had renewed
his term at St. Thomas's and Guy's.   Soon Keats would be
getting his diploma to practise, and then —   For the present
he gave every spare moment to poetry.   The time might come
when he could give all.

Clarke brought the young worshiper to Hunt and the two
became fast friends.   For Keats it was like being transported
to the abode of the immortals when he found himself in Hunt's
tiny cottage in the Vale of Health in Hampstead.   The house
itself charmed him with its books, paintings, busts, and the
piano.   Wherever he turned he saw something to capture the
imagination.   He felt at home.   Here, soothed by the peace of
the gentle countryside, in surroundings that harbored all the
arts, here was his true abode.   After the first visit he came
often, and Hunt was happy to welcome his young admirer.
Even Marianne, the hard to please, yielded to one who, besides being a thoroughly pleasant companion for her husband,
had the makings of a great poet.   Libertas, Keats called him
who had worn the chain for Freedom's sake, and, punning
upon his name, Hunt called him Junkets.

Leigh Hunt was enjoying a certain fame in the year 1816.
Together with the halo of his recent martyrdom he wore the
poetic laurel won him by the *Story of Rimini*, which had been
published in January.   He had written most of it in prison,
relying for his local color on Lord Byron's gifts of travel books,

combined with reminiscences of his beloved Hampstead. His release brought on an unavoidable interruption. After two years in prison it was hard for him to readjust himself to the cares and responsibilities of a free life. On the whole the period of confinement had been pleasant. He had had his treasures about him, his friends had made regular and munificent pilgrimages, and he had had more leisure for his writing than ever before. The choice spirits of the day had visited him, some from curiosity, some from a sense of duty; he was a notable figure. Thrown back among the free, he became like thousands of others but for his quickly fading martyr's crown. Worse, he had to bestir himself to earn a livelihood, for while friends will be reaching into their breeches' pockets when one is in prison, they inconsiderately leave one to make the best shift of things in a harsh and competitive free world. Wordsworth sent a fine set of his works, it's true, and Byron, more practical, supplied the table with a few brace of partridge; Cowden Clarke still contributed his baskets of fruit and vegetables. But with a wife and hungry children the supply had to be constant.

After a few trying months, however, Leigh Hunt resumed his pre-prison routine, wrote his regular articles, and set to work on the last lap of the *Story of Rimini*. By October of the previous year he had done enough of it to show Byron a nearly completed tale.

"I will back you as a bard against half the fellows on whom you have thrown away much good criticism and eulogy," his lordship characteristically encouraged. Better, he recommended the manuscript to Murray. "I think it the *safest* thing you ever engaged in," he heartened his publisher. Murray, however, preferred to hold at least a financial reservation. Instead of the four hundred and fifty pounds asked by Hunt for the first edition, he offered him fifty. Hunt, however, was in no position to stand by his price. He accepted, and wrote a dedication to Byron.

The poem had an immediate vogue. Young ladies, to whose tender passions it was chiefly addressed, read it and wept. Samuel Rogers quoted it — with what innuendoes it is not known — at his fashionable breakfasts. The critics damned it. The *Quarterly Review,* while dealing superficially with the poem, stabbed mercilessly at the poet — for the dedication. "We never, in so few lines, saw so many clear marks of the vulgar impatience of a low man, conscious and ashamed of his wretched vanity, and labouring with coarse flippancy, to scramble over the bounds of birth . . . and fidget himself into the *stout-heartedness* of being familiar with a Lord." And all because Hunt had addressed his lordship as Byron, simply.

The noble lord, then in the thick of his troubles, had still the heart to think of his fosterling and would have had Moore say a good word for it in the *Edinburgh.* Careful for his own laurels, Moore fought shy of the task. "With respect to Hunt's poem, though it is, I own, full of beauties . . . I really could not undertake to praise it *seriously.* There is so much of the *quizzible* in all he writes, that I never can put on the proper pathetic face in reading him."

Ungracious though the refusal was, Tom Moore nevertheless struck at the core of Hunt's chief fault as a poet. Owing to a peculiar weakness in his character, Leigh Hunt robbed of strength everything he treated and converted it to prettiness. He was incapable of the majestic sweep. The hard chisel stroke of the sculptor was not his; he preferred, rather, the effects of the clay modeler. In his hands the mighty relief of Dante's Francesca da Rimini story, hewn with the strength of a titan, became rococo frippery wound with fruits and flowers that crowded the essential design till it became insignificant. He took a cathedral frieze and tricked it to the uses of a ladies' embroidery circle.

Hunt's style, however, came not to him by accident. It was his literary manifesto against the enslavement of classicism. Poetical language, he felt, held no longer any meaning for the emotions; it had become a pattern through the uses and abuses of Pope and Dryden. For poetry, to be great and moving, to reach the heart and elevate the spirit, had to make use of the vital tongue, the common language which Shakespeare had not been afraid to employ in his day, the speech that is kept alive by the fireside and in the streets. Hence readers of the *Story of Rimini,* instead of the rolling poetic

numbers to which they had been accustomed, found themselves
regaled with pedestrian couplets that went their storytelling
way without knocking against any classical stumblingblocks: —

> The prince, at this, would bend on her an eye
> Cordial enough and kiss her tenderly;
> Nor to say truly, was he slow in common
> To accept the attentions of this lovely woman;
> But the meantime he took no generous pains
> By mutual pleasing to secure his gains;
> He entered not, in turn, in her delights,
> Her books, her flowers, her taste for rural sights. . . .

Hunt had turned the tragic story to a boarding-school exercise.
It was pretty, interesting, inoffensive, and a little silly. And
it was permeated with Hampstead scenery. Indeed, the handsome Paolo was another Leigh Hunt, stopping to gather daisies
and enjoying the beauties of the landscape.

> How charming, would he think, to see her here,
> How heightened then, and perfect would appear
> The two divinest things the world has got,
> A lovely woman in a rural spot.

If the reviewers were unkind, friends were prodigal of their
praise. Benjamin Haydon, unsparing of his wretched eyesight,
stole enough time from his canvases not only to read the poem,
but to favor Hunt with one of his "reactions." Haydon never
felt anything like other human beings. He believed himself of
the race of giants, and every emotion was in the nature of an
earthquake. "I have read and re-read your exquisite pathetic
tale, till my Soul is cut in two — and every nerve about me
pierced with trembling needles." It is flattering to a poet to
be told that he can cause such agonies of delight; it makes him
something of a god. Leigh Hunt was sufficiently human to
yearn after the attributes of divinity, and Haydon's praise
rose, a grateful incense to his nostrils. When the artist offered
to paint a picture from the poem, Hunt rewarded him with a
minor miracle — he wrote him a sonnet.

Now Haydon had had a number of sonnets written to him,
the most recent a sequence of three by none other than Wordsworth. True, Haydon had desired the lines less impersonal,

more sparing of the glories of leaf and nipping air and crystal-
line sky, a trifle less detailed on the effluence from yon distant
mountain's head — in short, generous in praise of his own
glory.   Leigh Hunt's more specific literary compliment struck
the right chord.   After all they had been friends for well-nigh
five years, since that controversy in the *Examiner* wherein
Haydon had affirmed against Hunt that the negro was the
link between animal and man.   They had laughed together
and they had quarreled, and their friendship had stood the
test.   For love of him Benjamin Haydon had temporarily put
aside High Art to paint his portrait: Hunt must bear that in
mind — his was the only portrait that the great Haydon had
ever stooped to paint.   Hunt's sonnet, therefore, was no more
than the artist's due.   The delighted Haydon read and reread
it till he had every verse by heart; he copied it out.   Overflowing with gratitude, he let Hunt know how he felt about it.
"The more I reflect on your sonnet, the more I am convinced
that is the very best thing you have done."   And so farewell
to the exquisite pathetic tale that had brought out his arsenal
of refined tortures.

Despite critical contrariness the poem had a good sale, and
for a while the wolf was kept from the studio-museum-work-
shop of the Hunts.   Lamb and his sister Mary, Hazlitt and
Vincent Novello, the half-English, half-Italian organist of the
Portuguese Embassy's chapel in Grosvenor Square, came frequently to spend the evening in Hampstead, and Keats, now a
member of the circle, met them all.   The two veterans of the
old literary guard liked the youth but paid little attention to
him.   Lamb was too much engrossed in his glass, and Hazlitt,
his mind full of the genii of England whom he was thinking of
compressing into the hour-jar of the lecture platform, could
spare no time to make discoveries.   James and Horace Smith
were often of the company, matching their quips with Hunt's
puns.   In 1812, on the reopening of the Drury Lane, for which
a competition for an address in verse had been held among the
poets, they had attained a well-deserved success with their
parodies, *Rejected Addresses,* as just as they were clever.   Besides the old guard, there was a staff of youths who reached
out for the literary standard.   John Hamilton Reynolds, whom

Byron had implored a critic to spare, had produced, besides his Oriental tale, another volume of verse on which the printer's ink had scarcely dried when he met Keats, still unpublished but for a sonnet, yet with ambitions rivaling his own. To Keats, Reynolds, nearly a year younger than himself, must have seemed a prodigy. But he knew that he had the power to excel him.

Other young men, with or without poetic aspirations, and a bevy of admiring female relatives, formed the Hunt circle, which made Haydon grumble that one of his friend's defects was "a love of approbation from the darling sex bordering on weakness." He himself had no patience with women except when he saw them in pigment and marble. The living examples annoyed him. In vain, however, did he shake his *antique* head and speak out his displeasure. His voice was drowned by the shrieks of admiration with which Hunt's female following greeted his singing of Mozart in his rich, flexible voice, or a reading of choice passages from the pathetic tale.

Haydon, indeed, had no great gift for friendship. Knocked about as he had been by opposition which he had met with clenched fists, he challenged everyone as an enemy. His whole heart he had laid at the feet of High Art and her daughter, Historical Painting; he could love human beings only with his mind. Lamb and Hazlitt were among his warmest friends, but he mistrusted them and preferred to see them together that the one might counteract the effect of the other. A frustrated artist, Hazlitt looked coldly on ability in others, chiefly in him, Haydon thought, so that the man's presence in his painting room obscured the light like a cloud. Haydon listened eagerly for some word of praise. "Why did you begin it so large?" Hazlitt would ask about a nearly completed painting. "A smaller canvas might have concealed your faults." And while Haydon bit his tongue in suppressed anger, "You'll never sell it," Hazlitt predicted. "Why — why — why not?" stammered the kindly Lamb.

For some reason Haydon responded to Keats without the usual preamble of suspiciousness, perhaps because he discovered in the young poet as great a passion as his own for

Greek art — perhaps, too, because for the first time in his
thirty years he had been moved by a woman of flesh and blood.
He had but recently seen by the bedside of a dying husband
one whose face was "the loveliest that was ever created since
God made Eve." Moved by her beauty made holy by her
grief, Haydon, the woman scorner, fell down in worship.
There was the helpmeet God had destined for him. What if
Haydon was at the moment too poor to provide for Mrs.
Hyman and her orphaned brood? He would help her as much
as his borrowings would allow; later, when the great canvas on
which he was working had been sold, he would marry her and
rear her children as his own. The sorrowful widow listened to
his suit and bowed a sweet assent. Haydon was lifted to the
skies with happiness; the world grew suddenly brighter. Love,
while opening that obdurate heart, had also let in friendship.

Moreover, at that time Haydon was at the peak of triumph.
After years of striving against the bitterest antagonism, he had
succeeded in rousing the interest of the nation in the Elgin
Marbles. Throughout the past year, before the inspiriting
figures of his colossal unfinished "Christ's Entry into Jerusalem," he had sat, after laying aside his brushes, and, losing
all sense of proportion, had attacked great and little in articles
defending Lord Elgin's treasures. These apostrophes to the
public that had the fire which his painting lacked had been
translated into French, Italian, German. Reprints appeared in
the most important cities of the Continent. Canova took up
the cause; Goethe sent forth his thunder. The name of Haydon reverberated through the world of art. At last the nation
decided to purchase the marbles.

"It has saved the marbles, but it will ruin you," Lawrence
warned him on his success. But Haydon had no ear for
warnings in his victory. He rejoiced to see his painting room
crowded with rank, beauty, and fashion, and ordered his front
doors left open to this incursion of opulence. "I was an object
of curiosity whenever I appeared in a public place," he recorded
for the future. "My vanity was tickled."

It was no wonder young Keats, arriving from Cheapside to
the studio overshadowed by the dimly seen figures of the
Christ canvas, in an atmosphere still breathing of the day's

triumphs, felt himself one with the mighty and wrote of the great spirits that on earth were sojourning — Wordsworth, Leigh Hunt, Benjamin Haydon.

> And other spirits there are standing apart
> Upon the forehead of the age to come.

And where, where would he stand in the future? Where was he now in the time of mighty workings? Was the beloved Libertas a true prophet when he said,

> As surely as all this I see, even now
> Young Keats, a flowering laurel on your brow. . . .

Keats heard the answer in himself and knew it to be true.

XVII

CROSSCURRENTS

RETURNED from her adventure with Byron, Clare kept her secret. Shelley, with his belief in the sacred freedom of love, would perhaps have understood, but Mary might have frowned upon it and found it as licentious as her father still found her living with another woman's husband. Mary, like Mr. Godwin, had an exaggerated respect for the opinions of society, and although with Shelley to keep up her spirits and her love of him to sustain her courage she made the best of her unconventional situation, she would have preferred that the blessings of Church and State had sanctified the otherwise perfect relation. Clare said nothing, therefore, and laid her scheme. Shelley's health had again been giving occasion for alarm, and Mr. Godwin, with his chronically gaping pocket and his hypocritical obduracy, further deprived him of peace of mind. There was talk of their going abroad. "Why not to Geneva?" suggested Clare, advancing many inducements, but withholding the most important to her — that Byron would be there.

And toward Geneva they traveled, Shelley with Mary, baby William and a nurse, and Clare. By the time they had arrived in Paris the first week of May, Clare knew she was with child by Byron, whom she informed of her progress with "the whole tribe of Otaheite philosophers." For Clare never hesitated to have her little joke at other people's expense.

Meanwhile Lord Byron, in the company of the lad Rushton, the excellent Fletcher, and his young doctor, was making slow progress. Now that England was being left behind, he fell into his Childe Harold mood, and while munching the bread of exile pondered over his lot. Life is a pilgrimage. He was resuming it not as the Harold of the glorious beginning, but as a hated outcast. Newstead Abbey, his London house, wife, child, friends, Augusta — all were being severed from his life, the Gordon wraiths whispering in his spirit, "Forever." Defiant among the wrecks of his defeat, he still clung to the only being who loved him and whom he still loved above, beyond, more deeply than anyone else the world contained. If he had any regret that the sea bore him from his native shores, it was only that it separated him from Augusta. She was the star of his fated bark, steadfastly shining over his dark way. Though others had turned from him, she had ever been true, bowing under the lashing of society, yet drawn the closer to him for his suffering, doubled because she must share it.

> Thou stood'st, as stands a lovely tree,
>   That still unbroke, though gently bent,
> Still waves with fond fidelity
>   Its boughs above a monument.

Love and death, the two had been indissolubly linked in his thoughts of Augusta. As the constant Medora she had been made to sing of the sepulchral lamp burning eternal but unseen. Now, to his spirit's anguish, she was the tree waving above the grave of their love.

He had sent the stanzas to Murray with the rest of the domestic pieces, but not yet for publication. Lady Caroline Lamb, whose charm the otherwise staid Murray could not withstand, succeeded in having them shown her. At once, as his guardian angel, she had cautioned Byron against their being made public. "You will draw ruin on your head and hers. . . . Believe one who would perhaps die to save you." To the last, to the very last, his sins pursued him. Would she, the little viper, *perhaps* die to save him? He did not answer her. Far from dying, however, Lady Caroline was at that very moment setting up a tiny cornerstone to immortality, as she added the final flourishes to the proof sheets of *Glenarvon*, a fictional account of her romance with Byron that she had made haste to write as soon as she had seen the tides rising against him. He had been cruel to her for the sin of loving him. He was soon to feel the sting of a scorned woman's revenge. "Be steady," counseled the symbolic figure on her seal, as it teetered across an abyss.

If Childe Harold set out in melancholy gloom, there was one with him who footed the pilgrimage with elation. Dr. John Polidori had never until then been far from the parental leading-strings. Now, wonderful to think of, at the age of twenty-one he embarked on high adventure with the greatest romantic in England, a poet, a phœnix among men. His father had looked on disapprovingly when Sir Henry Halford had given the young doctor a recommendation to Lord Byron. However, once his lordship had agreed to engage him as his companion and traveling physician, neither the pleading of his English mother nor his father's prohibitions in sounding Italian could stop the young medico, though even if they had, Mr. Murray's promise of a goodly five hundred pounds for his travel diary would have sent him off like a bolt. For Dr. John, having won the caduceus from Æsculapius at the age of nineteen, lusted after the laurels of Apollo. In his traveling box he took with him an unfinished poetic tragedy which, if not better than anything of Lord Byron's, he knew was at least as good. In the confidence of his youth and early success in his medical studies, Dr. Polidori took himself at his own worth.

Piccadilly Terrace was scarcely out of sight when the commissioned journal was begun with the upstanding pronoun *I* very much in evidence. "I left London at 10 in the morning with Lord Byron. . . ." Such notations, however interesting to oneself, make dull reading, a fact which forced itself upon the doctor's critical faculty after a number of lines. Inspirited by the vision of Mr. Murray's royalties, he put on the grand style at a receding vision of the Thames, whose "chalky banks were alternated with the swelling hills, rising from the waves, of the pleasing green-brown, the effect of the first dawn of spring on the vegetable creation."

With a man like Byron to observe, Dr. Polidori soon forsook the pleasing aspects of the vegetable creation for records of a livelier nature. "As soon as he reached his room," he noted two days later, "Lord Byron fell like a thunderbolt upon the chambermaid." That was at Ostend. At Ghent, the following day, both vegetable and animal nature bowed gracefully before the fine arts, when Lord Byron and Dr. Polidori visited l'École de Dessein. Neither his lordship, however, nor Polidori had the true artist's eye. They cared little for color and composition and looked, rather, for representations from life. A beheading of Saint John struck Dr. Polidori above everything else because "all the interest and beauty consisted of a dog smelling the dead body." Byron, on the other hand, was moved by a "Judgment of Solomon," where, commented the doctor, "the child was painted dead with most perfect nature; so much so that my companion, who is a father, could not bear the sight." Did the little stark painted body remind Byron of his own child, as irrevocably lost to him?

> Is thy face like thy mother's, my fair child,
> Ada! sole daughter of my house and heart?
> When last I saw thy young blue eyes they smiled,
> And then we parted, — not as we now part,
> But with a hope. . . .

Childe Harold rued with a sorrow sharper than had been felt by Byron, in whose harassed heart, during those last days of parting, the child had shared the hate he bore the mother. But now, with the waters heaving between him and England, it was as if rancor and cruelty had been washed away, and there were room for love alone. So is it with our feelings for the dead. The reality is forgotten and only transmuted beauty remains. Ada was dead to him, for was there indeed hope that in life she should ever call him "Father"? He knew that at Kirkby his portraits were kept shrouded lest the infant eyes see and question. Would she ever look again upon his living face?

Byron's traveling coach with its bed, library, plate chest, and dining table lumbered upon the uneven roads from city to city. At Antwerp once again he and Polidori paid their respects to the arts, only to outdo each other in ludicrous exclamations of horror before the ample forms of Rubens's women. Monstrosities and worse, they thought them, his lordship judging from experience, and the innocent doctor from the rarefied conceptions of his still virgin mind.

On the way to Waterloo the carriage broke down and they

went on in a *calèche* provided by the doctor.   The plain spread
before them.   Hardly a year had passed since it had been red
with blood and heaped with corpses, yet now it greened again
with the all-merciful oblivion of nature, like one vast grave.
Here and there the flowers were beginning to appear; the
plough had leveled the hollows, and grain was shooting up as
if the battle had never been.   Here it was that the escaped
Eagle had sought to regain his grip upon the world; here he
bit the dust of defeat.   Mournfully Byron gazed upon the
scene.   He stood not only on an empire's wreck, but on the.
very grave of ambition.   Once more the parallel: Napoleon —
himself.   Both, risen so high, were pedestaled only on a place
of skulls.   Napoleon wore the links of the world's broken
chain, while he, Childe Harold, self-exiled, wandered forth —
to what new destiny?   Frederick Howard, a young kinsman
of his, had lost his life in the battle.   Byron was shown the
spot where he fell, between two trees now in full leaf and the
stump of another, shivered in the fray.   His young blood,
Byron blood, had fed the plain.   "Poor Frederick, the best of
his race," the Childe elegized.   What was he now but a handful of earth, mingling with the English soil where the corpse
had been reburied?   "I never saw or heard but good of him."
And now Frederick Howard was but a name, the sap in yonder
flowering plant, a memory, fast fading, to those who had loved
him.

Man's work more than nature's bore the scars of the conflict.   On the houses left standing, ghastly splotches of plaster
filled in the wounds the cannon had made in the brick.
Children, seeing the two foreign gentlemen, ran after them
with brass buttons in their hands, souvenirs for the curious
in such things.   Byron preferred more personal mementos.
As on his first pilgrimage he had collected skulls of Athenian
heroes, again he bought a collection of bones.   Platæa, Troy,
Chæronea, Marathon: on such cornerstones was their glory
raised.   Mont St. Jean, Hougoumont: their gory halo lay still
too fresh upon them.   Byron carved his name in the chapel of
Hougoumont, and Polidori, the Childe's faithful shadow, aped
him.

The traveling carriage mended, they drove on, stopping

at Cologne to visit the cathedral where Polidori fell down a step and broke a glass "for which they at first would not take anything — which at last cost me three francs." He kept his countenance so well through the misadventure that he complimented himself for it in the journal. He was an exceedingly awkward youth, always stumbling into some difficulty out of which Byron helped him with extraordinary patience. He liked the impudent, self-centred young puppy, humored him, and encouraged his writing mania. The last night in England he had spent listening to a reading of Polidori's half-finished tragedy, amid the jeers of Hobhouse and Scrope Davies, who could not be made to see any virtues either in Polly-Dolly or in his work.

On the twenty-fifth of May the Napoleonic coach arrived at the inn in Sécheron where Shelley and his party were already installed. Byron put his age down in the register as a hundred, a fact which so amazed the innkeeper that he sent up a letter to this hale Methuselah within half an hour of his arrival — "a thing that seems worthy of a novel," noted the doctor, who found wonder in everything. Several days later, while Byron and he were out walking, they met Shelley with Mary and Clare, who introduced the two poets to each other. At dinner that evening Shelley visited Byron. "Bashful, shy, consumptive," Polidori described him. "Separated from his wife; keeps the two daughters of Godwin, who practise his theories; one L. B.'s."

Lord Byron had evidently lost no time in informing his companion of his liaison with Clare. It was just another affair, like that with the chambermaid at Ostend, except that, like everything connected with it from the beginning, it boded no good. But Byron could never resist women, even when he had no love for them. Clare had battered down every defense that he had set up. Now, with the forced intimacy of their living under the same roof, she promised to become a habit, a state not unwelcome, however, to one who had been treated with "two courses and a *desert* of aversion" by his moral Clytemnestra. Clare was with child? Well, he would be responsible for the infant. But he did not want another woman hanging round his neck. He would take whatever love women offered by way of novelty; none would again make a dupe of him.

Gone was the magnanimity with which he had spoken of Annabella. She had cast him off; she had stood, relentless and unforgiving, when he had humbled himself. She should now see that she was less than nothing to him, except as a thing to hate and curse. He would not stir himself to bring retribution upon her head, but fate would take care of it for him. One day she would suffer for the sin of her hard-heartedness, as Lady Noël, her mother, would suffer, and the fiend, Mrs. Clermont. And Samuel Romilly, who had made justice out of the wrong done to him, Byron. In themselves and in their children would they be visited. It was a Gordon who cursed them, and Gordon curses were as relentless as other people's piety.

Clare could no longer keep her secret, and confessed it to Shelley and Mary. What was to be done? In the charmed region of Geneva the moral codes of England melted as flakes in the sun. Shelley and Mary lived as sinless in their own eyes as the first occupants of Eden; they loved, and their love made everything right. It was not so between Byron and Clare. She had given herself in romantic caprice; he had taken her in moral apathy. A child, an innocent victim, was coming into the world. Shelley was ready to provide for it if Lord Byron shirked, as he had been providing without a murmur for the foolish girl who had thrown herself upon his protection the day he bound his life with Mary's. He did not condemn Byron for his human frailty, whatever he might think of him as a man and a Christian, that most hated of creatures.

Together the two poets read Rousseau's *Héloïse* while Mary was helped over the difficulties in Tasso by Polidori. Clare, in her own room, copied out her lover's poems and brooded over her condition. She was living like the heroine of a romance, her unhappiness affirmed — a tragic romance. But she too was touched with the beauty of the place where, at every step, ghosts of the past awoke, dispelling even one's sorrow. With a keen pang she must have copied the new stanzas of *Childe Harold*.

Here the self-torturing sophist, wild Rousseau,
The apostle of affliction, he who threw
Enchantment over passion, and from woe
Wrung overwhelming eloquence, first drew
The breath which made him wretched; yet he knew
How to make madness beautiful, and cast
O'er erring deeds and thoughts a heavenly hue
Of words, like sunbeams, dazzling as they past
The eyes, which o'er them shed tears feelingly and fast.

She, too, was trying to make madness beautiful. But how would it end? She could not but be aware that Byron did not love her. Her happiness had lasted ten minutes,[1] but she knew that those ten fleeting minutes would loom darkly over the rest of her life.

The two men soon left the inn at Sécheron, Shelley taking a cottage at Mont Alègre and Byron the Villa Diodati, a pleasant country seat where Milton had been the guest of his friend Diodati on his return to England. The two houses were only a ten-minute walk apart, Shelley's nearer the lakeside and Byron's on a terrace of vineyards fragrant with the budding grape. They met constantly, usually without the women, at Lord Byron's wish. He was not drawn to Mary. Did she perhaps remind him of another small, rigidly upright woman, nursing his Ada, just a little older than Mary's blue-eyed William? The Childe softened before babyhood, for

he had learned to love . . .
The helpless looks of blooming infancy.

Another babe, now two years old, before whom Annabella had seen his face softening to spiritual tenderness, had perhaps taught him that love.

Ere long Shelley and Byron became joint owners of a keeled boat. It became a source of unending joy to them, and also of peril when the sudden squalls rose up, making the lake a miniature ocean in its wrath. In the warm noonday, until far into the night, they rode the great lake, talking of life and poetry and the things that were their daily breath. Shelley's face, thrust forward eagerly, lighted up with the exhilaration

[1] From Clare's letter to Jane Williams, 1827.

of the adventure and the thoughts that at last he could express
to one his equal in intellectual daring.   Byron, sitting opposite,
his curling hair disarranged, his dark brows arched over his
pale grey eyes, looked as if only a heavenly spirit could gaze
out from within him.   He would sit silent, and then his voice,
that voice that was like music, poured out his thoughts in turn.
They spoke of Wordsworth and of his oneness with the spirit
of nature, Shelley quoting him with such inspired fervor that
Byron wondered whether he had not judged rashly in com-
paring the *Excursion* to "rain upon rocks — where it stands
and stagnates, or rain upon sands — where it falls without fer-
tilizing."

Sometimes Mary and Clare were with them, listening mute
and worshipful, and sometimes Polidori joined them, breaking
into their talk with some opinionated commonplace, feeling, as
he often had occasion to feel beside Byron, "like a star in the
halo of the moon, invisible."   He was jealous of the shrill-
voiced young man who seemed daily to be growing more necessary to his lordship, more even than himself, the picturesque
and brilliant Polidori.   He did not neglect his function of
diarist, however.   Obscurely aware that Shelley might some
day be remembered, he set him down for Murray's edification
as a well-meaning idealist who had "paid Godwin's debts and
seduced his daughter; then wondered that he would not see
him. . . . All clever and no meretricious appearance. He
is very clever," he repeated, observing the influence the twenty-
three-year-old youth was having on the mind of the great
Byron.

In the course of their acquaintance Mary entrusted baby
William to the doctor for vaccination.   She called him, Polidori, her brother.   His heart was touched.   Before such endearments he became tractable, especially after Shelley presented him with a handsome gold chain and seal for his services.
In the growing friendliness Polidori was encouraged to bring
forth his tragedy from his portmanteau and lost no time in -
reading it aloud.   Alas, hope was not permitted to spring in
his breast by Shelley's frankness, or indeed by the hilarity of
the others.   For who could preserve a respectful countenance
before such lines as " 'T is thus the goiter'd idiot of the Alps"

— broken by Lord Byron's solemn eulogy: "I assure you, when I was on the Drury Lane Committee much worse things were offered us." Through it all the author watched with the jealousy of a parent for the effect of his offspring's beauty upon his audience. Unhappily neither their faces nor their words offered him the balm he sought. "Talked of my play, which all agreed was worth nothing," he noted disconsolately, and that after he had got himself a sprained ankle jumping a wall to help Mary in the rain.

Shelley and Byron reacted powerfully on each other. While admiring the older poet and granting him all the attributes of genius, Shelley was not blinded to his deficiencies of character. He would have had him godly and was pained to find him human, allowing selfishness, prejudice, even baseness to color his acts. He did not condemn Byron for what had passed between him and Clare; each was equally responsible. At the same time he thought him less than manly for his harshness to a woman whose chief fault had been that of being dazzled into rashness by his romantic aura. He who would not tread upon a worm was horrified at Byron's cruelty to a fellow creature. He lectured him shrilly and long upon the nobler life and on intellectual beauty, losing sight, in the splendor of the argument, of the moral with which he would have adorned his eloquence. God and man, Christianity — another name for Intolerance — and the true religion of Universal Love, the cosmos and its genesis, human perfectibility and the ideal republic — everything entered the scope of his brilliant analysis.

How was a fallen angel to respond? Fallen glory posited a supreme power to reward and punish. The God of vengeance of his early Calvinistic teachings seemed too strong an opponent for Shelley's frail Good. Predestination, perfectibility: Byron teetered in the balance. He had none of Shelley's fervent faith in man. Rebellion against the Biblical Jehovah was all that Byron could offer. In spite of himself, however, he was drawn into a maze of daring speculation, losing himself in a new form of ecstasy. His energetic imagination took loftier flights. His poetry gained in depth and meaning. Using the earth as a springboard for flight, he attempted the universe.

Murray and his synod in Albemarle Street were astounded
and dismayed as they read the new poetry of their erstwhile
earthly poet. *Darkness, Prometheus,* visions of the world's
end, pæans to lawless daring. . . . What was happening to
Byron?

> I had a dream, which was not at all a dream.
> The bright sun was extinguish'd, and the stars
> Did wander darkling in the eternal space,
> Rayless, and pathless, and the icy earth
> Swung blind and blackening to the moonless air:
> Morn came and went — and came and brought no day,
> And men forgot their passions in the dread
> Of this their desolation; and all hearts
> Were chill'd into a selfish prayer for light:
> And they did live by watch fires — and the thrones,
> The palaces of crownèd kings — the huts,
> The habitations of all things which dwell
> Were burnt for beacons.

A succession of apocalyptic visions bewrayed the mind, while
the mention of burning thrones and palaces disturbed the good
Briton, still unrecovered from the horrors of vile republi-
canism across the Channel, not so long since. Walter Scott
was genuinely pained. "To speak plainly, the framing of
such phantasms is a dangerous employment for the exalted
and teeming imagination of such a poet as Lord Byron," he
cautioned. Byron should be Byron and not the mouthpiece of
strange philosophies. Hobhouse and Scrope Davies went forth
in great alarm to visit him and find out for themselves what
company he was keeping.

However, the days sped happily for the two poets, and the
summer nights as well, when they sat up talking until the early
hours. Formality set aside, the friendship attained the intimacy of familiar names. Albè, the women called Byron,
after he had startled them with a weird, savage howl that had
purported to be an Albanian song. The boat was in constant
requisition. Leaving Mary and Clare behind, the two men
made an excursion to Chillon, whose grim underwater dungeons
gave Byron the impulse he needed for composition. Bad
weather kept them two days at Ouchy; by the time Byron had

returned to Villa Diodati he had the complete manuscript of the *Prisoner of Chillon.*

In the shadow of the elder poet Shelley wrote little. However, the voyage round the Lake of Geneva, surrounded by ever-varying beauty, with the inly heard echoes of its presiding genius Rousseau prompting his thoughts to high reflection of man's power for good in this imperfect world, and a sense as of the veil of an unseen presence enfolding him, made manifest to him his own seeking, and in the glow of creative ecstasy he beheld the goddess he had long been worshiping. The *Hymn to Intellectual Beauty* took shape within him, but it was not until the afterglow of memory had reëvoked the moment's rapture that he wrote his solemn dedication of himself to her service. As Demon, as Ghost, as Heaven, that supernal Beauty had been half seen by sages and poets. Always he had sought her, until suddenly her shadow fell upon him.

I vowed that I would dedicate my powers
  To thee and thine — have I not kept the vow?
  With beating heart and streaming eyes, even now
I call the phantoms of a thousand hours
Each from his voiceless grave: they have in visioned bowers
  Of studious zeal or love's delight
  Outwatched with me the envious night —
They know that never joy illumed my brow
  Unlinked with hope that thou wouldst free
  This world from its dark slavery,
  That thou — O awful *Loveliness*
Wouldst give whate'er these words cannot express.

Byron looked upon Shelley as a visionary. He thought him a lesser poet than he was. On the other hand Shelley esteemed Byron more highly than he deserved.

Toward the middle of July inclement weather kept them all at home, and to speed along the tedious evenings they looked through a book of stories of the supernatural. Byron was present with the inevitable Polidori, and Shelley, and with him too were Mary and Clare. Half in jest Byron proposed that they should each write a ghost story, and all agreed. Night after night they gathered about the fire, reporting progress, though Mary and Polidori had done nothing and Byron, after outlining his plot for a vampire tale, entertained them with gruesome legend or recited Coleridge's *Christabel*. On one occasion the overwrought Shelley fancied he saw eyes peering out at him from Mary's breast and ran out of the room, shrieking, until Polidori threw water on him and calmed him with ether. Shelley's ghostly narrative was early given up. The doctor began a fantastic tale, but early abandoned it. Besides, there was Byron's workable plot, which his lordship seemed willing to cede to anyone who would have it. Polidori saw his advantage at once and memorized the salient points of the narrative for later expansion. Still Mary made no progress. One night she sat silently listening to Byron and Shelley discussing the nature of the principle of life. Could it be infused into the dead? Would it be possible to endow inert matter with the vital spark? The questions fixed on her imagination. All night long they kept her awake, and visions passed before her of a monster, a dread Adam, created out of inanimate matter and endowed with the principle of life by a student of the occult. Here was the theme for her romance ready to hand. She told Shelley about it and he urged her to write it, and so *Frankenstein* was begun by the eighteen-year-old girl.

Shelley and Mary were just returned from a visit to the valley of Chamouni, whose wreath of mountain peaks made the poet's soul overflow in the lines of *Mont Blanc*, when they found a new guest at Diodati — M. G. Lewis, the author of the *Monk*.

Outside his family circle and a few intimate friends who called him "Mat," Matthew Gregory Lewis was known as "Monk" Lewis after the protagonist of the Gothic romance with which he had chilled a world already greatly shaken by the nearer horrors of the French Revolution. The tale of the wicked monk Ambrosio, who under the cloak of piety concealed a satanic ambition and a devouring lust, took complete possession of the British reader, whose dreams, for more than a generation, continued to be haunted by the shrieks, dungeons, phantasmal bleeding nuns, and tortured heroines of Lewis's cabinet of horrors. Shelley in his inquiring boyhood had reveled in the book, which he had paid the compliment of imitation with his preposterous *Zastrozzi*. He had reread it with Mary the first year of their elopement. Scott, later a friend of Lewis's, had found it highly imaginative. Byron, on reading it over in his maturity, could not understand how a boy of twenty had been able to write a book that would have put to shame Tiberius at Capri. Tom Moore, the dainty philanderer, dismissed it with loathing as impious and libidinous. *The Critical Review* had early expressed the temper of the eighteenth-century *fin de siècle*, and, while deploring the hunger of the public for the horrible and the preternatural, granted Lewis genius though he had employed it "to furnish a mormo for children, a poison for youth and a provocative for the debauchee." Perhaps for these very reasons the *Monk* continued exhausting edition after edition through the succeeding years, adding royalties to Lewis's considerable wealth.

Shelley met a sinister-looking dwarf of uncertain age, — Lewis in 1816 was forty-one years old, — with lantern jaws, a wide, fleshy mouth, beetling brows, and great, outstarting, queerish eyes — like those of an insect, Scott had described them. Had Lewis himself been a creation of the horror school he could not have been more perfect. He dressed neatly, affecting the dandy. His white ruff spread immaculately over his bosom, and his little black coat with the double row of buttons enclosed his small figure as neatly as a nut holds its kernel. He might indeed have popped out of a magic shell like the imps in fairy tales, so queer and unreal he seemed.

Since the publication of the *Monk*, followed by other prose tales and plays, Lewis had been wrapped in a nimbus of mystery not unmingled with dread, people, especially the women, believing him to possess the attributes of his infamous characters. As a matter of fact a chaster and kindlier man did not exist in his day. Imbued with the spirit of philanthropy, he practised charity in secret, as others would commit a crime, and there were no slaves in Jamaica, indeed, no white laborers, who enjoyed the privileges of his two hundred blacks. When his father left him his extensive plantations, Lewis went to see them for himself, formulated a code of laws, and established a little black Eden in the wilds. He would have set his slaves free but that he knew they were happier under his care.

Oddly enough, together with his democratic spirit, he had a reverence for rank that prostrated him, a man of good family, before a title. He was never so happy as among lords and ladies, when his high-pitched voice, for he was an excessive talker, shrilled like a linnet's in a flowery bower. Byron had a patronizing fondness for the grotesque manikin. "Poor fellow! He is really a good man — an excellent man," he sighed. But he could not tolerate his ceaseless talk, talk, talk. Nothing, nobody, had power to check it except another with the same trait. During the Diodati visit Byron lost no time in taking him to Madame de Staël at Coppet, where he had the satisfaction of seeing the two, little Monk Lewis and the Epicene, pitted against each other in a battle of words that made the walls resound.

Of course the ghostly pastimes were entered into with keener zest with Monk Lewis now of the party. Far into the night the little company listened to weirdnesses that made the flesh creep with delightful thrills. For the host's delight Lewis translated parts of Goethe's *Faust*, ignorant of what visions were rising in Byron's brain. Mephistopheles, the scene on the mountain, the unholy pact, love, disaster — figures and deeds unrolled themselves before his fancy. He, Byron, would write his own "Faust," a mightier, because a more human, tragedy. And so the germ of *Manfred* was sowed.

Then one day the four men met for serious business when Lewis added a codicil to his will providing for the humane treatment of his slaves after his death. Byron, Shelley, and Polidori witnessed it. Little did any of them suspect how short was the time allotted him on earth. After visiting a sister in Italy and seeing Byron once more, Lewis reëmbarked for Jamaica. He had a pianoforte in his cabin, and a library, and a provision of medicines which he dispensed to fellow passengers who suffered on the journey.

In the West Indies his slaves welcomed him as if he had been a god, and wept to see him take ship again for the cold land which he preferred to their paradise. But he was never to reach England. On the boat he contracted yellow fever, and in a week he was dead. The crew, fearing a spread of the disease, placed the body in a wooden coffin, covered it with canvas, and grappled weights upon it. No sooner was it lowered into the sea than, instead of sinking, it floated on the waves, the canvas swelling to a sail in the wind, as the strange barge, with its spectral cargo, made its way back toward Jamaica. Trembling with superstitious fear, the crew watched its course to the edge of the horizon, where it was engulfed from view. Weird and conflicting were the tales recounted of the Monk's spectacular last voyage. Byron heard of Lewis's death two years later, and, paraphrasing Scott, wrote with his characteristic levity of the departed, truly Apollo's sexton, —

> I would give many a sugar cane
> Monk Lewis were alive again.

At the close of the summer of 1816, as the weather was turning rainy and cold, Shelley with his party left Switzerland for England. Almost at the same time Scrope Davies and Hobhouse arrived at Villa Diodati.

XVIII

TWO VIRTUOUS WOMEN AND A SINNER

THE first week in September, 1816, Shelley's household, increased by the presence of Elise, a Swiss nurse for William, arrived at Portsmouth by way of Fontainebleau, Versailles, and Havre. On the ninth of the month Harriet Shelley quitted Mr. Westbrook's house, where she had been living with her children, and left no address.

Since Skinner Street remained closed to Mary and Field Place forbidden to Shelley, the little clan sought the hospitality of Peacock at Marlow, where they stayed till Mary found lodgings at Bath. Shelley had business in London for Lord Byron, who had commissioned him to deliver some manuscript poems to Murray and to see them safely through the press. More, he was to feel the moral atmosphere and test the temperature of current sentiment toward the banished lord.

"I saw Kinnaird and had a long talk with him," Shelley wrote to Byron. "He informed me that Lady Byron was now in perfect health, and that she is living with your sister. I felt much pleasure from this intelligence. I consider the latter part of it as affording a decisive contradiction to the only important calumny that was ever advanced against you." Had Byron, so boastful to Lady Melbourne, denied his guilt to Shelley? It is conceivable. Shelley had no horror of a theme with which he had been made familiar in his reading of the ancients. He saw beauty, as he was later to show in *Laon and Cythna*, in a brother-and-sister relation in the forbidden degree: it was perfectly acceptable in poetry. Nonetheless his eyes would have widened and his voice risen to its shrillest in condemnation of incest in real life. In Byron's case he preferred to believe the rumor a calumny.

Meanwhile, as Shelley's letter indicated, Lady Byron and Augusta were seeing each other constantly, though either Kinnaird had misinformed Shelley or he had not understood aright about their living together. With the infant Ada, Lady Byron had left Kirkby for Lowestoft shortly after Byron's departure. Her health had suffered severely in her trials, and there had been no balm for her at Kirkby with Lady Noël and Mrs. Clermont losing no opportunity to speak ill of his lordly scapegrace and his "blessed set" — Hobhouse and Kinnaird and Davies and the whole Piccadilly crew that, according to them, had helped to lure Byron from the path of righteousness.

On the thirty-first of August Annabella came to London and took rooms for two weeks in Lower Seymour Street. There was a frequent interchange of visits between her and Augusta at St. James's Palace, a circumstance which served to quiet gossip, though had the true reason of their intercourse transpired, the scandalmongers would have been treated to a choicer subject.

In May Augusta had been brought to bed of another child. No sooner was she risen from her confinement than she received a note from Annabella which, through a mist of pious evasiveness and the invocation of God's blessing on Augusta and her children, announced the threat that Lady Byron would see her less often unless . . . for there was an implied unless. . . . Augusta understood, as who, in her situation would not, the meaningful closing sentence: "Should your present unhappy dispositions be seriously changed, you will not then be deceived in considering me as one who will afford every service and consolation of your most faithful friend." In other words, let Augusta do as Lady Byron wished, and she would not be thrown to the mercy of public opinion — the inevitable result if she, Lady Byron, denied her friendship. "I have been assured," answered the helpless woman, "that the tide of public opinion had been so turned against my Brother that the least appearance of coolness on your part would injure me most seriously — & I am therefore *for the sake of my children* compelled to accept from your *compassion* the 'limited intercourse' which is all you can grant to one whom

you pronounce no longer worthy of your esteem or affection."
A costly acceptance it was to prove to the victim at bay.

Since Byron's departure Augusta had been receiving from
him letters full of love and passionate encouragement. "My
Heart," the burning epistles began, "My dearest Augusta,"
ending with fervent assurances that whatever might happen
on this earth his whole being was consecrated to her. "Do
not be uneasy — and do not 'hate yourself.' If you hate
either let it be *me* — but do not — it would kill me — we are
the last persons in the world — who ought — or could cease
to love one another."

Whether in London or in Geneva the thought of her still
went through . . . In the sincerity of his emotion he echoed
the pulsations of his heart in the unaffected rhythms he adopted
in his most personal utterances. Beat, beat, beat, and a pause
as for a sigh. It might not be poetry; it was himself, talking
to himself, and saying what with his living voice he could not
speak to another. Society might condemn as it would. He
was unrepentant; he had pride in his sin. Augusta they might
take from him, but the memory of her and of his love none
could destroy.

> From the wreck of the past, which hath perish'd,
>   Thus much I at least may recall,
> It hath taught me that what I most cherish'd,
>   Deserv'd to be dearest of all:
> In the desert a fountain is springing,
>   In the wide waste there still is a tree,
> And a bird in the solitude singing,
>   Which speaks to my spirit of *thee*.

The waste of his life, the fountain springing, a bird singing in
the solitude. . . . That had been when Clare came to him,
for the moment loved, as she charmed away the desert with
her lovely voice and awoke thoughts of that other, "dearest
of all." In some such softness of mood, gratefully he had
written to the unhappy girl one of his finest lyrics.

But something alien had come over Augusta. The gayety,
the nonsense, no more enlivened the letters now laden with
piety and "damned crinkum-crankum," as Byron in annoyance

called a maddening indirection that betrayed another voice, imposed upon her own. Hobhouse in a manner explained the enigma. Lady Byron and Augusta had joined forces. The repentant sister had reformed and was now trying to work out her brother's salvation with her own. By depriving herself of all charm, she would spare him temptation. . . . It was easy to see who was her moral guide.

Byron was furious, not with Augusta, who could be persuaded into anything with her complacent philosophy, but with Annabella. During the summer, at Madame de Staël's prompting, he had written to his wife in a final attempt at reconciliation. Nothing had come of it. Wroth at having humbled himself once more in vain, he turned more bitterly against her, his rancor intensified to hate by wounded pride. Never in his life had he come upon such fortitude as that little being showed; and he who had been with women as a wind with reeds knew no bounds in his mortification. Hobhouse told him that Lady Byron had been ill. Instead of feeling pity, he rejoiced that the curses he had heaped upon her had in part been realized. "I am too well avenged!" he exulted in lines to her that reëchoed the incantation he had woven about her and included in *Manfred*. Whatever his sins, she had not been chosen to be his Nemesis on earth. Her virtues were her destruction, for she converted them to vices: —

> Trafficking with them in a purpose cold,
> For present anger and for future gold —
> And buying other's grief at any price.

Now she was turning Augusta against him. "And so — Lady B. has been 'kind to you' you tell me — 'very kind' — umph —" he answered one of his sister's letters mockingly. "It is well she should be kind to some of us, and I am glad she has the heart and the discernment to be still your friend; you were ever so to her." But she must be put on her guard against the woman. Hobhouse — a word from Hobhouse would carry weight. The obliging Hobhouse accordingly wrote, speaking evasively of the "Lowestoft correspondent." "Pardon me, my dear Mrs. Leigh, if I venture to advise the strictest confinement to very *common* topics in all you say in that quarter," he cautioned. "Repay kindness in any other way than by confidence. I say this, not in reference to the Lady's character, but as a maxim to serve for all cases."

Unhappily the warning came too late. By the middle of September, when Hobhouse wrote from Switzerland, Augusta had made a full confession of the incest not only to Lady Byron, but also to Mrs. Villiers, her friend, who under the illusion of helping her had, in her abhorrence of the truth, gone to Annabella's side. The two embattled ladies under the banner of righteousness had laid siege on the never-too-resisting stronghold of Augusta, in the devil's camp; nevertheless it had taken them three months of strategy before they could cry victory.

From the day Lady Byron had had the first suspicion of the relations that had existed between her husband and Augusta, she had lost all peace of mind. The lure of the subject possessed her waking thoughts. It deprived her of sleep. Like the red sun of an hallucination, it held her fixed upon its sight, fascinated and appalled. A morbid desire to know, to pry into the beginnings and perhaps discover the cause of Augusta's power over Byron, drew her. She wanted Augusta near that she might study her, capture her secret, and, by converting her to a *good* woman, rob her of her perilous charm. If an experimenter may be said to love his subject, Lady Byron loved Augusta. Certainly, as Mrs. Clermont admitted, Lady Byron had reason to feel kindly towards Mrs. Leigh, to whom, during those terrible weeks before Ada was born, she owed everything, "even her life." And Lady Byron was grateful. Her letters, after she left Piccadilly Terrace, had solicitude, even affection for one who, willingly or not, had been at the root of the evil in her marriage. Then had come the separation procured by herself and her parents, and Byron's departure.

Another woman, her purpose accomplished, would have placed a period after this episode, and begun anew. Not Lady Byron. She was twenty-four years old, but all her life was circumscribed by those thirteen months with Byron, which, like a magic ring, cut her off from the past and future. In that narrow circle was confined all of deep experience she had ever

known or was ever to know. Wherever she might be, the fatal
boundaries separated her from ordinary mortals, and if her
actions were strange, it was the strangeness of one marked
out for an uncommon destiny. Byron the magician, waking
his ghosts on the Alpine heights, had ensorcelled her. He had
had her before him when a Voice uttered an incantation: —

> "Though thy slumber may be deep
> Yet thy spirit shall not sleep;
> There are shades which will not vanish,
> There are thoughts thou canst not banish. . . ."

And indeed her thoughts were never from him, as his were
never from Augusta. He need not have called on the powers
of Hell to do what he had already too well accomplished,
simply by being Byron.

In the spirit of the spell, Lady Byron, her husband gone,
called up the months of her intense life through his counter-
part, Augusta, deriving a sterile gratification from her evasions,
then her tacit admissions, finally her spoken confession. It
was the struggle of a helpless mind in the closing coils of a
relentless justice. Why did Lady Byron wish to know what
had occurred in the past while she was yet Miss Milbanke?
The sin had been committed. With Byron's marriage to her
there had been an end — at least so Augusta swore, and so
she could recall from Byron's bursts of passion against his
sister, who, dreading the discovery of the secret, with quivering lips tried to turn his demands to a jest.

"You say my dear A. *I have been the cause of your sufferings*— if I have it has been innocently. . . ." Thus at first
Augusta had answered Lady Byron's accusations after the
letter threatening a limited intercourse. She neither denied
nor protested. "If I have, it has been *innocently*" — for
certainly there had been no thought of hurting Miss Milbanke
in London, at Newstead.

"In the last part of the time we were under the same roof,"
Lady Byron spoke more explicitly, "you will now remember
some things by which I intimated that I knew more than you
thought, and almost offered myself to your confidence. . . .
As you do not and never have attempted to deceive me re-

specting previous facts, of which my conviction is unalterable, I rely the more on your simple assertion of having 'never wronged me' intentionally." Nevertheless Lady Byron could not exonerate her from all guilt. "I lament that you *mis-judgingly* pursued a line of conduct so difficult for yourself — so dangerous and I believe so prejudicial to the ungoverned feelings of another — and inevitably tending to continue or renew his criminal recollections." But let the past be understood now, and buried, she added, only to reopen the subject in her next letter, exacting, though never directly, further details of that past which would not let her rest. Augusta's letters were all compliance and humility, abject humility. She was at the mercy of Lady Byron, who, despite her assurances, Augusta knew would be capable of wrecking her socially with her "principles of justice."

The sinner's regeneration, fully attested by the pious tone of her conversations, comforted the two righteous women. Mrs. Villiers impressed upon Augusta that Lady Byron was her Guardian Angel, and she must do as that guardian angel dictated, for her soul's sake. It was little Lady Byron demanded as the salve to her past suffering and her present sorrow: that Augusta abjure Byron. "Till you feel in reality that he has been your worst friend — indeed, *not* your friend — you cannot altogether think rightly — yet I am far from thinking any uncharitable feelings are to follow — forgive him — desire his welfare — but resign the pernicious view of being his friend more nearly." Above all Augusta must not use endearing phrases or marks that might bring back his "criminal recollections." Too well Annabella recalled the brooches of woven hair with the three mystical crosses worn constantly by brother and sister. And Augusta must be warned against the "levity and nonsense which he likes for the worst reason, because it prevents him from reflecting seriously." Mrs. Villiers had informed the Guardian Angel of a thick unsealed letter addressed by Augusta to Byron which she had seen on her writing table. Had Lady Byron been told of it? For however sincere the sinner's penitence, she was bound to confide explicitly in her Guardian Angel.

During Lady Byron's London visit the subject of the correspondence was resumed. She saw Augusta almost daily, plying her with questions in her desire not to leave one stone of that *via crucis* unturned. And Augusta answered, her distraught hand brushing away her hair oftener than ever from her pained forehead, as the methodical young woman coldly proceeded with her analysis. "There had been connection previous to my marriage?" "Yes . . ." "Subsequent to my marriage?" "No! Never!" "During the separation proceedings had he made any criminal proposals?" "No . . . No."

After these interviews Lady Byron communicated the outcome to Mrs. Villiers. Her success was truly edifying. But Mrs. Villiers, too, must be told by Augusta. She too must have the confession from the guilty lips. And it was arranged for the friend to put the wretched woman through another interrogatory. Of course Mrs. Villiers must not mention from whom she derived her suspicions. . . . She had heard from authority she could not doubt . . . from one who had been told by Byron himself of the crime. Augusta could say nothing in her own defense. Again she confessed.

What motive could Lady Byron have had in inflicting this added indignity upon Augusta? Was it that she still feared Ada might be taken from her if Byron should ever bring the divorce proceedings to court, and that since she would not be permitted to testify against her husband Mrs. Villiers might be called upon to do her the service? The validity of such testimony would have been dubious. Or was it that, since confession is good for the soul, Augusta's was thus obtaining a double benefit through the charitableness of her Guardian Angel and her friend?

The unhappy woman bore the inquisition without a murmur, in exemplary abasement of spirit, and with a "God bless you" at the end of her notes to "Dearest A" after she had been permitted to return to the comparative haven of Six Mile Bottom. According to the compact, she showed Byron's letters to her protectress and asked advice upon her behavior. They were absolute love letters, Lady Byron communicated, with firm underlining, to her confidante. Augusta must be adamant in her reformation. She must not encourage, she

must never *see* Byron more. At this the penitent relapsed.
Never see Byron? How could she promise never to see him
when at his least desire she knew herself ready to fall at his
feet?

Something of Augusta's real suffering must have shown
through her censored crinkum-crankum letters for Byron to
cry out to her: "All I know is — that no human power short
of destruction — shall prevent me from seeing you when —
where — and how — I may please. . . . Anything which is
to divide us would drive me quite out of my senses. . . .
Hope the best — and love me the most — as I ever must love
you." Self-abasement, repentance: where was their power
against words of such impenitent passion? Had even the least
of them been addressed to her, Lady Byron, who knows what
miracles might not have happened in her life, and his? But
she was not his kind. As she stood isolated within her magic
ring, so did he stand, with Augusta, apart from the world of
common loves and hates. Annabella half believed his fallen-
angel boast.

The third canto of *Childe Harold* was brought out by Murray, and Lady Byron read it. The outcast could still sing
in the land of banishment. Partly in jest, she had once told
him not to give himself up to the "abominable trade of versifying." Composition always made him irritable and impossible to live with. Never would she forget his rudeness when
once she interrupted him at his work, and on her asking
whether she was in the way, "Damnably," he had flung at her,
"Damnably!" It is perhaps understandable that on reading
the new canto she should have fixed only on his personal
allusions to her. "Cruel and cold," she complained to Lady
Anne Barnard, another secret-sharer. "It is said in this poem
that hatred of him will be taught as a lesson to his child. . . .
It is not my duty to give way to hopeless and wholly unrequited
affection; but, so long as I live, my chief struggle will probably
be not to remember him too kindly."

Not a word of the change in the poetry itself. The deeper
voice, the wider scope, the identification of self with the
universe, a revealed nobility of mind that declared at last
what in spite of acclaim he had not been until then, a poet —

all escaped her. To her he was still the Byron of *Lara*. "Egotism," she pronounced in one of her favorite character studies, "egotism is the vital principle of his imagination. . . . His constant desire of creating a sensation makes him not averse to be the object of wonder and curiosity." He was nourished by the praise of the populace, she thought, in spite of the lonely grandeur he affected. And she accused him of insincerity. "I know no one more habitually destitute of that enthusiasm he so beautifully expresses, and to which he can work up his fancy chiefly by contagion." The words are a portrait of Lady Byron herself. Had Augusta never existed, had Byron not suffered that first refusal, had their marriage been even conventionally successful, the rift would ultimately have come. In disbelieving his basic sincerity Lady Byron disbelieved the man.

The public too read the new volume and was puzzled, even as Hobhouse had been when he was shown the manuscript. He had at once perceived the greater power in it, but he had discovered as well an unfamiliar overtone. Shelley's influence, Wordsworthian pantheism . . . he pooh-poohed. A Byron should have nothing to do with metaphysics. What Hobhouse, Lady Byron, and a good part of the public failed to discern was the growth of the man. The idol of the populace who had held the pinnacle for three years — a longer season than is granted to fortune's darlings — had in his fall found wings. He rose again, beyond the reach of scorn, and, happily, beyond the praise which had proved its emptiness. A pretender, as Lady Byron saw him, an egotist avid for popular favor, would have dwindled into the miserable figure he was when deprived of the manna that sustained him. Byron was re-created.

While Augusta was being put through the question by the two well-meaning ladies, she was summoned in spirit to the heights of the Alps by the despairing conjuring of her brother. What was happening to her in that despicable world which, because he was a man, he had been able to spurn as it had spurned him? Her letters told him nothing definite, yet enough to fill him with uneasiness. He mistrusted the "kindness" of Lady Byron, following so close upon his parting adjuration, and looked upon her relations with Augusta as those of the snake with the dove. Poor, fluttering, childlike Augusta — what match was she for the wily one? To his way of thinking, Lady Byron, far from being sinned against, had sinned. Augusta had been her sacrifice and was now her victim, and his — yes, his — for having loved.

> If I had never lived, that which I love
> Had still been living; had I never loved,
> That which I love would still be beautiful. . . .

Again, as before, he was transmuting personal remorse and grief to poetry, this time to magnificent poetry. No longer a futile cry, it rose to a challenge against society, against the Creator, with a cosmic daring that robbed the denunciation of presumption. God and himself: he had been made in the image of that God. If now he rose to arraign, it was as one with a right for the essence of godhood in himself, and for the suffering imposed upon him. "My pang shall find a voice!" And from the depths of his bitterness it was lifted, and it spoke with the tongues of men and of angels, and not wholly of fallen angels. He was Manfred now, whose spirit from youth upwards had walked not with the souls of men.

> The aim of their existence was not mine;
> My joys, my griefs, my passions, and my powers
> Made me a stranger.

He had loved, as such a being would love, a sister-soul among mankind: —

> She was like me in lineaments — her eyes,
> Her hair, her features, all, to the very tone
> Even of her voice, they said were like to mine;
> But soften'd all, and temper'd into a beauty:
> She had the same lone thoughts and wanderings —
> . . . nor these
> Alone, but with them gentler powers than mine,
> Pity, and smiles, and tears — which I had not;
> And tenderness — but that I had for her . . .
> I loved her, and destroy'd her!

Again, again, it was the fatal thought giving him no rest. On the Alpine heights, as in his midnight room, he could not escape the stern Calvinist conscience. Even as much as Lady Byron he was concerned with Augusta's spiritual welfare. For himself he cared little; he was of the damned. But Augusta, his sweet sister? No power could wreak upon her a vengeance which he alone deserved. She came, beautiful as in her innocence, — yet now guilty, damned, through his sin, — and stood before him, silent to all his questioning, with passionless eyes that had gazed on eternity. What secret did she hold? For she must know — she had been with the dead.

> Astarte! my belovèd! speak to me . . .
> . . . We were not made
> To torture thus each other, though it were
> The deadliest sin to love as we have loved,
> Say that thou loath'st me not — that I do bear
> This punishment for both — that thou wilt be
> One of the blessèd.

But no answer came.

In spite of the phantoms that haunted a conscience that never slept, one had to live one's life, and Byron lived it, as fully if less wisely even than before. Scrope Davies, after a short visit, returned to England, the bearer of gifts from Byron to Augusta and the children and a special granite ball "for Ada — the love." Hobhouse remained with his lordship, who, thank goodness, finally got rid of Polly-Dolly. In November the two friends, with Fletcher and the addition of a dog whose sole recommendation was its ugliness, took the road toward Italy, the imperial carriage, more cumbrous than ever for the freight accumulated on the way, making slow progress. By the middle of December from Venice, "the fairy city of the heart," Byron was writing to his Astarte, "I have fallen in love with a very pretty Venetian of two and twenty. . . . She is married — and so am I — which is very much to the purpose. . . . I forgot to tell you — that the *Demoiselle* — who returned to England from Geneva — went there to produce a new baby B, who is now about to make his appearance."

XIX

"HARRIET SMITH"

Why did Harriet Shelley leave her father's house so soon after the return of her husband from the Continent that September of 1816?

For more than two years Harriet had been separated from Shelley, and whatever hope she had nursed that he would at last come back to her had long since faded. With the little girl Ianthe and the baby Charles Bysshe, she had found refuge, like any other young wife in distress, in the home of her parents. Her allowance, furnished both by Shelley and by her father, sufficed for herself and the children, so that on the score of money she had no need to worry. Eliza, as usual, looked after her. But soon the relations changed. It was one thing to take charge of the fortunate wife of a prospective heir, and quite another to have on one's hands a helpless woman saddled with two children and in an ambiguous social position that threatened to become definitely embarrassing as time went on. There was Harriet, a wife yet not a wife, given liberty by her husband and yet not free to marry anyone else if she chose. She was only twenty. With the memory still fresh of her three romantically full years of life with Shelley, she could not be expected to go willingly into retirement. Nevertheless, appearances had to be kept if one wished to profit by a final settlement. Therefore Eliza kept stern watch over her sister. She knew from her novel reading what recklessness one might be led to by bitterness and despair.

And Harriet had been desperate when, on Shelley's return from his first flight, he not only came back unrepentant, but convinced that he had made the right choice in Mary. Harriet had loved him, the Prince Charming of her girlish dreams, her awakener and her moral guide. Without him she found herself the common Harriet Westbrook, thrown back to her status and with the fine ideals she had learned from him making a mockery of themselves and her. What wonder she had no faith in them when, from her point of view, they could lead to such immorality as Shelley not only preached, but practised? She shrank back at first to the safety of middle-class decency. But alas, she had inhabited, if only for a short time, a heavenly region with Shelley, and she rebelled against her prison house guarded by Eliza, the keeper of the keys. Shelley no longer came to see her; she felt wholly forsaken. In her despair she spoke against him and thought of death as her only release.

"I am still at my father's house, which is very wretched . . ." she complained to Catherine Nugent. "Everyone goes against me. I am weary of life. I am so restrained here that life is scarcely worth having. . . . How many there are who shudder at death. . . . Is it wrong, do you think, to put an end to one's sorrows? I often think of it — all is so gloomy and desolate." A distressing sincerity spoke through the naïve dramatization of her feelings. Not even Hogg could have accused her now of putting on the mantle of tragedy to make herself interesting.

Because she was young, however, and sorely tried, she was easily persuaded by life to turn from her wooing of death. There were pleasures it could yet give her. Why should she not take them, like Shelley? Had he not written to her that some day she might find one who would be better suited than he had been to make her happy? Evading the vigilance of Eliza, and while Mary and Shelley were at Geneva, she formed a new connection. The man abandoned her in a few months, perhaps after she had confided to him that she was with child. It may be that, suddenly alive to her degradation on hearing that Shelley had returned, and unable to confront him with her shame, she ran away from her father's house and went into hiding to avoid a meeting. However it was, on the ninth of September she rented the second-floor lodgings at number 7 Elizabeth Street from Mrs. Jane Thomas, a widow, and gave her name as Harriet Smith.

Shelley made no inquiries after Harriet on his arrival, supposing, probably, that since he had no news of her all was going well with her and the children. He had hardly been home a month when he heard that Fanny Imlay had committed suicide, in a small hotel at Swansea. None knew why, and many reasons were advanced, though the note Fanny left spoke all too clearly: "I have long determined that the best thing I could do was to put an end to the existence of a being whose birth was unfortunate, and whose life has only been a series of pain to those persons who have hurt their health in endeavouring to promote her welfare. . . ." The name was torn off and burnt.

She had lately learned the circumstances of her birth from her aunts, and the knowledge had shocked her sensitive nature. Unlike Mary, she had always shrunk from asserting herself and, patiently humble, she had tried to make herself useful if not loved in that family where she had never felt anything but an alien. Godwin, after his own daughter left him, learned to depend upon the kindness of Fanny for his little comforts, and grew genuinely attached to her. Her death was one of the blows he felt severely in his long and much tried life.

Shelley assisted at the last painful offices. A little Swiss watch he had brought Fanny from the Continent was one of the few trinkets she had taken with her to her death. That, a red silk handkerchief, a brown berry necklace, and a small leather purse containing a few shillings were all her worldly goods; of the spiritual, only the memory of her mother, whose initials, M. W., she wore on her stays against her flesh, symbols of the suffering her birth had brought that brave and tragic figure. In July Fanny had written to Mary: "My mind always keeps my body in a fever; but never mind me." The words had been so long the poor girl's apology for existing that none ever minded her, unless something were required of her, when she would appear, gentle and uncomplaining. Even her death was planned so that it would not give much trouble to the living. At the Mackworth Arms Inn she went to her room and told the chambermaid she did not wish to be disturbed because she was tired. Next morning they found her lying dead, fully dressed, with her long brown hair covering her face, that none might be shocked at any trace of anguish on her features. An empty bottle of laudanum lay on a table beside her.

She had had no compunction about taking her life. Godwin had preached suicide as a justifiable act; Mary Wollstonecraft had attempted it. To the unhappy girl it offered itself as the only way out of a crowded earth that had no room for her. "I dread to unfold her mind, lest it should render her unfit for the world she is to inhabit" — Had Mary Wollstonecraft seen into her child's future when she expressed those fears? Godwin and his wife, and even Clare, said it was a hopeless love for Shelley that had made Fanny take her fatal decision. Shelley wrote only a sorrowful stanza commemorative of their last leave-taking.

> Her voice did quiver as we parted,
>   Yet knew I not that heart was broken
> From which it came, and I departed
>   Heeding not the words then spoken.
>   Misery — O Misery,
>   This world is all too wide for thee.

The poem remained a fragment.

After the brief stay at Peacock's, Mary went to Bath and Shelley to Leigh Hunt, who had long been asking him for the pleasure of a visit. Shelley had met him while Hunt had been serving his sentence, but the acquaintance had not had time to ripen into friendship. A mutual love of freedom attracted the men to each other. They had literary tastes in common. What is more, each respected in the other a loyalty to men and ideals that rose above creature comfort. Hunt had suffered for his right to speak freely; Shelley had made an enemy of society for daring to live according to his convictions.

Hunt's ménage was of the sort to delight Shelley's fancy. The crowned busts, the books in orderly rows on the shelves, — the only regions where chaos did not reign in that curious house, — surveyed by their monarch in his flowered dressing gown, breeches, and red slippers, made a colorful island in the green serenity of Hampstead. In a remoter region Marianne modeled her heads, or cut silhouettes out of paper, while the children, in flowing tunics, like their father, made free of the

rest of the cottage in a largeness of upbringing that gave them
their way till they were old enough to be reasoned with. That
liberal educational system suited the lively young barbarians
admirably, though Haydon, and other pedagogically correct
visitors, might have wished the rod had not been left to gather
dust. Bessie Kent presided in the background, a Minerva-
Cinderella, according to the part she was required to fill.
Oftenest, since Hunt's release, she had had to be sick nurse.

A morbid fear obsessed him, a dread of being afraid. Before his imprisonment he had suffered from a kindred melancholia, but in the security of the prison walls which, while
protecting him from the world that frightened him, stood also
as the solid proof that he *could* suffer for his principles, the
obsession slowly left him. Once more restored to liberty, he
had sunk into his old dread. For weeks he had been afraid to
leave his room, where he moped, incapable of casting off the
apathy that held him there. What would he do if he were
challenged to show physical courage? Would he shrink back,
a coward? He was in terror of being put to the test. Though
he could bear moral suffering with fortitude, physical pain set
him whimpering like a child. If he were to walk in the streets,
among people, provocation might be offered him — At last
he was prevailed upon to go out, and gradually his self-confidence returned, though there were times when he thought
with longing of those painted rooms in Horsemonger Lane
which shut out life's dangers and his own morbid cowardice.

Nevertheless he and his brother had not flagged in carrying on the battles of the *Examiner*. Pen in hand, Leigh
Hunt felt himself another man. Now, however, he devoted
himself to literary matters, although his political opinions remained unaltered, and persisted in wearing the soft turn-down
collars of liberalism as a challenge to the stocks and huge
cravats of the conservatives. On the first of December, 1816,
in an article entitled *Young Poets,* Leigh Hunt set himself
down forever as a discoverer of genius when he wrote of
Shelley, Keats, and Reynolds as poets who would be remembered in the future. True, he stressed Shelley's *original*
thinking rather than his poetry. Nevertheless in his case, as
in Keats's, the prediction proved true. Reynolds, after a

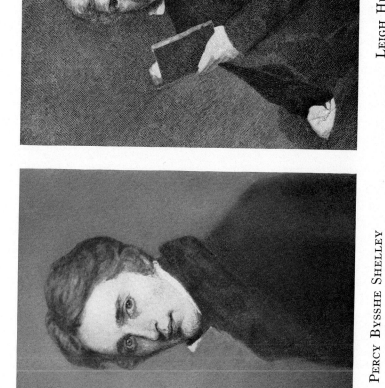

LEIGH HUNT

A PORTRAIT BY SAMUEL LAWRENCE

PERCY BYSSHE SHELLEY

A PORTRAIT BY W. E. WEST

burst of promise, was, even in the sun of Hunt's praise, showing signs of decay.

Shelley ransacked all of Marlow for a copy of the *Examiner* containing the precious article. There were back numbers galore, but not a trace of that important issue. It was the first time anyone had written a word of encouragement about his poetry, so that his curiosity was excusable. "I hear there is one at a village five miles off," he wrote Hunt hopefully in a letter containing a self-portrait in words, the gift of a five-pound note "for some little literary luxury" of which in the depressed state of his finances the friend of liberty might have been depriving himself, and details of the loan he was negotiating for him. It seemed Shelley's destiny to cement friendship with gold. Godwin, strictly speaking no friend, had given his shop a new lease through Shelley's bounty. Peacock found leisure for his writings with the help of an annuity from the same source. Now Leigh Hunt joined the ranks. His need, however, was real and urgent. The trial and the fines had thrown him heavily into debt. It was now a question of keeping a roof over his head, not to mention his progeny's and the venerable plaster immortals' on the bookcases.

Shelley arrived at Hunt's toward the middle of December, after having made unsuccessful inquiries about Harriet in London. No one seemed to know where she was. Peacock, through whom he had arranged that she receive the quarterly payments of her allowance, had seen nothing of her since June. Hookham had been unable to find any trace of her. Shelley had hardly returned to Bath from Hampstead when a letter came for him with news at last. "Harriet Smith" had been found, drowned in the Serpentine.

Little is known of the unfortunate girl's last days. From the time she had taken lodgings with the widow Thomas none seems to have cared what became of her, not even the once-devoted Eliza. Perhaps she had too much to do nursing Mr. Westbrook, then dangerously ill, to heed the actions of a girl as lost to honor as to fortune. There was more advantage in caring for a dying father. Yet soon after Saturday evening, the ninth of November, she must have known that Harriet was in extreme peril, that she might be already dead. There was no doubting the genuineness of despair in the letter the wretched girl addressed to her.

"My dearest and much beloved sister, — When you read this let^r I shall be no more an inhabitant of this miserable world. . . ." With touching words she told of her degradation, imploring Eliza's forgiveness. She sent a last message to Shelley. "I have not written to Bysshe. Oh, no, what would it avail, my wishes or my prayers would not be attended to by him, and yet should he rec. this, perhaps he might grant my request to let Ianthe remain with you always. Dear lovely child, with you she will enjoy much happiness, with him none. My dear Bysshe, let me conjure you by the remembrance of our days of happiness to grant my last wish. . . . Do not refuse my last request, I never could refuse you and if you had never left me I might have lived, but as it is I freely forgive you and may you enjoy the happiness which you have deprived me of. There is your beautiful boy, oh! be careful of him, and his love may prove one day a rich reward. . . . Now comes the sad task of saying farewell. Oh! I must be quick. God bless you and watch over you all. You dear Bysshe and you dear Eliza. May all happiness attend ye both is the last wish of her who loved ye more than all others. . . ."[1]

Did Shelley ever see the letter? The communications he sent to Mary showed no signs of affection or sorrow for Harriet, although he deplored her miserable end and denounced the Westbrooks as guilty of her death. "It seems that this poor woman — the most innocent of her abhorred and unnatural family — was driven from her father's house, and descended the steps of prostitution until she lived with a groom of the name of Smith, who deserting her, she killed herself. There can be no question that the beastly viper her sister, unable to gain profit from her connexion with her, has secured to herself the fortune of the old man — who is now dying — by the murder of this poor creature." It may be that because he was addressing Mary he refrained from any ex-

[1] Quoted from *Cornhill Magazine*, January 1922, where the letter was published for the first time by W. Courthope Forman.

pression of the grief he must be feeling for one who had once been dear, and whose self-inflicted death atoned for her transgressions. He did not condemn her. He could not. But deep within, remorse whispered that some share of the blame in that death was his. "If you had never left me I might have lived. . . ." Seen or unseen, the words of the dying girl burned in his conscience. Hunt saw the remorse on his face. He heard things that Shelley could not tell to Mary, whose position, by that death, would at last be righted in the world. For the sake of the unhappy woman whom he had never known, Hunt published after Shelley's death the stark little elegy in which, simply and poignantly, the stricken poet had lamented the misery of it all. He evoked the wintry scene with its presage of dissolution under the cold light of the sky, and he saw her, Harriet, once beloved, floating with scattered hair upon the stream, dead, with none to close her eyes fixed on the heavens.

> Thine eyes glowed in the glare
> Of the moon's dying light;
> As a fen-fire's beam on a sluggish stream
> Gleams dimly, so the moon shone there,
> And it yellowed the strings of thy tangled hair
> That shook in the wind of night.

The last of the four brief stanzas broke out with the pity so markedly absent from his letters.

> The moon made thy lips pale, beloved —
> The wind made thy bosom chill —
> The night did shed on thy dear head
> Its frozen dew, and thou didst lie
> Where the bitter breath of the naked sky
> Might visit thee at will.

Thus the *Times* report of a nameless woman's suicide and the secret lament of Shelley ushered Harriet out of the world.

But legal formalities had to be undergone before she could be suffered to lie at rest. After her body had been found floating in the river, it was carried to the Fox and Bull Inn, a receiving house for the Royal Humane Society. Many was the corpse that had been borne through the wooden gate behind the inn, opening into Hyde Park, where the Serpentine lured its victims to oblivion. An inquest was held, at which the widow Thomas gave her affidavit, saying that Harriet Smith appeared "in the family way and was during the time she lived in my house in a very desponding and gloomy way." Mary Jones, her servant, said the same, adding, "I saw nothing but what was proper in her conduct." Harriet, it seemed, had left her rooms between four and five o'clock on the afternoon of November 9. Where she had gone, whether she had walked through the streets till nightfall and then under the concealment of the dark had taken the fatal step, or whether she had deferred her decision for a time, none could tell. Her body showed no signs of decomposition, and the letter she had sent Eliza bore only "Sat. Eve." as the date.

None came forward to claim her either as Harriet Shelley or as Harriet Westbrook. By the compassionate mercy of Ann Phillips, the landlord's daughter at the Fox and Bull, who said that she knew the deceased, Harriet was spared a suicide's grave. But not the onus of her deed. She was buried as Harriet Smith, whose unwept and untended plot mingled in the lapse of years with the surrounding dust, beyond the need of posthumous piety.

No record of the tragic event found its way into Mary's diary, where she noted every progress made in her novel and in the drawing lessons she was taking from Mr. West. Then, for the latter part of December, the pages were left blank until a day or so before the end of the year, when, with Godwinian orderliness, she noted: "A marriage takes place on the 29th of December 1816." What made her mistake the date — in reality the thirtieth?

William Godwin, however, outdid himself surprisingly on the subject of that same marriage. He spread the news to all who knew him, far and near, and, after long desuetude, corresponded with his brother Hull. Mary had become the wife of Percy Bysshe Shelley in St. Mildred's Church. "Her husband is the eldest son of Sir Timothy Shelley . . ." Godwin crowed. "So that, according to the vulgar ideas of the world she is well married, and I have great hopes the young man will make her a good husband. You will wonder, I daresay, how a girl without a penny of fortune should meet with so good a match. But such are the ups and downs of the world." Thus spake the philosopher of Reason. Yet that his elation be not misconstrued, "for my part," he added, "I care but little, comparatively, about wealth, so that it should be her destiny in life to be respectable, virtuous and contented." Only two short years back he had called Mary's elopement a crime and had expostulated with Shelley "to give up his licentious love and return to virtue." Now, by the power of that ceremony in St. Mildred's Church, past crimes had been assoiled, and Mary and Shelley, white as new-washed lambs, were folded to the bosom of the forgiving shepherd. Poor Harriet, who used to fill the dinginess of Skinner Street with the sheen of her purple satin gowns, was forgotten. That same river that had cleansed her of her sins made possible Shelley's absolution. There's no ill wind, Godwin must have sighed and said. Had his good mother still lived she need no more have feared that London would one day be filled with "begging Godwins." One Godwin, at least, had married the son of a baronet. It was some satisfaction to the strangely mundane philosopher to sign his name as witness to the marriage document, endorsed, too, by the hand of M. J., garrulous on her stepdaughter's good luck. Well might she have echoed Godwin about the ups and downs of the world. Whatever her thoughts, she was so overcome with the sudden fortunes of Mary that she served the bridal pair breakfast before the wedding, then dinner, and supper too. The ceremony was indeed "magical in its effects," as Shelley commented with cynical humor.

Clare, meanwhile, was staying at Bath with Elise and "'Itty Babe" in rooms over a barber's shop in Bond Street, as she disconsolately awaited the birth of her own child. No one at the Godwins' suspected her condition, and both Mary and Shelley answered guardedly the few questions asked about her health. Indeed, not in their wildest surmising would Godwin and M. J. have conceived of any relation of intimacy between her and the famous Lord Byron.

Clare often wished she had never met him. The discomforts of her pregnancy worked havoc with her nerves, and the

quarrels between her and Mary never ceased. This war of
words, however, was the least of Mary's worries. The constant presence of a third person in the house, and that a pretty
woman, pregnant, and without any visible husband, raked up
a malignant curiosity wherever they lived, with scandal hissing
at their door. People had long had it that Shelley had run
off with two of Godwin's daughters, healing the father's hurt
with money. To such sordid allegations Shelley replied with
the silent scorn of innocence. But there Mary was not at
one with him. She craved the good opinion of her neighbors,
the more since for over two years she had been suffering
under their ostracism. If only Clare were placed somewhere,
somehow . . . if only Shelley could be made to realize the
awkwardness of their position with that girl eternally in their
house. "Give me a garden," she pleaded when he went house
hunting for their new quarters, "give me a garden and *absentia*
Clare, and I will thank my love for many favours." The sub-
stitution of the Latin word did not modify the unkindness of
her wish at a time when Clare, unfriended and wholly dependent upon them, had the greatest need of sympathy.

On Sunday, the twelfth of January of 1817, Clare was
brought to bed of a child, not the male "baby B" of whom
Byron had written so blithely to Augusta, but of a little girl
whose sweet infant mouth and deep blue eyes gave promise of
great beauty. Clare called her Alba, as an augury that the
dawn of that life might be propitious of a brighter day. Too,
it was an echo of that other name, Albè, which had brought
Byron humanly closer during those months of comparative
happiness at Geneva. "Four days of idleness," Mary noted
in her diary after this event which kept her at Clare's bedside to the sacrifice of her writing and studies. She penned
a precise little note to Byron, announcing his new fatherhood,
and with evident pleasure signed herself "Mary W. Shelley."
From London Shelley too wrote Byron, a long letter full of
the "exquisite symmetry" and beauty of the baby in whom,
though at the date of his writing she was scarcely five days
old, he had already discovered "a vigor and sensibility very
unusual." That Byron might not have been as enthusiastic
as himself never entered his mind. He was fond of Clare, he

admired Byron, he felt drawn to the child. Her unhappy birth made her the dearer for the demand it made on his protection.

After Harriet's death he renewed his plea to the Westbrooks for the possession of Ianthe and Charles, and there Mary was wholly with him, knowing how dearly he wished his children out of the toils of Eliza, whom he had come to regard as the malignant spirit behind her sister's suicide. The Westbrooks, however, held on firmly to their charges. Little Charles, in the event of Shelley's death, would fall heir to Sir Timothy's possessions. With Shelley out of reach, they could at least cling to his son, although, in her dying letter, Harriet had charged her husband to "be careful of him." It was a case for the courts. And to the courts the Westbrooks brought it, as they had long threatened.

Armed with a number of letters from Shelley to Harriet after their rupture, with a copy of *Queen Mab* and the story of Shelley's expulsion from University College, further re-enforced by the scandal of the young reprobate's practice of anti-matrimonialism with a daughter of the notorious perpe-trator of *Political Justice,* the lawyers of the Westbrooks brought their suit before Lord Chancellor Eldon. On his side Shelley had only his love for his children, the purity of his motives, and the testimony of William Godwin, who had sud-denly unearthed evidence that Harriet had been unfaithful to Shelley four months before he had left England with Mary. The fact that he was now *married* to Mary bore also in his favor.

Unfortunately, however, there was small likelihood that the rebel who had defied in his twenty-five years all the sanctities of British morality should find mercy in the eyes of the law. Sir Samuel Romilly, that evil comet of Byron's legal heavens, shed his lurid lustre in Shelley's case — on the Westbrook side.

On the twenty-fourth of January, baby William's birthday, Shelley's plea for the possession of his other children was heard before the Lord Chancellor. On March 27 the verdict was given. His lordship could not, under any circumstances, turn over the infant plaintiffs to their father, whose principles he reprehended as highly immoral. Neither did he deem the

Westbrooks fit guardians. Had not Mr. Westbrook kept a coffeehouse? As for Miss Eliza, she was "illiterate, vulgar, and . . . it was by her advice and with her active concurrence . . . that Mr. Shelley, when at the age of nineteen, ran away with Miss Harriet Westbrook." After much temporizing Ianthe and Charles were entrusted to the care of a respectable Dr. Hume, physician to the Duke of Cambridge, and his very virtuous wife, Shelley and Mr. Westbrook paying yearly for their maintenance. Once a month Shelley would have leave to visit his children, but always in the presence of the worthy doctor and his wife, that he might not infect their young minds with his heterodox opinions. "So beautiful! What a pity he is so wicked!" Such seemed the final decree of justice, words that on another occasion had been pronounced by her champion, Godwin.

Lord Eldon's judgment, however, had been in strict accord with the morality of the day. Shelley had affronted public opinion. It was now its turn to take revenge, even if it had to wound through Shelley's own flesh and blood.

XX

THE COCKNEY SCHOOL

SOME time after John Keats had received his diploma to practise, he shocked Mr. Abbey out of his customary stolidness by announcing that he did not intend to be a surgeon.

"Not be a surgeon!" the good man cried aghast. "Why, what do you mean to be?"

"I mean to rely upon my ability as a poet."

"John, you are either mad or a fool, to talk in so absurd a manner."

"My mind is made up," said Keats with quiet decision. "I know that I possess abilities greater than most men, and therefore I am determined to gain my living by exercising them."

Before such self-confidence Mr. Abbey could do nothing. He had long given up hope of making a staid citizen out of this, his eldest ward. He could, however, keep him from contaminating his sister Fanny's mind with his dangerous notions, and henceforth he limited John's intercourse with her. He could see her only at stated times and under proper surveillance. Mr. Abbey was not going to have her turn out like her mother.

His surgical instruments laid away and his fat medical books dispossessed to make room for his beloved poets, — his Chaucer, Spenser, Shakespeare, Chatterton, Hunt, and Mrs. Tighe, whose *Psyche* he admired for its gentle music, — he settled down in earnest to become a poet. Under Hunt's influence he had written a number of sonnets that won his enthusiastic praise and his friends', for Hunt kept nothing of beauty to himself. Horace Smith, the Novellos, the Ollier brothers, who were establishing a publishing house for the encouragement of fledgling poets, all were told of the young wonder, Keats, and were invited to meet him. And Keats walked on clouds. Following the Huntian fashion, he sent and received laurel wreaths and posies. He discoursed on the pleasures of the imagination, and agreed with his dear Libertas on the superlative rapture of a lovely woman in a rural spot. With him he deplored the abject state of the animal, man, extolled the blessings of freedom, and even celebrated the patriot Kosciusko in a sonnet. Wars and all wanton destruction he condemned, and would have had the world an idyllic realm of peace where flourished the arts and divinest poetry.

Just such a region in miniature had he found in Hampstead. Whenever possible he walked from Cheapside to Hunt's, spending the evening with him, now talking of books while the coals glowed on the hearth, now competing with him in the writing of a sonnet on a given subject. The friendly rivalry helped to weld their friendship. One evening they chose as their theme the Grasshopper and the Cricket. Friends dropped in, and Hunt praised before them with genuine delight Keats's first line, "The poetry of earth is never dead." Sometimes they tried to bring to Hampstead a little of ancient Hellas, and going out to the garden Hunt would return laden with laurel sprays which they made into wreaths for their heads. As they were both sitting together one evening in their crowns, some ladies entered. Quickly Hunt removed his wreath and motioned Keats to do the same. "I'll not take it off for any human being," he cried in a fit of prankish stubbornness, and throughout the visit sat solemnly with the laurel circling his ruddy curls. He knew it was no mockery that he wore Apollo's tree. In his veins he felt Olympian ichor flowing. Might he not be himself a son of the gods? He intimated as much in "I stood tip-toe," that first pæan of recognized power, when with the ecstasy of youth in a glorious spring day he gave full voice to his premonitions of greatness.

> Cynthia! I cannot tell the greater blisses,
> That follow'd thine, and thy dear shepherd's kisses:
> Was there a poet born? — but now no more,
> My wand'ring spirit must no further soar.

Often, when the two men found the midnight surprising their conversations, Keats was invited to stay till morning.

A bed was made up for him on chairs in the studio-library, and there, with the busts of the immortals watching over his sleep, he realized in dreams what he had yet to attain. Sometimes in the brisk winter nights he would take leave of Hunt and, his face bared to the wind and the dark, make his way across the Hampstead fields, through the long distance to the city. He had no care for the night and the cold, the rustling of the dead leaves and the pale, lonely glimmer of the stars. He was brimful of warmth for the friendliness he had found in the Hampstead cottage, as thoughts of Milton ran through his head, the godlike Milton, a lock of whose hair Hunt treasured among his possessions. And dispelling the wintry countryside, he dreamed

> Of lovely Laura in her light green dress,
> And faithful Petrarch gloriously crown'd.

At 41 Great Marlborough Street, the chaos over which Haydon was god, Keats's imagination expanded under other experiences. The studio was a jumble of casts, lay figures tricked in historical costumes, masks, studies, cartoons, and there, where the light was best, rose the vast new painting, still unfinished. Haydon fell at once upon Keats as a model. He would immortalize him, he said. Together with the great heads of Wordsworth and Hazlitt, he would place his in the crowd that watched Christ's entry into Jerusalem. "If I sell it," he would say, "you'll never lack anything." He was genuinely smitten with the youth whose eye had an inward look, "perfectly divine, like a Delphian priestess who saw visions." Keats, on his part, placed him on a pinnacle with the age's wonders. There were three things to rejoice in, he said — Wordsworth's *Excursion,* Hazlitt's "depth of taste," and Haydon's painting. Haydon was pleased, though he would have desired to occupy the height alone.

In the stirring atmosphere of the studio Keats moved like a wanderer in an antique land. Here a copy of some classic frieze brought to his rapt sight a glimpse of the life he had reconstructed only in his imagination. The cast of an heroic head contained infinity in its pupilless eyes. The past lay hidden there, as if time had never been. It gazed on him, intimate yet ageless, as it had gazed on youths and maidens whose very dust had perished.   Long before this, however, the horizon of that desired region had opened for him when, with Cowden Clarke, he had sat entranced through a reading of Chapman's translation of Homer.   Though much traveled in those realms of gold, never had he experienced the glory of Greece till he had heard Chapman speak.   He had discovered the land of his poetic choice.   Now he was treading its hallowed soil, as his eyes feasted on its actualities.   With Haydon he went to see the Elgin Marbles, and, urged by his guide to write about them, answered only in a feeble sonnet, deploring his unworthiness before their beauty.   No, he could not speak about things for whose greatness he could find no words; but he would give praise to one who had beheld "the Hesperean shine of their star in the East, and gone to worship them."

Haydon showed his disappointment.   He had expected a cry of exultation and heard a plea of despair.   Keats must assert himself.   Was he not, like him, a son of immortality?   Under the influence of Haydon's mood Keats wrote again, this time a wearied titan, pining in exile for his sun-lit heights.

> My spirit is too weak — mortality
>   Weighs heavily on me like unwilling sleep,
>   And each imagin'd pinnacle and steep
> Of godlike hardship, tells me I must die
> Like a sick Eagle looking at the sky.

Who was he?   Only John Keats, obscurely born, cursed with the worship of sun and moon where mists alone surrounded him.   How could he soar when hereditary taint held him down?

Happily it was a transient fit of depression, one of those which would seize him suddenly without warning when he had most reason to rejoice.   "Truth is, I have a horrid morbidity of temperament," he confessed to Haydon. . . .   "It is, I have no doubt, the greatest enemy and stumbling block I have to fear; I may even say it is likely to be the cause of my disappointment."   A portentous discovery.

For these periods Haydon would offer the faith that had solaced him in times of trial — and he had experienced many.

A force directed one's every act from above, he maintained. Everything he did had a shadowy finger guiding him toward it. By degrees he had metamorphosed the God of his faith to a Socratic dæmon and the great spirits of the past to familiars of his painting room who told him what to do, even to the planning of a canvas. Keats, who had no settled religion and had at first inclined to the urbane skepticism of the Hampstead set, found himself held by Haydon with the clutch of an angel fighting for the possession of a soul against the Prince of the Powers of the Air. A rivalry, not always friendly, sprang up between him and Hunt for ascendency over Keats's beliefs. The young man gave each his way, now favoring the one, and now the other. One Sunday in the closing year he wrote a sonnet on hearing the church bells toll, calling the people "to some other prayers, some other gloominess, more dreadful cares. . . . " "Surely the mind of man is closely bound in some dark spell," he reflected, as he saw the crowds forsake fireside joys to listen to the "sermon's horrid sound." He comforted himself, and incidentally the prompting spirit, Hunt, with the thought that vulgar superstition, in the tolling of the bells, was dying like an outburnt lamp, and that flowers would be growing over its ruins. Later he salved Haydon's jealousy. "I remember your saying that you had notions of a good genius presiding over you. I have lately had the same thought, for things which I do half at random are afterwards confirmed by my judgment in a dozen features of propriety. Is it too daring to fancy Shakspeare this presider?"

One day in January while Keats was correcting the proof sheets of the book of poems he was bravely launching upon its fate under the insignia of the Olliers, there occurred over Horace Smith's hospitable board a clash so momentous between Haydon, the defender of the faith, and Shelley, the infidel, that back in his studio the artist jotted down a vivid and not impartial account of the fray. Smith the host, Hunt with his wife and Bessie, Shelley, Keats, and he, Haydon, made up the party, perhaps the first at which Shelley and Keats had ever been together, though Hunt had already linked their names in his article. Haydon, blustering in after the rest had begun eating, found himself seated opposite "a hectic, spare, weakly yet intellectual-looking creature," who was carefully carving a bit of broccoli on his plate. Quite unexpectedly that gentle-seeming man raised a boyish treble and uttered words that made Haydon rear his squat frame like a baited bull. "As to that detestable religion, the Christian —"

Haydon listened no further, but looked about him. Hunt, between his admiring nymphs, smiled with roguish enjoyment while the youth continued his tirade. Who was he? Shelley? Haydon had been invited expressly to meet him. If it was Shelley, Haydon would soon show him what stuff he was made of — but not while the servant was present. His lofty arguments were not meant for vulgar ears. The dessert served and the servant gone, Haydon, like a stag at bay, resolved to gore his antagonist. But he reckoned without Shelley's serpent wiles. Shrill, subtle, agile in mind and body, he led the breathless Haydon through a dizzying dance round the pillars of established religion, calling upon the ancient philosophers and even Shakespeare for support. The bull in the china shop blundered no less clumsily than Haydon, but what he could not accomplish by quickness he strove for by stubborn force.

"The Mosaic dispensations are inconsistent with Christianity," Shelley darted.

"By Heaven, they are not. The Ten Commandments have been the foundation of all the codes of law on earth."

Shelley confuted him with arguments he had once used on the unsuspecting ministers of the church with whom, as Jeremiah Stukeley, he had corresponded in his Oxford days. Hunt lightly seconded him, the while Haydon roared and bellowed in exasperated impotence.

Neither Keats nor Smith took part in the contest which continued between the two main adversaries with now and then a goad from Hunt, until, "finding I was a match for them in argument," Haydon recorded, "they became personal, and so did I." He never forgave Shelley for differing with him, and from then on gave him up for lost. Genius he might have, and many virtues. In his private reckoning Haydon put him down among the goats.

One lamb, however, he was bent on saving from such evil influences, and every day his zeal for Keats's salvation increased. Haydon had nothing to fear from Shelley, as Keats did not take to him. He was the son of a baronet, and Keats felt too keenly his own humble origin, though it must be said for Shelley that he had as much contempt for rank as the veriest republican. Again, Shelley had made the tactless mistake of warning the younger poet against rushing into print — gratuitous advice to one who had been given ampler praise in Hunt's article, and whose book was already being bound in neat boards with a label reading *Keats's Poems*. The danger lay in Hunt's airy skepticism, which he made a snare, like his reading of poetry and his singing of Italian songs to the accompaniment of the pianoforte. How singular, reflected Haydon — the fiend had taken possession of Hunt's soul, and was now employing every artifice to seize those of his friends. Many an evening, after the bowl had gone round, Hunt would take his Bible, and, pointing to some passage, ask Haydon in his sweetest voice, the Serpent himself speaking: "Do you really believe this?" as one might say, "Now, really, with your intellect, you could n't . . . " "Yes!" Haydon would sputter, fixing him with terrible eyes. "By Heaven, is it possible . . . " And shaking his head pityingly at such a mind become a slave to superstition, Hunt would saunter to the piano and break into, *"Addio, il mio cuore."*

Keats, preoccupied with the fate of his firstling, paid scant heed to the continued struggle for his soul. He was civil to Shelley, though not sympathetic, posed for Haydon, and wrote a dedication to Hunt, who made much of the book and its coming success. His friend Reynolds, and Bailey, the Oxford student who helped him with the spelling and stressing of Greek names, his brothers, and Georgiana Wylie hailed him a poet. Even Charles Ollier, unlike his publishing brethren, was infected with the common enthusiasm and wrote a sonnet to the author, extolling his eager grasp at immortality.

The days passed, and the weeks. All the important literary reviews were thumbed over for some notice of John Keats's poems; not a mention enlivened the dreary pages. Hunt and Clarke tried to conceal their apprehension. The book, so far as critic and purchaser were concerned, might have emerged in the Sahara. And yet the little volume of 1817 contained better poetry than either Byron or Shelley had written at Keats's age. It was not only a promise, but a fulfillment. It had a sonnet, "On First Looking into Chapman's Homer," which was destined to take an honored place in the literature of England, and it contained lines that for grandeur bore comparison with great names. A delicate fancy invested his descriptions; he captured the very breath of nature in his wild-flower verses. He made one see, and feel, and breathe them.

> Open afresh your round of starry folds,
> Ye ardent marigolds!
> Dry up the moisture from your golden lids . . .
> Here are sweet peas, on tip-toe for a flight:
> With wings of gentle flush o'er delicate white,
> And taper fingers catching at all things,
> To bind them all about with tiny rings.

In one of the long poems, "Sleep and Poetry," he tore down the respected standards and set up his own. He had not yet the ardor of the battle for social freedom, like Hunt and, better, Shelley, but here, in the struggle for the liberation of verse from its vassalage to the past, he could strike a lance against the foppery and barbarism that had entered the lists where those who could not understand Apollo's glories

> . . . swayed about upon a rocking-horse,
> And thought it Pegasus!

He had no liking, either, for the "strange thunders from the potency of song" heard in his day, alluding indirectly to the followers of Byron's romantic violence.

> A drainless shower
> Of light is poesy,

he declared against their rumblings,

> . . . 'T is the supreme of power;
> 'T is might half slumb'ring on its own right arm.

Though marred by Huntian lusciousness and occasional disregard for the accepted meaning of a word so that it serve the exigency of rhyme, though embarrassed with echoes from his favorite authors, Keats's poetry contained an individual excellence that should have brought the critical lions out of their lairs, if only to growl. They remained for the moment quiescent. A family censor, however, let his voice be heard.

"Well, John," said Mr. Abbey, "I have read your book, and it reminds me of the Quaker's horse which was hard to catch, and good for nothing when caught. So your book is hard to understand and good for nothing when it is understood."

Haydon, as usual, brought out his stylistic hyperboles. "I have read your 'Sleep and Poetry' — it is a flash of lightning that will rouse men from their occupations, and keep them trembling for the crash of thunder that *will* follow." Not content with giving a private opinion, he penned a laudatory review which appeared in the *Chronicle,* unsigned. But Haydon would have been greater than himself had he resisted the temptation of doing himself a service at the same time. With bland effrontery, he closed his article by reprinting the sonnets Keats had written on him and the Elgin Marbles.

Unhappily the flash of lightning was seen of but few, and as the months passed and Ollier saw the stacks of Keats's volume undiminished in his storeroom, he was inclined to believe it a flash in the pan. George Keats, jealous for his brother's fame, blamed the financial unsuccess on the publisher's lethargy and wrote to tell him so in no mincing terms. Ollier, wounded, answered rashly, and the cordial relations between him and Keats came to an end.

Keats must get away from the Hampstead group; he must live in solitude and find himself, Haydon counseled. Hunt and his set could do him no good. Already people were pointing out influences in his work — a bad thing for a new poet. Moreover, Hunt was a red rag before the bullish conservatives, and he, Keats, had made a fatal error in dedicating his book to so unpopular a patron. He needed quiet and leisure for study. Did he not realize that his knowledge was scant, his rich mind still unexplored? Had he had a good classical background like Bailey, or that infidel Shelley, Keats would not have stood in wordless awe before the Parthenon marbles. Haydon lent him Goldsmith's *History of Greece*. Let him go, now, and plumb his depths.

Keats had himself seen his deficiencies. "O for ten years," he cried,

> ". . . that I may overwhelm
> Myself in poesy; so I may do the deed
> That my own soul has to itself decreed."

Ten years. . . . It seemed a long time to a youth of twenty-one. Many were the works he might accomplish. He and Shelley had decided each to write a long poem in friendly competition during the rest of that year. The subject of *Endymion* was seething in his mind. He would leave London and begin work upon it, that the indifferent world be roused by Haydon's prophesied crash of thunder. Shelley, who had found a house for himself and his family at Marlow, invited the younger poet to stay with him. Keats refused. He was breaking away from one influence and would not subject himself to another. After consulting with his brothers, who urged him to do what was best for himself, he set out in April, on the Lymington and Poole Mail, from Holborn for the Isle of Wight.

All night long he did not sleep, but gazed in the vague light on the unfamiliar landscape — the long heath broom furze, the hurdles, the reflected windows of a house upon the lawn grass. Toward sunrise, as the coach rumbled through the sleeping town of Chawton, in Hampshire, he passed unknowing a trim little cottage with drawn blinds, behind which Mrs. Austen and her daughter Jane were still sleeping.

At the Isle of Wight the primroses were in bloom, spreading to the edge of the sea, which he had never seen. He had not written anything for weeks, but now, with the surge of Shakespeare, whom he had been reading, beating in his ear, and the louder crashing of the billows on the shore, he felt his own song awakening. He wrote on the sea, and came out new-bathed as if from a plunge in the ocean. The change had done him good. Haydon was right. How distant seemed the tame hills of Hampstead and the prettinesses of Hunt, under whose shepherding he had felt himself becoming "a pet lamb in a sentimental farce"! Perhaps the world had been justified in ignoring the first offering of Keats, the Hunt disciple. He would soon show what he could do.

In the rooms he found at Carisbrooke with a good woman by the name of Cooke, he unpacked his books and *lares,* and placed them about him — his volumes of Shakespeare, a "glorious" Haydon which he pinned on the wall, a Mary Queen of Scots, and Milton, with his daughters in a row. But there was something he coveted — a head of Shakespeare which he found hanging in a passage of Mrs. Cooke's house. Would she let him have it? Seeing his eagerness to possess it, the kind woman gave it to him, though he stayed with her no more than a week. With this treasured relic he left for Margate, where his brother Tom joined him. "Do you not think this ominous of good?" he asked about his find to Haydon, believer in guiding spirits. He told his brother George about the picture, and Georgiana, who knitted the bard a pair of handsome tassels which hung on either side of the frame like very long and very colorful ears. For love of Georgiana, Keats kept them there, though he was not sure that the Swan of Avon might not have preferred his effigy unadorned.

Before quitting London, Keats had been introduced to the firm of Taylor and Hessey, who were Hazlitt's publishers. Mr. Taylor, a cultured literary dilettante redeemed by a shrewd business sense, had, with the help of his partner Hessey, who ruled over the retail department, made of his publishing house a thriving concern. At first Taylor had demurred at opening his doors to a young, unsuccessful poet whose only recommendation seemed to be a passion for poetry. But Mr. Taylor was not inaccessible, especially after Richard Woodhouse, his friend and literary advisor, made himself Keats's advocate. The Olliers had not done justice to the young man's book, he pleaded. He himself had read it, and had known at once that this was no ordinary talent. Taylor listened and was convinced. One of that rare type of literary man incapable of envy, Woodhouse had early discovered his own shortcomings as a poet, and thenceforth directed his efforts toward the encouragement of his betters. He still versified, without false illusions, kept chambers at King's Bench walk in the Temple, where he practised as solicitor, and acted as the power behind the Taylorian throne. From the time he met with Keats's work he dedicated himself to preserving every scrap that came his way. He knew that some day posterity would be grateful to him.

On the strength of Woodhouse's enthusiasm, Taylor and Hessey had elected themselves the publishers of Keats's *Endymion*. Heartened by an advance of twenty pounds with which "to destroy some of the minor heads of that hydra the dun," Keats began work in earnest on the poem by which he was to stand or fall. Poetry had become the breath of his life. "I find I cannot exist without poetry — without eternal poetry," he wrote. "Half of the day will not do — the whole of it. I began with a little, but habit has made me a Leviathan." Under his poetic frenzy he wrote on steadily in spite of distractions and constant changing of scene. Tom returned to London, his health improved by his stay in the country. Before the hectic face and too bright eyes of his brother, Keats trembled lest the curse which had carried away his mother had fallen on poor Tom. "Poor Tom . . ." he was never to read the words in *Lear* without a catch in his heart.

George, who had quarreled with Mr. Abbey, found a place in Well Walk for himself and Tom, and, his sojourning over, Keats went to live with them. He took another brief vacation, this time at Oxford with Bailey, and then to Stratford-on-Avon, where a visit to the birthplace of his presiding genius inspired him to renewed activity. On his return to London in October, three books of *Endymion* were completed. One book more, and then —

In the meantime a few tardy critics had deigned to make some slight reference to the *Poems* that had appeared that spring. The *Monthly Review* and the *Scots and Edinburgh Magazine* gave a modicum of praise, seasoned with friendly advice on the part of the Scotch reviewer that the poet cast off the "uncleanness" of Hunt's influence. The *Eclectic Review*, though less explicit, drove the point home when it regretted "that a young man of vivid imagination and fine talents should have fallen into so bad hands as to have been flattered into the resolution to publish verses, of which a few years hence he will be glad to escape from the remembrance." The allusion to the bad hands escaped no one. In three issues of the *Examiner* during June and July Hunt had been reviewing his protégé's volume at some length. He could have done Keats no greater disservice.

It was not until October 1817, however, that the challenge to a fray that was literally to continue to the death was given by the débutant *Blackwood's Magazine* in the first of a series of articles on the "Cockney School of Poetry," introduced by the posy: —

> Our talks shall be (a theme we never tire on)
> Of Chaucer, Spenser, Shakspeare, Milton, Byron,
> (Our England's Dante) — Wordsworth — HUNT and KEATS
> The Muses' Son of promise; and what feats
> He yet may do.

Hunt and Keats. The linking of the two names signalized mischief.

The article fell like a shower of mud upon Hunt's unsuspecting head. True, the cloud had been gathering, looming blacker since the publication of the *Story of Rimini* and now and then scattering a few thick drops. Never had abuse come down in such a torrent. *Z*, the writer of the article, took it upon himself to stand godfather to a school which he observed growing. "This school has not, I believe, as yet received any name; but if I may be permitted to have the honour of christening it, it may henceforth be referred to by the designation of THE COCKNEY SCHOOL. . . ." Mr. Leigh Hunt was given the dubious fame of being at the head of it because of his typical cockney writings. "One feels the same disgust at the idea of opening *Rimini* that impresses itself on the mind of a man of fashion, when he is invited to enter, for a second time, the gilded drawing-room of a little mincing boarding-school mistress. . . . The extreme moral depravity of the Cockney School is another thing which is forever thrusting itself upon the public attention. . . . How could any man of high original genius ever stoop publicly, at the present day, to dip his fingers in the least of those glittering and rancid obscenities which float on the surface of Mr. Hunt's Hippocrene? His poetry resembles that of a man who has kept company with kept mistresses. His muse talks indelicately like a tea-sipping milliner girl.

"The founder of the Cockney School would fain claim poetical kindred with Lord Byron. . . . How must the haughty spirit of *Lara* and *Harold* contemn the subaltern sneaking of our modern tuft-hunter. The insult which he offered to Lord Byron in the dedication of *Rimini* . . . excited a feeling of utter loathing and disgust in the public mind, which will always be remembered whenever the name of Leigh Hunt is mentioned."

Who was this *Z*, so tender of the haughty spirit of a man who had had to flee England on the same accusation of moral depravity that was now being hurled, unjustly, against Hunt? How did he constitute himself the guardian of the reading public? Hunt, angered by the brutal indecency of the attack, demanded to know *Z's* name, but *Blackwood's* would not divulge it. The following month a continuation of the Cockney School article appeared, more personal and, if possible, more abusive. Hunt made a counterattack. He was on the defensive, however, and fighting in the dark against he did not know whether one or many enemies. Backed by his friends, and his morbid dread of cowardice overcome, he challenged *Z* to a duel, but no satisfaction could be obtained from a letter of the alphabet.

In the opulent era of the fat Adonis of Carlton House, magazines had perforce to act as political mouthpieces for one party or the other. Despite — rather, because of — the wave of prosperity on the wake of the war, interests had to be safeguarded by a tactful directing of public opinion. Discontent must not be suffered to find voice, and thus the powerful Tory journals were ever ready to drown in a loyal roar any defense of the lower orders that came from such leveling sheets as the *Examiner,* notorious since its founding for its disrespect to the British lion. *Blackwood's* and the *Quarterly,* in their staunch adherence to the *right,* held out leonine paws, ready to crush. With the *Quarterly* the chastening had begun at home when an ardent republican was made first a conservative, and then laureate. Of course, unfortunate accidents sometimes occurred, as when, in that same year of 1817, Southey's revolutionary *Wat Tyler* attained unauthorized publication after twenty-three years, sold sixty thousand copies, and was read by a liberal in the House of Commons who contrasted its fiery idealism with Southey's current writing in the *Quarterly,* to show how a turncoat could play a profitable game. Against the insidious cunning of such disloyal party members, and against such policies as the *Examiner* held, Britannia had to defend herself through her Tory henchmen.

Now two young men had lately found employment in *Blackwood's,* promising talents both, with pens which in their hands could be made to run vitriol instead of ink. John Wilson, thirty-two years old, the son of a wealthy Glasgow merchant, had distinguished himself at Oxford. John Gibson Lockhart, in his early twenties, besides possessing a degree from the same university, had come back from a cultural accolade bestowed at Weimar by no less a hand than Goethe's. Wilson and Lockhart had met two years earlier in Edinburgh when they were both pacing the Hall of Lost Steps preparatory to being called to the bar. Wilson had published two poetic volumes that had made Crabb Robinson break out with, "A female Wordsworth is the designation of this author," who in everyday life was a swashbuckling giant, athletic and unkempt. Lockhart, sharp-witted and unscrupulous, audacious and with a poisonous stylus, had won himself the name of Scorpion, an appellation made public in the mercilessly cutting satire, the "Chaldee MS," in the first number of *Blackwood's,* where, beside Wilson, "the beautiful leopard . . . there came also from a far country, the scorpion which delighteth to sting the faces of men."

Both the Leopard and the Scorpion had been following the career of Hunt since his liberation. They had seen him becoming a celebrity by his poetry; now they observed young men dedicating their books to him. Something had to be done, and Lockhart, with or without the aid of the beautiful leopard, chose the Z method of attack to do it. Hunt's parrying roused him to further virulence. One victim did not suffice; he wanted more. In January 1818, *Z* published an open letter to Hunt, enumerating the charges he had still to make against him. "I mean to handle each of these topics in turn," he promised, "and now and then to relieve my main attack upon you, by a diversion against some of your younger and less important auxiliaries, the Keatses, the Shellys [*sic*]. . . ."

Endymion, nearly completed, was in the hands of Taylor and Hessey, while Keats wrote on. Shelley's *Laon and Cythna* had but lately been published. The Scorpion sharpened his sting.

XXI

THE PARADISE OF EXILES

WHILE he was still harboring the hope that his children by Harriet might come to live with his little Blue Eyes, Shelley had rented a house in Marlow ample enough to accommodate the numerous offspring of the Old Woman in the nursery rhyme. He was charmed with the handsome building and the near-by beech woods, which his imagination already revealed to him in the foliage of the coming spring, and with his customary faith in the permanence of enthusiasm, he would have taken the place "for ever." The landlord, however, was satisfied with a twenty-year lease. As the months passed and there seemed little likelihood that the Court would reverse its judgment, misgiving crept in that the house was indeed too large. But that fault, if fault it were, proved an advantage in the friendly incursions from Hampstead when Hunt, in the throes of removing his museum to Lisson Grove, filled every available chamber at Marlow with his troupe.

Mary Shelley and Marianne Hunt became fast friends. Besides having poet husbands, they shared common interests in their drawing and modeling. And then there were the children, an endless source of conversation. Throughout the summer of 1817 the Hunts were scarcely out of Marlow, as they enjoyed the country and Shelley's unstinted hospitality. Nor was that all. Gradually, in tinkling golden channels, Shelley's money, raised from post-obits when the yearly allowance from Sir Timothy gave out, ran its way into the sea of Hunt's debts.

Every day, with clockwork regularity and usually at dinner time, came another guest — Peacock, their neighbor. He ate heartily, drank his bottle of wine, and, perhaps under its stimulation, uttered unpleasant truths. He was young, just entering his thirties, and yet he allowed himself to accept the monetary help of a younger man who had too many parasites attached to his purse as it was. Shelley, however, welcomed his company. Since the spring both had been working on long narrative poems, and had been marking their progress in lengthy readings under the changing beech trees.

A few weeks after her confinement, Clare, "corseted" once more, came to join Mary in London, giving no inkling to Mrs. Godwin that she had recently become a mother. No sooner was the Marlow house taken than, with her baby, she came to occupy the rooms set aside for her. She was no longer Mrs. Clairmont, as she had let herself be known at Bath, but, once more assuming her maiden appellation, she passed herself off as the aunt of the infant, whose mother, she said, had sent her into the country for her health. Even though the baby lived in the house of the notorious Mr. Shelley, the good folk of Marlow might have exerted themselves to believe the story. When, however, Clare was seen nursing the child and behaving toward her as would any devoted mother, they began giving tongue to their suspicions. "Was the child really a niece?" they asked rhetorically. What if she should be the fruit of sin between *Miss* Clairmont and Mr. Shelley? Soon they preferred to believe the hideous lie and looked evilly at the strange household, the while they willingly accepted the charities of Mr. Shelley, who visited the sick himself and provided for the wants of the poor. They looked upon him as a being out of the common order, to be humored in his fancies in much the same way as one propitiates a mischievous fairy with a dish of cream. They watched him wandering by himself through the fields or hiding daylong in the woods, coming back toward sundown with his wicked books in his hand and a wreath of old-man's-beard twined about his wild hair. Surely he had been about no work of the Lord's.

Byron, meanwhile, maintained an ambiguous silence, and Clare, to the impatience of Mary, sank into her "croaking humor." What was his lordship going to do about the little girl? Did he intend forgetting about her as if she had been none of his? He had said, before the little group left Switzerland, that he would undertake to support the child, and that he was willing to have it stay either with Clare or with him to the age of seven. However, to the letters that Shelley, Mary, and Clare herself had written him there had come no response. What could the silence mean? In her despair Clare gave it the darkest interpretations. In July Shelley wrote again to Byron, hinting gently that it was time he did something about the baby. "She continues to reside with us under a feigned name. But we are somewhat embarrassed about her," he added, with gallant understatement. "We are exposed to what remarks her existence is calculated to excite." Then, to rouse slumbering tenderness in Childe Harold's breast, he gave a pretty picture of the tiny girl in the garden with his own little William, under the watchful care of Elise. She had already been initiated to the Spartan habits of the Shelleys by daily immersions in cold water. "Alba has blue eyes," Shelley went on, "and had dark hair which has fallen off and there is now a dispute about the colour. Clare says that it is auburn." Perhaps from that fact she designated Lord Byron's daughter as "Miss Auburn."

Weeks went by and still the child remained unacknowledged by her father. Not knowing what to think, Clare turned her anguish to blame and her blame to hate of Byron, forgetting that when she had wooed him so importunately she had absolved him of all responsibility and had assured him that she would ever love him "gently and with affection." Too late, however, had she discovered that Byron was not a Shelley. In her situation she was no whit different from those unhappy girls whom virtuous mothers hold out as the shame of their sex. Her poor little Alba, the daughter of the most famous poet of the age, could only look forward to a bastard's lot.

During these months of anxious waiting on the part of Clare, Byron, in Venice, was living the life of a man who could hardly have been identified with the melancholy Childe, still less with the Corsair or even Manfred, the last act of whose drama he found it difficult to write. The fairy city of the heart had cast her spell over him and metamorphosed him into what he had struggled all his life against becoming — a man content with common pleasures. Hobhouse had gone, early in December, to prowl among the ruins of Rome, leaving Byron to settle down in the house of a linen draper by the name of Segati who boasted comfortable lodgings and a young, clever, and very pretty wife. Over Segati's shop in the Frezzeria hung a handsome sign, "Il Corno." It was not long before, by the noble Englishman's prowess, it became known as "Il Corno Inglese." [1] Signor Segati, like most Venetian husbands, accepted the honor with becoming modesty, pocketing it, as well as others of a more tangible nature, in mute thanksgiving. After all, it was not every shopkeeper who had such a jewel of a wife as Marianna, who knew on which side her bread was buttered and went halves with her husband. By virtue of her charms, her easy compliance, and a good singing voice, she had risen in the world, and even Signor Segati was admitted to the *conversazioni* of the Venetian bluestockings, where Marianna, amid a circle of plain women, sang, while he stood at the other end of the salon with the gentlemen, congratulating himself, and drinking the Adriatic equivalent of English punch.

Byron knew appeasement. Marianna, generous of herself, though perhaps too fond of money, was everything that his lordship at the moment desired. "She is pretty as an Antelope," he described her to Murray. "She is very handsome, very Italian, or rather Venetian, with something more of the Oriental cast of countenance," he confided to *"Goosey my love,"* adding further that the adventure had come opportunely to console him as he was beginning to be "like Sam Jennings very *unappy,* but at present . . . I have been very tranquil, very loving, and have not so much embarrassed myself with the tortures of the last two years and that virtuous monster Miss Milbanke, who had nearly driven me out of my senses — curse her." But Augusta must know that she was always first in his affections. "You can have no idea of my thorough wretchedness from the day of my parting from you till nearly a month ago though I struggled against it with some strength. At present I am better — thank Heaven above — and woman beneath — and I will be a very good boy." Marianna, in other words, was only the opiate to calm his hidden torments.

[1] The English Horn.

He knew Augusta would understand. Little did he suspect what other eyes read his letters.

Marianna cared not what she was so long as milord remained generous and did not divide his favors. Through the gay weeks of the Carnival she went with him everywhere in his gondola, shared his box at the Opera and his bed at home, wishing that providence would keep the Englishman many months beside her. Years she did not dare hope. What Venetian woman, after all, was faithful to her lover for more than a few weeks? If she kept him for months she was deemed a model of virtue. A year's fidelity made her the heroine of legend. Such a heroine she aspired to be. She did not look kindly, therefore, on Byron's daily visits to the Armenian monastery, where he made friends with the friars and studied their language. She could have taught him things more profitable than might be found in books, trash fit only to *"forbirsi i scarpi"* — clean one's shoes withal, as she pronounced appreciatively in her Venetian dialect on the subject of the higher learning.

Very soon Lord Byron became a well-known figure in Venice. The female intellectuals, Madame Benzoni and Madame Albrizzi, quarreled for the privilege of having him adorn their salons. Gondoliers disputed the right of showing him the more intimate places of interest on the orange-shaded isles. Sisters-in-law of Marianna, seeing her good fortune with the Englishman, spied the time when she was away to pay nocturnal visits to milord, resulting in the surprise entry of the *dama*, a scene, a skirmish between the ladies, screams, and volleys of asterisks. In spite of temptation, however, Byron remained reasonably faithful to his Adriatic nymph and well content with Venice. The seething in his breast was quieted by his strenuous living. The past seemed canceled — for the moment. Yet he could not write. "As for poesy," he explained to Murray, "mine is the *dream* of my sleeping passions; when they are awake, I cannot speak their language . . . and just now they are not dormant."

By the beginning of the Lenten season, he found he had to pay for the excesses of the Carnival in abstinence and sacred music, as he lay in bed with a slow fever brought on, thought

Marianna, by the climate. Byron knew better. "I find 'the sword wearing out the scabbard' though I have but just turned the corner of twenty-nine." Now no more nocturnal gliding with Marianna in the gondola by the light of the moon on the hushed waters. . . .

> For the sword outwears its sheath,
> And the soul wears out the breast,
> And the heart must pause to breathe,
> And Love itself have rest.

In the delirium of fever, England, the past, the triumph and the fall, came back and kept his mind in a ferment. Lady Frances Webster, the White Rose, Lady Caroline Lamb. . . . Strange that at this time he should think of them. . . . But then, Lady Caroline always saw to it that she should be as a thorn in his flesh. He had read at last her outrageous *Glenarvon*. Though to one who asked him whether the likeness was good he had answered, "The picture can't be good — I did not sit long enough," he masked annoyance in his flippancy. It is not flattering to be presented to the world on a public title-page as one who

> . . . left a name to all succeeding times,
> Linked with one virtue and a thousand crimes.

Such things one could write of oneself in the rôle of the Corsair. But they were not weapons for the hand of a scorned woman to use. One sleepless night during convalescence in the care of Marianna, he amused himself by writing a few nonsense verses for Moore.

> I read the *Christabel,*
>   Very well:
> I read the *Missionary;*
>   Pretty — very:
> I tried at *Ilderim;*
>   Ahem!
> I read a sheet of *Marg'ret of Anjou;*
>   Can you?
> I turn'd a page of Webster's *Waterloo:*
>   Pooh! Pooh!

I look'd at Wordsworth's milk-white *Rylstone-Doe:*
Hillo!
I read *Glenarvon,* too, by Caro. Lamb —
God damn!

A strange world, my masters. Here was a mistress aveng-
ing herself by publishing what she had better kept to herself,
there a man indulging in literary heroics on Waterloo when
he had been best employed tending his White Rose. . . .
What was she doing now, the chaste Lady Frances? Webster, he knew, was busy pamphleteering on the suspension of
the Habeas Corpus Act. . . . But then, beyond being jealous
of his wife, he had never really prized her.

Byron's passions dormant, his poetry awakened, and he
wrote the third act of *Manfred.* He was not pleased with it.
The fine frenzy, the reaching after the sublime of the first
two acts, was not there. It was as if the magician had closed
his book of spells and diminished to a mere man. He felt
his deficiency, and when he sent the manuscript to Murray
he wrote apologetically. The publisher showed the work to
Gifford, who was emphatic in his adverse judgment. "The
third Act is certainly damned bad," Byron admitted at once,
blaming his fever for it. But it had not been his fever. He
had already worked out in his poetry the inner conflict that
had motivated it; the inspiration was gone. He promised
to rewrite the rejected act, and went off to Rome for a change
of air and a visit to Hobhouse. Marianna made the parting
difficult, though he assured her he would return. She offered
to leave her husband, her child; she would follow milord to
the ends of the earth. He had to use all the persuasions in
his power to dissuade her. "It is only the virtuous . . ."
he commented on the affair, "who can give up husband and
child, and live happy ever after."

In Rome, four months after the event, Byron received the
announcement of little Alba's birth. "By the way," — he informed Augusta casually while on the subject of "your children and mine," "it seems that I have got another — a daughter. . . . I am a little puzzled how to dispose of this new
production . . . but shall probably send for and place it in a
Venetian convent, to become a good Catholic, and (it may be)

a *Nun,* being a character somewhat wanted in our family." [1]

No balm there for Clare, had she been able to see the letter. Byron's reasoning was of the simplest. His blood flowed in the child; she was a Byron. But there was a chasm of convention between Ada, "Little Legitimacy," and "my daughter, the last bastard one," as he described Alba to Kinnaird. "Will you think of some plan of remitting her here, or placing her in England?" he asked. "I shall acknowledge and breed her myself, giving her the name of *Biron* . . . and mean to christen her Allegra, which is a Venetian name."

He answered Shelley in due time, signifying his willingness to provide for the child. He said little of Clare's part in the matter, and the reticence was not reassuring.

With Hobhouse, the old traveling companion, Byron made the rounds of the Roman sights, revealing not a shade of the emotion that infused his whole being as he stood amid the ruins of the Coliseum or under the shadow of the gods at the Pantheon. Hobhouse, he knew, would have mocked his poetry into prose — had he not, in the Greek voyage, turned that flight of eagles to vultures over the holy mount? There was in Rome material for a fourth canto of *Childe Harold.* He did not begin it then, but reality was working at white heat in the crucible of his imagination. Glory and decay — they had always been the song, cradling his boyish dreams in half-ruined Newstead. He had awakened to its meaning on the dust of ancient Greece.

For the present, however, that final act of *Manfred* had to be recast, an unpleasant task to him always. "I am like the tiger in poesy. If I miss my first spring I go growling back to my jungle." He could not do that now. *Manfred* was close and precious. He forced himself to make the end worthy of the theme, and sent on the finished work to Murray, who brought it before the public by the middle of June.

On the whole the Italian journey had not been poetically fruitful — a few lyrics, a long poem, the *Lament of Tasso,* composed at Ferrara en route to Rome, and the last of the poetic drama. But a new energy seemed surging within him, an active clarity of mind like that which after confession and

[1] Thus early Byron was thinking of a convent for his daughter.

absolution possesses the sinner. Byron had made a clean breast of his tormenting past. Though he had not been absolved, — no absolution existed for his deed, — he knew his punishment as he knew his guilt.

> What I have done is done . . .
> The mind which is immortal makes itself
> Requital for its good or evil thoughts,
> Is its own origin of ill and end. . . .

He had not been the dupe of a higher power, nor had he been its prey. He was his own destroyer, and had created his own punishment. He could now, knowing his fate, live out the rest of his life not only as a poet but as a man. Conscious of a mighty calling, he had the courage, nay, the zest, to face the future. "If I live ten years longer, you will see . . . that it is not over with me," he had recently written to Moore. "I don't mean in literature, for that is nothing. . . . But you will see that I shall do something or other . . . that will puzzle the philosophers of all ages. But I doubt whether my constitution will hold out." Ten years longer. That would mean three years beyond the time set by the fortune teller's prophecy — too much for a Gordon to expect.

Hobhouse had commissioned Thorwaldsen to make a bust of the poet. After the sitting he would take him to Frascati and up the heights of the Alban mount. How like those early days of youth it was, and yet how different! Then Childe Harold had hardly found himself; now it seemed as if his whole story had been told.

Before leaving Rome Byron went to see three robbers guillotined. The spectacle of death had always lured him. Here, however, was something of solemn pageantry to the forced exit from life of the three poor wretches. Bellingham's execution had been as nothing to the scene of the masked priests, the half-naked executioners, the black Christ carried in slow procession, the soldiery, and, in the midst, the victims, blindfold. Byron stood close to the scaffold, trembling so that he could hardly hold his opera glass. He was determined to see. The first execution turned him hot and thirsty; the second and third had little effect of horror.

Life was good in spite of a burdened heart and a mind that knew no quiet. He thought of Marianna, fresh and eager, waiting for his return, and wrote her to join him on his way back. Strange how he could be attached even to a woman who, he knew, loved him more for his money than for himself. Yet shrewd, grasping Marianna gave him what love she was capable of. Had she not been willing to abandon her home for him? One woman alone was cold and implacable. Under the crumbling arches of the Coliseum, in the starlight peopled with shades, he called upon Nemesis to avenge him upon Lady Byron and her parents, on Samuel Romilly for sanctioning the separation, and upon all whom he believed to have been instrumental in his downfall. Only recently he had learned from Hanson that a bill had been filed by Sir Ralph to make Ada a ward in Chancery, depriving him of his paternal right over the child. The communication had stirred up his smouldering hate. He wrote at once to Lady Byron. "If you think to reconcile yourself to yourself by accumulating harshness against me, you are again mistaken: you are not happy, nor even tranquil, nor will you ever be so. . . . Time and Nemesis will do that, which I would not, even were it in my power. . . . No one was ever even the involuntary cause of great evils to others, without a requital: I have paid and am paying for mine — so will you." Meanwhile he retired with the purchased wifeliness of Marianna to a little country place at La Mira, on the outskirts of Venice.

At Marlow, Shelley, trying to drive from his mind the persecutions of fate and law, had been transmuting his private griefs and the world's wrongs into the poem which he had begun that spring. The Lord Chancellor's decision had had loud reverberations. Because of the prejudice it aroused in the public, Shelley was filled with dread lest the hand of the law snatch from him his own little William as it had Charles and Ianthe. And indeed, for a time his fears did not seem ill-founded, in the face of the Chancellor's accusation that the immoral youth was unfit to be trusted with the care of any child.

Shelley was near a breakdown. He could not give way to

his feelings because Mary, about to be confined, had to be spared painful emotions. He did unbosom himself to Leigh Hunt and to Peacock, but from the latter he could obtain only limited understanding. Reserve lurked at the base of his sympathy like the shadow of accusation. Shelley had to turn inward for comfort. On the deserted chalk hills over-hanging the Thames, he poured out his grievances in the weather-worn notebooks that always went with him like a part of himself. When the decree was passed, depriving him of his children by Harriet, in the first burst of resentment against the Chancellor he wrote a curse whose stanzas echoed the *Zastrozzi* vehemence, invoking impious hells and angels of vengeance. But the fire of a haughty indignation burned through them, and the tenderness of a father's love. Unlike Byron, he would not make the public his confidant. He wrote for himself alone. Nor did he in his clear-sighted justice con-found the instrument with the law. "I curse thee — though I hate thee not. — O slave!" he apostrophized the Chancellor,

> "If thou couldst quench the earth-consuming Hell
> Of which thou art a dæmon, on thy grave
> This curse should be a blessing."

William, now the only son left him by the law, became dearer to him in his dread of losing him. In that same note-book he addressed a strangely haunting half-ballad, half-lullaby to the child, summoning him to embark with him and Mary for a kinder land than home.

> We soon shall dwell by the azure sea
> Or serene and golden Italy. . . .

There, in the paradise of exiles, peace would be theirs, and security, and freedom. He might find health, too, perhaps. Worry over Godwin's rapacity, bolder now that Shelley was his son-in-law, fear of arrest for the debts which Harriet had left, Clare's anxiety to see her baby settled, and his own inner grieving, gave him no rest. As always when under a strain, he fretted to be on the wing. He was pent in, however, by a stronger cage than ever in Albion House with its twenty-year lease, a stock of new furniture, and a host of noisy, unpaying guests.

Mary's confinement in September drove away the Hunts for the period of her convalescence, only to have them reappear in full force, with the addition of Bessie Kent to keep order among the youth, when the patient had hardly been a week out of bed. Mary was happy in her little girl, who even as an infant of a few weeks bore an extraordinary likeness to Shelley. Perhaps she might make up to him the loss of that other blue-eyed girl, Harriet's child.

No sooner did Shelley think of Italy than he began his preparations for the departure. True, he had paid twelve hundred pounds on the lease of the house, but then he could rent it and get back some of the money. The furniture could be sold, and as for the books, they would be very useful in a foreign land. Two things had to be done before the new exodus. Definite plans had to be made for Alba's future, and Mary's *Frankenstein* and his own *Laon and Cythna* had to be seen through the press. With Clare, the tireless companion of his wanderings, Shelley went to London.

Mr. Murray failed to see the commercial advantage of issuing *Frankenstein* under his imprint; so did the Olliers, who with fear and trembling had undertaken to publish Shelley's poem. Eventually Shelley found an enterprising firm in Lackington, Allen and Company for Mary's novel, which came out in the late autumn anonymously, but with a dedication to William Godwin that pointed as directly as any name to the source. Godwin was pleased. In this novel by his daughter he could not fail to see the power and vision that had animated his own *Caleb Williams*. What was Franken-stein's creature but his own Falkland, transfigured by an amazing imagination? He had always known that Mary would some day make a mark in literature. But his horny heart was most deeply touched by her filial piety; and a self-centred exultation possessed him that he, rather than Shelley, had the dedication of the book. An unphilosophic jealousy had rankled in him since Mary had left his house, and in spite of his semblance of friendship to Shelley after the visit to St. Mildred's, he had no love for him. Gone were the days when

Shelley had considered him a luminary too dazzling for the darkness that surrounded him. That the dazzle had been quenched by his own greed made the obscurity no easier for Godwin to bear. Furthermore, Shelley had also opened Mary's eyes.

Laon and Cythna, later called the *Revolt of Islam,* came out toward the end of 1817. A number of review copies had been sent to the magazines when, in December, they were hastily recalled by Charles Ollier, who feared, at the very least, arrest and prosecution because the hero and heroine were represented in the unconventional rôles of brother, sister: husband, wife. Shelley felt he had done his duty when he forestalled objections in the preface by the caution that "the sentiments connected with and characteristic of this circumstance" had no personal reference to the author. Charles Ollier found that it was not enough. The very denial of a thing often makes the perverse public believe it. Either Shelley consent to alter the poem or it must be withdrawn from publication. High on his Pegasus, Shelley at first would not dismount for the exigencies of public and publishers, but as Peacock somewhat acidly commented that he had no hope of any firm but the Olliers', he reluctantly complied by omitting the incest theme, which in the end was nonessential.[1] "It is ruined! Ruined!" he moaned as he excised words and lines.

But the poem was not ruined. It was too glorious a thing to mar. Like a sky scintillant with a million stars, it lost no splendor by the clouding of a few points of brilliance.

In a sense the *Revolt of Islam* was Shelley's apology for the failure of the French Revolution to bring about the reign of universal brotherhood. A great triumph might have been achieved. Yet disaster supervened, not because of a fallacy

---

[1] The following will indicate the nature of the changes made by Shelley: —

Original Line	New Version
I had a little sister whose fair eyes . . .	An orphan with my parents lived whose eyes. . .
To love in human life — this sister sweet	To love in human life — this playmate sweet
What thoughts had sway over my sister's slumber	What thoughts had sway o'er Cythna's lonely slumber

in ideals, but in the means of murder and hatred — tyranny's weapons — employed to achieve it. All was not lost, however. By his errors man would learn. A bloodless revolution, motivated by love, not hate, soon would hail the dawn of the golden age when oppression and intolerance would be forgotten words, and the nations of the earth, bound by fraternal ties, would form a sublime confederacy such as would cast into the gloom of barbarism the chronicled pasts of the poets' songs. Laon, a young poet, — Shelley himself, — moved by a passionate benevolence, inspires an oppressed nation to rise against tyranny. Hand in hand, Cythna, — Mary, — his sister soul, wife and comrade, goes with him through triumph and disaster. Might conquers over their just cause. The lovers are seized and immolated for their yet unrealized ideals. But death is only an awakening from the darkness of life. Guided by a child soul, Cythna's daughter, they reach the Temple of the Spirit.

Of human aspiration, hope, defeat, and death Shelley wove his twelve glowing cantos, enriching them with the rainbow hope of future triumph. As poet and man he had lived and suffered. Impact with life had softened the asperities of his *Queen Mab* intolerance, so that now, like that other Idealist whom he was beginning to estimate justly, he could understand and forgive. Love, stronger than hate, cut him loose from the chains of his youthful fanaticism, leaving him free to pursue a higher, if more arduous, path. He had taken the first step when, in his aching indictment against the Chancellor, he had cried, "I hate thee not!" Its nobler expression was to follow in the greatest poem of the trilogy begun with *Queen Mab*.

To Mary the new poem, a celebration, too, of the omnipotence of love, was dedicated in stanzas aglow with the sincerity of his devotion, as he told of how he had worshiped and been betrayed until she came and reawakened his faith. Harriet Grove and the later, more tragic, Harriet were accused, in the original version, with hard directness: —

> She whom I found was dear but false to me,
> The other's heart was like a heart of stone
> Which crushed and withered mine.

But the kindliness of suffering tempered the allusion to the dead, though not to the indifference under which his soul had chilled.

> Yet never found I one not false to me,
>   Hard hearts, and cold, like weights of icy stone
> Which crushed and withered mine, that could not be
> Aught but a lifeless clod, until revived by thee. . . .

Never had he reached the heights of rapture or sounded the deeps of feeling as in the farewell duet of the lovers when death itself surrendered before the sublimity of their passion.   Meaning and music, image and mood, mingled in an unearthly ecstasy never before uttered in English poetry.   Shelley owed nothing to any predecessor.   He had found his voice.

Appreciation was not his, however.   Godwin, requested for his opinion of the new poem, found it too far removed from life and advised Shelley to exercise his powers in argumentative prose, basing his judgment on the Chancery paper the irate father had written on being deprived of his children.   But Shelley, clear-visioned as an eagle in his skyey pursuits, was not duped by the words of reason.   "I listened with deference and self-suspicions to your censures," he wrote to his father-in-law.   ". . . But the productions of mine which you commend hold a very low place in my own esteem. . . .   The poem was produced by a series of thought which filled my mind with unbounded and sustained enthusiasm."   Neither did Mary show the approval Shelley expected.   Dazzled by Lord Byron's success, she would have wished Shelley had exerted his genius in poems that touched the heart as well as the mind of man. He soared too high, till man could no more follow him.   He should endeavor to write of real living men and women.   More to please her than out of any inner urge, he began *Rosalind and Helen,* a modern eclogue, as flat and colorless as a shadow against the sun of his true genius.

Like the critics at home the professional reviewers showed no enthusiasm.   Some accumulated their poison against the heretic Shelley until the time when it should have most effect.

Discouraged in his poetry and harassed by financial troubles, he dwelt heartsick on the thought of Italy.   In Marlow

poverty trailed him to his very door. But single-handed he
could do little toward remedying the injustices of an indifferent
system. If misery was so severe in the little town, how much
worse must it be in the cities where the larger population
made for greater suffering. In the manufacturing towns riots
occurred daily against the long hours and miserly pay by
which the industrial magnates sought to increase the gains
already amassed by a profitable war. Paid government
agents grew fat on the discord they instigated.

In November 1817, a riot broke out among the weavers in
Derbyshire, fanned to flame by one Oliver, an official spy,
when three poor weavers, Brandath, Turner, and Ludlam, were
immediately arrested as the scapegoats. With the barest
excuse for a trial they were condemned to death, and before a
horrified public they were first hanged and then beheaded.
The day their execution was reported, the British papers
came out with wide black bands, not as a sign of mourning for
the murder of English liberty, but to announce the death of
the Princess Charlotte in childbirth. The contrast drove itself home to Shelley's mind, ever alive to social injustices.
In the heat of indignation he dashed off *An Address to the
People on the Death of Princess Charlotte,* wherein, while
deploring the untimely decease of the princess, he pointed out
pertinently the greater cause the nation had for grief in the
rottenness at the government's core. "We pity the plumage,
but forget the dying bird," he cried out to the people, quoting
the words Paine had used on another historical occasion.
With *A Proposal for Putting Reform to the Vote,* published
earlier in the year by the "Hermit of Marlow," it was the last
public expression of Shelley, the political reformer.[1]

At long length Byron signified his desire to have his child
sent to him in Italy, to the relief of Mary, on whom the
scandalmongers wrought with deleterious effect. Clare took
the decision with mixed feelings. She was devoted to the
lovely, vivacious, intelligent Alba, who grew every day more
endearing with her baby ways. However she, a woman of no

---

[1] If we except the letter sent by Shelley to the *Examiner* from abroad,
November 3, 1819, protesting against the conviction of Richard Carlile,
a publisher of free-thought literature.

means, had nothing to offer her. Shelley, who so far had taken care of both her and the baby, could not be expected to make himself responsible for the future of Byron's child, though he had more than once suggested rearing Alba with his own children. Under Byron's care the little one would be given all that belonged to her — a comfortable home, a father's love, and a position in the world. Who knows, if the child succeeded in penetrating into that stony heart, she might even be looked upon by him as no less precious than Lady Byron's daughter. Shelley, who read between the lines of Byron's letters, had his misgivings, and urged Clare to consider well before deciding to surrender her baby. For Alba's sake she stifled her own forebodings.

Byron, in expectation of the daughter whom he had never seen, wrote to Hobhouse, back in London, to look after her transportation. Newstead Abbey was again being sold, this time to Wildman, a boyhood friend of Harrow days, and while asking for the legal papers to be sent him in Italy, Byron suggested that his child by Clare be shipped at the same time. "Pray desire Shelley to pack it carefully — with *tooth-powder, red only;* magnesia, soda-powders . . . and any new novels good for anything."

Hobhouse was spared the task when Shelley, ready at last to leave for Italy with his family and Clare, proposed bringing his lordship's daughter part of the way. On the ninth of March, 1818, two days before Shelley saw the chalk cliffs of England losing themselves on the horizon, he and Mary and Clare celebrated a wholesale christening of the children at St. Giles-in-the-Fields. Clare's little girl, so soon to be parted from her, was named Allegra in the baptismal register, which further entered the "Right Hon. George Gordon, Lord Byron, the reputed father."

The Hunts, and Mary Lamb, who came later to help with the packing, were the last friends who visited the Shelleys in London. It was with keen regret that Hunt saw them go. Would Shelley stretch out a helping hand from across the sea? During the past year Hunt had received from him no less than fourteen hundred pounds.

XXII

BEYOND THE CHAMBER OF
MAIDEN THOUGHT

" 'A THING of beauty is a constant joy.' . . . What do you think of that, Stephens?" Keats, then a medical student, had asked from his favorite seat near the window.

"A fine line but wanting something," answered Stephens.

Keats thought it over and then broke out with an inspired "I have it. 'A thing of beauty is a joy for ever.' " The line, planted so long ago in his imagination, expanded into the opening of *Endymion*.

> A thing of beauty is a joy for ever:
> Its loveliness increases; it will never
> Pass into nothingness; but still will keep
> A bower quiet for us, and a sleep
> Full of sweet dreams. . . .

Bright with hope and the affirmation of the eternality of beauty, her most fervent lover had begun his long poem, on a scale as heroic as Haydon's canvases. He had just entered life in the fullness of manhood. Another Endymion, he was beginning his quest of the goddess who since his childhood had cast her magic over his eyes. Beauty was the only truth. Let the wise reduce the colors of the rainbow into a formula. For himself, he preferred gazing spellbound at its unanalyzable wonder. Unlike Shelley, who would have seen the work of the sublime principle and a richer poetry in the searching of science, Keats shut his mind to it. "What the imagination seizes as Beauty must be Truth — whether it existed before or not, for I have the same idea of all our passions as of love: they are all, in their sublime, creative of essential Beauty. . . . The imagination may be compared to Adam's dream — he awoke and found it truth."

Again, unlike Shelley, Keats aimed not at bringing a message to humanity, but at solacing it with a beautiful story beautifully told. He was not primarily concerned with liberating man from his manifold tyrannies, although he knew that some day he would have to bid farewell to the joys that entranced him and pass them for a nobler life — the agonies and strife of human hearts. But that was not to him the singer's first mission.

> And they shall be accounted poet kings
> Who simply tell the most heart-easing things.

It was such a heart-easing tale that he had meant to write in *Endymion*.

The shepherd of Latmos, awakened by the kiss of Diana, has thenceforth in his blood the restless memory of her. Unable to live without the appeasement she alone can give, he seeks through land and sea the vision of her who has so enthralled him. Lovers of myth and legend he encounters in his seeking, Venus and Adonis, the nymph Arethusa and Alpheus, Glaucus and Circe, all the beautiful and dread presences that had peopled the world of Keats's own dreaming. The gods of the underworld, the divinities of the sea, pass by in a rainbow-hued poetic frieze, deepening to the wine-red triumph of Bacchus. In the end Endymion, recognizing something of his unearthly love in an Indian maid, yields to her wooing. But misgiving mars his joy. He has proved unfaithful to the ideal of his search. In pity of his suffering, his earthly love reveals herself in her true heavenly shape as the goddess of the moon.

No moral there to enlighten the ages; no philosophical kernel for the wise to seek out. More than one who had had a preconceived idea of what Keats's first ambitious work was to be murmured in disappointment. "I think," Shelley said of the poem, "if he had printed about fifty pages of fragments from it, I should have been led to admire Keats as a poet more than I ought, of which there is now no danger." But then Shelley, like Hunt, had been piqued by Keats's defiant resolve to pursue his own unfettered scope. The would-be curate, Bailey, was shocked out of countenance by what he considered Keats's indelicacy — and indeed the guardians of decency, the critics, found much to fume at in such faults of taste as marked him a disciple of the Cockney King. What difference was there between Hunt's description of Francesca's kiss, "To his cold clammy lips joining her balmy twins," and Keats's invocation of "those lips, O slippery blisses . . ."? Bailey's objections had more than offended taste behind them. He saw the horns of the arch-fiend in his innocent friend's work, and cried out against them in capitals, exclamations, and italics. "The second fault I allude to I think we have noticed — The inclination it has to that abominable principle of *Shelley!* — that *Sensual* Love is the principle of *things* — " a profound misconception of Shelley's poetry, which proved once more that one has only to obtain a shady reputation to have every error laid at one's door.

Blackwood's crew treated poem and author with the expected barbarity, calling Keats "Johnny" and offering sarcastic advice. "It is a better and a wiser thing to be a starved apothecary than a starved poet; so back to the shop, Mr. John, back to the 'plasters, pills and ointment boxes.' . . . But, for Heaven's sake, young Sangrado, be a little more sparing of extenuatives and soporifics in your practice than you have been in your poetry." It remained for Byron, however, two years later, to throw a handful of ordure at "Jack Keats or Ketch or whatever his names are," and to make an indecent pun on Keats's motto from Shakespeare, "The stretched metre of an antique song," when the *Edinburgh* gave the ill-starred youth a word of praise that came too late. "Why," Byron exploded in a letter to Murray, "his is the onanism of poetry. . . . Such like is the trash they praise and such will be the end of the outstretched poesy of this miserable self-polluter of the human mind." [1] Keats had dared in an audacious moment to attack Pope. Byron had never forgiven this sin against the holy ghost of poetry.

Keats had done his best, and again his best had failed. Too honest not to see the flaws in his work, yet too sensible of his powers to be discouraged, he made the mistake of pointing out

---

[1] A quotation usually brilliant with asterisks, like other Byronian references to Keats, except in T. J. Wise's privately printed *Bibliography of Byron*, from which the excerpt has been taken.

his weaknesses to those whose business it was to judge of them, while he promised to do better in the future. "This may be speaking too presumptuously, and may deserve a punishment," he wrote in his preface, "but no feeling man will be forward to inflict it." He reckoned without the Weimar-bred, culture-mad Edinburgh critics. He spoke without knowledge of the *Quarterly* Attila, scourge of poets, William Gifford, who thought the highest success of a poet was conferred with a court livery — Gifford, "a retainer to the Muses; a door-keeper to learning; a lacquey in the state." Hazlitt, like many another, had smarted under his lash, but having a whip of his own he gave stroke for stroke. Keats bore the onslaught with the proud defiance of silence. After the *Quarterly* attack a man in Dartmouth sent the poet twenty-five pounds. A lady known to Haydon went immediately to Gifford with the news, hoping to propitiate him toward Keats. "How can you, Gifford, dish up in this dreadful manner a youth who has never offended you?" she entreated. Peering up at her through his green eye shade, "It has done him good," he said coldly. "He has had twenty-five pounds."

At Haydon's instance a copy of Keats's early poems had been sent to Wordsworth. A word from him could have done much toward restoring the self-confidence of a youth to whom he was a god of the age. Wordsworth cut the first few pages and left the rest untouched: at his death the silent witness proved that before one of the brightest promises of the century he had been obstinately blind. But Wordsworth was notoriously self-centred. He knew himself the patriarch of the romantic movement and cared not to share his laurels even with one who had a legitimate claim. Crabb Robinson, visiting at the Lambs' when Coleridge and Wordsworth had been there together, was struck by his preoccupation with himself and his work. "I heard a long time Coleridge quoting Wordsworth's verses; and W. quoting not Coleridge's, but his own." Wordsworth was no discoverer of genius. Praise, he believed, was best bestowed at home.

Yet he had had another opportunity to set himself down as a generous man as well as a great poet. Haydon, that pursuer of fame, had seen to that. At the *immortal dinner* he gave in

his new and larger quarters at Lisson Grove, he invited Keats
that he might meet Wordsworth face to face.   Lamb was there,
delightfully merry from too frequent quaffs at the bowl, and
Monkhouse, Wordsworth's friend, and Ritchie, who was about
to set out for Africa.   And there was, too, a comptroller of
stamps, a stranger to Haydon, who had forced himself into the
party that he might have the happiness of meeting the bard.
Haydon was at the height of his felicity.   He had prepared a
fine dinner.   The canvas of Christ's entry glowed from its
austere vastness upon the collection of greatness in the studio.
He beamed officiously.   Lamb, who had been vexed by the
foolish questions the comptroller of stamps had flung at Wordsworth, and had hardly believed his ears, held up a candle to
the bewildered man's face, crying in his tipsiness, "Let me
have a look at this gentleman's organs — *Hey diddle diddle,
the cat and the fiddle* —   Do let me have another look . . ."
until Haydon and Keats had to shut him up to subside in the
painting room.

In the quiet, Wordsworth quoted Milton and Vergil, safely
dead, intoning them most solemnly, when Haydon called on
Keats to give the Hymn to Pan from *Endymion*.[1]   The youth
got up shyly and, walking up and down the room, recited in his
hushed half-chant the vigorous processional of Bacchus and
his crew, bringing into the studio the gayety of the laughing
rout, and life, and sunlit youth, through the medium of a rich
and supple music.   Then, while the room still vibrated with
the echoes of the finished song, Wordsworth spoke.   "A very
pretty piece of paganism," he said aridly.   Keats was mortified.   He knew that the hymn deserved more than this dry
crumb of superiority.   He was yet to realize that genius may
be limited in its greatness.   .

Nevertheless, though the living denied him praise, Keats
heard the dim murmurings of posterity in his ears.   "I think
I shall be among the English poets after my death."   Through
Wordsworth's alliterated faint praise, through the shrieking
attacks of the Tory reviewers, the thought persisted.   When
he himself was dust, his name would shine in gold in the scroll

[1] I give Haydon's earlier account.   He changed his setting in a letter
of 1845, first published in Amy Lowell's *Keats*.

of the future. "Ritchie," he requested the African traveler, "promise to carry a copy of my *Endymion* to the desert of Sahara and fling it in the midst." Even in the remote corners of the globe he would make his name known. Did Ritchie keep his promise, and, in the desert where he was so soon to perish, sow the fame of the ambitious youth?

Thousands of miles across the Atlantic, in a yet virgin tract of America, the name of Keats was to be planted in flesh and blood when George Keats, twenty-one, with his sixteen-year-old bride, Georgiana, set out to make his fortune. Morris Birkbeck, the Quaker, had bought some sixteen thousand acres of land west of the Mississippi, and had called to youth to quit the war-exhausted Continent for the unlimited opportunities of an unexploited country. A new President, James Monroe, had been inaugurated in 1817, and an era of good feeling had set in. The people of America were going westward. Every day from the Eastern states caravans of prairie wagons started out with men and beasts and portable goods, toward the pioneer acres sold to the settlers on easy terms. Log cabins dotted the virgin lands. At night the friendly lamp threw its glow from the oiled paper of the windows and the smoke of the chimneys wreathed upward to the skies. Fields of wheat and corn soon grew where only the prairie grass had spread, the log cabins united into settlements, and the wilderness was tamed.

George Keats had been out of employ for a long time. Possessed of a quick pride, he had quarreled with his fellow clerks at Mr. Abbey's warehouse and had finally broken with his guardian. Mr. Birkbeck's project beckoned. With some of the money left by old Mr. Jennings, he would buy his own tract in America and work it as a gentleman farmer. Georgiana, with a man's courage in her girl's frame, promised to follow wherever George would go. In August the two inexperienced but inspired emigrants left London for Liverpool, accompanied by John and his friend Charles Brown, who saw them sail, and then proceeded on a walking tour through Scotland.

The little orphan clan was breaking up, with George gone to America, Fanny still under the guardianship of Mr. Abbey, and Tom — John could not bear to think of the youth — wasting away in a fatal illness. That spring John had been constantly at his side in Teignmouth, nursing him and easing his pain — a cure was not to be thought of. Wind, fog, and a ceaseless downpour from the heavens worked on his nerves until he felt himself drenched and rotting like a grain of wheat. He had not been well. At Oxford with Bailey, in a youthful desire to know all of life, he had plunged incautiously into a reckless adventure that had sent him home ailing.

"The little mercury I have taken has corrected the poison and improved my health," he wrote Bailey while undergoing treatment, "though I feel from my employment that I shall never be again secure in robustness." [1]   At first he had linked his ailment with the disease his mother had left as a dread heritage to her children. His friends were certain that, like Tom, he was suffering from the same cause — Marianne and Jane Reynolds particularly. But then, sheltered young girls had no thought of what perils may lie in the way of pleasure. "I think Jane or Marianne has a better opinion of me than I deserve," Keats honestly admitted, "for, really and truly, I do not think my Brother's illness connected with mine — you know more of the real cause than they do." Although he recovered, his physique was impaired, and it was with growing apprehension for himself that he watched Tom's relentless journey toward the grave. The Devonshire climate did the invalid no good. A violent hemorrhage decided John to hurry him back to London, where he could at least have medical attention and the companionship of cheerful friends. He felt himself sinking in a morbidity of soul that made him fear the worst.

Yet for all his wretchedness he had not been idle during the dreary vacation. A long poem, from a tale of Boccaccio's, lay in his knapsack. Forced in parts, touched with his dejection, *Isabella* moved quickly, nevertheless, to a tragic climax. But Keats was not at his best out of the region of antique faëry. "Too much inexperience of line, and simplicity of knowledge," he commented on this, his first ambitious attempt to treat of real men and women, with whom, so far, he had had but little to do. Perhaps under the influence of Shelley's

---

[1] W. M. Rossetti in his *Life of John Keats*, 1887, was the first to draw an inference of syphilis from this letter.

social consciousness he put his pen to work in an indictment against economic injustices.   But he had no satisfaction in the writing.   His imagination, strayed from its chosen path, fretted to return to it.

> . . . Though no great minist'ring reason sorts
> Out the dark mysteries of human souls
> To clear conceiving: yet there ever rolls
> A vast idea before me.

He had written those words when he had first become sensible of his poetic mission.   They held true now as then. A mighty drama was beginning to unfold itself within him, palely as yet, like some faint sketch of one of Haydon's pictures — a vast fragment of Greek mythology, when in the struggle for supremacy the younger gods of beauty overwhelmed the primitive deities.   He needed leisure, however, and a tranquil mind to have the poem come forth in its pagan grandeur. When Charles Brown approached him with the proposal of the Scottish tour, he found it hard to refuse.   Tom was in the hands of loving friends at Well Walk; he wanted John to go. Packing his knapsack with a few essentials and one book alone, Carey's translation of Dante, he joined Brown, whose traveling library consisted of a Milton.

Brown, a friend of short standing, had nonetheless won Keats's reticent affection.   Though only thirty-two years old, he presented the aspect of middle age, what with his corpulence and a prematurely bald pate.   The son of a Scotch stock-broker, he had started out in life as that ambiguous magnate, a Russia merchant, with an elder brother, and at the age of eighteen he had journeyed to distant St. Petersburg as a repre-sentative of the firm.   After the Napoleonic invasions, business failed to prosper, and for a time Charles was so close to poverty that he had to make a shilling do the service of a pound.   His brother James, however, made him an agent for the East India Company, and on his death left him a very com-fortable competence.   In spite of his business experience, Brown had no love for it and looked wistfully toward Apollo's laurel bough.   So far he had produced only the libretto for an opera which had enjoyed a brief success at Drury Lane,

chiefly on the merits of the popular Braham, who sang the
lead, but his literary ambition was not quelled.

With an old schoolfellow, Charles Wentworth Dilke, he
had joined in the building of two houses connected by a party
wall, the larger for the married Dilke with his wife and son,
the smaller for his own bachelor uses. In honor of Dilke's
forbears they named it Wentworth Place. Brown's was a com-
modious house whose wide windows opened upon a common
garden and the slopes of Hampstead. Besides providing him
with a pleasant home, his half of Wentworth Place brought
him a neat income every summer when he sublet it to responsible tenants. Following his custom, before setting out on
his pedestrian tour with Keats, he had rented the house to a
well-to-do widow, Mrs. Brawne, with her three children —
Fanny, the eldest, entering into womanhood, and a younger
girl and a boy. So Brown made up in advance for the expense
he might incur on his holiday. A prudent epicure, he obtained his pleasures with laudable husbandry.

The light-hearted bachelor was just the companion Keats
needed at the time. Depressed after the departure of his
brother and Georgiana, and morbidly preoccupied with Tom's
health, he was grateful for the joviality of Brown. Nor was
the comic element wanting in this gay enterprise. With their
knapsacks on their backs, in their old clothes, and with a plaid
thrown over their shoulders, they were everywhere taken for
peddlers, a lure to the curious country folk, who wanted to
know what they carried in their bags to sell. Spectacles, perhaps, to judge by the impressive pair Brown wore on his
nose.

A tireless walker, blessed with a tough constitution, Brown
crossed bog and mire with the ease of the fairy-tale boy in
seven-league boots, regaling himself at the end of the day's
journey with heavy peasant fare and plenty of strong waters.
Keats bravely kept up with him, or tried to. He had brought
only one coat with him besides the plaid. When that was torn
and had to be left with a local tailor for repairs, he had to get
on as best he could without it. Often the weather was bad.
On the way to Oban they tramped fifteen miles in the rain,
ankle-deep in mud, soaked to the skin. Brown enjoyed it, and

Keats thought he did, though his mind reverted time and again to a quiet room, and books, and some blank paper to write his thoughts upon. However, he had left London to find himself in new surroundings. He would not prove a weakling and falter on the way. Brown saw the bright eyes grow brighter, and the cheeks flush as if with fever; but because Keats made no complaint, he thought no more of them. Then Keats's voice took on a peculiar hoarseness. A passing cold, perhaps, that would soon go of itself.

Keats's acute sensitiveness responded to the majesty of the Northern landscape. So far in his life he had seen only the gentle downs of Hampstead, the Devonshire hills, and the primrose banks of the Isle of Wight spreading down to the sea. Nature in her sublimity he beheld now for the first time. The mountains made him rise to his full height in an impulse of greatness. "I never forgot my stature so completely," he confessed, differing with Hazlitt, who had affirmed that scenes of grandeur made man conscious of his smallness. Keats felt himself a giant in a young and glowing world. His imagination, which dwelt constantly with the denizens of his poetic realm, beheld them moving about amid the vastnesses. At Fingal's Cave he spoke of them in a description of astounding vividness. "Suppose now the giants who rebelled against Jove had taken a whole mass of black columns and bound them together like bunches of matches — and then with immense axes had made a cavern in the body of these columns . . . such is Fingal's Cave, except that the sea has done the work of excavations and is continually dashing there — so that we walk along the sides of the cave on the pillars which are left as if for convenient stairs." Against a background of such elemental majesty would he build his drama of the rebel gods of Greece.

Keats's sore throat became worse, but still neither he nor Brown saw cause for alarm. They continued their tour, climbing to the top of Ben Nevis on the brisk stimulus of repeated drams of whiskey, — thus equaling the feat of Mrs. Cameron, who, though the fattest woman that ever was seen, as the guide told, had nevertheless panted to the very crest of Nevis and there sate herself down. Amused at the lady's adventure,

Keats celebrated her in a mock dialogue with the mountain. He was gayer than ever, but at last Brown had to admit that it was an abnormal merriment. Keats was indeed very ill. The doctor he agreed to consult ordered him home at once. Reluctantly he parted from Brown and, taking passage at Cromarty on a fishing smack, sailed for London.

Mrs. Dilke was very much alarmed when the wanderer returned to Well Walk, where she had been taking care of Tom. "John Keats," she wrote to a friend, "arrived here last night as brown and as shabby as you can imagine." He had scarcely any soles left in his shoes, his coat was patched and torn, while a great fur cap in the middle of August added to the pathetic grotesqueness of his appearance. However, the voyage of more than a week by water had helped to restore his health, so that though he did not feel strong, he was able to hide it from the searching eyes of Tom, as once more he took his place at the poor boy's bedside.

It was a time of great mental and spiritual anguish for Keats. The fury of the reviewers, then at its height, made him doubt the genuineness of his gifts — but only momentarily. The *vast idea* rolled before him, dispelling the envious shadows of little minds that knew enough to recognize the advent of something new and strange, yet had not the courage to accept it without fear. As they had done with Shelley, they did with Keats, looking on the rising genius through the smoked glass of their prejudices, soothing their feeble vision, but robbing him of none of his light.

Hunt and Haydon, neighbors at Lisson Grove, still vied with each other for control over Keats. Neither succeeded. In his long hours of self-exploration by Tom's bedside he dwelt moodily on the men and women he knew, searching out their little flaws with bitter satisfaction. No longer did Hunt figure as the beloved Libertas. Keats now saw him critically as the dilettante, the chirping philosopher of the hearth who takes everything lightly because he lacks the depth to feel profoundly. "Hunt does one harm by making fine things petty and beautiful things hateful," the dejected youth condemned. He had a grievance against Hunt. While the reviewers had been voiding their poison, Hunt had said little or nothing in his defense,

Keats complained, not reflecting in his suspiciousness that the better part of friendship at the time was silence in a man whose every word would have bred a thousand enmities. Haydon wearied with his fanfaronade of self, his large promise and slow achievement. The Smiths and the Novellos bored, as they twisted meaning for the sake of a pun.

He saw a little of Joseph Severn, an artist a little older than himself and a close friend of Tom's. And he saw Brown. Otherwise he shut himself up in unhealthy solitude, inquiring for motives in the least reflected chitchat of friend and acquaintance. If one said, "Keats, I shall go and see Severn to-day," he quickly retorted, "Ah! you want him to take your portrait." And seizing upon the friend's words and his own, he exhausted himself with analysis.

The soreness in his throat returned when again he caught cold. Dreading the worst, and afraid of betraying his fears, he assumed a feverish merriment before Tom. But he could not bear the questioning of the hollow eyes in a face already pinched with death. "His identity presses on me so all day that I am obliged to go out," he told George and Georgiana in one of his long, affectionate letters. He was soon driven home again by his disillusionment in company and the fear that Tom might die in his absence. Mr. Abbey grudgingly allowed Fanny to visit the brothers at Well Walk. To the dying boy such unprecedented clemency could mean only one thing. Before Keats's letter had reached George in America, Tom was no more.

"I have Fanny and I have you — three people whose happiness to me is sacred," Keats wrote them. "It does annul the selfish sorrow which I should otherwise fall into. . . ." The moon had been shining full and brilliant as he had been writing. "She is the same to me in matter, what you are to me in spirit." He was still Endymion, her worshiper.

Yet he was human and thought of an earthly love. Even his Endymion had succumbed to an Indian maid. At twenty-three he, Keats, had had no real outlet for his emotional life. George, younger than himself, was expecting soon to be a father; Bailey and Reynolds were engaged. Haydon was only waiting to finish his painting to marry the beautiful woman he

had met at her husband's deathbed. He alone had found no
one to love him.

Like all susceptible youths he had begun by elevating women
to divinities in the first fervor of ripening manhood. Little by
little he had seen them as ordinary mortals and had become
critical of them for self-protection. Too well he knew that if
ever he fell in love the flame would consume him. He was not
one to take any life experience lightly. Consequently he put
his young blood to the rein. "When I am among women I
have evil thoughts, malice and spleen," he confided to Bailey,
with whom he could unburden himself after their common
escapade at Oxford. "I cannot speak, or be silent — I am
full of suspicions. . . . You must be charitable and put all
this perversity to my being disappointed since my boyhood. . . . After all, I do think better of womankind than to
suppose they care whether Mister John Keats, five feet high,
likes them or not."

Mister John Keats, five feet high: there hid the secret of
his inferiority. Ever since he had grown conscious of passion in the fleeting glimpse of the woman at Vauxhall, he had
struggled to overcome it. Unhappily men and women brought
it bitterly to his notice. "Had I a man's fair form!" The
cry was ever to reëcho in the presence of a desirable woman.
For a brief spell, that autumn, he had been able to still it in
the gust of passion that carried him away before an Indian maid
in the flesh. He had gone on a visit to the Reynolds', where
he met Jane Cox, a young cousin of theirs recently come from
India. Proof of her unusual beauty lay in the circumstance
that the Reynolds girls, who had spoken generously of her
before Keats had appeared on the scene, grew spiteful with
jealousy when they perceived her effect upon him. She
ravished his senses. "She has a rich eastern look; she has
fine eyes and fine manners. When she comes into a room she
makes an impression the same as the beauty of a leopardess."
The memory of her kept him awake at night "as a tune of
Mozart's might do." But Keats knew it was not love he felt —
only the keenness of desire. Some time previously he had been
stirred by a fair incognita at Hastings whom he met again in
London. He had kissed her. Beyond that and presents of

FANNY BRAWNE

FROM THE ORIGINAL MINIATURE IN THE
POSSESSION OF HER GRANDDAUGHTER,
MRS. OSWALD ELLIS [1]

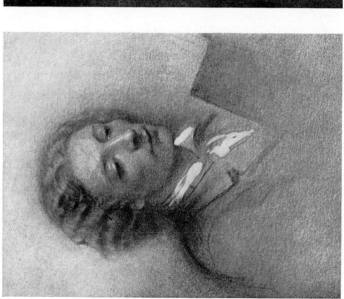
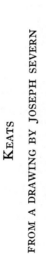

KEATS

FROM A DRAWING BY JOSEPH SEVERN

([1] *Reproduced, by special permission, from Keats's "Letters," edited by Maurice Buxton Forman, Oxford University Press*)

game which she had made him for his invalid brother, there had been only friendship.

Goaded by frustration, Keats would pretend that the physical life meant nothing to him. He had to strive for nobler aims that demanded the sacrifice of sensual happiness. What had he to do with a wife and children? His was the sublime solitude of creativeness. "The roaring of the wind is my wife and the stars through the window pane are my children," he comforted himself. But his body, which made its own demands, was not satisfied.

The world and his part in it kept him in long communion with himself. Why is man born? What is his place in the grand scheme of things? In the bleakness of the rain, as he had watched by the side of Tom at Teignmouth, his ideas had taken shape as he had endeavored to feel "the burden of the Mystery." "I can compare human life to a large mansion of many apartments, two of which I can only describe, the doors of the rest being as yet shut upon me — the first we step into we call the infant or thoughtless chamber, in which we remain as long as we do not think. . . . We no sooner get into the second chamber, which I shall call the chamber of maiden thought, than we become intoxicated with the light and the atmosphere, we see nothing but pleasant wonders and think of delaying there for ever in delight: However among the effects this breathing is father of is that tremendous one of sharpening one's vision into the heart and nature of man . . . whereby this chamber of maiden thought becomes gradually darken'd and at the same time, on all sides of it, many doors are set open — but all dark — all leading to dark passages."

After Tom's death Keats went to live with Brown at Wentworth Place. Little did he know that even then a door of the chamber of maiden thought was being set open for him as the Indian Maid of the leopardess walk made way for the true Diana.

John Keats met Fanny Brawne.

XXIII

JULIAN AND MADDALO

THROUGH southeastern France and Switzerland the Shelley household, with three infants in tow, made its way to Italy. But first Godwin had had to be propitiated. Worried lest the removal of his son-in-law to a foreign land stop the flow of currency in the direction of Skinner Street, he demanded assurance that the needs of his old age would still be respected across the Channel before he gave his paternal blessing. The day before the sailing he came in person to bid farewell to the voyagers, unaware that of them all two alone were ever again to see England.

It had been Shelley's dream to make a home for his family on the shores of Lake Como, the jewel of northern Italy, but nowhere could he find a suitable residence. His experience with Albion House, whose damp had mildewed his books, had taught him to look for more than a picturesque exterior. Ruefully he rejected the Villa Pliniana, set at the foot of a romantic precipice, crowned with a forest of chestnut and cypress, and cooled by a fountain whose mystical ebb and flow had been described by Pliny the Younger. He settled for a brief period at Milan, whose pinnacled cathedral, "a most astonishing work of art," roused his facile enthusiasm. But it was the interior he loved. Behind the altar, where the light of day fell in a golden glow beneath the stained-glass windows, he, the self-confessed *atheos* of the visitor's book at Montavert, sat in the holy quiet, reading his Dante and thinking his thoughts.

On the twenty-eighth of April, 1818, Alba, now Allegra, the fifteen-months-old baby whom they had nicknamed the "bluff little Commodore" for her radiant health and liveliness, had been sent in the care of Elise to join her father in Venice. Shelley had been full of qualms. An acquaintance whom he had met by chance at the Milan post office told him incredible tales of Lord Byron's scandalous life. Byron's own letters had been far from reassuring. A cruel resentment against Clare forbade his writing to her, and his allusions to her in his letters were such that Shelley kept them prudently out of her sight. However, before Clare made her final decision to part with Allegra, he called her to him, and with kindness and tact and an extraordinary common sense that forsook him when dealing with his own affairs he gave her his view of the matter. She must not give up the lovely child who had grown so dear to them all. He spoke of the rumors he had heard, of Lord Byron's feelings toward herself, of the difficulty of reclaiming Allegra once Clare waived her maternal rights. With his customary generosity he renewed his proposal to bring up the little girl with his own children in any land where he should make his home and where, far from such persecution as she had suffered at Marlow, Clare might look after her in safety. But Clare hardly listened. Employing Godwinian reasoning, she reiterated that her womanly weakness was not to stand in the way of her child's welfare. She would be strong and bear her suffering in silence, but Allegra must be given her chance. Against Clare's arguments, expressed with contemptuous vehemence whenever she was crossed, Shelley could do nothing.

Two days after leaving Milan, Elise arrived in Venice with Allegra and was received at the Palazzo Mocenigo on the Grand Canal, whither Lord Byron had removed his servants, his increased menagerie, and his current mistresses, establishing himself as a citizen of the fair city. His private gondola, moored to a painted post, was guarded by Tita Falcieri, a youth with the body of a boxer and the moustachios of a pirate, well learned, withal, in the chase of the sort of game milord seemed to fancy these days. Within doors a new queen reigned, succeeding by dint of tooth and nail the wife of Signor Segati. It had not taken Margarita Cogni long to usurp Marianna's unsteady throne. His lordship, wearied of the incurable itch of Marianna's pretty palm, decided to take his pleasures elsewhere — at smaller expense. For he liked saving his money now that Newstead Abbey had been sold for nearly one hundred thousand pounds. In the beginning of his "scribbling career" he had made the noble gesture of giving away his copyright money. Now he preferred to make use of it himself and drove shrewd bargains with the genteel Murray, the better to fill a well-furnished money box. For once in his life Childe Harold betrayed a resemblance to Catherine Byron, widow of Mad Jack, counting her shillings in her Aberdeen lodging.

There was one who looked on with approval. Margarita Cogni, as jealous as a tigress of his lordship's favor, terrorized the servants in her zeal to protect his interests. Even the learned Fletcher submitted to her ascendency. What else could he do, poor fellow, against the keen claws of this Italian wildcat? He rued the hour when his master had let her into the house and prayed for the day when she should be out of it, though he had to admit that the expenses of the management were reduced to less than half, and that the other female inhabitants of the Mocenigo toed the mark with padded paws and never a mew of disobedience.

Lord Byron had met Margarita in the summer of 1817 while riding with Hobhouse along the Brenta in the cool of the evening. She was standing with a group of peasant girls who, when they saw milord, knew him at once for the immensely rich *inglese* who had been helping their people with his money, that year of great distress. As he rode past, one of them, probably Margarita, called out after him in graceful Venetian, "Why don't you, who relieve others, think of us also?" It was not long before his lordship came to the rescue of Margarita, who, besides want's burden, had to bear a consumptive husband, a man so jealous that he scarcely minded his oven. When Margarita came to the first rendezvous his lordship stated his terms. "I have no objection to make love with you," declared that truthful daughter of the earth. "I am a married woman, and all married women do it. But my husband — " The baker was ferocious, she said, and would certainly do her mischief, a fear so belied by her Amazonian proportions that Byron was amused.

He liked the tall, healthy, primitive girl, dark and fiery as if made of the soil and sunlight of Italy. She was twenty-two, with a superb figure unspoiled by childbearing — a circumstance which in his lordship's eyes put her above the Signora Segati. Moreover, the *dama* had become wearisome with her explosions of jealousy which made her no better than a wedded wife. Not that Margarita, the stately Fornarina, was free of the vice. Fierce as a tiger, she tolerated no rival. "If she found any women in her way," said Byron complacently, "she knocked them down." But these were not her chief charms to the Childe. The girl, innocent as Eve of the scrivener's art, and perhaps as contemptuous of it in the scheme of life as that first of women would have been, treated him like a man, and loved him for himself. None of the languishments of a Caroline Lamb there; none of Lady Byron's learnedness. Margarita gave herself with the devotion of an animal, amused him with her pantaloon humor, mothered and spoiled him and looked on him, the most celebrated of English bards, as her master and her child. Murray in London was puzzled by the letters his lordship sent from the wicked city. Perhaps when he saw the picture of the Fornarina which George Henry Harlow made of her, he understood a little of her hold. She was the antithesis of Lady Byron, amoral where the other was moral, pagan where the other was devout — though Byron did mention in one of his letters how the superb hussy had a way of crossing herself when she heard the church bell strike, "sometimes when that ceremony did not appear to be much in unison with what she was then about." As a matter of fact Lord Byron was working out through Margarita, and the other nine muses whom he discreetly kept from her knowledge, another aspect of his revenge against that wife who thought herself too pure for him.

So far Nemesis had been propitious. Not in vain had he invoked her aid that night at the Coliseum. He learned by the merest chance that Sir Samuel Romilly had cut his throat in grief over his wife's death. Fiercely gloating, Byron seized his pen and etched his acid triumph to Lady Byron, who must be warned that a Gordon curse was no empty breath. Sir Samuel Romilly, her legal adviser, had deprived him of wife and child and sent him to exile. Now the crime had brought him its reward. Little had this man thought "in the radiance of fame, and the complacency of self-earned riches — that a domestic affliction would lay him in the earth, with the meanest of malefactors, in a cross-road with the stake in his body, if the verdict of insanity did not redeem his ashes from the sentence of the laws he had lived upon by interpreting and mis-interpreting, and died in violating." In the magic of distance he, Byron, transformed himself to the white lamb, sacrificed for the sins of others — but avenged by the powers of justice.

Lady Byron, meanwhile, had not broken by a word her implacable silence. With Mrs. Villiers she still looked after that erring soul, Augusta, read the letters Byron sent her, and ruled her conduct no less zealously now that she knew all. Whenever any new work of Byron's appeared, she exchanged comments upon it with Mrs. Villiers, made her own exegesis till she had interpreted to the full its every word, and then sent Augusta counsel. Indeed, Mrs. Leigh could scarcely trust herself to take a step except under the shadowing wing of her guardian angel. What should she do, what should she say, when people asked her about her brother's works and the terrible allusions the reviews made to *her?* There was that distressing season when *Manfred* had appeared, with B.'s feelings so fearfully portrayed about his wife, about her. . . . "You can only speak of *Manfred*," advised the angel, "with the most decided expressions of your disapprobation." It was easy for her, the strong-willed, to give advice. She had God on her side, and could therefore live with composure in the same house with Byron's portraits, shrouded under their green coverings, and not ache to have him back again. But Augusta loved her brother, and he, even in the midst of his riotous life, still loved her. Yes, it was easy for Lady Byron to remain cold: loathing of her blackened every letter he sent. But to herself he was all charm and tenderness. He could write, in ludicrous jealousy, "Hobhouse tells me that at your levee he generally found Ld. F. Bentick — pray, why is that fool so often a visitor? is he in love with you?" — and in another letter tell of his *fifty* mistresses. In her muddle-headedness Augusta felt she knew her brother better than did anyone else, however learned.

At the Palazzo Mocenigo, undisturbed by the shrieks of the parrots and the competitive vociferation of Margarita, Lord Byron was writing his new poem — new in more than one sense. In fact, the Venetian Sardanapalus had awakened to a poetic energy that threw down as so many tin soldiers the Laras and Corsairs of an earlier day, as he exulted in the creation with which he was grappling. It was the second of his vigorous mood. *Beppo,* that Punchinello of the Carnival nights when with the Signora Segati Byron had looked through the worldly wisdom of Venice, — and of humanity, — had come, with his tricks and turns and canny levity, as a precursor of *Don Juan,* the true hero of disillusionment. As yet only the first canto had been written of what was to prove his most vital poem and, oddly, the most essentially Byronic. Again it was Byron writing of Byron, but now a mellowness had come into his work, tingeing with ripeness the experiences of his youth just as the grey hairs were touching his auburn curls with age. A sharper realism cut each stanza of mock-heroic *ottava rima* to neat wedges of satire, eagerly apprehended by the mind that savored the pungency which made even truth palatable.

The frank animalism of his Venetian life, a reaction from the primness of Seaham and Piccadilly Terrace, had proved a catharsis. He was not wholly free, however, of his tormenting antipathies. One and all, they crept into his verse, held their stage, and were hooted off by Don Juan mocking Byron — a salutary sign when a hero can laugh at himself. Of course Byron had to take his little revenges. Lady Byron appeared as Don Juan's mother, a learned lady "famed for every branch of every science known"; nor was the hapless Sir Samuel spared.

> Some women use their tongues — she *look'd* a lecture,
>   Each eye a sermon, and her brow a homily,
> An all-in-all sufficient self-director,
>   Like the lamented late Sir Samuel Romilly,
> The Law's expounder, and the State's corrector
>   Whose suicide was almost an anomaly —
> One sad example more, that "All is vanity," —
> (The jury brought their verdict in "Insanity.")

In cynical but urbanely impeccable stanzas, he drew his life
and hers, as he now saw it, the blame of course — for Don
Juan was no martyr to gallantry — falling upon Donna Inez.

> Perfect she was, but as perfection is
>   Insipid in this naughty world of ours,
> Where our first parents never learn'd to kiss
>   Till they were exiled from their earlier bowers,
> Where all was peace and innocence and bliss,
>   (I wonder how they got through the twelve hours),
> Don José like a lineal son of Eve,
> Went plucking various fruit without her leave. . . .
>
> Now Donna Inez had, with all her merit,
>   A great opinion of her own good qualities;
> Neglect, indeed, requires a saint to bear it,
>   And such, indeed, she was in her moralities;
> But then she had a devil of a spirit,
>   And sometimes mix'd up fancies with realities,
> And let few opportunities escape
> Of getting her liege lord into a scrape. . . .
>
> Don José and the Donna Inez led
>   For some time an unhappy sort of life,
> Wishing each other, not divorced, but dead;
>   They lived respectably as man and wife,
> Their conduct was exceedingly well-bred,
>   And gave no outward signs of inward strife,
> Until at length the smother'd fire broke out,
> And put the business past all kind of doubt.

As a result Lady Byron was concerning herself with good
works and bringing up Ada ignorant of her father, while
Byron, in the city of vice and folly, kept his mistresses and gave
the affection of which Little Legitimacy was deprived to
Allegra, his new toy. He grew very fond of the child, who
soon learned to greet him with a pretty *"Bon dì, papà,"* like a
little Venetian. He had expected the little Byron to be pretty,
but was beyond measure delighted to see how far she exceeded
his expectation. In the unconventional palazzo Allegra became a favorite and the special pet of Margarita, to whom
everything was dear, from the fierce dog to the monkeys, if

only it belonged to his lordship. All of Venice soon learned that *il giovinotto inglese* of the extravagant reputation had lately received *two* of his daughters from England, one of whom looked nearly as old as himself — a story Shelley himself was to hear from Lord Byron's gondoliers.

Many another tale reached Clare at the Bagni di Lucca, where the Shelleys had gone to find refuge from the Italian summer. Byron wallowed in unbelievable vice. Allegra, the poor innocent babe, was at the mercy of kept women. Alas, was it for this Clare had sacrificed herself? Anguished by her thoughts, she fell into her moody silences, speaking neither to Shelley nor to Mary for days at a time as she brooded, the image of despair. Life, indeed, seemed to hold little for her. She had succeeded in nothing. Her hour of love had resulted in a lifetime of grief. The stage career she had so ambitiously planned had come to an end in an assignation. None listened to her voice but Shelley, who wrote for her those beautiful stanzas, "To Constantia, Singing," and ungrudgingly paid for her music lessons. She was a failure as an author. The novel she had finished could find no publisher, not even when Shelley submitted it with his recommendation both to Lackington and to Taylor and Hessey. Emptiness, nothing but emptiness, opened before her, intensified by envy of Mary's good fortune in having a husband who loved her, and pretty babes. No wonder the two women were always at odds. Wretchedness shortened Clare's patience, while happiness made Mary feel less for another's woes.

Shelley found refuge in the Tuscan woodland. Every morning, carrying his books and writing materials, he would walk with great strides through the chestnut alleys and climb over the alder-covered ledges to a pool in the thick of the forest. Steep rocks enclosed the natural basin, stirred and replenished by the perpetual dashing of a mountain torrent. On an overhanging rock Shelley, his clothes thrown off, lay reading Herodotus until his body cooled, and then leapt into the vivifying waters. Toward dusk he returned home, when Mary went riding with him through the beech woods near their house until the stars came out and the vivid Italian fire-flies lighted their way home. There, by lamplight, they read

and studied together.   Mary, whose Italian had improved, exercised herself in a translation of Alfieri's *Mirra*, while Shelley,
to open for her the portals of that ideal love of which she was
still the living symbol, translated Plato's *Symposium*.   With
less pleasure he finished the modern eclogue she had set him as
a task at Marlow.

In the midst of this studious peace came the news that
Allegra was no longer with her father.   Clare's anxiety grew
to despair.   No more did she think of Allegra's brilliant future
in her yearning to have the child in her arms, safe from the
indifference of strangers.   She must see Byron at once and
demand back her daughter.   Shelley, dubious of her success
with a man who took no pains to hide his intense dislike,
offered to accompany her.   With the despondent woman who
changed her plans with every breeze, he started out for
Florence, where he took a gondola to Padua.   His sailor's
heart delighted in the graceful boat, painted and hung with
black, whose steel beak, the only touch of brightness, gleamed
in the lights from the lamps.   A violent thunderstorm, one of
those sudden irruptions that can wreak mischief even in sheltered waters, held Clare trembling with terror in the cabined
dark, made eerie by the sudden flashes of lightning that not
even the black cloth blinds could shut out.   It was midnight
when they reached their hotel.   Next day the journey toward
Venice was resumed, the talkative gondolier, one of Lord
Byron's, entertaining his passengers with the latest scandals
of milord.   The morning of the twenty-second of August
Shelley beheld the wicked city, its pink façades flushing like
coral in the morning light.

He breakfasted with Clare at a hotel.   Then, taking another
gondola, he accompanied her to the house of the British
Consul General, Richard Belgrave Hoppner, whose wife, a
pretty Swiss with an infant of a few months, had wrested
little Allegra from the influences of Palazzo Mocenigo.   The
Hoppners listened sympathetically to Clare's story and called
for Elise, who brought in the child.   How had the bluff little
Commodore changed in the four months that had elapsed!
Her cheeks were pale.   She was no longer the lively, high-

spirited imp of the Marlow days when she had played with little Blue Eyes. Shelley, however, found his favorite "as beautiful as ever though more mild." But it was that very mildness that determined Clare to fight for her possession. The Hoppners counseled moderation. Often, said the officious Consul General, Byron expressed "extreme horror" at the possibility of Clare's arrival in Venice, saying that if she came he would instantly quit the town. It would be better if he were not told of her presence there.

That afternoon, while Clare stayed with Allegra, Shelley called on Byron, who was delighted to see him, although the first subject the loyal Shelley broached was the unpleasant one of Clare. Of course his lordship would be glad to oblige his friend. But he did not like to have Allegra leave him for a long stretch. You know these Venetians. . . . They would think he had grown tired of her and sent her away. He already had the reputation of being capricious. But then, said he lightly, he really had no right over the child. "If Clare likes to take it, let her take it. I do not say what most people would in that situation, that I will refuse to provide for it, or abandon it, if she does this; but she must surely be aware herself how very imprudent such a measure would be." A veiled threat, but a threat nonetheless. Byron held Clare in his power through her love of Allegra; he would have none forget it.

Shelley for the moment did not press his plea, as Byron was anxious to be off to the Lido and insisted upon having his company. The two men got into Byron's private gondola and the stalwart Tita steered them across the *laguna* to the long sandy barrier that protects Venice from the Adriatic. Here alone in the horseless city could Byron indulge his only exercise of riding. On the Lido his horses were waiting. The two mounted and renewed their olden talk of God and destiny, as they rode now by the fort at one end of the Lido, and now, on the opposite mole, past the Jewish cemetery where once a year the light-hearted Venetians danced on the graves in some mad ritual. Hardly a month was to pass before Shelley's one-year-old Clara, who looked so much like him, found burial on that barren island, the first of his family whom Italy was to claim.

Happily the future was veiled. As he mused with Byron on the subjects that used to hold them in nightlong vigils at Geneva, thoughts of Clara and Allegra mingled with his reflections, all of them bound up with the slowly closing day, the wave-washed beach, the faint tolling of the vesper bell from the island of San Servola, whose sad pile, the madhouse, rose out of the dusk. Who was this man Byron, and why had fate linked him with his own concerns?

Shelley recalled that evening in the tranquillity of his days at the villa that Byron had turned over to him near the ruins of the castle at Este. There Mary, bereaved of her daughter, clung desperately to William, too beautiful, too delicate a child. There Clare snatched at her brief happiness with Allegra. In the summerhouse at the end of the garden overlooking the plain of Lombardy with its amphitheatre of hills, Shelley assuaged grief and ill-health in poetry. *Julian and Maddalo:* under the two names he painted idealized portraits of himself, "a complete infidel," and Byron, whose religious views no one exactly knew, reproducing in a conversation their twilight excursion.

> I rode one evening with Count Maddalo
> Upon the bank of land which breaks the flow
> Of Adria toward Venice. . . .

The slow bell tolls from the island of the madhouse, where, as Maddalo tells Julian, at this hour each maniac leaves his cell for the vesper service — a thought that rouses Julian's scorn against the injustice of divinity that can impose so dark a lot on man.

> "You talk as in years past," said Maddalo.
> " 'T is strange men change not. You were ever still
> Among Christ's flock a dangerous infidel,
> A wolf for the meek lambs — if you can't swim
> Beware of Providence."

Fateful words.

The next day they set out for San Servola to see the Maniac,

that Julian might hear his tale. But first Count Maddalo's little daughter (Allegra) comes to them, and at the sight of her
Julian, whose thoughts had been darkened by Maddalo's skepticism, pleads: —

> " . . . See
> This lovely child, blithe, innocent and free
> She spends a happy time with little care
> While we to such sick thoughts subjected are
> As came on you last night — it is our will
> That thus enchains us to permitted ill —
> We might be otherwise — we might be all
> We dream of happy, high, majestical.
> Where is the love, beauty, and truth we seek
> But in our mind? and if we were not weak
> Should we be less in deed than in desire?"
> "Ay, if we were not weak — and we aspire
> How vainly to be strong!" said Maddalo:
> "You talk Utopia." "It remains to know. . . ."

On, on, the two voices Mary had heard for the first time together at Geneva, and that were to haunt her to her dying
day, traveled the spaces of philosophy. *Julian and Maddalo*
and the exquisite *Lines Written among the Euganean Hills*
ended the month of October.

But there was another work that had been conceived, one
whose opening lines rolled like mighty thunders over primeval
space. He knew he had begun his masterpiece, and his heart
was in elation to complete it.

> Monarch of Gods and Dæmons, and all Spirits
> But One, who throng those bright and rolling worlds
> Which Thou and I alone of living things
> Behold with sleepless eyes!

The Promethean voice filled the overwhelming night with a
marvelous music, and Shelley knew, as surely as he knew
only the poet was worthy of the name of Creator, that with
Prometheus Unbound he should earn immortality.

But with the closing autumn a wintry mood descended on
his spirit. The leaves of the vine-trellis that led to the gar-

den study rattled in the cold; the flowers were fading. Mary
and Clare in inconsolable sorrow mourned, one the loss of
a child by death, the other, by something as irremediable —
a proud man's tyranny. Allegra was unwillingly brought back
to the Hoppners as Shelley started out on another peregri-
nation —southward, to the sun. He had had enough of Venetian life. The spectacle of a people dancing on the wreck
of their freedom pained that heart overflowing with the
benevolence he would have poured over the world. Venice,
the tyrant, after an ephemeral struggle, had become, what
was worse, a slave, first to the French, now to the hated Aus-
trians, who taxed her people and quartered their soldiers
upon them. Who could blame the oppressed for concealing their chains in motley? Shelley loathed their hollow
gayety.

Moreover, he was disillusioned in Byron, who seemed all
candor while one talked to him, — "But unfortunately it does
not outlast your departure," — and shocked by his private life,
infinitely more depraved by contrast with the purity of his own
with Mary. "He associates with wretches who seem almost
to have lost the gait and physiognomy of man, and who do
not scruple to avow practices which are not only not named,
but I believe seldom even conceived in England," he wrote to
Peacock after leaving Este. But the rebel puritan laid in his
shadows too thick.

True, a seeker after intellectual beauty found but meagre
pasturage in Lord Byron's fields. Shelley, however, failed
to find there beauty of any kind. Women like Margarita
Cogni horrified him, whereas Byron poetized them to Junos,
or at least Medeas. Certainly Margarita was epic. Worthy
of Homer was the picture of her standing in the storm on the
open steps of the Mocenigo, her hair wet and lashed by the
wind, her rain-drenched clothes, moulding her to nakedness,
flapping like wings behind her as lightning and the waves
played at her head and feet, watching where 'Celenza [1] and his
gondoliers were struggling against an ugly squall in the *laguna*,
while not another soul of the prudent Venetians was to be
seen outdoors. *"Ah! Can della Madonna! Xe esto il tempo*

---

[1] His Excellency.

per andar al Lido?" [1] she cried when she saw his lordship safe, and then let out her fury upon the boatmen for not having known better than to imperil their master in a storm. Fierce and tender, the tigress rejoiced at recovering her noble Cub.

Thoughts of England with their accompanying nostalgia had troubled the two poets when they had been together. The bread of exile, for all it kept the body whole, had a bitter taste that not all the beauty of the surrounding landscape could sweeten. Yet neither entertained seriously the idea of returning home. Perhaps friends might be coaxed to join them, and help create in Italy an intellectual circle that should compensate for the loss of England. Who better than Leigh Hunt could be invited? "We talked a good deal about you," Shelley wrote him, "and among other things he [Byron] said that he wished you would come to Italy, and bade me tell you that he would lend you money for the journey." The scheme was not to be put into effect till four years later.

Little else besides a want of friends tempted the two exiles to turn their thoughts from Italy. Byron wished the Channel wider at the memory of his "cold wife," while echoes from Skinner Street made Shelley grateful that Mary was spared the sound of the actual voice. She had written to tell her father of her little girl's death. "You must recollect . . ." responded the Olympian, "that it is only persons of a very ordinary sort, and of a pusillanimous disposition, that sink long under a calamity of this nature." She followed his advice by withdrawing into herself with her grief.

After a short stay in Rome, where Shelley distracted himself with a prose fragment on the Coliseum, he decided to remove his family to the more healthful Naples. The ruins of Rome had communicated to him their impressive desolation and roused the slumbering revolutionary. In the English cemetery, near the pyramids of Cestius, he found a melancholy appeasement, as he contemplated the tombs, mostly of young

---

[1] "Ah! Dog of the Madonna! Is this a time to be going to the Lido?" Some of Byron's biographers, misapplying Margarita's words, have inveighed against the fair Medea for having called him a dog. Literally, where an Elizabethan would have said *'Sdeath* or *'Sblood,* Margarita invoked the dog of the Virgin, it seeming no anomaly to the Italian mind that the Madonna should have a dog.

men and women who had come to Italy in search of health, covered over with bright grass and flowers. "One might, if one were to die, desire the sleep they seem to sleep."

In Naples his dejection increased. Besides the spiritual malaise, he suffered physically from a return of the old complaint that no doctor had been able to diagnose. The medical practitioner in Naples into whose hands he placed himself made him suffer worse pain without bringing him any benefit. Shelley had little doubt that he had not long to live — a thought that caused him no poignant emotion except that of having lived, as he believed, in vain. He seemed to have lost his eagerness to write. He began a poem and laid it aside. He set to work on another, only to leave it half finished. His black mood penetrated every line he wrote, and he carefully kept them from Mary, not to aggravate her sorrow. There was still another reason for his despondency, a secret shared by Clare, and later revealed to his cousin Medwin. A lovely woman of noble birth had fallen in love with Shelley in England. Several times their paths had met and she had confessed her passion, only to be told that her love could not be returned. Like some unhappy maiden under a spell, she followed him wherever he went, letting neither water nor mountain bar her way. Sometimes she preceded him to his destination, and there waited for a sight of him she loved but could never win. She was in Naples when Shelley arrived, in time to see her die, leaving a very young infant in his care. Shelley never revealed the lady's name. Clare, who alone knew it, kept her secret to the grave.

No wonder his sensitive spirit took refuge in the shadow of death, where, alone with Misery, the companion of his years, he should find rest at last. "Hasten to the bridal bed," he wooed his dismal bride.

> Underneath the grave 't is spread:
> In darkness may our love be hid,
> Oblivion be our coverlid —
> We may rest and none forbid.

By the waters of Naples, still the thought and the desire persisted, as he gazed into the transparent waves, watching the

green and purple seaweeds moving with the motion of the noontide seas. He had nothing, he meditated — "Nor fame, nor
power, nor love, nor leisure." Nor love? Mary in her affliction forgot everyone, even him. His longing for peace,
expressed in the *Stanzas Written in Dejection, Near Naples,*
reached the gods, who remember all.

> Yet now despair itself is mild,
>   Even as the winds and waters are:
> I could lie down like a tired child,
>   And weep away the life of care
>   Which I have borne and yet must bear,
> Till death like sleep might steal on me,
>   And I might feel in the warm air
> My cheek grow cold, and hear the sea
> Breathe o'er my dying brain its last monotony.

He found power to work at last, and by the end of January,
1819, he had finished the first act of his Promethean drama.
The fire of inspiration burned out his bodily fever; he must
write or be consumed. Change always did him good. Thus,
the warm Neapolitan winter over, he took Mary and his little
William to Rome for the glorious Roman spring and the renewal of his energies. Over the graves of the Protestant
cemetery wildflowers brightened the vesture of death and
festooned with fresh green the crumbling towers of the old
Roman wall bordering the tomb of Caius Cestius. The whole
hill slope at that season burned, a springtime conflagration,
with its thousand flames of hyacinth and jonquil.

But Shelley had found himself a wilder seclusion for the
writing of his drama in the ruins of the Baths of Caracalla, of
whose magnificence only the ivied piles remained, like moun-
tainous wrecks of some destroyed cosmos. "In one of the
buttresses that supports an immense and lofty arch . . . are
the crumbling remains of an antique winding staircase, whose
sides are open in many places to the precipice. This you
ascend," he described to Peacock, "and arrive on the summit
of these piles." There, enwrapt in the scent of the many
flowering shrubs, a free Prometheus on his promontory, he
accomplished the unchaining of his Titan, as in the pauses of
his thought he interspersed the pages of his notebook with

drawings of tree and flower. Little did they know, those mortals who spied fleetingly the long-striding youth in his schoolboy's jacket and open collar, with his large eyes staring and his hair flowing wild, that a presence was walking among them. April saw the poem concluded but for the lyrical outburst of the fourth act, which was added toward the end of the year. Shelley's message, voiced haltingly in *Queen Mab* and with ampler music in the *Revolt of Islam*, at last found perfect expression in deathless verse. Whatever the world might think, he knew he had created something that would endure as long as men's hearts beat in a living earth. And like his Prometheus, he freed himself when he had only pity for the forces of evil, Jove's furies, which tortured mankind.

> I weigh not what ye do, but what ye suffer,
> Being evil.

While in Rome the Shelleys met Amelia Curran, the young Irishwoman whose liveliness in Skinner Street had made poor Harriet decry her as a coquette. She was studying art, and, finding good material in the Shelleys, engaged on portraits of the whole family, including Clare. Hers was no great skill. Nevertheless, in the painting of Shelley she conveyed something of the compelling purity of his face — the great brow with its shock of hair through which his hand seems newly to have run in poetic distraction, his gentle mouth and the large spirit eyes full of intellectual fire, yet also of a strange sadness.

Shelley, indeed, was at the time in an exalted state of mind. He had but recently obtained possession of a manuscript telling the story of the terrible Count Cenci, and in his visits to the galleries and palaces he had seen a portrait of Beatrice Cenci, that unnatural father's victim. The girl's angelic beauty and her monstrous fate so possessed him that when, as he walked through the streets of Rome and heard the old-clothes men cry, *"Cenci! Cenci!"* he thought the words the echo of his own soul. He had urged Mary to write Beatrice's tragedy, but she felt unequal to the demands of the appalling story. Shelley set to work upon it.

As the debilitating Roman summer drew nigh, Shelley felt

SHELLEY IN ROME

PAINTED BY JOSEPH SEVERN

the effects of it in a recurrence of his spasms. The doctors urged a removal North, a change welcomed by Mary, who had been uneasy not only about Shelley, but also about her little son, whose delicate constitution gave her cause for alarm. Moreover, she was expecting the birth of another child in the autumn and wished to be where she could have adequate medical care. Her friends the Gisbornes recommended an English doctor in Florence. Miss Curran's portraits, however, kept them in Rome a month longer. On the day set for their departure, William Shelley died of the Roman fever. "Monday, June 7, at noonday." Clare set down the day and the hour, as her thoughts flew, perhaps, to that other frail child, in the hands of strangers, of whom Mrs. Hoppner wrote, "Allegra . . . has become quiet and serious, like a little old woman, which saddens us greatly."[1] Mary, Clare: both were childless now.

They buried the little corpse beneath the pyramidal tomb of Caius Cestius, among the young men and women who had come to Rome — to die. Italy had claimed her second victim.

[1] "*Allegra . . . est devenue tranquille et sérieuse, comme une petite vieille, ce qui nous peine beaucoup.*"

XXIV

THE ROAD TO ROME

FAR out in the American wilds George and Georgiana read at great length in Keats's letters of the Indian maid who, though not a Cleopatra, was at least a Charmian. Visualizing, perhaps, an arch lift of Georgiana's brows, Keats denied emphatically that he was in love. He was just physically stirred. "I should like her to ruin me," he avowed, "and I should like you to save me." In his next letter, however, all reference to the enchantress had vanished. Instead, a new figure entered upon the stage, ushered in by naïvely disingenuous preliminaries. "You may like a little pic-nic of scandal, even across the Atlantic. Shall I give you Miss Brawne? She is about my height, with a fine style of countenance of the lengthened sort; she wants sentiment in every feature; she manages to make her hair look well; her nostrils are very fine though a little painful; her mouth is bad and good . . . her shape is very graceful, and so are her movements. . . . She is not seventeen, but she is ignorant; monstrous in her behavior, flying out in all directions, calling people such names that I was forced lately to make use of the word — Minx." Not a flattering portrait, but then, Romeo ceased his lover's ravings when Juliet supplanted Rosaline.

"She is about my height. . . ." The first words Keats had to say of Fanny Brawne at once leveled and raised her to his heart's height. He might admire like a lovesick swain the opulence of an Eastern leopardess. He could only love a woman who made him forget his stature. Allusions to it angered him more than ever. At about this time a woman of his acquaintance was reported to have said of him, "Oh, he is quite the little poet." "Now this is abominable . . ." Keats fumed. "You see what it is to be under six feet, and not a Lord."

Fanny Brawne could not have been called beautiful, though to Keats, once he acknowledged to himself that he loved her, she became the perfect Helen whom every man coveted. He was violently, self-devouringly, in love. His letters, when he began writing to her, embarrassed with the abjectness of his adoration, terrified with the violence of his passion. He rhapsodized on her beauty on the one hand, declaring himself unworthy, and cursed it on the other for having enslaved him. Gone was his faith that the wind and the stars would have sufficed his desire for wife and children. He could not live without Fanny; yet he was unhappy with her.

He had seen her for the first time after his return from the Scottish tour, when, on Brown's coming home, he had gone to live with him at Wentworth Place. Mrs. Brawne, who had occupied the house for the summer, had liked Hampstead and its society so well that, when the time came for her to leave, she took her family but a short distance away to Downshire Hill, where her newly made friend, Mrs. Dilke, might come to call. Visits were exchanged, and often Mrs. Brawne and her eldest daughter were to be found next door to the two bachelors. The meeting occurred. Keats, in the presence of an elegantly dressed, intelligent young woman, obviously of good family, found his heart touched, and bridled in self-defense. Some instinct told him that he must take care. In the beginning, therefore, they quarreled, the high-spirited Fanny, accustomed to admiration, resenting Keats's seeming antagonism. He, on his part, flouted her for being light and frivolous, for loving dancing and society. Nevertheless, on Christmas of 1819, they were engaged.

London, since Waterloo, had been brilliant with the military. The winter seasons were enlivened with balls and gay parties, and in Hampstead routs and dances took place almost nightly, when the heroes home from the war, together with visiting Frenchmen, enjoyed the adulation of the ladies. All England seemed to have gone mad after the great victory, following fads with the same passion it had devoted to war. During the previous winter a wave of Egyptianism had swept over the land, people of fashion setting the pace by decorating their homes and themselves *à l'orientale*. Hampstead, in its humbler way, had followed suit, the craze entering even the domain of the immortals when Leigh Hunt and Keats and Shelley had competed in writing each a sonnet on the Nile. The present season, though less Egyptian, was no less gay. Fanny Brawne threw herself into it with a will. She liked dancing, she liked Frenchmen, — who but a jealous lover could condemn her at her years? — and she enjoyed creating a flutter in masculine hearts. Keats was destroyed with suspicions. In the intensity of his love he exaggerated her fascination, and could scarcely bear to have her out of his sight. Was she not beautiful? Did not everyone desire her? Who could love *him*, John Keats? "I am not a thing to be admired," he was to write her in self-abasement. "You are; I love you; all I can bring to you is a swooning admiration of your Beauty. I hold the place among Men which snub-nosed brunettes with meeting eyebrows do among women — they are trash to me." And to the other Fanny, his sister, he wrote asking to be taught a few common dancing steps.

Fanny accepted his idolatry. But she was a very modern young woman, as fond of her freedom as of compliments. She read voluminously, new books and old, talked of them with glib readiness, and was never at a loss in witty repartee. Moreover she knew the art of making her natural charms show to best advantage. Her light brown hair, waved and curled in the latest fashion, towered above her retreating forehead. She dressed exquisitely, often designing her own gowns from books on the history of costume. A shepherdess dress that she made haunted Keats in later days, as he lay ill in his room, crucifying himself with visions of her in the arms of another. That torture, however, had been his from the first. In vain she swore that she loved him, and him alone. Let her be absent from him and his suspicions were let loose.

> Who now, with greedy looks, eats up my feast?
> What stare outfaces now my silver moon!

he broke out one evening in January after Fanny had gone to a dance.

Ah! keep that hand unravished at the least;
  Let, let, the amorous burn —
  But pr'ythee, do not turn
The current of your heart from me so soon.
  O! save, in charity,
  The quickest pulse for me.

He knew himself enthralled; but do what he would to drive
the thought of Fanny from his mind, go where he might, his
love obsessed him, making him suffer excruciating pangs when
he compared his own chained state with Fanny's freedom.
He wanted her as much a prisoner as himself. Her name,
Frances, bridged the past to Dante's time. Like her of
Rimini, she should have been inextricably bound to him by the
might of their love, so that even in the whirlwinds of hell they
could not have been disunited. Fanny Brawne, however, in
the glow of youth and health, had no love for shadows, even
eternal ones. The music of the dance, the arm of a uniformed
man about one's waist, a whispered compliment — all these
were things that youth feeds on. She loved her exacting lover
no less by appearing attractive to other men's eyes. In this,
her lack of understanding, she did Keats the greatest injury.

Unconsciously he would have freed himself from a love
that was become a shirt of Nessus on his spirit. Not that he
failed in poetic power. Indeed, during the year after his
meeting with Fanny he wrote his best poetry. By some inexplicable process, while despising himself for his love-weak-
ness, he put himself to the test as a poet, and, unfurling his
spirit, left the other suffering, humbled self to struggle with
its bonds. He looked to distance, if not to free him, at least
to lengthen his chain. Early in 1819, shortly after his engagement to Fanny, he left Hampstead on a vacation to
Chichester and Bedhampton, to prove to himself, perhaps,
that he was not yet wholly the thrall of love. His friend Haslam, when the postal duties increased, had made him a present
of some thin paper for his letters. Some of it Keats took
along with him.

The twenty-first of January, St. Agnes's Day, found him at
Chichester, among simple people versed in olden lore. Perhaps some goodwife, referring to the day, told him of the

belief that if a maid went to bed fasting on St. Agnes's Eve,
she should be vouchsafed a vision of her future husband in
a dream.   The bare bones of legend were enough for Keats's
transfiguring imagination.   Taking Haslam's thin paper, he
composed his *Eve of St. Agnes*.   It may be the witchery of
the season possessed a mind already too full of one young girl
and of his unfulfilled desire.   The Madeline of his poem, innocent, beautiful, he enshrined in a moonlit room of old
romance, while music, scarce heard, came from the revelers
below, in the great hall.

> A casement high and triple-arch'd there was,
> All garlanded with carven imag'ries
> Of fruits, and flowers, and bunches of knot-grass,
> And diamonded with panes of quaint device,
> Innumerable of stains and splendid dyes,
> As are the tiger-moth's deep-damask'd wings;
> And in the midst, 'mong thousand heraldries,
> And twilight saints, and dim emblazonings,
> A shielded scutcheon blush'd with blood of queens and kings.

Madeline kneels down in prayer, bathed by the science-defying
might of a poet's fancy, in rose bloom, and soft amethyst cast
by the moonbeams through the painted casement.[1]   She re-
moves the pearls from her hair, and loosens her bodice.

> . . . By degrees
> Her rich attire creeps rustling to her knees:
> Half-hidden, like a mermaid in sea-weed,
> Pensive awhile, she dreams awake, and sees,
> In fancy, fair St. Agnes in her bed,
> But dares not look behind, or all the charm is fled.

It is no wraith of a lover that has been gazing on these moving
rites, but Porphyro, faint at the sight of her beauty.   Dream
and reality, fusing in an intenser life, carry Porphyro and his
Madeline to the happiness Keats knew was never to be his with
Fanny.   Perhaps because of that knowledge he let his fancy
pasture in those swooning blisses which were later to shock
the virginal Woodhouse for the verity of their portrayal.

---

[1] Science put Keats's effect to the test and found that moonbeams
through stained glass do not cast "rose bloom" and "soft amethyst."

Originally Keats had drawn a veil over the awakening of Madeline. As he reworked it in London, Woodhouse, appalled, read of how Porphyro "winds by degrees his arm round her, presses breast to breast, and acts all the acts of a bonafide husband, while she fancies she is only playing the part of a wife in a dream."[1] . . . "I do apprehend it will render the poem unfit for ladies," he bewailed to Taylor. "He [Keats] says he does not want ladies to read his poetry: that he writes for men — and that if in the former poem there was an opening for a doubt what took place, it was his fault for not writing clearly. . . ."

Keats, exasperated by jealousy and pent-up desire, goaded also by the critics, spent himself in defiance. In the end the offending stanzas were by his better judgment excluded from the published poem, leaving it the thing of pure, magical moonlight and young love which, with its unfinished companion-piece, the *Eve of St. Mark,* was to wake British art and poetry from a prolonged slumber, and create a new school with the Pre-Raphaelites.

Meanwhile friends and enemies led their little lives and *pressed* themselves upon Keats's identity only when they came in contact with his own deeper life. Hunt he saw occasionally and would have seen oftener, though not with the old cordiality, were it not for Marianne, to whom Keats took a strange dislike, stimulated perhaps by Haydon, whose silver Mrs. Hunt had fallen into the habit of borrowing without returning.

However, the friendship between Keats and his would-be spiritual guide was also becoming strained, unfortunately on account of money. Haydon's painting, always on the verge of completion, yet still with wide, unpainted areas, had been costing him health and sight, besides keeping him from exerting himself in more lucrative, if less ambitious, work. Now and again, by overworking his weak eyes, he had been compelled to take periods of rest in the country, whence he would return to find the dun at the door, and, worse, the execution server a-prowl, ready to fall upon him. Some time before

[1] Letter of Woodhouse to Taylor, Pierpont Morgan Library MS., first quoted by Amy Lowell.

Christmas Haydon had made bold to approach his young friend for a small loan, hinting that unless help were forthcoming he would be obliged to sell his drawings — to him a deed as drastic as that of selling a child of his blood. Keats, however, was himself in straitened circumstances. His *Endymion,* thanks to the critics, far from selling, fared little better than his first book of poems. His little patrimony was rapidly dwindling, and Tom's share, which on his death had fallen to his brothers and sister, had unfortunately been tied up in a Chancery suit. Keats, nevertheless, showed himself willing to help Haydon. "Ask the rich lovers of art first — I 'll tell you why — I have a little money which may enable me to study. . . . I never expect to get anything from my Books. . . . Try the long purses — but do not sell your drawings or I shall consider it a breach of friendship."

Unhappily the long purses had come undone by Haydon's perpetual pullings, so that they gaped empty at his renewed trials. In vain he assured the rich lovers of art that for the glory of England and the public encouragement of historical painting he would "lay his head on the block." They remained deaf, maliciously hoping, no doubt, that he would carry out his threat and leave them in peace. Haydon had to resort to Keats. "My only hope for the concluding difficulties of my Picture lies in *you,*" said he. Keats did not discourage him. He told him, however, that he loathed going to town and standing in the bank an hour or two — "to me worse than anything in Dante." But, "Do not be at all anxious," he comforted the expectant Haydon, "for *this* time I really will do . . . business in good time and properly." Nevertheless the weeks passed, with Haydon still waiting and Keats yet hoping to *do.* Mr. Abbey held on tighter to the moneybags, so that the proffered help which the despairing artist had been expecting, like "nectar and manna and all the blessings of gratified thirst," threatened to vanish in a mirage.

Angered by the delay, and worn out with working against actual privation, he reproached Keats. "Why did you hold out such delusive hopes every letter on such slight foundations? — You have led me on step by step, day by day . . . you paralyzed my exertions in other quarters." Keats was hurt.

He had lent friends nearly two hundred pounds which he was not sure of ever getting back. Now Haydon, one of his closest, reproved him for something beyond his control. "You seem'd so sure of some important help when I last saw you, — " he answered, "now you have maimed me again: I was whole, I had begun reading again — when your note came I was engaged in a Book." If he had paralyzed Haydon's exertions to obtain a loan in other quarters, he, Haydon, had dammed the very current of his inspiration. Little did he know, little did anyone know, how the tiniest mote, in the diseased state of Keats's nerves, loomed to a beam in the way of his effort.

Some time in April, however, he was able to lend Haydon thirty pounds, on a bond which Haydon would have had payable in two years, confident that by the expiration of that term his "Christ's Entry" would be finished and he could satisfy all claims. Brown, the businessman, insisted that the bond be made to mature in three months. On such a rock did the friendship of Keats and Haydon split. Haydon had scarcely had the sum two months when Keats, himself in want, wrote him to "borrow or beg some how what you can for me." Haydon had nowhere to turn and did nothing. Keats sent his complaint across the Atlantic. "He did not seem to care about it — and let me go without my money with almost nonchalance when he ought to have sold his drawings to supply me. I shall perhaps still be acquainted with him, but for friendship that is at an end." [1] The two men met occasionally, nonetheless, but the warmth of friendship, at least on Keats's side, was gone.

On the other hand his intimacy with Charles Brown increased, and he saw, too, more of Joseph Severn, who painted a miniature of him to exhibit with his canvas of "Hermia and Helen." Severn was well though slightly built, with a sensitive, romantic face. After winning the Academy medal, he

---

[1] These are the bare facts of a circumstance that has caused Keats biographers to heap infamy upon Haydon's head. Amy Lowell's portrait of Haydon is the black shadow that emphasizes the white radiance of Keats. In this instance, however, Haydon can no more be blamed than Keats. Haydon was no parasite. He borrowed that he might work and pay his debts, in spite of Miss Lowell's assertion that "he never paid" them.

had enjoyed a certain glory. Keats dreaded his effect on Fanny Brawne. When the two met he was gnawed with jealousy and chided Fanny, who answered, soothing, "You must be satisfied in knowing that I admired you much more than your friend." It gave no alleviation to the wretched lover, who made matters worse for himself by his impenetrable reserve. Just as he never alluded to his parents, he let no word escape him of his consuming love, not even to Brown, who, himself a master of dissimulation, had early guessed the secret. Keats said nothing, and Brown, so far as his personal life went, kept his counsel, though had he wished he could have told Keats a tale of his own clandestine intrigue with an Irish girl, Abigail Donohue, whom he was going to marry secretly that summer. Love, however, hardly entered into the arrangement. The girl was healthy and unspoiled by education. Charles Brown, feeling the natural urges of manhood, desired to perpetuate himself in a child. He may have felt that Keats, with his exalted concepts of love, might not have entered into the spirit of the adventure. Thus the two men, living under one roof, were in their intimate lives planets apart, if in all else as close as brothers.

Then something momentous happened. Dilke, who carried his paternal devotion to extremes, wished his son to go to school in London, and in order to be near him removed his family to Westminster. Mrs. Brawne, thereupon, rented the Dilke house, and Keats and Fanny had only a wall dividing them. For a time the nearness of his love, which enabled him to watch her every move, brought Keats a security that he had not enjoyed from the moment of their meeting. He could sit in his room near the open window and watch her as she came and went on her many little duties. He could see her gathering flowers in the garden, or sit reading under a tree. And on those unhappy evenings when there was a ball in town, he could look after her till she was out of sight, and listen, the rest of the night, for the click of the latch and the sounds of voices that told him she had returned and would soon be sleeping on the other side of the partition. They were not happy months, — Keats in love was incapable of happiness, — but at least they left him the strength to work.

And he worked as never before, one poem following the other in an efflorescence that seemed to have in it something of magic. *Hyperion*, begun before December of 1818 and resumed at intervals, had, like the sacred oak, a slow but noble growth. In the intervals of its evolution Keats brought other poems to completion, writing in May alone four odes, *On a Grecian Urn, On Melancholy, To a Nightingale,* and *On Indolence.* During the summer, away from Hampstead and the again-disturbing presence of Fanny, he finished *Lamia* and collaborated with Brown on *Otho the Great,* a tragedy which they hoped Kean would find worthy to play. It was a commercial venture, undertaken to fill Keats's rapidly diminishing coffers, although he tried to bring to it his artist's sincerity. Alas for schemes made in defiance of fortune! Kean, though pleased with the rôle of Otho, left for America. No one else offered to produce the play. In September Keats wrote the ode *To Autumn* and would have resumed *Hyperion,* but he soon desisted. "I have given up *Hyperion* — there are too many Miltonic inversions in it." Factors other than the one he gave were powerfully at work within him, forces for good and ill. *Hyperion* remained, a mighty oak blasted at the height of its growth, showing what it was, and what it might have been.

No one, not Keats himself, realized the greatness of the poems he produced during those few wonderful months. The *Ode to a Nightingale,* written in the Wentworth Place garden, Brown rescued from behind some books where Keats had thrust it, crumpled to a ball. The critics had wounded too deeply for him to care what the fate of his works might be. He found joy and an ineffable satisfaction in writing; that, while the world did not press upon him, was enough. Through that miraculous year every sense in him seemed to have been renewed. He felt, he saw, as if for the first time, sensual nature in all her manifestations. A blade of grass, the song of a bird, a heaping autumn granary, rapt his senses; he was a nympholept, worshiping eternal beauty, made one with her in his all-yielding rapture. "A thing of beauty is a joy for ever. . . ." The words had been the dogma of his faith, repeated with slight alteration in his most personal writings.

With his sudden and destructive experience of love, come like an alien in the temple of his worship, a heretic whisper made itself heard, rising louder till the prayer, as in some demoniacal rite, became the converse of itself. "Beauty — Beauty that must die." He set down the words of rueful wisdom in his *Ode on Melancholy*.

> She dwells with Beauty — Beauty that must die;
> And Joy, whose hand is ever at his lips
> Bidding adieu; and aching Pleasure nigh,
> Turning to Poison while the bee-mouth sips:
> Ay, in the very temple of delight
> Veil'd Melancholy has her sovran shrine. . . .

So had it been with him when one of the many doors of the chamber of maiden thought was set open, revealing the temple of delight. Even while his vision into the heart of nature and man, into himself, had been sharpened, he had been bound in the chains of his painful knowledge. Early that spring, "La Belle Dame sans Merci," the title of a song found in an old book, had rung its mysterious meaning in his mind. It seemed the name of some fair enchantress who, with wiles of love, ensorcelled unwary youths till, though they lived in the world, they were no more of it, as he had not been from the time Fanny, by virtue of that same power, had made him her bondsman. Vaguely dissimulating, he told his hidden throes in his own *La Belle Dame Sans Merci*. He was the "wretched wight, Alone and palely loitering." To him the kings and warriors cried, "La Belle Dame sans merci Hath thee in thrall!"

Four months passed between the writing of the ballad and *Lamia*, the third and last of his tales. The germ of the narrative he had found in a passage of that Pandora's box, Burton's *Anatomy of Melancholy*. Its meaning he, by his own knowledge, had been endeavoring to wrest from life. Lamia, beautiful mistress of the delights of love, is only a glistering shadow, a serpent who has wound herself about the living heart of Lycius. Apollonius, the sage, has no sensual beauty to counteract Lamia's hold over the youth. But he is reality and can make Lycius see beyond the tinsel shadow. The wedding feast is spread. Lamia and Lycius are sitting in the place of honor. From across the table Apollonius fixes his truth-compelling eye upon the lovely and deceptive form of Lamia and uncovers what she is.

> And Lycius' arms were empty of delight,
> As were his limbs of life, from that same night.

Lycius had been saved from Lamia, but his salvation had killed him. The parallel between Keats and Fanny was not far to seek.

In hopeless efforts to save himself, he took long absences from Fanny, thinking that with her out of sight he could keep her out of mind. Fanny let him go. It may be she did not regret those jealous eyes watching her every step, that husky voice reproaching her for not loving as he loved. But if she found respite from her trying lover, she was not long left to enjoy it. Letters would arrive in close succession after intervals of distressing silence. "Ask yourself my love whether you are not very cruel to have so entrammelled me, so destroyed my freedom. . . . For myself I know not how to express my devotion to so fair a form: I want a brighter word than bright, a fairer word than fair. I almost wish we were butterflies and liv'd but three summer days — three such days with you I could fill with more delight than fifty common years could ever contain." A few weeks would pass, and his ardor turn to suspicion. She did not love him as he loved her; she was too young. Perhaps the time would come when she would experience such love, but then, woe unto him. "If you should ever feel for a Man at the first sight what I did for you, I am lost. Yet I should not quarrel with you but hate myself if such a thing were to happen."

Months had passed since their engagement and there was still no prospect of their marrying. Keats's financial position was going from bad to worse. Very little of his grandfather's legacy remained, as Mr. Abbey did not tire of telling him, reminding him at the same time that he had better leave chasing the Quaker's horse for a more remunerative exercise. Thoughts of going to Edinburgh to prepare himself for the practice of medicine conflicted in Keats's mind with ideas of becoming a journalist. For the first he needed money which he had not; the alternative offered no security which should be the hearthstone of marriage. True, Fanny was well off and would not have scrupled to share with him all she had. Keats in his fiery pride would sooner have died than accept. He toyed with the venture of embarking as a surgeon on an Indiaman. Taylor tactfully dissuaded him. What was to be the ultimate solution? "I tremble at domestic cares," he told Fanny, "yet for you I would meet them, though if it would leave you the happier I would rather die than do so. I have two luxuries to brood over in my walks, your Loveliness and the hour of my death. O that I could have possession of them both in the same minute!"

He was then deep in a refashioning of *Hyperion* and the mechanical versifying of *Otho,* the one to appease his exacting muse, the other to tempt blind fortune. There were moments when in his desire for Fanny he felt he could succeed in making money by his poetry, and he wrote with a high heart to Taylor, "I feel every confidence that if I choose I may be a popular writer; that I will never be; but for all that I will get a livelihood — I equally dislike the favour of the public with the love of a woman — they are both a cloying treacle to the wings of independence." How desperately, even while he spoke of freedom, the prisoner of love beat against the bars!

By burying himself in work he refrained from dashing off to Wentworth Place. In October, however, a strong pretext offered itself when discouraging tidings came from America. He must see Abbey about George's affairs. But he could not trust himself to live under the same roof with Fanny and therefore asked Dilke to find him rooms in Westminster. A vain precaution. Though Dilke obtained him lodgings in College Street, Keats found himself straying toward Hampstead and Fanny. Sunk were the high hopes of a journalistic career and a bachelor life. The Wentworth Place garden flushed with the crimson of late-blooming roses; the tree under which he had sat listening to the song of the nightingale with its message of eternal beauty, even though, like Tom, like himself, "youth grows pale, and spectre-thin, and dies"; Fanny's window, behind which he caught a glimpse of her, like Diana behind a transparent mist — all these wrought upon him like the honey wild and manna dew of La Belle Dame Sans Merci. He spent near Fanny three charmed days, his will in a cloud. "I am living to-day as yesterday: I was in a complete fascination all day," he wrote her from his gloomy lodging. "I feel myself at your mercy. . . . You dazzled me. There is nothing in the world so bright and delicate. . . . I have had a thousand kisses, for which with my whole soul I thank love — but if you should deny me the thousand and first — 't would put me to the proof how great a misery I could live through. . . . Ah, hertè mine!" he ended the lambent note. More quietly he wrote,

> The day is gone, and all its sweets are gone!
> Sweet voice, sweet lips, soft hand and softer breast. . . .

And in the recollection of the day's vanished bliss, he soothed his wild desire. Storms of passion with difficulty controlled made of his meetings with Fanny the preludes of anguished hours. Love alone was a destructive power in a man of Keats's temper; unfulfilled love laid him on the rack.

> I cry your mercy — pity — love! — aye, love!
> Merciful love that tantalizes not,

he begged in the fire of his suffering.

> Yourself — your soul — in pity give me all,
> Withhold no atom's atom or I die.

It was Keats's dedicated being crying for the loved one's immolation on the altar of love. Fanny may have understood. She had, however, the virtues and the faults of the society in which she lived, and the conviction that only the marriage vow made such a sacrifice sacred. She was engaged to him, she reflected, and she was willing to wait for him — years, if necessary.

Mr. Abbey, whenever Keats approached him for money, threw in subtle hints of how much more gainful it was to follow commerce instead of poetry. Why did n't Keats go into the tea-brokerage business with him, he suggested, or perhaps become a hatter? He, Abbey, had some concern in a hatter's shop in the Poultry. In his advocacy the old man went so far as to quote the devil, Byron, for his purposes, when he took up a magazine containing extracts of *Don Juan* and read them — with emphasis on one against literary ambition — to the astonished Keats. "I do believe if I could be a hatter I might be one," said Keats sincerely.

Brown, who had now come back to London, — a married man, though he had left his Abigail in Ireland, — induced Keats once more to live with him, and the tenor of the old life was resumed. And yet how different! The wonderful fertility of the spring and summer months had left Keats exhausted. He had to force himself to write a line. Alone in his room he would take up the fragment of *Hyperion*, but could add not one verse to those he had submitted to Woodhcuse, who had an unbounded admiration for it. "It is that in poetry which the Elgin and Egyptian marbles are in sculpture," he declared. Surrounded by his fallen giants, Keats spurred himself to action. Woodhouse had spoken of issuing another book; *Hyperion* might be finished in time. But instead of completing the old version Keats tried to reshape it into the *Fall of Hyperion, A Dream*. That, too, remained a grand, unrealized idea, pierced with the blood-red light of a new vision. Man now entered the twilight of the gods. He spoke the questions and he would be answered.

> "What am I that should so be saved from death?
> What am I that another death come not
> To choke my utterance sacrilegious, here?"
> Then said the veiled shadow — "Thou hast felt
> What 't is to die and live again before
> Thy fated hour, that thou hadst power to do so
> Is thy own safety; thou hast dated on
> Thy doom." — "High Prophetess," said I, "purge off,
> Benign, if so it please thee, my mind's film." —
> "None can usurp this height," return'd that shade,
> "But those to whom the miseries of the world
> Are misery, and will not let them rest."

John Keats in his own misery had learned pity for mankind's.

Meanwhile in America George's speculations had proved so rash that he had to leave his wife and child and come to England to claim what money still remained from the original Jennings fund. The affair was in a hopeless tangle. Keats, perhaps for Georgiana's sake, gave his brother full power to settle the business, with the result that when George, shortly afterwards, left England, he took with him not only his share of Tom's money, but also John's, leaving in lieu of the precious cash a promise of repayment. George could not have despoiled his brother at a more disastrous time.

Late one February night, a few days after George had sailed, Keats returned to Wentworth Place from London in a state that to Brown looked like fierce intoxication. He saw in a moment, however, that Keats was fevered. Deceived by a warm day, he had gone out without his greatcoat and, staying late in town, came back on the stage, sitting on top, as he always did, at the mercy of the chill February wind. Brown advised him to go to bed, and Keats obeyed. He had hardly laid his head on the pillow when he coughed. "That is blood from my mouth," Brown heard him say. "Bring me the candle, Brown, and let me see this blood." A moment of tense examination of the bright red drop, and Keats, the medical student, diagnosed his case. "I know the colour of that blood," he said, calmly. "It is arterial blood. . . . That drop of blood is my death-warrant — I must die." From that moment he knew that the name of John Keats had been added to the rolls of the dead. And his "posthumous life" began when in years he had hardly entered what in youthful daring he had called the Vale of Soulmaking.

The death warrant did not take him unaware. By Tom's bedside he had known what it was to die, so that this second death had no terror — only despair and regret that he had not been given longer to prove his claim of heir to eternity. Years later Leigh Hunt was to remember Keats studying his hand, which was bloodless and swollen in the veins. "It is the hand of a man of fifty," he would say. Even then he had known his body had exceeded its life.

And there had been another who had known. One Sunday in April of the bygone year, Keats had been walking toward Highgate in the tree-shaded lane by the side of Lord Mansfield's park, when he met Mr. Greene, a demonstrator at Guy's, in the company of Coleridge. Mr. Greene introduced them; their hands touched. "There is death in that hand," the sublime visionary remarked to his companion when Keats had gone. For the two miles they had walked together Coleridge's beautiful voice, that Hazlitt called the music of thought, rose and fell as he touched on a thousand themes — poetry and nightingales, dreams and nightmares, monsters, the kraken, mermaids, and wonders that inhabit life and sleep. Of the phenomenon walking beside him he had been unaware except for that moment of second-sight. But then, Coleridge was only a visitor in the world of reality where for years he had been wandering like a stranger. In Highgate he lived in the care of Dr. Gilman, who controlled his use of the key of dreams except when, amoral as a child, Coleridge would smuggle in supplies of opium with his cases of books. He had collected about him a circle of young disciples over whom he presided, a sage — more than a sage, an arch-magus wrapped in mystery, uttering his music of thought for ears too dull to hear its unearthly nuances. Like a hidden current, however, his influence flowed through the age's poetic streams. Without him even the poems of Keats would not have been what they were.

For many weeks Keats was confined to his room by the doctor's orders, forbidden to write or to do anything that excited his mind. But his creative zest was gone. The pathetically merry satire, *Cap and Bells,* in imitation of *Don Juan,* gave him no pleasure, and ignoring Brown's encouragement he abandoned a task so foreign to his genius. Better than Brown he knew that the jingling rang false. His work was done. "If I should die," he would say to himself during the anxious sleepless nights when, in spite of the doctor's optimism, he knew himself marked for death, "if I should die, I have left no immortal work behind me — nothing to make my friends proud of my memory — but I have lov'd the principle of beauty in all things. . . ." If he had had time — Gone was the faith that had made him cry out boldly against the critics' scorn that he would be among the poets after his death. He brooded upon their cruelty and could scarcely trust himself to open any letter addressed to him for fear of painful reactions. He felt the whole world against him. Brown opened his mail and answered Keats's publishers, whose letters would else have remained unread. Woodhouse and Mr. Taylor waited anxiously for the doctor's reports. "I am happy to tell you," Brown told them with incredible optimism, "that we are now assured there is no pulmonary affection, no organic defect whatever, — the disease is on his mind and there I hope he will soon be cured." Perhaps during these sieges of emotional chaos Keats exclaimed to Reynolds, "If I die, you must ruin Lockhart." [1]

Fanny would come to see him in his sickroom, but that was soon forbidden. Her presence agonized him as much as her absence. A thoughtless word, a glance at Brown, kindled the fires of his jealousy. Until he should get better he begged her to write her *good-night* on a slip of paper to lay under his pillow. Tenderly, she obeyed. She would have done anything to sweeten what she knew must be the last months of his life. Moved by a sense of honor, Keats had offered for her sake to break the engagement; she had refused. And Keats loved her the more for her self-sacrifice. Love was scarcely the name for what Fanny now felt for him. It was pity, rather, for one whose mighty soul nature had put into so weak a vessel.

At first Keats begged her not to go out. The thought of her at a gay gathering was more than he could bear. She obeyed. When he was well enough to lie on a sofa-bed in the parlor, he begged her to be at a certain hour in the garden. Then through the frosty windows he charmed his sight with gazing at her, made remote and unreal by the wintry haze. "Do you hear the thrush singing over the field?" he asked in the middle of winter. "I think it is a sign of mild weather — " Thrushes, spring, summer, health, walks in the garden with Fanny, perhaps . . . these were the anticipated joys that gave him the strength to fight to convalescence. He was grateful to Fanny for every tenderness. "Do I not see a heart naturally furnish'd with wings imprison itself with me?"

[1] Pierpont Morgan Library MS.

he wrote to her. "No ill prospect has been able to turn your thoughts a moment from me." What comfort these words must have brought her in after years when those who did not know accused her of cruel indifference to Keats!

On Saturday, the twenty-fifth of March, Keats ventured out to London to witness a long-awaited event. Haydon was exhibiting his "Christ's Entry" at the Egyptian Hall in Piccadilly. It took three Life Guardsmen to carry the rolled canvas on their shoulders. When it was put up, the six-hundred-pound frame snapped an iron ring which had looked strong enough to have supported the world. Haydon, as penniless as ever, had had to indulge in more epic borrowing to enable him to exhibit his work at last. The private showing, if only for the spectacle, was an immense success. Carriages choked up Piccadilly, Haydon having chosen his invited guests from the Court Guide. Footmen in livery thronged the entrance. Lords and ladies filled the exhibition room, talking excitedly of nothing but the painting. In the midst of the bustle in came the Persian Ambassador in full regalia and an overplus of black beard. Standing before the canvas, he pronounced loudly in good English, to the artist's delight: "I like elbow of soldier." With less pleasure, surely, he heard sly Northcote's compliment: "Mr. Haydon, your ass is the savior of your picture."

Aloof from the fashionable crowd, in a corner, Haydon spied Hazlitt and Keats, "really rejoicing." Both, as well as Wordsworth, appeared among the painted crowd that followed Christ's entry. Keats's face, intense and eager, as Haydon had seen it many a time, must have seemed a mockery of his wasted self to the poor youth so rashly out of a sickbed to see the triumph of a friend.

With life and time slipping from him, Keats prepared his third and last book for the press. Sometimes, when Brown was away, — for Keats could not bear to have him in the same room with Fanny, — she looked over volumes of poetry with him to find an appropriate motto. What did Fanny think of her lover's genius? She had heard Brown and Dilke speaking highly of his gifts; she must have known of his publishers' faith in him. But then, there were those reviews. . . . Perhaps she did not trouble herself about his work and really loved him for himself, as Keats liked to believe. To him that had been the miracle of it all from the beginning — that Fanny, a thing of beauty, should have found him admirable.

As the summer approached, Keats, apparently improved in health, sickened with anxiety at the thought of Brown's letting his house. Where could he go then? Not to Well Walk, where he had seen Tom die. Surely not to Abbey's. Perhaps Brown, knowing his condition, would not leave him. But Brown showed no signs of changing his plans. Besides, Abigail was expecting a child. Again Keats played with the idea of joining an Indiaman. The farthest he went by sea was to accompany Brown on the voyage down the river to Gravesend, where the two parted, one to go on a second Scotch tour, the other, for the time, to rooms near Hunt's in Kentish Town.

A bunch of flowers from Fanny, while bringing her near, spoke sharply of her absence. No more would he watch her through the window or listen for her step behind his door. He had told her that she should go out again, for her health, and not let a sick man deprive her of the pleasures that belonged to her youth. She had too readily taken him at his word. The loneliness of his room became the theatre of distressing phantoms — Fanny dancing, Fanny smiling to another. He wrote her endless notes, scorching with passion. "I am greedy of you. Do not think of anything but me. Do not live as if I was not existing — Do not forget me. . . . Your going to town alone, when I heard of it was a shock to me — yet I expected it — *promise me you will not for some time, till I get better.* . . . Confess your heart is too much fastened on the world. . . . You must be mine to die upon the rack if I want you." That was the way he loved. He was asking for no more than he gave. But it was a terrible martyrdom to the young girl. Her heart, furnished with wings, longed for the light outside of the chamber of death; her every flight toward life brought Keats a step nearer to the grave. He hated every healthy man who could make Fanny smile — even Brown, for the hours of jealousy he had unwittingly made him suffer. "I feel the effect of every one of those hours in my side now: and for that cause, though he has done me many services . . . I will never see or speak to him until we are both old men, if we are to be."

An abnormal secretiveness cut him off from his fellows. He had told no one of his love, yet he dreaded that through carelessness on Fanny's part his secret should be discovered and profaned. In writing his letters to her now, he would fill the page and add "My dearest girl" last, that none look over his shoulder and learn whom he was addressing. And always he poured upon Fanny the burden of his suspicions and despair. "I wish I was either in your arms full of faith or that a thunder bolt would strike me!" He did not want to live, yet he could not bear the thought of parting with her. Would that parting be the end of all, or would another life follow, where the happiness that had been denied him on earth should be mercifully granted him? He had always leaned on the side of skepticism. But now he longed to believe in immortality. "I shall never be able to bid you an entire farewell," he wrote her. "I wish to believe in immortality — I wish to live with you for ever."

His health had grown steadily worse, and the hemorrhages he had had convinced even the doctors that there was no hope. He must go to Italy or perish in another London winter. Hunt, deeply affected, persuaded Keats to live with him until arrangements should be made for the journey south. But Mortimer Terrace, in spite of Hunt's good intentions, was hardly the place for a high-strung invalid. The cries of the hucksters, the ballad singers, and the street music distracted him, and Marianne's housekeeping was not of the sort to make for comfort. Keats would take short walks with Hunt up and down Mortimer Terrace. Then, back home, he would sit on an improvised sofa of two chairs in the parlor, as he turned, distraught, the pages of a book while Marianne cut out paper silhouettes of him. When alone, he sat with his eyes fixed on Hampstead, dwelling on the vision of that bright star whose light consumed him. One day, while out with Hunt, Keats, unable to bear longer his secret suffering, turned

on him a face of anguish and confessed he was dying of a
broken heart. Indeed, the frequent heart attacks told too
well how great was the strain upon it.

Shelley was informed by the Gisbornes, whom he had met
in Italy and who had recently returned to London, of Keats's
desperate plight. He wrote him immediately, inviting him
to be his guest in the quiet little city of Pisa, where he had
temporarily taken root. "This consumption is a disease particularly fond of people who can write such good verses as
you have done," he said gently, adding that he had lately
reread *Endymion*, "and ever with a new sense of the treasures
of poetry it contains, though treasures poured forth with in-
distinct profusion." He was the elder poet, and therefore
he could still give a little word of advice. "This, people in
general will not endure, and that is the cause of the comparatively few copies which have been sold. . . . In poetry I
have sought to avoid system and mannerism: I wish those who
excel me in genius would pursue the same plan."

Nothing, for all its delicacy of intention, could have
sounded more tactless to a man preyed upon by disease and
discouragement. A poetic rivalry had always kept the two
youths at a distance, more, perhaps, owing to Keats's extreme sensibility, which saw offense where none was meant,
than for lack of sympathy on Shelley's side. There was,
moreover, a fundamental difference in the core of their genius.
Keats wrote for beauty's sake; Shelley used beauty as a
cloak for truth. No matter how well meant, it could not
have been pleasant for Keats to be reminded that his books
were not selling. Shelley had always been too free of counsel,
and the younger poet still bore him a grudge for his earlier
solicitude. He answered Shelley's letter, neither accepting
nor rejecting the invitation, and then attacked the important
subject. "I am glad you take any pleasure in my poor poem,
which I would willingly take the trouble to unwrite, if possible, did I care so much as I have done about reputation."
Very deftly he turned advice upon Shelley's hands. "A modern work, it is said, must have a purpose, which may be the
God. An artist must serve Mammon; he must have 'self-
concentration' — selfishness, perhaps. You, I am sure, will

forgive me for sincerely remarking that you might curb your magnanimity, and be more of an artist, and load every rift of your subject with ore. . . . I remember you advising me not to publish my first blights. . . . Most of the poems in the volume I send you have been written above two years. . . ."

The *Lamia* volume came out in July 1820. In August, Jeffrey, high mogul of the *Edinburgh Review,* gave Keats the first favorable critique from the pen of an impartial reviewer. Hunt, of course, and Lamb, though anonymously, wrote of the volume. The *New Monthly* praised *Hyperion;* other magazines found it in themselves to speak fairly of the "cockney apothecary." Alas, it was too late for the dying youth to find joy in the recognition of his work. Praise and blame — for the *Quarterly* and *Blackwood's* leopard and scorpion remained hostile — showed themselves for the futile things they were. In spite of success, however, the new volume sold but poorly, though the inferior work of an obscure youth called Clare, published also by Taylor and Hessey, made a great stir. But Keats, in spite of the mob's acclaim, knew whose should be the final triumph.

His stay at Mortimer Terrace came to an abrupt end when a note from Fanny was brought to him by Hunt's son Thornton with the seal broken. It is said a maidservant had broken it out of malice. No matter whose the blame, Keats, his secret so brutally revealed, fled to Hampstead in a fever of wrath. Too plainly Mrs. Brawne saw that the pitiful ghost was no longer of the world. With admirable unconventionality, she took him into her house, where, by the side of Fanny, his joy and torment, he passed his last blissful days in England.

On the seventeenth of September, in the season when the late roses of Wentworth Place were again kindling their torches of flame, Keats embarked on the *Maria Crowther* with Joseph Severn, the only one of his friends whose devotion followed him to the end. He would continue the study of art in Rome, Severn assured him, to minimize his sacrifice. He had no money but twenty-five pounds and a letter of introduction to Canova to pave his progress to a foreign land.

JOSEPH SEVERN

A SELF-PORTRAIT IN PENCIL

(Reproduced from a photograph made for the collection of Louis A. Holman by Arthur Severn, the artist's son)

Keats, through the generosity of his publishers, had enough to relieve his dread of dying in poverty.

As far as Gravesend the faithful Woodhouse accompanied the poet, and in farewell, as one does with the dead, cut off a lock of his hair. Charles Brown, Keats was nevermore to see. Twice, by a strange chance, they might have spoken — once when the fishing smack which brought Brown to London lay at anchor beside the *Maria Crowther* in the night, and again when the brig moored at Portsmouth near where Brown was staying.

Keats had not said a final good-bye to Fanny, and his friends, covetous of his affection, and attributing his suffering to her, spoke unkindly of the young girl. "I can not now but hold a hope of his refreshed health," Reynolds wrote to Taylor, "which I confess his residence in England greatly discouraged, particularly as he was haunted by one or two heartless and *demented* people. . . . Absence from the poor idle thing of womankind, to whom he has so unaccountably attached himself, will not be an ill thing. . . ."[1] But in his hand Keats clasped a white carnelian that Fanny had given him.

Before the boat sailed Keats sent Severn ashore for a bottle of laudanum to take with him to Rome, whence the pyramid of Caius Cestius beaconed him to the land of the immortal.

[1] Pierpont Morgan Library MS.

XXV

EHEU FUGACES . . .

AFTER long years of a shadowy life in death, old King George III, blind and insane, sank into his grave in January 1820, leaving his throne to the fat Adonis of more than fifty who became George IV. Magnificent preparations were going forward for the coronation festivities, all London talking of nothing else. Such are the subtle workings of destiny that an event of greater significance to the British nation had occurred but a few months earlier at Kensington Palace, without creating a stir except in the bosom of Victoria Mary Louisa of Saxe-Coburg and her husband, Edward, Duke of Kent, who may have wished that the newborn princess Alexandrina Victoria had been a boy. Lord Byron, living in Ravenna a novel kind of family life, thought half seriously of attending the coronation to claim his right of being "a puppet" in the show, but the consideration that Lady Byron would have had to share the privilege drove the desire from his mind.

Quite unexpectedly, however, the coronation was put off by a scandal that sent a flush over the face of the civilized world. The new king wished to rid himself of his wife, Caroline of Brunswick. His first legal act, therefore, was to call for a bill of divorcement. To his chagrin the Cabinet refused to pass upon it. Undeterred, when Parliament convened in April the king sent a "green bag" of infamous evidence to each House, in his endeavor to prove that Queen Caroline had been more than indiscreet with her Italian chamberlain, Pergami. Meanwhile Queen Caroline, in Italy, informed of the proceedings, chartered a vessel, when she was refused passage on a royal ship, and sailed to England to prove her innocence.

Talk of the coronation gave way to spicy gossip, the whole

nation dividing itself into partisans for king or queen in a chess game of undue proportions. The "green bag" Queen Caroline balanced with accusations against her husband. Months passed, with the queen's trial still pending. From Edinburgh, *Blackwood's* launched rhetorical questions of a high morality — "Was the moral name of England to be insulted by a perpetual reference to the free and unquestioned career of its first female, through what was universally alleged to be the most barefaced and debasing licentiousness?" — while in London, its cockney enemy twitted, through Leigh Hunt: —

"You swear — you swear" — "Oh Signor si — "
"That through a double door, eh,
You 've seen her *think* adulterously?"
"Ver' true, Sir — Si, Signore."

Shelley, at the Baths of San Giuliano, heard echoes of the proceedings and was vastly, if cynically, amused. He was reading his *Ode to Liberty* to a friend when a procession of pigs being led to the fair passed under the windows, punctuating with grunts and snorts the verses as he read them. How like the chorus of the frogs from Aristophanes! Why should not he, Shelley, write a political-satirical drama of the queen's trial, introducing the pigs as a chorus? No sooner thought than done. *Swellfoot the Tyrant* was his commentary on the royal Punch and Judy show. There was no Englishman, at home or expatriate, who had not something to say. Even Keats had been able to jest feebly on the affair in his *Cap and Bells.*

Byron not only observed, but took sides. "We are both Queen's men at bottom," he wrote with charming all-inclusiveness to Moore. Some zealous politicians had gone so far as to invite him to England to participate in the ungallant badgering. He was too chivalrous for that. Besides, there was plenty to be done nearer home had he a mind to it. Eventually the trial was discontinued when Queen Caroline put a definite end to it — by dying.

From his foreign post Byron kept an eagle eye on everything that went on at home. With scandalized amusement he watched Hobhouse as a radical in Parliament doing things so dangerous that they had already procured him lodgings in gaol. So, Hobbie now loved the "people"! It was a fit topic for a ballad.

> When to the mob you make a speech,
>   My boy Hobbie O,
> How do you keep without their reach
> The watch within your fobby O?
> But never mind such petty things,
>   My boy Hobbie O;
> God save the people — damn all Kings,
> So let us crown the Mobby O!

A strange state of affairs when Parliament sent one to Newgate, and Newgate to Parliament! But that was the way of life, playing many a prank, before shutting her Jacks in the box from which there is no coming out in this world.

In his thirty-second year Byron felt the weight of the past. Of the friends of his youth the dearest had died. Others were scattered like leaves in the wind of England's righteousness — even dear stuttering Scrope, the last of the tree. His inveterate gambling had done for him. Encouraged by the huge winnings that at night he used to deposit in his chamber pot, he had gone on wooing fortune for the sake of the sport until she turned and made him flee the wrath of his countrymen. He was now at Bruges, an inglorious exile.

Sometimes people Byron had known became alive for a moment in a flash of news from England. He had heard, for instance, of Polidori and his diary, which Murray had refused to ennoble in print. Undismayed, however, the ambitious medico had worked over the plot of the vampire of Geneva days, and with numerous improvements of his own had had it appear in the *New Monthly Magazine* as a work of Lord Byron's, gulling even the Olympian Goethe, who pronounced it the best thing his lordship had ever done. Another prose tale came out the same year. A volume of verse followed, and an *Essay on Positive Pleasure,* in which the melancholy Polly-Dolly took so gloomy a view of life and love that the absurd womankind took umbrage.

Indeed the poor doctor had had no luck with the sex. At Norwich, where he set up his practice, to the vaticination of Byron, —

I fear the doctor's skill at Norwich
Will hardly salt the doctor's porridge, —

he fell in love with a young lady far above his station. Instead of wooing her in the effective manner of his lordship, he stumbled in front of her gate and broke his leg, necessitating his being nursed in the house of his adored one till he could be moved to his own home. Whether the young lady was cautioned by his brittleness, or whether he was destined to prove the dictum of the path of true love, his devotion remained unrequited. Life, sweet to some, was wormwood to him. At the age of twenty-six the poor youth, sickened with a Byronic fever he could not cure, brought it to an end with a strong dose of prussic acid, as he had often threatened at his lordship's scoffing.

Sometimes a visit from England rejoiced the exile, as when Hobhouse had stopped with him on the way to some political or antiquarian exploit. After the sale of Newstead, Hanson and his son had come to the Mocenigo bringing the deeds, magnesia, and Byron's favorite red tooth powder. They were astonished to see the tears of welcome in the eyes of the Childe who had boasted of the hardness of his heart. Thomas Moore's advent in the autumn of 1819 had moved him to rapture. Moore, on the contrary, suffered a momentary disappointment. He had expected to see again the slim, romantic Childe with a face of alabaster and that expression of seraphic spirituality that had been his chief beauty. He found instead a robust foreigner with hair flowing down his neck and a face which, though still handsome, was more of the earth. He was happier than Moore had ever seen him. Was it possible that this time he was really in love? Moore was presented to a buxom young girl with the complexion of a rose, and thick, loose curls of a deep gold framing her face. "The Countess Guiccioli," said Byron. During his stay at the Mocenigo Moore was to hear more of her, and was to observe, too, that while Byron stayed with him all day, he rode out

toward nightfall to La Mira, where Teresa Guiccioli waited.
The Venetian salons were in a flutter about the affair, begun so discreetly, so delicately, in the traditional manner —
only to degenerate into what threatened to become mere vulgar domesticity. And right under the nose of the Countess
Guiccioli's venerable husband! Surely his lordship's good
friend must do something to bring him back to the ways of
honest adultery! Moore did nothing but enjoy, while he
could, the company of Byron in the few days that were his,
and carry back with him memories of that last night in Venice
when, in the moonlight that whitened the coral of the palaces
and shed a holiness on St. Mark's, they floated in their gondola through the sleeping city. Something more tangible
Moore took with him on parting — a sheaf of manuscript in
a white leather bag. "My life and adventures," said Byron,
at the time engaged in one of his most puzzling.

One evening in the spring of 1819 at the salon of that
Madame Benzoni who had taken Byron's Fornarina under her
protection, to polish the diamond, he was introduced to the
Countess Guiccioli, née Teresa Ghisleri Gamba, a name as
ancient in Ravenna as it was noble. She was seventeen,
large-eyed, with the longest lashes in the world and the mouth
of a Grecian statue that became even more beautiful when she
smiled, showing her perfect teeth. She was not tall, a trifle
overplump and full-bosomed, but radiantly womanly. Byron
lost no time in making a conquest. That night, before the
countess took her leave, he had arranged for their next meeting, alone.

He liked to believe he was Teresa's first lover. She did
not disillusion him. Her husband, Count Guiccioli, an agreeable, cultured gentleman, had snatched her from the convent
threshold to ensure himself, if God willed, legitimate offspring
to crown his autumn years. He had been twice a widower
— rumor had it that he had sped his good ladies' journey
heavenward. He owned rich estates in Romagna, drove a
coach and six, and liked to mix sentiment with his affairs,
which, at least on two suspected occasions, had ended with
the deft turn of a knife at the hands of his *sbirri*. But a
nobleman can do no wrong, hedged about as he is by wealth

and influence. He had had nothing to complain of during the
year he had been married to Teresa. She had been a good,
respectful wife who went with him on his tours through his
domains; and when by ill chance he had been forced to leave
her behind, she lightened his absence with dutiful letters
breathing of Dante and the French romancers. Yea, Count
Guiccioli discovered that he had reason to flatter himself on
his marriage.

But Teresa, after closer knowledge of "the noble and exquisitely beautiful" English poet, made discoveries of her
own that altered the tone of her address to her revered Guiccioli. Proud of her conquest, she attended the Venetian *conversazioni* flagrantly hanging on her lover's arm, until there
was not a woman but lifted her brows at such indiscretion.
Teresa, in her happiness, threw all petty caution to the winds.
What if, in the hushes of astonishment, her *"Mio Byron"*
rang out through the salon? She was doing nothing more
shameful than did the other married ladies: she was claiming
her lover. For a whole year as a virtuous wife she had
served her novitiate toward her full accession as a matron.
Now that she had fulfilled her part of the contract there was
no one, not even Guiccioli, a papal count, who could object
to her acquiring a *cavalier servente*.

It was a new part for the Childe, one better suited to his
Don Juan. Something in Teresa's daring brought to his
mind the amour of his triumphal season. Indeed, the countess
was another Caroline Lamb — "much prettier, and not so
savage." Otherwise there was that same rashness, the same
disdain of public opinion. But unlike other women, she had
an asset that was likely to enhance her in the eyes of one who
had taken up the "gentlemanly vice" of avarice. "She is the
queerest woman I ever met with," he told Kinnaird, one likely
to appreciate the communication, "for in general they cost
me something one way or another, whereas by an odd combination of circumstances, I have proved an expense to *her,*
which is not *my* custom." Still, the gold pieces were increasing in his strong box, and it redounded to a woman's credit to
know that she loved *senza interesse.*

At the Mocenigo the Fornarina became unmanageable when

she scented a rival in the offing. Alas, in spite of the gowns
colla cua[1] which she had learned to wear like a grand lady,
and the sumptuous hats, — far less becoming than her plebeian veil, — *'Celenza* was tiring of her. She could see it.
And she made such scenes that Byron had to tell her to go,
not without a goodly provision for herself and her mother.
She would not hear of it. She wept and vociferated, and
when she saw that he was in earnest, she seized a knife while
he was having dinner and would have stabbed him or herself
had not Fletcher seized her by the arms. Calmly Byron
called his boatmen with the gondola and ordered them to
take her home. She swept down the stairs without a word,
while he resumed his dinner. Suddenly there was a great
commotion below, explained when a few minutes later Margarita was brought up, drenched and suffocating. She had
thrown herself into the Canal. Byron did not believe that
she had seriously tried to destroy herself — Caroline Lamb
had taught him not to take such bravado to heart. Still, it
had required courage for a woman, and a Venetian, of all
races the most afraid of water, to fling herself into the lagoon
on a cold, dark night, before men who would have made no
great struggle to save her had she resisted. After that she
tried several times to ingratiate herself. But now that Byron
had his *contessina* he weaned himself of the lure of his
Medea.

The course of the new love, though smooth in one channel,
showed troubled waters in another. As a mistress Teresa
Guiccioli was all that could be desired. She was of a lineage
equal to his; she was tender, pliable, and not clever. On the
other hand she was saddled with a husband who under a suave
exterior hid the craftiness of a de' Medici. She had, moreover, a father and a brother more than ordinarily ticklish in
the matter of honor, and five sisters whose future chances of
married respectability depended upon her example in that
state.

From the beginning Byron had seen that she cared little
what the Albrizzis and the Benzonis, the Italian Grundys,
thought. She had proclaimed her independence and was de-

[1] With a train.

termined to maintain it with éclat. The situation was likely
to prove embarrassing to one who, like Byron, had a horror
of appearing ridiculous. As it happened, Count Guiccioli
had to betake himself to Ravenna in the late spring, and the
lovers were perforce separated.

Byron felt as sentimental as a schoolboy at Teresa's departure, working himself into the conviction that he was
desperately in love with her. Indeed, after his Venetian
debauchery, the fair-haired young girl was another Beatrice,
Teresa feeding the illusion further with her love letters, whose
commonplaces, written in the tongue of Dante, must have
seemed pure poetry to the lover. She must see him. He
must come to her who was ill, perhaps dying — not from love
alone, but from a dangerous miscarriage which she had suffered on arriving at Ravenna. Byron, scornful in his writings, of the sighing swain, set out at once to be at his lady's
side. A poetical lugubriousness descended upon him on the
way, making him pause at cemeteries to indulge in the spectacle of death. Was it Childe Harold amid the ruins of
Greece, or the young, innocent Byron, dreaming on Peachey's
tomb at Harrow? At the Campo Santo of Bologna he admired the monuments as he listened to the loquacious sexton
telling of how the grave of a Princess Barberini, dead two
hundred years, had been opened, and her hair found, as yellow as gold. At Ferrara he was moved by the epitaphs,
"*Martini Luigi Implora Pace . . . Lucrezia Picini Implora
Eterna Quiete.*" Such simple words he would wish inscribed
above his ashes in some Italian burial ground. "I am sure
my bones would not rest in an English grave, or my clay mix
with the earth of that country." His bitterness was still
terribly, unforgivingly alive. Meanwhile, as he fed his gloom,
he delayed his journey toward Ravenna.

When he arrived there he found Teresa thinner but more
beautiful. The count, who came to visit him, feared she was
dying of a consumption. Very graciously Byron sent for his
own doctor from Venice. In a few weeks, however, in spite
of the alarming symptoms, Countess Guiccioli was as well
as ever. It was Lord Byron's presence, as even the count
could see, that had acted as a marvelous tonic. Byron sent

out bulletins to acquaintances in Italy, to Hobhouse and Murray across the Channel, to Augusta. "The G. is better — and will get well with prudence. Our amatory business goes on *well* and *daily*. . . ." "*She* manages very well. . . . By the aid of a priest, a chambermaid, a young negro-boy, and a female friend, we are enabled to carry on our unlawful loves. . . ." "I see my *Dama* every day at the proper (and improper) hours. . . . I don't know what I *should* do if she died, but I ought to blow my brains out." He was in earnest, at least in intention. Indeed, when the countess had been in danger, he had supplied himself with a powerful poison for the final emergency. He had it still, laid away in a drawer.[1]

The count he found politer than ever, calling for him at his inn and displaying him before the scandalized Ravennese in his coach, "like Whittington and his cat." An unfathomable personage, the count, and not to be trusted. "If I come away with a stiletto in my gizzard some afternoon, I shall not be astonished."

However, with Teresa riding on a pony beside him through the legendary pine forest of Ravenna, he was as romantic as the Annesley Byron. Poetical memories lingered in that wood where the unhappy Francesca must have walked in the days of her girlhood before Paolo the handsome came to woo her for his hunchback brother. Through those dim recesses, if one ventured out of a Friday night, one might still see, perhaps, the apparition of the girl whose heart neither pity nor love had moved — the ghostly hunter following fast, the phantom hounds upon her. And as they caught and held her naked body and the huntsman tore that cold heart from her breast, he might speak, as he had spoken to Nastagio degli Onesti: "Thus, as often as I overtake her, I slay her with this same dagger which I turned upon myself. . . . But it does not end there. . . . As though she had not died, she rises again, and as God's righteousness and power decree, begins once more her dolorous flight, while I and the hounds renew the chase." In this country it was a sin not to love. Times had not changed the hushed little town. A Cardinal

[1] Pierpont Morgan Library MS.

legate administered what government foreign oppression allowed, while the people, as Byron observed, still "made love a good deal and assassinated a little."

He was allowing himself to sink into the soft comfortableness of habit when Hoppner threw into it a handful of nettles in a letter from Venice. People were talking, said he, and the purport of their talk reflected no glory on la Guiccioli. As a friend, Hoppner must warn "my dear hero." "I am very sorry for the distress you feel on the G——s account, not only because I think in almost every such case they are good feelings thrown away on an unworthy object; but because I have reason to think it is particularly so in the present instance. . . . While it is merely for your amusement, and that the impression was only to be momentary I should never interfere with your pleasures: but to hear you talking of a serious attachment to a woman, who under the circumstances would be unworthy of it . . . and who in the present instance, it is reported, avowedly not to return it, but to have entrapped you in her nets merely from vanity, is what the friendship you have honored me with does not allow me to witness without remonstrance. . . . I see you overwhelmed in a passion which is in every way unworthy of you, and for one, who when she thinks herself sure of you, will leave you in the lurch — & make a boast of having betrayed you." [1]

This piece of gratuitous intermeddling threw Byron into one of his epic rages, making him, in his wrath, overlook a grave and wholly unwarrantable charge against two innocent individuals with which the consul closed his scandal sheet. "The Shelleys have lost their eldest boy which has left them for the moment childless and in deep despair: the lady however is about to replace the wife. I do not know whether Miss Claire has gone quite crazy or not; but it is certain that both Mrs. Hoppner and I would willingly ascribe what we must otherwise attribute to innate wickedness in her, to folly." [2] The lie was to have a later revival, fouler with the added gross-

---

[1] This letter was published in part from the Pierpont Morgan Library MS. by the late Earl C. Smith in the PMLA for December 1931.

[2] It is my opinion, and I voice it boldly, that Mr. Hoppner was at the root of the Shelley and Clare scandal which in September of 1820 he tried to make Byron believe, and which Byron, in 1821, retailed to

ness laid to the spite of discharged servants, but pointing too
plainly to the original source. Byron, for the present, was
tender of only his wounded pride. It was bad enough for the
consular Diogenes to seek to direct his conduct. But to be
told that he was playing the part of a dupe to a woman's
scheming was more than he could tolerate.

In all his relations with the sex he demanded the upper hand,
revealing himself in that respect as the eternal masculine.
A tactful woman who wished to control him played the submissive, like Augusta. Lady Byron had opposed her will
against his, and there came the clash of thunderbolts. "It
is very odd," observed the learned Fletcher on that point,
"but I never yet knew a lady that could not manage my Lord
except my Lady." Fletcher made too generous an estimate.
Clare should have been included in his exception. At any
rate, Byron gave most to the women who yielded most. He
thought he had found such an one in the Guiccioli, when here
came a counselor who, with unprecedented effrontery, told
him he was a vain woman's fool. He must vent his fury or
explode. Alexander Scott, an acquaintance then in Venice,
was chosen as the recipient of his unbosoming. He wrote
at white heat, beating out one postscript after another as refutation followed refutation, and dashes and underlinings
streaked the pages with the lightning of his rage. He did
not choose his words. Italianisms crept in, translated borrowings from the parlance of the street. Catherine Byron's
son knew the idiom of the Venetian Billingsgate.

"I never supposed that the G. was to be a despairing Shepherdess — nor did I search very nicely into her motives — all

---

Shelley. See below, pages 425, 446. The above quotation, never before
published, is contained in Hoppner's MS. letter in the Pierpont Morgan
Library. It is dated July 9, 1819 — a year before the maid Elise
was ever thought of by Hoppner as his informant. According to the
later accusation, moreover, Clare had long since, allegedly, "replaced the
wife," at Este. She should have been by now about to give birth to the
child which, according to Elise, or rather Hoppner, was torn from her by
Shelley and placed in the Neapolitan Foundling Hospital. How can he
therefore *ex post facto* and paradoxically *a priori* say in July 1819 that the
lady was about to do what, according to his machinations, she should have
done long since? The present bit of evidence is important in laying the
guilt where it obviously belongs.

I know is that *she* sought me . . . so that if there is any foolmaking on the occasion — I humbly suspect that *two* can play at that. . . . I have no hesitation in repeating that I *love* her — but I have also *self-love* enough to be cured by the least change or trick on her part when I know it. . . . I suppose this may possibly be some *cookery* between H. and Menghaldo. . . . What does he mean by *'when she is sure of me'?* how 'sure'? when a man has been for some time in the habit of keying a female — methinks it is his own fault if the 'being left in the lurch' greatly incommodes him. . . . If the lady takes another caprice — *Ebbene?* can't one match her in that too think you? then let her boast of 'betraying &c.' Give me but proof — or a good tight *suspicious confirmation* — and I will rejoin you directly and we will village at the Mira. . . ."[1]

Scott, like a good friend, acquainted him with the Venetian rumors which, with unloverlike candor, Byron retailed to the Guiccioli. Teresa denied everything with great spirit, as she had denied the allegations in Hoppner's letter obligingly translated for her benefit by his furious lordship. More, she rose to her own defense, penning a sentimental and foolish justification to Scott, whom she "milorded," to Byron's amusement. "Byron has read me some parts of your letter that concern me," she began. "You cannot imagine what sentiments it aroused in me. Certain it is . . . I felt how great is my obligation to you, and how great should be my esteem. Therefore I neither blush nor fear to take the liberty of sending you these two lines;[2] indeed, I deem it my duty. To all your kindness I hope, however, that you will add another favor, that is, to advise patience to those who condemn me for future deeds." Ah, there was a master stroke of irony! Her life, she explained, had begun but a few months back. She could not, in that time, have given her accusers occasion either for praise or for blame by any deed of hers. "I marvel much, therefore, at the sublime acuteness of these people, that permits them to look into, to enter, and to judge of the

[1] Pierpont Morgan Library MS.
[2] *These two lines,* the Italian formula, became nearly twoscore, in the countess's intoxication with her eloquence.

future." Irony came frisking back, wagging its tail like a pampered puppy. "But I place my trust in another judge to clear me," she declared grandly. "Time. If you could only see, Milord, with what strength I utter this word, and how wishfully I invoke Time!" Scott knew Byron, did he not? At least he had some idea of the sort of man he was. "How wicked I should deem myself if I feared that some day I should make such a man blush for having loved me!" Never, never! How could a poet's ideal betray him? "I am as sure of myself as of the fact that to-morrow I shall again behold the sun." There, that should settle the scandalmongers forever. "I do not wish to bore you further, Milord. Pardon the great liberty I have taken, feel with me, and continue in your courteous services toward me; say that my crime is but *one,* and will *always continue one.* I thank you, Milord, and I wish you every happiness, for you deserve it." [1] Thus, a Beatrice, if she had loved her poet as she, Teresa, loved Byron, would have defended herself against the lying tongues of Florence.

To her lover she proposed a step that would have made the Benzoni and Albrizzi habituées swoon with horror. Why not elope? she said. "Then instead of being at my mercy I shall be at yours. . . . You have every proof that a man can have of my having been in earnest — and if you desire more — try me." [2] Nothing more disastrous to her reputation could have been thought of than for Teresa to withdraw herself from the protection of a husband whose forbearance thus far had been angelic, and join a lover who by the act would have lost all standing as a gentleman. It was one thing, according to the moral code of the day, to be an honorably adulterous wife, and quite another to become that quintessence of unwomanliness, that creature without status: a wife who had left her husband for her *cavalier.*

Byron, soothed by such self-sacrificing generosity, refused to accept the offer, although his thoughts, after his purge of

---

[1] Translated by the author from the unpublished MS. in the Pierpont Morgan Library. The original is in Italian.

[2] According to Byron, Teresa herself, as early as July 12, 1819, suggested elopement, a fact completely lost sight of by all Byron biographers.

libertinism, turned toward an untumultuous life with someone
who loved him. Would he attempt marriage again? Perhaps.
To Augusta he wrote: "If you see my spouse, do pray tell her
I wish to marry again, and as probably she may wish the same,
is there no way in *Scotland*, without compromising her im-
maculacy?" He was sentimentally, adolescently in love. The
days when he could not see Teresa he sent her love letters that
lost not a spark of their fire by being in Italian. Meanwhile
his work lagged. At her bidding, and to do honor to the poet
whose bones lay entombed in Ravenna, he wrote the *Prophecy
of Dante,* of which Teresa was very proud, though she knew
not a word of English. Stanzas for another canto of the Don
increased desultorily. He was in no mood for writing; he
would not be until the fever of that new love had cooled, leaving
him the calm he needed for creation.

The count spoke of taking his wife to Bologna. Byron,
wearied of his subjection, himself now suggested elopement:
"C'è un solo rimedio efficace — cioè d' andar via insieme." It
was Teresa's turn to advise prudence, as she thought, perhaps,
of those five sisters who would by the deed be left to wither on
their maiden stalks. No, not elopement. Could n't she, somehow, manage to "pass for dead" like another Juliet, and have
her lover claim her? The count intervened by taking her to
Bologna, whither Byron followed soon after, a faithful, if not
a sighing, swain.

In Venice, Allegra, lovely as a pomegranate blossom, grew
taller and more grave, tended by Mrs. Hoppner or some female
servant of the Mocenigo. She resembled Byron with his expressive eyes and, the Hoppners vouched for it, a devil of a
spirit. At times the child's presence proved inconvenient.
Byron did not like to leave her to the servants, yet he could not
take her with him on his gallant peregrinations — this day in
Ravenna, to-morrow in Bologna. What else could he do when
his *dama's* husband was ever on the wing? A solution presented itself when a Mrs. Vavassour, a wealthy English widow,
proposed to adopt Allegra. At first Byron was willing. Mrs.
Vavassour, however, insisted that he renounce all claim to the
child, and here the arrangement fell through. He could not
disclaim a Byron, even an illegitimate one.

Under the influence of the Guiccioli, Don Juan softened to
weakness. Every emotion cut to the quick. One night at the
theatre, while witnessing in Teresa's company a performance
of *Mirra*, Alfieri's tragedy of incestuous love, he was seized by
such convulsive sobs that he had to leave the theatre. The
Guiccioli went into hysterics. "She has been ill, and I have
been ill, and we are all languid and pathetic this morning, with
great expenditure of Sal Volatile," he jested to Murray. Still
the thought. . . . There was no forgetting, not in distance,
not in the sentimentalities of a young girl nurtured on *Corinne*
and the *Vita Nuova*.

At the very height of his Guicciolian idyll, in May, he had
sent to Augusta a letter which she forwarded to her guardian
angel, not without awareness of how those delirious words
might affect Lady Byron. "Many would condemn the act as
an *insult*," she apologized on sending the letter. But the
guardian angel had to advise on her behavior toward the man
who was "surely to be considered a *Maniac*." Never had he
expressed himself so madly. "My dearest Love . . . I have
never ceased nor can cease to feel for a moment that perfect
& boundless attachment which bound and binds me to you —
which renders me utterly incapable of *real* love for any other
human being — for what could they be to me after *you*? My
own XXXX we may have been very wrong — but I repent of
nothing except that cursed marriage — & your refusing to continue to love me as you had loved me. I can never forget nor
quite forgive you for that precious piece of reformation — but
I can never be other than I have been — and whenever I love
anything it is because it reminds me in some way or other of
yourself. . . . It is heart-breaking to think of our long
Separation. . . . Dante is more humane in his 'Hell' for he
places his unfortunate lovers (Francesca of Rimini & Paolo,
whose case fell a good deal short of *ours* — though sufficiently
naughty) in company — and though they suffer — it is at least
together. . . ."

Was it Annabella or the reformed Augusta who erased the
name and substituted the crosses — how much more rightly!
One gleam of comfort shone for Lady Byron out of all that
passionate murk: Augusta had told the truth. Byron had not

sinned during his married life.   But he was unregenerate.   His
proud defiance cried out in every one of those terrible sentences.
"When you write to me speak to me only of yourself — and
say that you love me. . . .   They say absence destroys weak
passions and confirms strong ones — Alas! *mine* for you is
the union of all passions and of all affections. . . ."   How
different life might have been had that destroying torrent
been turned into a normal channel!   It was never to be.   The
fatalism of Byron's Calvinistic faith had so decreed.

Far into the autumn Byron's liaison with the Guiccioli progressed pleasantly and perilously under the winking eye of the
count.   Byron proved a most obliging *cavalier*.   He drilled
himself to learn the art of holding a fan and folding a shawl,
to know, too, when to propitiate marital frowns by making large
loans and requesting political favors on the count's behalf.
Would Murray be so good as to ask his government friends
whether they would not appoint an Italian noble as consul or
vice-consul of Ravenna?   You see, the count wished to have
British protection in case of changes — and changes, whether
at home or in the world, occurred with dismaying frequency.
The Guiccioli managed her side of the affair by recurrences of
her accommodating consumption for which there was no cure
but the company of Byron.   The count's vigilance, under the
circumstances, relaxed.   He went so far, in fact, as to permit
Teresa to accept the hospitality of La Mira unchaperoned —
to the horror of the salons and the amusement of the visiting
Moore.

Unhappily an intercepted letter told the count that the
rest of the world was privy to the doings of his household.
He sputtered with rage.   A papal count must not be horned in
the public streets.   Either Teresa choose the Englishman or
live with her husband as a proper wife.   Teresa was in high
dudgeon.   Whoever heard of being asked to make such a
choice?   Every married woman had her rights.   Was she the
only one to be deprived of them?   She would show his excellency her husband!   And once again Teresa offered the
expedient so many times suggested but never acted upon.   Now
it was Byron who magnanimously objected to the elopement.
He would not ruin her life.   She must go back to Ravenna

with her papal count, while he would return, a broken-hearted man, to England, or, with little Allegra, re-create his life in some jungle tract of South America.

The Mocenigo was dismantled while the menagerie shrieked and the servants cursed. Allegra, wondering at the adventure, was already in the gondola. Byron, in his traveling clothes, his cap on his head and his cane in hand, was standing at the top of the marble stairs waiting — for what? An omen? The servants had not yet brought the arms. If it struck one before everything was ready, he said, he would not leave. The hour struck. Had Lady Byron and Augusta heard it, how many weeks of worry at his coming they might have been spared!

Teresa, in deceptive peace with her husband at Ravenna, sent for her lover. And he came, with his servants, part of his livestock, and Allegra. Before long the unpredictable count had the inconvenient Englishman living — on payment of rent — in one of the floors of his grey stone *palazzo*. The people of Ravenna, "who loved a good deal," admired Lord Byron. They were less enthusiastic about the count, who, in spite of his great wealth, turned to lucre his wife's liaison with the foreigner. Of Teresa they were tolerant. It pleased their love of the picturesque to see her, beautifully dressed, hanging on the arm of the handsome milord in sumptuous costumes of velvet and gold braid; and it touched their hearts when, along the Corso, the Guiccioli carriage rode by, exhibiting to their view the fair-haired countess and milord's little daughter, for all the world like a Madonna and child.

Byron's resentments softened. He wrote to Lady Byron more kindly than he had yet done, asking for a picture of Ada. "This time five years . . . I was on my way to our funeral marriage," he recalled with melancholy but no bitterness. "I hardly thought then that your bridegroom as an exile would one day address you as a stranger; and that Lady and Lord Byron would become bywords of division. . . . That I think of you is but too obvious. . . ." He told her of the Memoir he had given Moore. Would she read it? "I have never revised the papers since they were written. You may read them and mark what you please." Lady Byron declined, considering the publication of such a work at any time as "prejudicial to her child's future."

New Year's Day of 1820 had been appointed by the revolutionists in Spain for their outbreak and the proclamation of the Constitution of 1812. The three leaders, Riego, Cabazes, and Quiroga, worked valiantly, but the time was not ripe and the insurgents were driven to the mountains. The spark was set, however; sooner or later revolt would become revolution. Accordingly, in March of that year, King Ferdinand was compelled by his people to swear fidelity to the Constitution; political prisoners were liberated, and a junta took the reins of state until a new Cortes was convened.

The news of the Spanish revolution spread like wildfire over Europe. In France, Louvel, thinking to cut off the reigning house of the Bourbons, plunged a knife into the heart of the heir presumptive, the Duc de Berry. In Naples and Sicily the secret society of the *Carbonari*, those freemasons of revolution, active against Bourbon oppression since the beginning of the century, gathered new members to their forces. In vain the government tried to oppose them by encouraging a rival reactionary society; the *Carbonari* only grew in power. Fired by the success of the Spanish revolutionists, they clamored for constitutional government. In July, General Pepe, a *Carbonaro* of high rank, took the lead, demanding that Ferdinand, King of Naples, who had signed the Constitution of 1812, in order to maintain his rights to the Spanish throne, proclaim that same Constitution for his kingdom. The strength of the people was too great. The old king yielded. Before the crucifix of the royal chapel in Naples, while the victorious populace stood in awe, King Ferdinand prayed that the vengeance of God smite him if he prove false to his oath. Little did anyone know how soon he was to repudiate his act as a mere farce.

Shelley, that worshiper of freedom, exulted in an *Ode to Liberty* and an *Ode to Naples*. Byron, relying rather on the efficacy of action, enrolled as a member of the Ravenna contingent of the *Carbonari*, who, perhaps in honor of the revolutionaries of 1776, called themselves the *Americani*. They received him with open arms. He was wealthy; he was a foreigner, hence free from Italian interference. The youth of Ravenna, including Teresa's brother, Pietro Gamba, adhered to his standard.

Before long Count Guiccioli lost all composure on seeing milord's apartment in his *palazzo* used as a storeroom for revolutionary arms. It was more than that wary gentleman could countenance. Again he posed to his wife the problem of choosing between him and the Englishman. Teresa chose the Englishman, seconded by her father and Pierino, who had had enough of the papal count's tergiversations. In July, the month of the Neapolitan declaration of independence, the deed of separation asked by the Gambas was granted by the pontifical court. The Countess Guiccioli was free. But it was a limited freedom. Now, if never before, did she have to respect the proprieties in the house of her father, where by papal edict she was compelled to live.

To romantic love, however, all things are easy. Count Ruggiero liked his daughter's poet. Pierino worshiped him. Accordingly, maintaining outward decorum, the lovers saw each other as often as before, either at the Gamba country place or at their city home. Byron, oddly enough, retained his apartment at the Guiccioli Palace and lived on terms of the utmost urbanity with the count, who, now that his wife was no longer under his roof and the amenities were observed, saw no objection to sheltering the Englishman and his armory.

In the mist-thaw-slop-rain of the Ravenna winter, *Don Juan* languished at the fifth canto. Alone, Byron varied the ennui of daily life, nursing his pet crow out of a temporary lameness and playing with his falcon and nine cats. In the past year he had sent to Murray an historical tragedy, *Marino Faliero*. In January 1821 he began *Sardanapalus*, an *apologia pro vita sua* in the Nineveh of Mocenigo. On the twenty-second of the month, at twelve of the clock, midnight, he rounded out his thirty-third birthday.

> *Eheu fugaces, Posthume, Posthume,*
> *Labuntur, anni. . . .*

XXVI

THE COLD HEARTH

GRIEF laid its two-edged sword between Mary and Shelley after the death of baby William. Mary was inconsolable. All her life had been bound up in that frail child, and when he was so cruelly snatched from her she shut the doors of her heart and let none enter to share in her grieving. In vain Shelley sought to comfort her. The sword lay between. He himself was ailing. Sorrow and despair fed on his frame, sparing only his imagination that kept the intense fire alive from the fuel of body.

At the Villa Valsovano on the outskirts of Leghorn, he and his depleted family spent the summer months of 1819. There, in a tiny glass-enclosed roof tower overlooking a green plain that stretched to the busy Tuscan seaport, he finished his *Cenci* while the sun beat upon him or the sudden summer squalls sounded their tattoos overhead. In his work he found forgetfulness. Cheer he had from the Gisbornes, who lived hard by, and Henry Reveley, the son of Mrs. Gisborne by a previous marriage. In the afternoon, after his work of composition, he would take lessons in Spanish from his amiable friend whom Godwin had once wished to make the second Mrs. Godwin, or plan some engineering feat with Henry, a student of the noble science. Between them they devised the building of a steamboat to navigate about Leghorn. And so the months passed.

In the autumn the Shelleys removed to Florence to await Mary's confinement. Disturbing news arrived from England. Godwin had sunk deeper into debt. His rent in Skinner Street, unpaid for years, was demanded with threats of the law. Shipwreck menaced the old bark. In his concern for himself Godwin's limited sympathy was spent, leaving only advice for others' woes. Mary's isolation in her sorrow irritated him.

"You have lost a child," he wrote peevishly, "and all the rest
of the world, all that is beautiful, and all that has a claim upon
your kindness is nothing, because a child of three years old is
dead!" What was it she wanted that she had not? She
had the husband of her choice, "a man of high intellectual at-
tainment, whatever I and some other persons may think of his
morality. . . . But you have lost a child — " Why did she
not think of her old father and help him in his need? As
always, Shelley wrote immediately, promising help as soon
as he could raise the money. Godwin waited. Time, which
weighed heavily upon his many years, made him short-
tempered. "Do not let me be led into a fool's paradise . . ."
he reproved Mary when the money failed to arrive at the expected moment. "If Shelley will not immediately send me such
bills as I propose or as you offer, my next request is, that he
will let me alone, and not disturb the sadness of my shipwreck
by holding out false lights."

Mary, within days of her lying-in, was so distressed that for
her good she requested, and Shelley agreed, that he intercept
all letters from her father. Godwin's complaints, from being
querulous, became insulting. In the few years of their rela-
tionship Shelley had sunk nearly five thousand pounds into the
bottomless pit of his father-in-law's obligations. Still it gaped
for more.

On the twelfth of November, 1819, Mary was delivered of
a boy, sent as if to take the place of that tiny corpse in Rome.
They called him Percy Florence. At first Mary dared not
cherish him. Three times she had been a mother, to be deprived of all her children one by one. Dangers besieged the
newborn on every side — his father's constitution, her own
morbid temper, the treacherous Italian climate. It was with
misgiving she saw the squirming little body wrapped in a warm
flannel petticoat in expectation of the layette Marianne Hunt
was sending from London.

Shelley, deprived of Mary's company, wandered about the
streets of Florence alone. He loved to walk in the Cascine,
watching the rising and falling of the Arno, and the autumnal
leaves whirled by the gusts. One day a fierce windstorm shook
the laden boughs. Rain clouds, driven by the mighty voice,

huddled in tumult overhead. The very weeds under the river swayed in terror. Suddenly naked, the boughs shivered in wintry cold. Yet though they seemed to die, the coming spring would bring to them renewal. With his poet's eyes Shelley saw through the rent vesture of mortality the soul of the immortal. He was the wind; he was the driven leaf. In an access of prophetic rapture he wrote his *Ode to the West Wind,* ending with the ecstatic invocation: —

> . . . Be thou, Spirit fierce,
> My spirit!   Be thou me, impetuous one!
>
> Drive my dead thoughts over the universe
> Like withered leaves to quicken a new birth!
> And, by the incantation of this verse,
>
> Scatter, as from an unextinguished hearth
> Ashes and sparks, my words among mankind!
> Be through my lips to unawakened earth
>
> The trumpet of a prophecy!   O, Wind,
> If Winter comes, can Spring be far behind?

Yet his poetry alone could not give him the warmth of human intercourse without which he found life intolerable. Clare, heartsick and embittered, proved a depressing companion. Besides, Mary again suffered from her old jealousy. The two women did nothing but quarrel whenever they were together, and Shelley's interference, as in all such cases, made matters worse. Mary spoke of sending Clare away, a procedure that the loyal Shelley could not approve. Where could the poor girl go, unfriended and with only the little money he could give her? Henry Reveley seemed interested in her. If, after her first hard experience, Clare could find it in herself to love again, life might offer some solution. In the meantime Shelley must shoulder the burden of her care.

Small wonder he sunned himself in every beam of light that he could find outside of home. And a brilliant ray suddenly shone for him in the person of Sophia Stacey, the ward of Robert Parker, one of Shelley's uncles. Sophia Stacey lived in a lower floor of the house occupied by the Shelleys in

Florence. With an elderly chaperon the buoyant young girl had come to study music in Italy, which was unfolding for her its first enchantment. She was all bright rapture, responding and taking color from the beauty about her. Shelley fell under her charm. He acted as her guide to the sights of Florence, gave her his own lyrics to set to music, and listened entranced when, to the accompaniment of her harp, she sang in her fresh young voice. For her he wrote the *Indian Serenade* to fit the music of Mozart's "Ah, perdona," and *Good Night*, in English and Italian, and a poem, *Thou art fair, and few are fairer*, in praise of her beauty and her singing. He was sensually awakened. His spirit, blighted in the gloom of home, expanded in the girl's sunny youth, so that whenever he left her after some jaunt in the woods, the contrast of his cold hearth struck him painfully.

> Is not to-day enough? Why do I peer
>   Into the darkness of the day to come?
> Is not to-morrow even as yesterday?
>   And will the day that follows change thy doom?
> Few flowers grow upon thy wintry way;
>   And who waits for thee in that cheerless home
> Whence thou hast fled, whither thou must return
> Charged with the load that makes thee faint and mourn?

He left the poem a fragment, fearful, it may be, of saying too much, though much was said. Happily Sophia departed before he felt too great a need of her. The cheerless home brightened as Mary found new joy in her baby. Shelley's fluttering wings were furled in the renewed love of her eyes.

He had done good work in the past year. The last divinely lyrical outpouring had been added to the finished *Prometheus Unbound* and he had found new strength in the *Ode to the West Wind*. Otherwise his poetry had been chiefly political. The Manchester riots in England inspired his *Mask of Anarchy*. *Song to the Men of England* sought to infuse his ardor into the oppressed. And he also indulged in a bit of levity. William Wordsworth had recently published *Peter Bell*, which John Hamilton Reynolds ridiculed before publication. Critiques and reviews reached Shelley in Leghorn, and he was so amused

that he began writing *Peter Bell the Third* — laughing at the
foibles of Wordsworth and Coleridge as Messiahs of simplicity.
Wordsworth's oneness with Nature woke in him the imp of the
perverse. Slyly, but with justice, he jested: —

> But from the first 't was Peter's drift
>   To be a kind of moral eunuch,
> He touched the hem of Nature's shift,
> Felt faint — and never dared uplift
>   The closest, all-concealing tunic.

Had Wordsworth had any inkling of the younger poet's
criticism when he met Trelawny at Lausanne the following
year?   Certainly he showed the same obtuseness that he had
betrayed with Keats. "What do you think of Shelley as a
poet?" Trelawny asked. "Nothing . . ." said Wordsworth
as he entered the *calèche* with his wife and sister. "A poet
who has not produced a good poem before he is twenty-five we
may conclude cannot and never will do so." *"The Cenci!"*
Trelawny challenged. "Won't do," came the inexorable voice.
Wordsworth, alas, in all but his poetry, had the myopic sight
of his contemporaries.

In April of that year the *Quarterly,* on the pretext of reviewing the *Revolt of Islam,* made an attack on Shelley's
character and ventured, in the best King James, to predict his
destruction. "Like the Egyptians of old, the wheels of his
chariot are broken, the paths of 'mighty waters' close in upon
him behind . . . he calls ineffectually on others to follow him
to the same ruin — finally he sinks 'like lead' to the bottom and
is forgotten. So it is now in part, so shortly will it be entirely
with Mr. Shelley." No, his countrymen did not love him.
He had seared their eyeballs with his lightning and they cursed
him.   Even abroad they carried their hatred with them, reviling
the atheist and attacking the man.   Like a thundercloud, abuse
against him gained weight and size, by whispered gossip and
the ominous threats of a discharged servant. Mr. Hoppner,
jealous for Byron's reputation, stood on the alert.

The cold winter driving them from Florence, the Shelleys,
early in 1820, went on to Pisa, where, except for brief vacations, they determined to make their home. The purity of its

waters as well as its temperate climate offered the chief inducements. But there was another reason, in a friendly colony of
expatriates and cultured Italians. Not that Shelley desired
society. In a drawing-room he was the unhappiest of pent
creatures seeking a loophole for escape. But Mary felt the
solitude of their life and yearned after brilliant intercourse.
What the ladies of fashion were wearing interested her as much
as news of the latest Neapolitan victory; a compliment restored her youth. She would have liked Shelley to go with
her to the theatres and give entertainments where she might
distinguish herself as a woman of great gifts, the wife of a
poet and in her own right a writer of repute. Shelley would
sooner have faced a battery. "The quick coupled with the
dead," he was to comment on her and himself when, in the
later tragic months, the contrast could no longer be ignored.
He hated society because he saw it for the sham it was. Mary
loathed solitude because it encouraged her sickly brooding.

However, life passed interestingly at Pisa. The small white
town, with its leaning tower and a bulwark of blue mountains,
seemed enclosed in its own sufficiency. Fields of golden corn
spread round it in the summertime. In the autumn the gar-
lands of the vine, swinging from tree to tree, hung their bunches
of misty purple half-hidden in their darkening leaves. The
Arno, spanned by its bridges, wound its dun waters through the
town, reflecting the ancient houses whose marble had taken on
a liquid shimmer. Many a legend still echoed round the walls
of those palaces. Next to the house that Shelley occupied, a
marble edifice bore the motto, *Alla Giornata,* that puzzled him
and still remains a mystery. It was said one of the founders
of the family had been held prisoner by the Saracens, and on
his return he built himself that palace with its dedication —
was it to the day of his release? No one knows. Near by,
in the old ducal keep, a murder had been committed. On the
same side of the river the Palazzo Lanfranchi hid behind its
pillared entrance memories of olden feuds and scenes of blood
that kept alive the dread of ghosts among the Pisan multitude.
The heavily barred ground-floor windows spoke too clearly of
other, more palpable, fears. Underneath, the dungeons preserved their secrets.

Ubaldo Lanfranchi, Archbishop of Pisa, it was said, had brought on his ships the soil from the Holy Land that covered the Camp Santo on the outskirts of the town, where in storied attitudes the patron saint of Pisa unfolded his life on the frescoed walls, and a Triumph of Death preached its silent sermon. Antiquity walked hand in hand with the modern world, and Shelley's spirit breathed.

He wrote tirelessly. The mists gathering and fading on the summit of the Pisan hills inspired him to the rushing lyricism of *The Cloud*. He sang with the skylark, heard on a walk with Mary in the sunset glow of a summer evening. He captured the spirit of ideal beauty in the *Sensitive Plant*, which throve in the light of the gracious presence, and died when it was gone. He spun, with the *Witch of Atlas*, a fleecy mist of magic about reality.

But he could not veil the perfidy of human nature. Even while he felt most at peace with his fellow men, Byron, from Ravenna, was trying to fathom the meaning of some new *cookery* that Hoppner gave him. What was it the fellow was aiming at with his innuendos against Shelley? "I regret that you have such a bad opinion of Shiloh; you used to have a good one," Byron wrote. "Surely he has talent and honour, but is crazy about religion and morality. . . . You seem lately to have got some notion against him." It was not long before Byron knew, though Shelley was not to learn the full extent of Hoppner's scandalmongering till the following year. Paolo and Elise, Shelley's discharged servants, had, according to the consul, been making grave charges against him and Clare. Shelley, they said, treated his wife brutally. While he had been occupying Byron's house at Este, he had had an affair with Clare, who bore him a child that he tore from her to place in the Neapolitan Foundling Hospital.

So much for the story. That Hoppner, who on a previous occasion had shown himself a gossip and an intermeddler, should have believed if not encouraged it was nothing to marvel at. He had, for his own aggrandizement, set himself up as the Cerberus of his lordship and therefore lent three pairs of ears to profitable evil-saying, and employed three maws for spewing it forth again. He was well aware that Byron was at the bitterest odds with Clare over Allegra. In the very letter where he regretted Hoppner's bad opinion of Shelley he had spared no words to show his wrath against her. "To express it delicately, I think Madame Clare is a damned bitch," he exploded. "What think you?" Hoppner made haste to set before his lordship his mess of scandal, of which the first course had been served in the early Guiccioli days. But Byron must keep the matter secret, he warned. Why the demand for secrecy? Byron acquiesced, and there the affair temporarily rested.

That summer, in Naples, had died a little girl whom Shelley had cared for as a ward — the baby daughter, perhaps, of the English incognita whom he had known and lost in 1818. A letter of his to the Gisbornes announced the event while alluding to Paolo's perfidy. "My Neapolitan charge is dead. It seems as if the destruction that is consuming me were as an atmosphere that wrapt and *infected* everything connected with me. The rascal Paolo has been taking advantage of my situation at Naples in December, 1818, to attempt to extort money by threatening to charge me with the most horrible crimes."

Though undated, the comment followed as a postscript to a communication of the second of July. Two days later Clare made a significant entry in her diary: —

> High-ho! the Claire and the Ma
> Find something to fight about every day.

The tension between the two women had become greater than either could stand. A break was inevitable. Even Shelley had to allow at last that, in spite of the innocence of all parties, Clare's presence in his house, far from protecting her, did her great injury before her detractors. Mary redoubled her persuasions, and a place was found for the unfriended girl as governess in Florence in the home of Professor Bojti. At first Shelley had thought of transplanting his household gods to the Levant or Greece, and asked Lord Byron if he could favor him with some letters of introduction. But the plan, one of those fairy threads snatched from the spindle of the Witch of Atlas, vanished into thin air.

In October, Shelley left Mary and baby Percy at the Baths of San Giuliano and escorted Clare to a stranger's hearth. It was a sad parting. The unhappy girl, an outcast from the only place she could call home, left with a heavy heart. Shelley, even Shelley, bowed to the demands of society. Everyone and everything conspired against her. Byron had long ceased to answer her broken-hearted letters pleading for a sight of Allegra, whom she had not seen since those briefly happy days, two years ago at Este. The Hoppners had turned against her and seemed to take malicious pleasure in retailing the parts of Byron's letters that would most wound her, as when he declared the child should not quit him again "to perish of starvation, and green fruit, or to be taught to believe that there is no Deity." A fine scruple, forsooth, from one who lived as he did. He disapproved of the careless management of Shelley's household with its vegetarianism, adding he would as soon send Allegra to a hospital as allow the Shelleys to take charge of her. "Have they *reared* one?" he asked brutally.

All his taunts would have been as nothing, however, had he not threatened to send Allegra to a convent. To Clare, raised in the prejudices of freethinking, it was like condemning the child to be buried alive. "I am willing to undergo any infliction rather than that her whole life should be spoiled," she broke at last. Instead of being propitiated, Byron flared vindictively: "Were it not for the poor little child's sake, I am almost tempted to send her back to her atheistical mother, but that would be too bad. . . . The girl shall be a Christian and a married woman, if possible." Thus Don Juan.

At twenty-two Clare had had too much of life. Her heart was dulled. Yet there were those who thought that because in artificial excitement she could throw off her gloom and laugh and sing louder than the rest, she could yet live as the living. One, knowing her past history, had proposed to marry her; but she had refused him. Henry Reveley, too, had fallen in love with her, but though she tried to like him, she could not, and again rejected an offer of marriage. A settled life was not for her. She had had her moment of happiness and she had been made unfit for common living. Sadly she took leave of Shelley, and with her own child about to be immured with women who had never known love, she went to rear another woman's children. Shelley wrote often to her, letters that Mary did not see, and so affectionate as to be almost lover-like. She answered, addressing him not at his home, but in the care of Mrs. Mason, Lady Mountcashel, who had be-friended her at Pisa. It was advisable for the peace of Mary, who would not have understood either Shelley's pity or Clare's gratitude.

On returning to San Giuliano Shelley found that a visitor had arrived — his cousin Thomas Medwin of the 24th Light Dragoons. For several months he had been corresponding with him, then staying at Geneva, but, as the climate affected his health, Captain Medwin had decided to try Italy. Italy, of course, meant the house of Cousin Shelley, whom he had not seen for nearly seven years, but whose hospitality could nonetheless be counted upon. Unfortunately, after the first few days, Medwin's company ceased to be interesting. In fact, he became something of a bore. Although he had donned the habit of Mars, his ambitions were unsatisfied. He yearned after the sacred singing robes which willy-nilly he must drape about himself. Since the days when he and Shelley had been schoolfellows and collaborated on the *Wandering Jew,* Medwin had been writing constantly. From Geneva he had sent reams of manuscript for his cousin to correct. Now that they were together he was never without a handful of his productions for Shelley to nurse into shape. Mary, hard at work on her novel about Castruccio, Prince of Lucca, nevertheless found time for the importunate guest and played chess with him. Life, with-out Clare, was beginning to be pleasanter.

The heavy rains that autumn at San Giuliano swelled the Serchio, broke through the dams, and flooded the village, carry-ing away furniture and cattle. In the midst of the confusion the Shelleys found their ground floor under six feet of water and their lighter movables navigating this sudden sea. The doors had been forced open by the pressure of the waters. Taking their baby, the Shelleys escaped through an upper window into a boat and so, with no little danger, made the four miles to Pisa.

At Casa Galetti, next door to the marble palace with its

cryptic motto, an eventful winter began. The house was large and comfortable, and a bargain at thirteen sequins a month. Mary, with the nurse and the baby, had the lower apartment. Medwin and Shelley occupied the two rooms on the fourth floor. Shelley was delighted to have again a study of his own and spent a happy day arranging his books and gathering his papers together. Even if the house should be full of guests, — and the season threatened to be a social one, — he could always escape without interfering with Mary's pleasure. "Poor Mary . . . she can't bear solitude, nor I society."

Society at Pisa, however, was sufficiently varied to interest even such a recluse as Shelley. There was Francesco Pacchiani, priest, professor, guide, philosopher, and friend — for profit. The tall, dark, angular social apparition of the middle-aged factotum alone warranted the name of the "Devil Pacchiani" by which he was commonly known. He had the midnight eyes of a Gothic hero, and his gloom, though he could be merry on occasion over a bottle of wine paid for by another. In his early days experiments with the galvanic pile had led him to believe he held the key to an important discovery that would enrich him, but further researches led to naught. Though he wore the priest's hat, he had long shaken off the restrictions of the order, and tales of his exploits shortened many an evening wherever men were gathered. A *bon mot* had cost him his professorial chair. "Who's there?" the guards had called one night on hearing the sounds of rioting. *"Sono un uomo pubblico,"* answered il Signor Professore, *"in una strada pubblica, con una donna pubblica."* [1] The description and circumstances fitted him only too well.

If ever a Pisan wanted a house disposed of, or a daughter married, he called on Pacchiani. Did he wish for a doctor? A confessor? Pacchiani brought him. Did a lover pine for a sight of his beloved, kept imprisoned like a bird in a cage? Pacchiani had the sesame to burst open the bars. He was the know-all and do-all in the little city, an Autolycus with the learning of a Pico della Mirandola. Shelley would listen entranced to the rogue's eloquence, which reminded him of

[1] I am a public man in a public street with a public woman.

Coleridge's, overlooking in his admiration the cloven hoof that stumped under the intellectual garb.

Pacchiani also acted as the Pisan catalytic agent. No advantageous stranger entered the town without his bringing him into contact with the others, working changes in human relationships, creating sympathies and aversions, loves and hates, he, the while, going among them, unchanged and unchangeable. If there were a few sequins to be got he pocketed them gratefully; success and failure, as a rule, brought their own rewards. Against some obstacles, however, even the devil Pacchiani was powerless: the prejudices of the English. Walter Savage Landor, when asked to meet Shelley, refused from moral scruples. He was no exception. Indeed, wherever Shelley went, his *crimes* cast their shadow before.

For some time Pacchiani had been telling the Shelleys about a beautiful Pisan girl of noble birth whose father, on his second marriage to a woman hardly older than his daughter, had shut her up in a convent until a deliverer should come. What an unhappy life for her, *la sventurata,* imprisoned in a cheerless cell by the tyranny of an unnatural parent! But what would you? Such are the customs in Italy with unmarried girls. They have to pine in *conservatorios* until they regain their liberty at the price of their body. The worst of it was that Count Viviani, besides this daughter just turned eighteen, had another waiting to be disposed of, and he was not overanxious to give them a dowry. Now it is well known that claimants do not come for brides as naked as Griselda, even when their beauty is as a resplendent taper in the darkness of a cell. For two years Teresa Emilia Viviani had been in her holy prison house, and still there glimmered no hope of freedom. It would be a blessing and a mercy, it would be bringing water to one perishing of thirst, to visit the unhappy Emilia. Shelley, no whit changed by experience from the passionate champion of the Harriet Westbrook days, saw in Count Viviani another Minotaur to be foiled. Mary must go to Emilia and bring her comfort. Poor, lovely prisoner! She had found her defenders against Intolerance.

Accordingly, one day in late November, Mary and Clare, who had come home for the Christmas holidays, set out for

the Convent of Santa Anna, escorted by Pacchiani, who, besides less honorable offices, held that of father confessor to
the Viviani family. The two women saw Emilia and were
charmed. She was indeed lovely, but — Mary sensed a
vague imperfection in that embodiment of all virtues. Several
days later, Shelley, with Medwin, conducted by Pacchiani,
went on the pilgrimage.

If the women had been charmed, Shelley was ecstatic. The
contessina was supremely, romantically beautiful. In a face
of classic purity glowed the eyes of a Beatrice Cenci, soft,
voluptuous, yet innocent as a child's. She was pale. Her
cheeks and brow seemed cut out of marble. Her heavy black
hair, caught in a knot at her neck, contoured a head that made
Medwin think of the Greek Muse in the Florence gallery. She
made quick, impulsive movements, however, that showed her
to be alive — ethereal, yet humanly, desirably alive. Shelley
was prostrate before her. What a heartless wretch that father
must be who could force so ravishing a creature to droop in
that dreary prison! In his sympathetic ardor he did not stop
to reflect that the prison could not have been so drear if foreign
gentlemen gained admittance into its parlor to talk freely with
a lovely inmate. But how was a lover of beauty to reflect
when a glorious vision bereaved him of sense? How could he
see anything but the cruelty of Emilia's situation as he heard
her pour out, in a language that itself was music, the burden of
her suffering, while she gazed in pity upon a captive lark.
"Poor prisoner! . . . How I pity thee! What must thou
suffer when thou hearest in the clouds the songs of thy parent
birds, or some flocks of thy kind on the wing, in search of other
skies. . . . But like me, thou wilt be forced to remain
here. . . ."

In the succeeding weeks Shelley traversed often the old road
leading to the outskirts of Pisa, where, in an unfrequented
street not far from the walls of the town, the Convent of Santa
Anna huddled its dingy ruins. But the garden in all seasons of
the year was a delight. Old-fashioned beds of sweet herbs,
basil, verbena, and mignonette, rewarded the loving care of
the nuns. Beyond, the low-growing fruit trees made a green
park of the orchard. There Shelley and Emilia walked, as the

Mephistophelian Pacchiani engaged the nuns elsewhere. Sometimes Mary went with her husband with gifts of books and flowers for Emilia, as uneasily she watched the domination of this new orb over her husband's inconstant planet. She grew jealous, and with reason. Shelley, no adept at concealment, showed too clearly how profound was the passion inspired by Emilia. She touched his inmost soul; she became part of his deepest life. "Would we two had been twins of the same mother!" he exclaimed in *Epipsychidion,* his testament of the ideal love. He felt that in Emilia he had found it — not only the ideal, but its most perfect expression in her mortal image. The heavenly and the earthly Venus were in her combined.

> Seraph of Heaven! too gentle to be human,
> Veiling beneath that radiant form of Woman
> All that is insupportable in thee
> Of light, and love, and immortality!
> Sweet Benediction in the eternal Curse!
> Veiled glory of this lampless Universe . . .
> Thou Wonder, and thou Beauty, and thou Terror!
> Thou Harmony of Nature's art! Thou Mirror
> In whom, as in the splendour of the Sun,
> All shapes look glorious which thou gazest on!

And Mary? His fidelity to her, his wife and friend, lost nothing by this seizure of platonic ecstasy.

> True love in this differs from gold and clay,
> That to divide is not to take away.
> Love is like understanding, that grows bright
> Gazing on many truths.

He loved her, the companion of his mortal days; he adored Emilia. In his heart and mind the two loves found harmonious coexistence, as the moon and the sun in the heavens. He was the passive earth, ruled by those twin spheres of light, waking into fruits and flowers as they darted their potency into his being.

> So ye, bright regents, with alternate sway,
> Govern my sphere of being, night and day!
> Thou, not disdaining even a borrowed might;
> Thou, not eclipsing a remoter light.

However, Mary, far from not disdaining the borrowed might of Emilia's orb, resented daily its ascendency over Shelley, for, too human to enter into his heaven, she interpreted his fervor in terms of everyday living. It is not flattering, after all, to a wife, even an extraordinary wife, to be made the celestial hand-maid of another woman whose flaws, however well hidden from the worshiper's eyes, lost none of their magnitude in hers. Emilia was young, and virginal, and beautiful. But she was also, consciously or not, somewhat of an actress. The fire of her Italian blood might be carried to the snowy heights of platonism; yet, since fire can melt snow, Mary had excellent cause for feeling concerned about her husband. Shelley and Emilia took solitary walks, a fact whose brief entry in Mary's diary spoke volumes for her fears. They corresponded with each other, Emilia writing soulful effusions on the nature of love that were belied by her addressing of Shelley as *"diletto amico"* and *"adorato sposo."* Both names, of course, appeared in Emilia's prayer books, where Christ, to whom the devout were mystically married, became the *adored spouse.* Did it hold the same mystical meaning when the girl applied it to an earthly friend?

Shelley's poem rhapsodized on this spiritual union with Emilia. On an island under Ionian skies, away from the tumult of the world, Emilia, vowed by him to be the lady of the solitude, should mingle the essence of her being with his.

> Our breath shall intermix, our bosoms bound,
> And our veins beat together; and our lips
> With other eloquence than words, eclipse
> The soul that burns between them; and the wells
> Which boil under our being's inmost cells,
> The fountains of our deepest life, shall be
> Confused in passion's golden purity,
> As mountain-springs under the morning sun.
> We shall become the same, we shall be one
> Spirit within two frames, oh! wherefore two?
> One passion in twin-hearts, which grows and grew,
> Till like two meteors of expanding flame,
> Those spheres instinct with it become the same,
> Touch, mingle, are transfigured. . . .

These were not the transports of mortals. Two souls, in the divine lambencies of ideal love, consumed themselves to unity. They became god.

Mary, limited by her human frailty, caught the material words, but was deaf to the immortal meaning. Time did not heal what must have been too deep a wound. Years later, when editing her husband's works, she had no word of comment for that poem of his soul.

Yet she had had the human satisfaction of seeing Shelley's Juno become a cloud. Emilia, unable to maintain her balance on the heights he reared, fell, and showed that she was clay. Before the year was out a bridegroom came knocking at the convent gate. She took the freedom he brought. *"L'anima amante si slancia fuori del creato, e si crea nell'infinito un mondo tutto per essa. . . ."* Such had been her words which Shelley found elevated enough to keep as a motto for his poem. What world did her soul create in the infinite with Signor Biondi? It was no Shelleyan paradise. For six years she endured her disenchantment in the poisonous swamps of the Maremma. Then, like Dante's Gemma, she wasted away in loneliness and died.

Shelley completed *Epipsychidion* before the end of December. By February 1821 the emotions that had lighted it were quenched, and in sending the poem to Ollier he wished it not to appear as his own. "Indeed, in a certain sense, it is a production of a portion of me already dead." Thus early the epitaph was inscribed over the grave of his soul's love. But by this time another star had risen in his firmament when some friends of Medwin's arrived at Pisa.

Edward Elleker Williams, a lineal descendant of one of Cromwell's daughters, as Medwin boasted, and his wife Jane, had journeyed to Italy on purpose to meet Shelley. They were charming young people both, entertaining and accomplished. Edward, a year younger than Shelley, had seen a good part of the world, served in the navy, and entered the 8th Dragoon Guard that took him to India. Many 's the tale he could tell of that wonderland where he had had his store of adventures. In manner he was gentle and frank, humble about what he did not know, but sure, perhaps oversure, in matters nautical. He had as great a passion as Shelley for the sea, and the same fearlessness, rendered somewhat rash by his two or three years in the navy. Like Medwin, though more modestly, he tried his hand at writing. In leisure hours he did a bit of water-color painting — nothing remarkable, but pleasing because he had not the arrogance of the amateur.

Shelley liked him at once, and from the first the two could be seen floating toy boats on the Serchio. Soon, however, they became the proud owners of a fine twelve-foot craft, "to go adventuring," Shelley said, through the many rivers and canals from Pisa to Leghorn. One was more venturesome than the other. The first day when they called for the boat at Leghorn, they decided to sail her home. It was night by the time they started, and the wind blew brisk. Raising a huge sail, they pointed the prow toward Pisa on the choppy, darkening waters, and sailed on gloriously — till the boat capsized. Shelley, who could not swim, was none the worse for the ducking and not the least discouraged from further adventuring. He played with the sea as innocently as a child, and with a child's trust in it. How could it harm one who loved it with his joyous love?

Jane Williams made herself a favorite both with Mary and with Shelley. "I like her very much," he wrote to Clare with unusual brevity after Jane had called on them. He found her extremely pretty, but "apparently not *very* clever." So far the idealizing eye had not deceived him. But then, it was only their first meeting and one must make allowances for embarrassment. Moreover, he was not seeing her at her best, fatigued as she was from a long journey, and nearing the time of her delivery. As the months passed and Emilia's light waned, he beheld Jane's splendor enhanced by that decrease, and he who had been blind grew blinder in his dazzlement. Jane became the corporeal ideal of his quest. She was the woman he had thought to find in others. Had he not described her as the ruling Grace in the *Sensitive Plant?* Surely, he had had a pure anticipated cognition of her, as in a magic glass, a year before she came upon his way. And he was lost.

The Jane of everyday life was by no means the portent of Shelley's idealization. Physically she would have been called lovely by those to whom expression means more than perfection of feature; others would have found her plain. Her forehead, broad and high, framed by silkily glinting light brown hair in the soft ringlets of childhood, and her large eyes whose enormous pupils overwhelmed them with a luminous darkness, gave her face a deceptive spirituality soon dispelled by some trivial utterance. However, she knew how to be silent intelligently, covering the flaws of a deficient education. And she sang exquisitely to the harp and guitar. Then, when music spoke for her and the glamour of her instrument communicated itself to her, she was all loveliness, a vision to wonder at, a Miranda, and the lovesick Shelley knelt at her feet. But he did not know — perhaps never knew — that the angelic Jane had left a husband, a British officer, at St. Helena for Williams's sake, and that in her domain of the household she could be a shrew. He saw only what he would see — the Miranda of his imagination, the Magnetic Lady whose healing touch had the power to charm away the pain from his heart and temples.

The heart's division again sundered him and Mary. Wounded, she grew cold toward him, and, as Harriet before her had done, she looked for comfort in society. Pacchiani had brought Prince Mavrocordato, a Greek exile and an ardent patriot, to the Shelley house. Mary made friends with him, impressed both by his title and by his breeding, and soon she was teaching him English in exchange for readings in the ancient dramatists of his country. For the first time in his life with Mary, Shelley evinced jealousy. But he offered no reproaches. How could he when, as Mary would have reminded him, his heart was always soaring on the wing of his fancy? He found release for an annihilating dejection in short personal lyrics strangely reminiscent of the Bracknell poems wherein he had rued his desolated hearth. "The serpent is shut out from Paradise," he unburdened himself to Williams, —

Therefore, if now I see you seldomer,
  Dear friends, dear *friend!* know that I only fly
    Your looks because they stir
    Griefs that should sleep, and hopes that cannot die. . . .

When I return to my cold home, you ask
Why I am not as I have ever been.
You spoil me for the task
Of acting a forced part in life's dull scene. . . .

The cold home. . . . Duty and dereliction again guided him back to solitude, as the drama repeated itself with other characters to sustain the leads.

XXVII

ADONAIS

Toward the close of February, 1821, in the Piazza di Spagna, Rome, a few shoddy pieces of furniture were carried out of the house on the right of the Spanish stairs that rise to the Trinità de' Monti, heaped to a pyre under the supervision of the sanitary authorities, and burned to the ground. A mound of smouldering ashes scattered by the guards was all that remained of the worldly possessions of John Keats, British poet, deceased in Rome on the night of Friday, February 23.

The following day casts were taken of his face, hand, and foot. Sunday morning the coffin was closed over the wasted corpse, bearing with it close to the heart under the shroud the last letters of Fanny Brawne, unread. Out of consideration for the faithful friend, exhausted from weeks of watching without rest or sleep, the regulation requiring a night funeral for non-Catholics was suspended, and at nine o'clock Sunday morning the body of John Keats, followed by a handful of Englishmen, was lowered to its grave under the shadow of Caius Cestius.

Joseph Severn's lifework was done, though he was to live to a great age. As a painter he left little of note. As a friend he raised himself a monument more enduring than brass. What memories were his when from the burial ground he returned to the now solitary lodging where for four months he had been constantly with Keats. Did he recall the weary journey from Naples to Rome when, to cheer the disheartened invalid, he had run beside the carriage gathering wild flowers to fill those thin, restless hands? There had been the nights when he had played Mozart on the piano, hired because Keats could not live without music. There had been — for a brief time only — those walks on the Pincio with the handsome Lieutenant Elton, so hale in appearance that none would have guessed he too was dying of

consumption.   Certainly the Princess Bonaparte, passing them
by at the same hour each day in her carriage, thought the lieutenant worthy of her languishing glances.   There had been
those months of hope, and then the dreadful weeks of despair
when, with a voice made hoarse by suffering, Keats asked the
doctor, day after day with increasing irritation, "How long is
this posthumous life of mine to last?"   Long since he would
have put an end to it with the bottle of laudanum which Severn,
hating himself for his cruelty, had hidden away.

Then despair had yielded to quietness as Keats held in his
hand a polished oval carnelian — Fanny's gift — and listened
to Severn reading the stern consolation of Jeremy Taylor.
He was able to face death and constantly prayed for it, greeting each dawn that woke him out of his earthly sleep with disappointment in his eyes, the only feature in which life yet
glowed, terrible and accusing.   Severn was long to remember
those eyes, opening in great doubt and horror from some dream
vision, and closing gently again after resting, reassured, upon
him.   Then there had been the night Keats bade him take
down his epitaph: "Here lies one whose name was writ in
water," not knowing that even then that name was being inscribed among the immortal.   Toward the end he desired to
know where he should be buried, and Severn, going to the
pyramid of Cestius, told him of the grass and the many flowers
on that holy hill slope, and of the flocks of sheep that young
shepherds, like his Endymion, drove past the cemetery.   He
described to him the violets that overspread the graves, and
saw the pained face relax to peace as Keats said in his husky
whisper: "I already feel the flowers growing over me."   He
slept more toward the end.   The sweat of death dampened his
forehead, matting the long hair upon it; the eyes seemed
mercifully closed at last to life.   It was during such a sleep
that Severn, to keep himself awake in the exhausting watch,
had drawn a last portrait of his friend.

His death was kept a long time from Fanny Brawne.   "It
is now five days since she heard it," Brown wrote to Severn.
"I shall not speak of the first shock, nor of the following days,
— it is enough that she is now pretty well."   But Fanny's
maligners were never silenced.   Her coldness, the false whisper

ran through the years, with the critics' fury, had killed Keats.

Shelley knew nothing of Keats's love, but he did know that, even more than he himself, Keats had suffered from the gross abuse of the press. Friends of Keats who corresponded with him stressed the fact, and in noble indignation Shelley rose to vindicate the memory of a brother poet whom, even after death, the critical vultures attacked. He had read the *Lamia* volume, and while not admiring the narrative poems which he thought written "in the bad sort of style" of Hunt's imitators, he bowed before *Hyperion*. "The fragment . . . promises for him that he is destined to become one of the first writers of the age." Alas, the presaging words fell on the deaf ears of fate. Keats wrote no more, but when his pen had dropped from his hand he was already one of the *first* writers of all time. Shelley's admiration increased the more he read the colossal fragment. It was poetry at its loftiest, in all respects fulfilling the exacting requirements he demanded of the art. In his *Defence of Poetry* he had said that the poet participates in the eternal, the infinite, and the one. Now more than ever, by his work and by the fate that placed him with the eternal, did Keats claim the title.

Through June, when the kindling buds of the Pisan spring had burst to summer flower, when, in the burial ground of Rome the daisies overspread the turf of the recent grave, Shelley wrote *Adonais*. Bion and Moschus, the pastoral elegists of Sicily's golden age, lent him the poetic form, and Spenser the stanza. The poetry, especially in the second half where he soared untrammeled by classical models, was purest Shelley. In his modesty he thought it the *least imperfect* of his compositions. The court of posterity whose severity he feared would pronounce upon him the verdict, "Guilty — death!" on the strength of *Adonais* alone, gave him enduring life.

The elegy was the expression of one who all his life had lived companioned by the shadow of death so that no terror darkened his conception. He wept for Adonais, and with him everything mourned that had loved beauty — spring, her lover, Urania, her beloved. All things that Adonais had created into loveliness, from shape and hue and odor and sweet sound, made his processional.

> . . . And the mountain shepherds came,
> Their garlands sere, their magic mantles rent;
> The Pilgrim of Eternity, whose fame
> Over his living head like Heaven is bent,
> An early but enduring monument,
> Came, veiling all the lightnings of his song
> In sorrow. . . .

Thus even Byron was made to lament for one whom he had reviled in life.

But Shelley did not know that while his praises of Keats would be sung for ages to come, Byron's remarks had to appear decently clothed in asterisks. "Mr. Keats, whose poetry you enquire after," Byron had written to Murray in November of 1829, "appears to me what I have already said. Such writing is a sort of mental masturbation, he is always ******** his imagination. . . ." "That dirty blackguard Keats," he had called him. To Shelley, on learning from him of Keats's death, he said, coloring chameleon-like to the occasion: "I am very sorry to hear what you say of Keats — is it *actually* true? I did not think criticism had been so killing. Though I differ from you essentially in your estimate of his performances, I so much abhor all unnecessary pain, that I would rather he had been seated on the highest peak of Parnassus than have perished in such a manner." "Are you aware that Shelley has written an elegy on Keats," wrote to Murray the incorrigible mocker of his better sentiments, "and accuses the *Quarterly* of killing him?

> Who killed John Keats?
> "I," says the Quarterly,
> So savage and Tartarly;
> "T was one of my feats."

Nonetheless Byron saw the wisdom of revising his opinion of one who had the discriminating admiration of Shelley. Moreover, there *was* something to *Hyperion*. "As he is dead, omit *all* that is said *about him* in any *MSS.* of mine, or publication," he cautioned his publisher. He could not wholly keep his resolve. In *Don Juan* finally appeared the mock-elegiac stanza, in spite of the protests of Leigh Hunt: —

> John Keats, who was kill'd off by one critique,
>   Just as he really promis'd something great,
> If not intelligible, without Greek
>   Contrived to talk about the gods of late,
> Much as they might have been supposed to speak.
>   Poor fellow! His was an untoward fate;
> 'T is strange the mind, that very fiery particle,
>   Should let itself he snuff'd out by an article.

His presence in Shelley's poem, however, like that of a sinner whom the painters of Italy's age of innocence would place among a glory of saints, ennobled him, if only by the holiness about him. Among those of less note came Shelley himself, his head bound with pansies overblown and faded violets.

>   . . . Of that crew
> He came the last, neglected and apart;
> A herd-abandoned deer, struck by the hunter's dart.

As Keats had suffered, so had he. But Keats now was gone where malice could not reach him; he was made one with Nature. Who mourns for Adonais? Mourn no more. For he is gathered to the kings of thought. "Die, if thou wouldst be with that which thou dost seek! Follow where all is fled!" Shelley now spoke his own despondency. Why linger, why turn back, why shrink from the invitation of death? He had little left to make him want to live,

>   . . . and what still is dear
> Attracts to crush, repels to make thee wither.

The breath he had invoked descends upon him —

>   . . . my spirit's bark is driven
> Far from the shore, far from the trembling throng
> Whose sails were never to the tempest given;
> The massy earth and spherèd skies are riven!
> I am borne darkly, fearfully afar;
> Whilst, burning through the inmost veil of Heaven,
> The soul of Adonais, like a star,
> Beacons from the abode where the Eternal are.

It was his own elegy as well as that of Keats that he had written.

He had *Adonais* printed at his own expense in Pisa from the "types of Didot," and sent to Ollier, who did not republish it. Neither the dead Keats nor the living Shelley had proved gainful investments for an ambitious publisher. The Pisa copies, therefore, circulated in England.

As caprice would have it, Shelley's *Queen Mab* had recently been brought out piratically by Clark, an unscrupulous publisher who squirmed out of every attempt to bring him to justice. Thousands of copies of the "atheistical" poem were sold, the press pouring out its foulest ink upon the poet. Once more the hounds were unleashed. When *Adonais* appeared, therefore, the critics were primed for their worst, and such was their fury that the parents of Joseph Severn, whose name Shelley mentioned with a tribute in the preface, besieged him with threats and prayers that he break off all acquaintance with the scandalous man. The *Cenci* and *Prometheus Unbound* had fared little better with the critical gang. One Steropes, in *John Bull,* delivered himself of a tasteless play upon words which, if by nothing else, made him remembered beyond his little day.

> Shelley styles his new poem "Prometheus Unbound"
> And 't is like to remain so while time circles round;
> For surely an age would be spent in the finding
> A reader so weak as to pay for the binding.

Meanwhile disquieting rumors had come from Ravenna. Lord Byron, finding the revolutionary town too dangerous for Allegra, had sent her to a convent in Bagnacavallo, several miles away. It was the only thing he could have done. In the uncertain state of the political situation, he might be called upon at any time to turn the Guiccioli Palace into a fort. He could not endanger the life of Allegra. That winter Del Pinto, a military commander, had been assassinated before his very threshold; he had died, in fact, in Fletcher's bed, where he had been carried by the mercy of his lordship to prevent the corpse's being left all night on the street by the terrified Italians. Soon afterwards, on the advice of the Countess Guiccioli, Allegra, wrapped in a little ermine coat, was sent to the nuns at Bagnacavallo.

The change could not have been distressing to the little girl who had been buffeted about almost from birth, by a woman's weakness and a man's pride. She loved her *caro papà*, who spoiled her as he did the rest of his pets. She remembered her *mammina* whom she had not seen for a long, long time. She recalled Shelley, too, with whom she had been so happy that day when, while waiting for *papà*, they had rolled the billiard balls on the marble floors. For a child of four Allegra had many memories.

The convent at Bagnacavallo, built on an elevation, had but recently been converted to a school for the daughters of the well-to-do. The nuns took charge of their little wards, taught them every detail of the heavenly hierarchy and as little about the world they lived in as would keep their minds free from sin until the day a husband should come to instruct them in all that was needful. Since Allegra was much younger than the rest of the children, she was turned over to Sister Marianna Fabbri, who did her best to play the part of both teacher and mother, a privilege for which Byron paid a double fee. A new life began for the little girl. Instead of the lavish disorder of her father's house, she found herself in surroundings as bare as they were gloomy. No fires were allowed the children even in the severest winter. Their food was of the plainest. In the changing world of the nineteenth century, the nuns of Bagnacavallo preserved the austerities of the Dark Ages.

Clare, wild with grief, sent to Byron one of her irritating letters. Had he not promised that the child should never be away from her parents? And tactlessly she reminded him that she had exacted the promise when he had suggested the lesser evil of placing Allegra under the protection of Mrs. Leigh. Carried away by despair and anger, she spared no words as she mustered the most powerful arguments to make him undo his deed. "How will Lady Byron . . . be soothed and rejoice in the honourable safety of herself and child and all the world be bolder to praise her prudence, my unhappy Allegra furnishing the condemning evidence!" Byron fumed, vented his wrath by saying and writing uncomplimentary things about her, and remained obdurate. He had removed

Allegra from Ravenna for her safety, and none too soon, as events proved.

At the Congress of Leibach in January, the representative diplomats of the European nations, much concerned with the restive state of Italy, determined on the plea of the traitorous King Ferdinand to restore absolute government in Naples by force of Austrian arms. In March an invading army, fifty thousand strong, was sent down into Italy; on the twenty-fourth it entered Naples. Piedmont and Lombardy flared rebellious in a last attempt to maintain freedom, only to be quelled by the armored fist of the Holy Alliance. Absolutism held Italy in its grip, its rigors enforced by courts-martial. Hundreds of conspirators were thrown into prison or transported to Austrian fortresses; and one, Silvio Pellico, poet and patriot, found himself in a dungeon at Spielberg. In Ravenna the *Americani* had perforce to lie low, but the government had its eye upon them. The Englishman at the Palazzo Guiccioli they could not touch; he was beyond their power. But in revenge they exiled Count Ruggiero Gamba and his son Pietro.

Political vicissitudes, however, failed to move Clare, whose heart was taken up only with her child. It had been a bitter winter, with snow deep on the roads. What anguish she suffered whenever she saw a bright fire with children playing about it, and thought of her little Allegra, shivering with the cold in her dismal prison. Shelley, however pained by Clare's torment, could not but see the justice of Lord Byron's measure in sending the little girl to safety. Still, something might be done to avoid much needless pain. Byron, too, evidently thought an interview advisable and requested Shelley to visit him at Ravenna, *alone*. It was not until the beginning of August that Shelley was free to go. From Pisa he rode in an open *calèche* under the summer sun as far as Bologna, not without a spill that sent the rotund coachman rolling down a slope while his own angular figure stuck where it was pitched. From Bologna he took a caravel to Ravenna, where he arrived at ten o'clock the night of August 6.

Byron, as always, was delighted to see him. He took possession of him at once, and the long conversations were renewed

as if they had never suffered interruption, until the sun paled
the light of their lamps and sent them to bed even while the
laborers were starting out for their work in the fields.   There
was indeed much to talk about — the poems they had both
been writing, Allegra, the situation in Italy, the Countess
Guiccioli.   Did Shelley know about the Countess Guiccioli?
And with his usual expansiveness in matters of the heart, Byron
told him of his liaison.   No, the countess was not with him.
Because her family was under an interdict, and because she
had no status now that she was divorced from her politically
unimpeachable papal count, the Guiccioli had been forced to
flee Ravenna.   She was now in Florence, whence she sent
whole flights of sentimental missives to her dearest George,
as she called his lordship.   Shelley was duly shown the letters,
from which he judged that the countess must be a very amiable
woman, an impression which was immediately conveyed to
Mary, to predispose her in the lady's favor.

Then, in the course of the night, a thunderbolt was sprung.
It may be that Byron, on seeing Shelley face to face, so pure,
boyish, and solemn, was conscience-stricken at what he had
been led to believe of him in the previous autumn, and, though
sworn to secrecy, he blurted out the whole of the Hoppner
scandal.   Shelley was aghast, not so much at the vile con-
coction, as at the perfidy of humanity.   He wrote to Mary the
moment he got up next morning, telling her without concealment all he had heard.   *He* could not defend himself, nor
could Clare, who was equally implicated.   It was for Mary,
if she believed him guiltless, to tell the truth.   "As to what
Reviews and the world says, I do not care a jot," he wrote, too
overwrought to be grammatical, "but when persons who have
known me are capable of conceiving me — not that I have
fallen into a great error, as would have been the living with
Claire as my mistress — but that I have committed such unutterable crimes as destroying or abandoning a child, and that
my own!   Imagine my despair of good, imagine how it is
possible that one of so weak and sensitive a nature as mine can
run further the gauntlet through this hellish society of men."

Mary rose nobly to the occasion, in a letter to Mrs. Hoppner,
repudiating the slanders with admirable spirit.   Shelley's in-

nocence was self-evident. As for poor Clare, "You ought to have paused," admonished Mary, "before you tried to convince the father of her child of such unheard atrocities on her part." She demanded a complete retraction from the Hoppners. The letter was consigned by Shelley to Byron, who charged himself with sending it to them with an enclosure of his own — a precaution required by his not having kept the slander from the person whom it most concerned. Mary waited, day after day, for a word from the Hoppners; none ever came. Instead, the magazines got wind of the story and sowed it abroad. Shelley could not contain a bitter reflection. "However cautious the Hoppners have been in preventing the calumniated person from asserting his justification . . . this was the utmost limit of their caution." [1]

The days — or whatever was left of them with the late rising of Lord Byron — passed pleasantly at Ravenna, so pleasantly that Byron began to long for the society of a few choice spirits. The Guiccioli, seconded by Pierino, who was desirous of seeing the world, had been planning a tour to Switzerland as a refuge from Italian persecution. Byron, however, had no desire to move out of Italy, and was inclined to think it rather inconsiderate of his *amica's* family to have got themselves banished. But he could not abandon them now. Besides, Teresa had become a habit too hard to break. He proposed to Shelley, therefore, that he find him a house in Pisa. Shelley wrote to Mary, who began house hunting at once. It must be a large and magnificent place to hold Lord Byron's furniture and contain, safe from one another, dogs, monkeys, cats, an eagle, a crow, a falcon, two guinea hens, and an Egyptian crane —

---

[1] Because Mrs. Shelley's letter was found among Byron's papers after his death, Dowden, Ingpen, and other Shelley biographers would conclude that Byron never sent it. Such perfidy was not in his character. Byron probably sent the letter, — the seal was found broken, — but because it concerned both Shelley and Clare, the mother of his child, he demanded to have it back, an understandable precaution in one who knew Hoppner's ingenuity in scandalous *cookery*. It is obvious that Hoppner never had any liking for Shelley or Clare, or even for Allegra, whom he designates, against the pleasing descriptions of Shelley, Byron, and the prioress of Bagnacavallo, "not by any means an amiable child." (See *Athenæum*, No. 2169, May 22, 1869.) Mrs. Shelley believed the Hoppners guilty, for years later, when she met them again, she cut them dead.

an assemblage which in its present ark had the bad manners of before the flood. There must be room, too, for the numerous Gambas and two households of servants. And for the expected and unexpected guest.

During their nocturnal meetings the two poets had talked of Leigh Hunt, who was in worse straits than ever. Byron renewed his offer of having him join them in Italy, with the added attraction of a new magazine in which they might all collaborate. The association of Byron with any review, Shelley reflected, would immediately make its fortune — a thing which Hunt could use better, almost, than any man except Godwin. Without giving Byron the chance to change his mind, he sent the invitation across the Channel. Leigh Hunt in Pisa — what more delightful prospect?

Light of heart, Shelley went to see Allegra at Bagnacavallo. Who knows but with Byron at Pisa the little one might be taken from her convent and brought to live with her father, for surely he could not leave so young a child alone among strangers. A shy little girl in a white muslin frock, pantalettes, and a black silk pinafore, was brought before Shelley and stared at him, not saying a word until he gave her a basket of sweetmeats and a gold chain he had bought at Ravenna. Then she brightened at once. He hardly recognized Allegra, she had grown so tall. But she was slight and pale, with a ready obedience and an alternating gayety and sadness that troubled him. Was that the romping, headstrong little Commodore, that delicate wisp of a child?

Yet, though altered, Allegra had lost none of her beauty. Her eyes had retained their deep blue, and her mouth, the Byron mouth, was exquisite. Her hair, in large fair curls down her neck, contrasted vividly with the dark braids of her companions. She seemed to Shelley a thing of a finer and higher order. In a little while Allegra remembered him. Then all shyness was lost. Before the amazed nuns, she led him through the convent, showing him her bed, the chair where she sat at dinner, the little cart in which she and her companions drew each other in the garden. Then she opened her basket of sweets and gave her little friends and the nuns a portion before she would eat any. Shelley marveled at the change.

Marveled and was saddened. And there was more to give him pause. That baby of four recited a number of prayers that she knew by heart, and hardly stopped talking of the Bambino and Paradise, telling over a list of saints that staggered the unbeliever.

"The idea of bringing up so sweet a creature in the midst of such trash till sixteen!" he exploded to Mary. Yet in spite of her preoccupation with saints and angels, Allegra showed that she still had a little of the Byronic devil in her. The nuns, who had been ordered to bed to hide from the temptation of the stranger, had nearly all obeyed the summons. Suddenly Allegra began ringing the bell that ordered them to assemble, and it took all the efforts of the prioress to keep them from obeying, in various states of disarray. Perhaps on account of the visitor Allegra was not scolded.

What should he say to her mamma, Shelley asked her on leaving.

"*Che mi manda un bacio e un bel vestituro.*"

"*E come vuoi il vestituro sia fatto?*"

"*Tutto di seta e d'oro.*" [1]

And what should he say to papa, asked Shelley.

"*Che venga farmi un visitino e che porta seco la mammina.*" [2]

Did Shelley give Byron the pathetic little message? Certain it is that Byron did not go to Bagnacavallo, not even when in a big, round, very careful hand that kept rigorously to the ruled pencil lines Allegra wrote him her first letter: "*Caro il mio Pappa* [sic], *Essendo tempo di Fiera desidererei tanto una visita del mio Pappa* [sic] *che ho molte voglie da levarmi; non vorrà compiacere la sua Allegrina che l'ho* [sic] *ama tanto?*" The lonely child asked for the least of joys — only a visit from that dear papa who used to pamper her. They were holding a fair at Bagnacavallo and she had "a lot of whims

---

[1] "That she send me a kiss and a beautiful robe."
"And how do you want the robe made?"
"All of silk and gold."
Vestitura (Shelley misspelled it) means not a dress, as it has always been interpreted with innuendoes on Allegra's vanity, but a ceremonial robe. Her description would fit such a garment. Besides, the child's concern with heavenly things would have made her desire the sort of garment she had seen on the Bambino.

[2] "That he come to see me and bring my dear little mamma."

to get rid of." Would he not oblige his little Allegra who loved him so? On the other side of Allegra's letter, Sister Marianna Fabbri wrote his lordship that the news of his impending departure had been kept from the "little Miss" to spare her pain. Since he had never been to the convent would he not give them all the *consolation* of a visit before he left, to satisfy the yearning of Allegrina? He should then see for himself how the child was cared for "and how well beloved she is for her fine and rare qualities." [1] Byron did not make the visit till the following spring, and only when a sterner voice than a child's longing commanded.

Meanwhile Leigh Hunt, in London, on receiving Shelley's letter inviting him in his name and in Byron's to start out for Pisa, did not wait to be asked twice. The inducements were enormous. "He [Lord Byron] proposes that you should come and go shares with him and me in a periodical work. . . . There can be no doubt that the profits of any scheme in which you and Lord Byron engage, must, from various yet co-operating reasons, be very great." Profits . . . great profits. The words rang a peal of freedom in Hunt's debt-ridden head. In the course of time Marianne had blessed him with a number of small Hunts, so that when the summons to ease and plenty arrived he had six children in tow, all nurtured on the principle of self-determination. Now Shelley, when proffering the invitation, pointedly said nothing about Marianne and the junior clan. But Hunt was too domestic a man to think of engaging on any venture without his family. When, therefore, he prepared to be tempest-tossed, he bade Marianne and the little Hunts to be in readiness as well. Money for the voyage arrived from Italy, and the Hunts prepared to embark in September.

In Pisa the Shelleys, domesticated at the Tre Palazzi with Edward and Jane Williams, looked impatiently for the arrival of their old friends. Just opposite waited the Lanfranchi Palace, engaged as the most suitable dwelling for Byron. September passed, and October. Neither Hunt, from London,

[1] Translated from the original Italian autograph letter at the Pierpont Morgan Library.

nor Byron, from Ravenna, gave any sign of appearing on the scene. Already the Guiccioli, established on an upper floor of the large *palazzo*, was torturing herself with suspicions as to why her dearest George tarried so long. His apartment had been fitted up for him, and every day, for six long weeks, the Arno had been scanned for his boat, and the streets for his carriage. Byron, deep in the mysteries of his lyrical drama, *Heaven and Earth*, on the fallen angels who loved the daughters of men, had no thought for that fair daughter of earth who was pining for his arrival. He enjoyed his bachelor peace and held it the more dear knowing he was so soon to lose it. Reluctantly he left the dismantled palace of the papal count, when he could no longer decently remain, and led his caravan Pisa-ward. Allegra — do not leave Allegra, Shelley reminded him. But Byron set out without her.

Slowly and ponderously the carriage lumbered on the road, across the Apennines. He had no desire to make the journey any faster. In Bologna, for a few minutes as intense as hours, he clasped the hand of Lord Clare, his old school friend, exchanged words that bridged the gulf of years, and parted, having held eternity in a moment of time. This chance meeting on a public road moved him deeply and proved to him how truly lasting were his sincerest affections. The processional went on at its funereal pace. Another chance meeting with Rogers, a risen ghost of the triumphal year, a visit to the Florentine galleries, and then on, to Pisa at last, and the sentimentalities of his *amica*.

November came and went, and still the genial Hunt and his less genial family came not. Had he sailed, or had he, as Fletcher feared, met a watery grave in the Channel? The waters about the Continent had wreaked great mischief that year. Shelley, and now Byron, waited, not knowing what to think. At last they heard that the Hunts had embarked in the middle of November, but the seas, protesting against what the reviews benignly dubbed a tribe of Jonahs, heaved and tossed as if anxious to make an end of every living soul on the brig *Jane*. Marianne, in a shattered state of health, was certain she would never make the voyage alive. And truly there was enough to worry even such an optimist as Hunt. The brig was small and unsteady and seemed dangerously overloaded. Worse, she carried, besides barrels of sugar, a cargo of gunpowder destined for the Greek revolutionists. Marianne, in vexation of mind and body, spat blood and seemed more than once on the point of giving up the ghost. Everything labored against them. At Blackwall a considerate friend had embarked a she-goat, that the young Hunts might enjoy their morning milk. Hardly had the *Jane* sailed than the creature, in her terror, ran dry, and lay disconsolately in a long boat, a caprine picture of misery. The captain, realizing the foolhardiness of going against such infernal weather, took shelter at Ramsgate.

For three luxurious weeks the Hunts stayed with Cowden Clarke, and on the eleventh of December the *Jane* started afresh. Unfortunately, so did the sea. If the brig had been buffeted before, she was now worried helpless in the huge maw of the terrier sea. The captain prayed and swore and confided to his passengers that his hair, once as dark as any man's, had turned white in a shipwreck. Marianne longed for Hampstead, resigning her soul to God each time she saw the cook rummaging with a lighted candle end among the barrels of gunpowder. Soon the waves rose so high that Hunt carried the goat into the cabin, where the wretched beast, unable to find foothold on the slippery floor, carried on a frantic dance. Marianne and the children, sunk in a stupor of exhaustion, heard and saw nothing, not even when an Indiaman nearly bore down upon the ill-omened brig. That was too much for Hunt. When the *Jane* anchored in Dartmouth harbor, he gathered his little Jonahs, more dead than alive, about him and turned their faces toward Plymouth.

Friends were not slow in discovering the *Examiner* martyr in his temporary seclusion, and, ferreting him out with the bait of a silver cup, lured him into society. A new Hampstead flourished in Devonshire, made easeful by the money received from Italy. Hunt thought it best to put a period to his Odyssey — for the present, at any rate. It had been better, perhaps, had he never set sail again. So the superstitious Haydon believed to the end of his days. Hunt was to him

what the Italians call a *jettatore*, an unconscious force for evil.
"Like Scylla, where he comes grass never grows." Keats
had been persecuted for associating with him; Shelley had
received the news of Harriet's suicide after a visit to him;
Byron had met his moral Waterloo; Haydon himself had
suffered in popularity. What mischief were the fates laboring
to avert in turning the sea against him?

The Pisan colony increased. In January of 1822 there arrived at the Tre Palazzi as guest to the Williamses, Edward
John Trelawny, a figure so striking as to draw Mary Shelley
out of an obsessing apathy. "Tired with the everyday sleepiness of human intercourse," she recorded with rare prolixity, "I
am glad to meet with one who . . . has the . . . merit of
interesting my imagination." Certainly nothing approaching
everyday sleepiness clung about the straight, dark, sinewy
personage who blustered into Pisa, a phenomenon as "terrible
and lovely as a tempest." By blood Trelawny was a Cornish-
man. In appearance he was Byron's Conrad redivivus. His
grey eyes had the piercing look of an eagle's; his strong forehead and nose gave him the profile of a bird of prey. Though
he was not yet thirty, he wore moustachios of prodigious
thickness, and his hair and beard of curly black wrapped the
vivid face as in a cloud broken through by the light of a keen
intelligence. Not only physically did he resemble the Corsair.
Fiercely independent even as a boy, he had run away to sea
at the age of eleven, missing the battle of Trafalgar by a few
hours. From then on he had traveled the four corners of the
earth, accumulating adventures and wives till he lost count.
The Mrs. Trelawnys, however, he suffered in no way to
restrict his mobility. He left them as readily as he found
them, usually with a living memento of himself to assure them
that it had been no dream, and resumed his carefree pirate
way. Impulse, not reason, he boasted, guided his life. Mary
found herself studying this incarnated denial of her father's
theories, and, in spite of her judgment, admired. A woman
must have someone to interest her imagination when her
Elfin Knight [1] proved errant.

Byron's fame had lured Trelawny to Pisa, but when he ar-

[1] Mary's pet name for Shelley.

rived he found, to his surprise, his idol outshone by an unexpected light, whose influence, even after the light itself had
faded, was to endure through a long, checkered life. The
night of his arrival he was sitting in the Williamses' parlor
talking over old times when he saw in a dark passage a pair
of glittering eyes fixed intently on his. Jane noticed his
startled face and, following his look, she said, going to the
doorway, "Come in, Shelley. It's only our friend Tre just
arrived." Trelawny had long known of the atheist Shelley,
had read his books and had questioned the oracle Wordsworth.
He was not prepared, therefore, to see, instead of the awe-in-
spiring figure he had anticipated, a tall, thin stripling, gliding
in blushing like a girl and holding out both hands in greeting.
Ariel met Caliban and made him his slave. The first moments
devoted to the social amenities troubled the youth, till Jane
asked him what book he had in his hand. At once Ariel's face
brightened. It was Calderón's *Magico Prodigioso* — and,
waving his enchanter's wand, Shelley transformed the four
walls of the room to a palace of dreams. The spellbound
Caliban forgot everything in the vision and was called to
reality only by a sense of emptiness. "Where is he?" he
asked, waking from the dream. "Who, Shelley?" asked Jane.
"Oh, he comes and goes like a spirit, no one knows when or
where."

Yet the wings of that spirit were weighed down. He was
discouraged with his work, disappointed in his friendship with
Byron, whose ruthlessness in matters of ordinary human behavior shook his confidence in man's inherent nobility. What
could one expect from common men if the sublimest spirits
failed? "Space wondered less at the swift and fair creations of
God, when he grew weary of vacancy, than I at this spirit of an
angel in the mortal paradise of a decaying body," he wrote of
Byron. Yet greater even than his admiration was his sense of
Byron's deficiency. An insurmountable barrier had always
divided them, which in the intimacy of their relations rose
more forbidding. The two men might discuss their work or
go out riding together, living outwardly in a genial companionship. Their noblest aims kept them apart.

As a poet Byron had been overwhelmed with success, and for the past ten years no name had rivaled his in popularity. Shelley, for the appreciative notice he received, might never have written a line. Beside Byron he lost the self-confidence that had spurred him on, and wrote hardly at all. Was not Byron doing work that none might hope to surpass? His Biblical mystery, *Cain,* had no peer for grandeur. Every word of the as yet unpublished cantos of *Don Juan* was stamped with immortality, fulfilling what Shelley had long hoped to do — "something wholly new and relative to the age, and yet surpassingly beautiful." What had he written? *Hellas,* a tribute to the Greek revolution, an unequal work, though one of his best for lyric beauty. But people hoped for more than inspired lyricism. With dimming zeal he dedicated it to Mary's friend, Prince Mavrocordato, who had left Pisa to win the solider laurels of the battlefield, and gave himself up to Misery, his woeful bride. Would he write more? "I have lived too long with Lord Byron, and the sun has extinguished my glow-worm."

Byron, on his part, had no such certainty of his own superiority. "Shelley has more poetry in him than any man living," he would say, and so valued his criticism that a word from the Snake, as he playfully called him, sufficed to change his opinion. While at Pisa he had been writing *The Deformed Transformed,* a Faustian drama in which, after lifelong struggle, he rid himself of the complex of his deformity. "Tell me what you think of it," he said to Shelley, giving him the play to read. Shelley read the manuscript attentively. "Well, how do you like it?" asked Byron. "Least of anything I ever saw of yours. It is a bad imitation of *Faust,* and besides, there are two entire lines of Southey's in it." Byron flushed and instantly threw the manuscript into the fire. Medwin, who was present, gasped at the holocaust, but was reassured to see the play, several years later, in print. For Byron was very tender of the children of his brain.

Trelawny, observing the two poets, asked Byron pointedly why he seemed afraid to couple his name publicly with Shelley's and would never write anything about him. "Some of

his best verses are to express his admiration of your genius."
"Ay, who reads them?" retorted Byron. "If we puffed the
Snake it might not turn out a profitable investment. If he
cast off the slough of his mystifying metaphysics, he would
want no puffing."

As it was, his friends in London were sending Byron
trepidant warnings about the proposed magazine with Hunt
and Shelley. *"Alone* you may do anything," Moore wrote,
"but partnerships in fame, like those in trade, make the strongest party answerable . . . and I tremble even for *you* with
such a bankrupt company."

The winter passed. Behind the Lanfranchi Palace the
orange trees were putting on the new bloom of spring, while
on the river's margin the sleeping wildflowers revived. Byron
was seen again taking his morning walk with Teresa, all in
white, in the palace grounds. Fletcher reflourished with a
new crop of hair amid his thinning grey locks. In the afternoon the Guiccioli called in her carriage for Mary and Jane,
while the men took their horses to a neighboring vineyard
for target practice, relieving the tyranny of words by talking
a barbaric language, neither English nor Italian. Pierino
Gamba, as much in love as his sister with his lordship, had become a trusty Achates, following him everywhere. Trelawny,
flashing his eagle eyes from his fallen idol to Ariel, gathered
impressions for posterity.

Not only was there no sympathy between Trelawny and
Byron, but a peculiar jealousy existed which soon developed
on Trelawny's side to dislike. A poet should be a poet, like
Shelley, and had no business swimming the Hellespont and
indulging in other spectacular feats which should remain the
province of an adventurer like himself. He took Byron up on
everything. If he demonstrated his skill in shooting, Trelawny must show that he could do as well, and never forgave
Byron when he failed. He challenged the poet to a swimming contest in which he claimed he came out the victor. In
rebuttal Byron remarked in company that if Trelawny could
be made to wash his hands and tell the truth, he might yet
be a gentleman. Trelawny stored the words in his vindic-

tive pirate mind, while outwardly he continued the friend.

As the weather grew fairer and the sea, seen from the high windows of Shelley's apartment, lured him, he longed for a boat in which, between wave and cloud, he might forget the pains of the world in the solitude where alone lay peace. Trelawny knew Captain Roberts of Genoa, who, he said, could build any boat from specifications, and undertook Shelley's charge, offering, with Edward Williams, to share the expense. Byron, not to be outdone, ordered a large decked schooner, and the shipbuilding got under way. Byron, indeed, could well afford to suspend his lordly vice of hoarding. With the death of Lady Noël the Wentworth estate was equally divided between Lord and Lady Byron, so that by 1822 his income alone exceeded seven thousand pounds a year. Financially, at least, his marriage had been no mistake.

At Genoa Captain Roberts executed his commissions. Lord Byron's *Bolivar* was the admiration of all who saw her, — a large, rigged schooner, too pretentious, perhaps, — but, as Lady Blessington was to remark when she met his lordship, he liked his belongings to show what they cost. And the *Bolivar* was an expensive vessel. Shelley's cockleshell had given the shipbuilder pause. Trelawny had advised building the boat from a model of an American schooner that he had in his possession. Williams, on the other hand, insisted on a sloop copied from plans he had obtained from a royal navy yard in England. They decided finally upon a graceful boat, twenty-one by eight feet, without a deck, but, to make up for that deficiency, with a splendor of sails. In honor of Byron it was to be called the *Don Juan*.

However, while the boats were a-building to seal a friendship, that friendship itself was going on the rocks with Clare again at the helm. Troubled with forebodings that she should see her child no more, she devised a fantastic plan of kidnaping her from Bagnacavallo and carrying her off to America. Shelley must help her, and Mary. It was the last resort of a woman crazed with frustrated mother love. Shelley reasoned with her, to bring her to her senses. He could not in any case make himself a party to a forged letter, as she suggested, to release Allegra from her convent. It would only mean a duel. Besides, Lord Byron, scenting a plot, was obstinate and awake about the child. In vain Shelley endeavored to make him see that it would be better for Allegra if she were transferred from that unwholesome place. Suspicious of his zeal for Clare, Byron remained obdurate. Allegra was happy at Bagnacavallo, he declared, and there she should remain.

Mary added her persuasions to Shelley's to make Clare give up her mad plan. Byron, she informed her, spoke of returning to England. With him at a distance it would be easier to effect what Clare sought. At present it was impossible; nothing moved him except to exasperation, when he would threaten that if Clare annoyed him further he would place Allegra in a secret convent where none might see her. Now was not the moment for desperate measures. "Spring is our unlucky season," the daughter of Reason cautioned, enumerating a catalogue of woes, from deaths to platonic episodes, that would have staggered one less impressionable than Clare. "Now the aspect of the Autumnal Heavens has on the contrary been with few exceptions, favorable to us. What think you of this?"

Clare had little time to ponder the question. When next she had definite news of Allegra it was to learn that she was dead. An epidemic of typhus, rising from the miasmic swamps about Ravenna, had spread to Bagnacavallo, attacking the nuns and their unprotected wards. A messenger sent to Byron to warn him of Allegra's danger arrived in time for his lordship to have hastened to the child. He waited, hoping for a notice of her improvement. The next message told him of her death. And then he paid Allegra the visit she had begged of him through Shelley, and in the painstaking little note which he had dismissed as a request for "paternal gingerbread." For the first time he saw part of himself, a Byron, dead, and as never in life he made the little corpse enter into, and share, his own childhood's dreams.

He sent the body to England to be buried in Harrow Church, where, on Peachey's tomb, another Byron, long dead, had thought on life and immortality. The churchwardens, how-

ever, would not receive within the holy precincts the body of a
bastard child; nor would they admit the marble tablet which
Byron had designed to keep alive her memory. In the little
green churchyard near the door, Allegra was buried with
nothing but a rose tree to mark her grave. Even there she was
to give displeasure. Lady Byron, who trailed like a ghost the
places linked with Byron, murmured at having his natural
child buried so near the door. But the little body was not
suffered to be disturbed, and to this day, with every passing
spring, the turf is covered with a rain of flowers.

Clare resigned herself to the inevitable. She begged only
a lock of hair from the head of the child who had been hers
so brief a time, and gathered up the wreckage of her life to
build anew. The Shelleys, with their friends, had taken a
house on the Gulf of Spezia for the summer. Clare would
stay with them till she had the strength to stand alone, and
then — she made no plans for the future. One could only
hope.

While the Shelleys were moving from the Tre Palazzi,
rendered odious by the nearness to Byron's palace, Leigh
Hunt with his family set sail for Italy on the *David Walter*,
saluted by the farewell shots of his *Blackwood* enemies whom
neither time nor death had propitiated. The beautiful
Leopard and the Scorpion probably joined forces in their
classical leave-taking, written for the occasion in what purported to be Italian.

Signor Le Hunto, gloria di Coccagna
 — Chi scrive il poema della Rimini,
  Che tutta apparenza ha, per Gemini,
D'esser cantato sopra la montagna
Di bel Ludgato, o nella campagna
  D'Amsted, o sulle marge Serpentimini
  Com'esta Don Giovanni d'Endymini
Il gran poeta d'Ipecacuanha?
Tu sei il Re del Cocknio Parnasso
 Ed egli il herede appanente,
  Tu sei un gran Giacasso ciertamente,
Ed egli ciertamente gran Giacasso!

Tu sei il Signor del Examinero
Ed Egli soave Signor del Glystero.[1]

[1] This macaronic production, a mixture of Spanish and Italian, appeared as the composition of Fudgiolo in the "Noctes Ambrosianae" No. 1 of *Blackwood's* for March 1822. For the benefit of those who would otherwise lose this bit of Wilsoniana, the author appends her translation.

Signor Leigh Hunt, thou glory of Cockaigne,
    That writ the poesie of her of Rimini,
    The which, I ween, sounds every bit by Gemini,
As it were sung from Ludgate's height amain
Or from the greening Hampstead's fair champaign,
    Or from along the marge of Serpentimini, —
    How fares it with Don Juan of Endymini,
The sovereign bard of Ipecacuaigne?
Thou art the King of Cockneydom's Parnasse,
    He verily is the apparent heir,
Thou art, no doubt, a great Jackass, I swear,
And eke thy friend, a sovereign great Jackass.
    Thou art the Lord of the Examinère
    And he 's the gentle Knight of the Glystère.

XXVIII

WHERE THE ETERNAL ARE

LIKE a fortress hewn out of the rock by the toil of the sea, Casa Magni stood partly in the waves and partly against the mountains, a rugged grey-white house whose grotto-like arches were crusted deep with the dried salt spray. A semicircle of rocks enclosed the small bay on the one hand. On the other the village of San Terenzo lifted its campanile over the church dome of the patron saint and the huddle of tall, narrow houses. Behind, rising gradually to the cloudy distances, the hills overgrown with the dense green of ilex and pine on their gentler slopes lifted rocky heads to the sky. On the east the tower of Lerici landlocked the greater bay. Portovenere on the opposite point flung its arm across the sea. Nothing more desolately beautiful could have been imagined than the site of Casa Magni. A halcyon rest, it seemed hardly of the earth, so close was it to the water. One walking on the terrace would catch the spray on face and hair. On stormy nights the booming of the surf echoed through the stone chambers, making the whole house vibrate like a buoy. Shelley loved the place. What if it contained only four habitable rooms and its only washbasin was the sea? He insisted upon renting it, and when Williams and Jane could find nothing for themselves in the vicinity, he took them in.

What accommodations were made for five adults — Clare joined them later — and three children, with nursemaids and housekeepers, still remains a mystery which Mary failed to elucidate in a plan which she sent to a friend. A large dining hall took up the centre of the house. Two bedrooms opened from it on the right, and one on the left, facing the sea. Of the two rooms on the right, one, with windows opening on the terrace, was Shelley's. The other, looking toward the hills, the Williamses'. Across the dining hall Mary and the baby occupied the other room. A primitive kitchen was shared by the two households, an unsatisfactory arrangement at best, but one that made for teapot tempests when Jane, an angel with the harp, turned vixen in those domestic precincts.

Mary hated Casa Magni from the moment she crossed its threshold. The solitariness, the awful beauty of the hills and sea, the mysterious lights playing upon the waves at night from the gloomy shores, overcame her with a sense of impending evil that she could not shake off. She was again pregnant, a condition that always aggravated her natural melancholy, now intensified by Shelley's marked attentions to Jane Williams. In Jane alone he seemed to find respite from a profound spiritual anguish. Only Jane could cure the spasms from which he suffered. When her hand was on his brow, then alone the tormented features relaxed, as if from her fingers flowed the vital forces necessary to his existence. Again and again she was called upon to *magnetize* him into sleep.

The cleavage between Shelley and Mary had widened, more and more since the Emilia episode. For the first time perhaps, with the Italian girl, he had experienced the passionate warmth of a woman's nature, and it had brought home to him Mary's lack. She was cold, though devoted. Years later, when in barren widowhood she sublimated those scenes of pain in transparent fictions, she had to avow that she had been to Shelley only as snow against Emilia's fire. But while she was living with Shelley she had no sense but that of his apparent disloyalty.

As for Shelley, his nervous system was keyed to the breaking point. Every emotion, every passing sensation, touched chords whose feeblest vibrancy caused him agonies of physical suffering. Pleasure and pain alike struck those chords, and in his state of nervous receptivity every moment brought its pangs. The sight of a flower, the hearing of music, touched abnormally wakened senses, making the flower larger and more bright, the song unbearably sweet. To keep his mind occupied between the pauses of *Charles the First,* the new tragedy he had begun, he translated passages from Calderón and the

Walpurgisnacht scenes from *Faust*. They were the food his imagination craved.

By some chance he fell upon a book of etchings by Retzsch, illustrating some of the most striking parts of the Goethian drama. Before the picture of Faust and Marguerite embracing in the summerhouse, Shelley felt himself overpowered with desire. "The artist makes one envy his happiness," he wrote, "that he can sketch such things with calmness, which I only dared look upon once, and which made my brain swim round only to touch the leaf on the opposite side of which I knew that it was figured. . . . The etching certainly excited me far more than the poem it illustrated." He was overwrought with unsatisfied longing, longing which Mary could not, and Jane would not fulfill: her love for Edward and Shelley's friendship stood between.

> . . . What would do
> You good when suffering and awake?
> What cure your head and side?

he had the Magnetic Lady ask him. And he answered explicitly: "What would cure, that would kill me, Jane."

Yet that cure that kills he desired above all things. In vain he reasoned with himself in those all-revealing personal lyrics that

> When hearts have once mingled
> Love first leaves the well-built nest.

Such had been his experience with Harriet, with Mary, but always love held out the promise that in the next essay it would dwell forever. He idealized Jane, seeing in her what his infatuate fancy would have him see: the true personification at last of the Ideal Beauty. All that had come before had been but a reflection of that orb of light. Now the star itself was shining. And in her light he sang, a thorn-pricked nightingale. *To Jane: the Invitation, To Jane: the Recollection* — poem after poem he consecrated to the hours spent with her, or the thought of her.

And Jane? She accepted the tribute of his worship, seeing no difference between it and the admiration of others but that this love came accompanied by poems whose flattery she could not miss, and by gifts delicately bestowed.

> Ariel to Miranda: — Take
> This slave of Music, for the sake
> Of him, who is the slave of thee,
> And teach it all the harmony
> In which thou canst, and only thou,
> Make the delighted spirit glow,
> Till joy denies itself again,
> And, too intense, is turned to pain. . . .

The verses had come with a guitar. One need not know the exact significance of the names of Ariel and Miranda to sense the exquisite compliment. Jane accepted it.

Late Sunday afternoon, the twelfth of May, 1822, all the inhabitants of Casa Magni were looking out toward Porto-venere, where, with sails in the breeze, a small schooner-rigged craft was rounding the cape. Was it, could it be? — Shelley and Williams looked at each other. It seemed too large, too handsome a vessel for the *Don Juan*. Perhaps it was Lord Byron's boat being sent them by mistake. But no, when it drew near enough for them to see, they could read the name *Don Juan* on the mainsail. Shelley could scarcely contain his desire to board her. There was no further question of joint ownership. Shelley paid the price of eighty pounds, and the boat became his property.

Trelawny looked the *Don Juan* over. She was fast, and strongly built. According to Mr. Heslop and the two English sailors who brought her, she had already weathered her first storm. But she was crank in a breeze, Trelawny remarked, and needed, moreover, two tons of pig-iron ballast to bring her down to her bearings. She looked, for all the world, like a great rigged nutshell with a kernel of metal. But Shelley and Williams would have no murmur against her. In their estimation she was the finest craft that sailed the Tyrrhenian seas. "I find she fetches whatever she looks at," Williams defended her. One thing alone displeased them — the swashbuckling name on the mainsail. It grew every hour more hateful. Byron or no Byron, they would rechristen the boat the *Ariel*, and at once got busy with knives and turpentine to scrape off the offending letters. Captain Roberts had done too thorough a job; or perhaps the demonic spirit of the Don undid at night what they accomplished by day. For nearly three weeks Shelley and Williams employed spirits of wine and all known paint eradicators to cleanse their sail. They had finally to have the piece cut out by a sailmaker and the new name set in.

There was no staying at home now. From dawn to dusk the two friends were on board the *Ariel,* driving Trelawny to distraction with their eccentric seamanship. Williams, as a practical sailor, took it upon himself to teach Shelley the secrets of the sea — how to steer, when to hoist sail and make himself useful. Shelley, as usual with a book in his hand, let the *Ariel* take care of herself while he communed with the elements and divine philosophy. Useless for Trelawny to tell him to throw his books overboard if he would be a sailor. Shelley insisted that he could both steer and read at the same time.

Williams was not so deficient as Trelawny had thought, though he wanted practice and was consequently slow in an emergency. However, they kept Charles Vivian, one of the English lads who had accompanied the boat, to help manage her. Still, Trelawny would have felt greater security if Shelley had known how to swim. But there was no teaching him. How could one teach a man wholly devoid of the instinct of self-preservation? One day, in a deep pool of the Arno, Trelawny had been exhibiting his prowess. "Why can't I swim?" Shelley had asked. "It seems so easy." Trelawny, seizing the opportunity, had told him what to do. Removing his jacket and trousers, and kicking off his shoes, Shelley dived in. A minute later Trelawny had seen him lying stretched out at the bottom, making no move to save himself. "I always find the bottom of a well," he said when Trelawny had fished him out, "and they say truth lies there. In another minute I should have found it."

To help the women reach the *Ariel* dry-shod, Williams, with the help of a carpenter, built a long frail shell of a dingey made of the wood that the Italians used for their sieves. It was so light that one person could carry it from the beach into the ground-floor storage room of Casa Magni. Shelley was almost as delighted with it as with the *Ariel,* and when not sailing on the bay he could be seen paddling about in the dingey, always with his book, as unconscious of danger as if he were resting on a grassy bank. The old sailors of San Terenzo shook their heads at the rashness of the mad Englishman and uttered dark sayings in their incomprehensible dialect.

Once on the sea Shelley regained his creative confidence. However, the drama of *Charles the First* had gone but poorly; he had not the heart to proceed with it. What had he to do with the mundane affairs of men? The mystifying metaphysics so deplored of Byron unwound their mystic scrolls before him. Discarding the tragedy, he began the *Triumph of Life,* a poem wherein again he questioned the pageant of existence for its meaning. One by one the driving forces of humanity passed him, a Dantean processional, with man everywhere in chains. Aboard the *Ariel,* with only the secret elements to witness, he interrogated the spirits of the mighty dead to solve the riddle of life as long ago the eager boy had sought to unseal the mysteries beyond death. Would man ever be free? Or was freedom only an illusion? Would the day ever dawn on the mortal world to find man perfect at last?

Back at Casa Magni he was taught the oft-repeated lesson that even the best are but faulty creatures. Jane and Mary disputed the right over the saucepans, whose sole monopoly Jane wished to enjoy. "It is a pity that anyone so pretty should be so selfish," he sighed. But when on a starlight night the bay was a moving crucible of emerald and silver, and Jane on the terrace sang to her guitar, accompanied by the lapping of the waves and the keen, low cry of the aziola in the pine woods, Shelley found himself translated to the paradise he was ever seeking; and with her as its goddess he realized moments of happiness. In her singing he forgot even the coldness of Mary and the dying embers of the spent hearth, as he longed only that the music go on, on till he was made part of it.

Though the sound overpowers,
Sing again, with your dear voice revealing
A tone
Of some world far from ours,
Where music and moonlight and feeling
Are one.

Mary, indescribably wretched, made "scenes." She was not well. The solitary location of the house, the long mysterious nights filled with the restless sea and the frightening noises of the woods, the festive howling of the half-barbaric inhabitants of San Terenzo, dancing on the waves in a weird ceremonial, the lack of common comfort, Shelley's attentions to Jane, everything produced a state akin to melancholia. She suffered more than ever from her pregnancy, and finally she had a severe miscarriage. For hours she fell from one swoon into another, and lost so much blood that Shelley feared she would die before the physician arrived. With a presence of mind that would have astonished those who mistakenly looked upon him as a visionary, he had Mary sit on ice until he succeeded in checking the hemorrhage, so that when the doctor came Mary was out of danger, though so feeble that for weeks she had to lie in bed, nursed by Clare, who had been hastily summoned from Florence.

Everyone at Casa Magni lived as under an evil spell. The air itself was accursed. Whether the close association of so many people in a house too small for them made for the wear and tear of their nerves, or whether the surroundings themselves, from their strangely affecting beauty, wrought too strongly upon their imaginations, they were, one and all, afflicted with visions and forebodings that made their days a nightmare. Shelley, the most sensitive, was also the most susceptible. One night, while with Williams on the terrace, he suddenly clutched his arm, crying as he pointed toward the sea in a shimmer of moonlight, "There it is again — there!" He had seen Allegra, naked, rising from the waves, clapping her hands and laughingly beckoning to him to join her. Williams could see nothing. Nevertheless he was shaken to see Shelley so unnerved.

Not only the ghosts of the dead, but living doubles walked

the earth.   Jane several times had had a vision of Shelley's other self passing her window, when she and everyone else knew that he had gone to Lerici with Williams.   Again, his phantom was seen to enter a little wood near by, while his body was elsewhere.   And Jane dreamed that he was dead.

Then one midnight the house was startled by Mary's screams, as she ran from her room across to Jane's, and fell in a faint at the door, while Shelley, in a trance of horror, stood over her with a lighted candle in his hand.   He had had a frightful dream — that Williams and Jane had drowned and their spectres, hung about with seaweed, had appeared to him. Soon after, in the shifting of the vision, he saw himself strangling Mary, and then, following a cloaked figure that had come to his bedside, he had beheld in the cowled phantom's features — his own!   "Are you satisfied?" it hissed, as it vanished.

It needed no Joseph to fathom the symbolism of that dream. Interpret it as one would, death was the key — Edward's, or Jane's, or Mary's, or his own.   Then, perhaps, that complex of emotions might be unraveled.   Death, someone's death. The lore of dreams pointed to his own.   Was it not death to meet one's phantom face to face?

And the thought never left him.   Why go on living?   Had he not, in his intense life, lived to be older than his father? Increase of years gave only increase of disillusion.   Where dwelt the beauty he thought so often to have found?   Not on earth.   Harriet Grove, the other Harriet, the Boinvilles, Mary, Emilia, and now Jane — what had he loved in them? He dared to answer in a burst of truthful scorn: —

> I loved — oh, no, I mean not one of ye,
>   Or any earthly one, though ye are dear
> As human heart to human heart may be; —
>   I loved, I know not what — but this low sphere
> And all that it contains, contains not thee,
>   Thou, whom, seen nowhere, I feel everywhere.

On June 18 he made a strange request in a letter to Trelawny.   "Should you meet with any scientific person, capable of preparing the *Prussic Acid, or essential oil of bitter almonds,*

I should regard it as a great kindness if you could procure me a small quantity. . . . I would give any price for this medicine; you remember we talked of it the other night, and we both expressed a wish to possess it; my wish was serious, and sprung from the desire of avoiding needless suffering. I need not tell you I have no intention of suicide at present, but I confess it would be a comfort to me to hold in my possession that golden key to the chamber of perpetual rest." That same day, in writing to John Gisborne, he pointed to the rift in his relations with Mary. "I only feel the want of those who can feel, and understand me. Whether from proximity and the continuity of domestic intercourse, Mary does not. The necessity of concealing from her thoughts that would pain her, necessitates this, perhaps. It is the curse of Tantalus that a person possessing such excellent powers and so pure a mind as hers, should not excite the sympathy indispensable to their application to domestic life." Shelley, unlike Byron, never took the world into his confidence in his personal experiences except in the transmutation of poetry. That he could complain so unreservedly to Gisborne argued a grave state of affairs. "Love is not akin to jealousy," he burst out with flashing eyes one day as he and Trelawny were walking together. "Love does not seek its own pleasure but the happiness of another. Jealousy is gross selfishness!"

Never careful of his personal safety, he now went out in search of danger. Jane was sitting one evening on the sand in front of Casa Magni waiting for her husband, when Shelley came out, carrying the dingey. "Come with me," he invited. Jane got in with her two babies, and Shelley followed, crouching at the bottom of the boat. Soon he was paddling away from the shore, round a jutting height of rock, to deep water. Jane looked uneasily about her. She could see no sail within a mile, and still he went into deeper water. She turned to him to urge him back, when to her terror she found him resting on his oars, his eyes staring into vacancy. Fearful of upsetting the boat by a sudden movement, she said nothing, waiting for him to come out of his abstraction. He spoke after what seemed an eternity of suspense: "Now let us together solve the great mystery." Jane knew him well. Let her but enter into his mood and they should all be lost. Instead, she laughed in amusement she did not feel, and said prosaically: "No, thank you, not now. I should like my dinner first, and so would the children." Her words brought him back from the ideal to what must have been a shocking reality. He paddled back without a word.

The June days passed, no fair, temperate days as in the North, but excessively sultry. The sun beat down upon the fields with such ardor that each blade of grass was as a flame. The sea gave off metallic lambencies — one might have said the sparks of its own heat. For weeks not a cloud had passed across the sky; no drop of moisture had fallen upon the earth, parched and cracked in a thousand thirsty mouths. Everywhere the brooks had run dry. The fields of corn looked as if a fire had swept them. In the villages round about Lerici special Masses were said for rain, and the relics of the patron saints were carried through the streets. But the heavens remained cloudless, a cupola of fiery gold.

And while, as it were, the earth held its breath, tidings came to the Shelleys that Leigh Hunt had landed in Genoa. From there he was going to Leghorn, to see Lord Byron, who was summering hard by, and for Leghorn Shelley and Williams, with the boy Vivian, set out on the *Ariel* the first day of July. A fresh breeze was blowing. Mary, just risen from her sickbed, crawled out on the terrace to see them off. As the sails swelled in the wind and the *Ariel* quivered eagerly in all her timbers, Mary felt herself sinking under a sense of dread. "Shelley!" she called weakly. "Shelley!" But the sound of the breeze through the sails drowned her voice. Out of the sheltered bay, beyond Portovenere, she watched the *Ariel's* sail, until she could see it no more. Somehow she wished that Shelley had not gone, and she wept.

On the voyage from Genoa to Leghorn the gods sent their omens to Leigh Hunt, when out of an evening sky of slumbering peace there suddenly darted lances of lightning, and rockets that fell, amid a roar of thunder, into the sea, almost on the spot where only a week later — But the gods deemed their warning sufficient. Though awed by this display of heavenly fireworks, Hunt reached Leghorn without mishap and placed

himself in the hands of Trelawny, whose aspect, had not the
thoughtful Shelley described him in advance as a wild but
kind-hearted seaman, would have made Libertas think twice
before entrusting him with the invalid Marianne and their six
"little souls."

At Monte Nero, where Byron was "villaging" with the
Gambas, Hunt found the celestial fireworks rivaled by some
of earthly make.   The whole household was in an uproar, the
servants screaming, the Countess Guiccioli flushed, with her
hair scattered like a fury's, Count Pietro, his arm in a sling,
vociferating, and Byron, grown so fat that Hunt hardly recognized him, trying in vain to make the peace, while at the
gate a terrible, red-capped ruffian, evidently the cause of the
mischief, was glaring tigerlike about him, daring anyone to
approach.   It seemed there had been a quarrel among the
servants.   Knives were drawn, and Pierino, on meddling in
the fray, had been gashed in the arm — a trivial wound, but
it drew blood, and everyone saw red.   As it was, the peren-
nially exiled Gambas were only on sufferance at Monte Nero.
The least disturbance, and who knows where they should
have to go next — perhaps to South America.

Certainly it was no auspicious welcome to a man who had
had to make three embarkations to reach the land of promise.
Byron, though glad to see him, spoke lukewarmly of the *Liberal* project.   He seemed, in fact, reluctant to part with any
more of his hoard to one who had only a deficit of sixty
crowns to show for the original loan of four hundred pounds.
Here was indeed a merry grasshopper who had sung away his
provisions in Plymouth and now came breezily for more!
Byron would willingly have given him the proverbial answer
— *"Eh, bien! dansez maintenant!"*   But Shelley, like an incarnate conscience, arrived that night, exacted Byron's promise
that he would help support both the *Liberal* and Libertas, and
whisked Hunt off to Pisa.

The ground-floor apartment of the Palazzo Lanfranchi had
been ready half a year for its tenants, but when they came
they were disappointed.   Instead of a Hampstead studio-
museum transplanted to Italy, they discovered a sprawling
flat whose barred windows had more the air of Newgate, fitted

up with furnishings that Marianne found decidedly mean. Was that the best his lordship could do? And was n't it considered very plebeian in Italy to live on the ground floor? They looked meaningfully up the grand staircase from where they caught glimpses of Byron's lavish furnishings, and thought their thoughts. Marianne was sure she would be miserable in Italy.

Shelley, in excellent spirits away from the depressing influences of Casa Magni, spent several days in Pisa, showing Hunt the places of interest. Never had he looked so much like a spirit walking the earth in mortal shape. In his presence Hunt found his cares magically fallen off, and it was with regret that he saw him go. Before they parted he gave Shelley a copy of Keats's last volume to read on the voyage home. "Keep it till you give it to me with your own hands," he said. Shelley got into the post chaise, and in the darkness drove off to Leghorn, where Williams, anxious to return to Jane, was impatiently waiting. Shelley had written her that same day a note touched with foreboding. "How soon those hours passed, and how slowly they return to pass so soon again, perhaps for ever, in which we have lived together so intimately, so happily! Adieu, my dearest friend!" At Leghorn he went to see a notary about his will, and on Monday, the eighth of July, at noon, he, Williams, and the boy Vivian were on board the *Ariel*, ready to sail.

Captain Roberts gazed diffidently on the horizon, darkening with lines and blots of cloud, and shook his head. It portended a storm, he said. The sea, unrefreshed through the long drought, looked like a rotting thing, sluggish as lead and covered with an oily scum. A gathering breeze hardly stirred it. But Shelley and Williams would be off, and between one and two o'clock the *Ariel*, together with two Italian feluccas, left the port at a good speed. Trelawny, prevented by the port authorities from following with the *Bolivar*, watched her receding, as he listened to the sailors talking among themselves. "Look at those clouds. . . . See how the water smokes!"

Climbing to the lighthouse tower, Captain Roberts saw with dread the approaching tempest. Huge drops of rain began to fall, hitting the oily scum and rebounding as from a solid surface. He could see in the distance the *Ariel's* mainsail being lowered. Then, like a curtain, the denseness of the storm hid her from the lenses of his glass. For twenty minutes thunder and lightning clove the skies. The rain fell in sheets. When again the sea fog lifted, the *Ariel* was nowhere in sight. Perhaps she had made Viareggio before the storm broke, and was lying in harbor. Yet it was strange that the other vessels should be there, all of them that Roberts had seen — and not the *Ariel*.

At Casa Magni the women waited. There, too, the storm had broken with great violence, lasting the night, but Tuesday dawned calm in spite of rain, and the sea, a fearful monster but a few hours since, came fawning on the shores. Their men could not have sailed yesterday. They had started early that peaceful morning. And like generations of seamen's wives who had stood upon those sands scanning the horizon for the familiar sail, Mary and Jane watched for the *Ariel*. She did not come that day, nor the day following. Every sail that entered the bay looked to their strained sight like the one they sought. She would arrive to-morrow. Shelley had not seen Hunt for so long. . . . There was so much they had to do and see. Then Friday's post brought a letter from Hunt addressed to Shelley. With trembling fingers Mary broke the seal. "Pray, tell us how you got home," she read, "for they say that you had bad weather after you sailed Monday. . . ."

Monday. They had sailed during the storm. The two women dared not look into each other's eyes, for that moment they knew.

But they would not betray their fears. Immediately they took a boat and crossed to Lerici, inquiring everywhere. None there had heard of any shipwreck. They posted to Pisa, where Trelawny had gone before them on the same errand. No news. Ah, yes — the dingey and the water cask belonging to the *Ariel* had been found off Viareggio. The little boat had been thrown overboard, perhaps, in the storm — but the cask . . . Dumb with despair, the two women returned to Casa Magni. The village of San Terenzo, in thanksgiving for the rain that had come, was lighted up for a festa and, nightlong, men, women, and children gathered on the sands, performing their barbaric ritual, running into the waves and back again, yelling a strange wild song to the sea's moaning.

Trelawny, indefatigable, wandered from town to town, inquiring of the authorities if any bodies had been found. He could no longer hope. Then, on July 18, he was sent for by the counselor of state in the Duchy of Lucca. The sea, wild and rough that day, had washed a body ashore off Viareggio. Trelawny viewed it, and as he looked at the poor wreck, battered by the waves and devoured by the fish, he could hardly believe it had once belonged to Shelley, whose spirit eyes from the first had captured his soul. The face and hands were fleshless, but the corpse could still — too surely — be identified. In one pocket of the double-breasted schoolboy jacket Keats's last volume, doubled back at the *Eve of St. Agnes,* was found as if hastily put away at the page he had been reading when death came; in the other, Sophocles. Three miles south, near the Tower of Migliarino, Trelawny had to view another corpse. It had no clothing but the fragments of a shirt and a black silk scarf with the embroidered initials "E. E. W." that proved it to be Williams's. Three weeks later the sea gave up the last of the *Ariel* crew, when the headless skeleton of the boy Vivian was thrown upon the shores of Massa.

But the living could not claim the bodies of their dead. According to the strict quarantine laws of Italy, whatever the sea cast up had to be burned on the shore for fear of the plague. Vivian's remains were hastily cremated where found. Shelley's body and Williams's were first buried in quicklime in the sands of the beach until Mr. Dawkins, the *chargé d'affaires* at Florence, obtained permission that the ashes be returned to their wives for burial.

It fell to Trelawny to accomplish the last rite. On the fourteenth of August Williams's body was consumed on the shore. The following day Mary was taken to see the three white wands that marked the spot under which Shelley lay buried, and then, when she had gone, the pyre was erected.

No grander scene could have been chosen for a poet's funeral. The waves in quiet sorrow moaned against a stretch of golden sand, luminous in the sunlight. Behind, a great line of pine trees lifted their branches, their trunks rearing back as with fear of the sea that had been known to rip off their living bark in anger. The mountains glistened in the sun, reflecting the light from their marble veinings. No human abode but the watchman's temporary hut near the graveside disturbed the immense solitude.

When Byron and Hunt arrived, the body was exhumed, the remains laid in the iron furnace, and the pyre lighted. Byron, bitterly cynical the previous day at Williams's cremation, on mankind's pride and folly in cherishing what in the end is but a mass of decay, stood silent and thoughtful while the flames wrapt all that remained of one who had been as a torch in the world's darkness. Where was that bright spirit? Not here, where the consuming heat laid bare the heart of him before whose purity all other men were as beasts. Not in that seething brain, uncovered by the burst skull. Not anywhere in those white ashes over which, with shrill cries, a sea bird circled, undaunted by the heat that made the air a quivering veil. Byron could bear no more, and, plunging into the sea, swam off to the *Bolivar*.

In Shelley's notebook his last poem broke off in the middle of a line.

"Then what is life," I cried —

And Death had answered him.

In September, with the help of Captain Roberts and a number of Italian seamen, the *Ariel* was raised from ten fathoms of water near the spot where she had been hidden by the sea fog. She had not capsized. The stern had a gaping hole where another boat must have struck it. With an injury of that kind, and the tons of iron ballast she carried, Trelawny knew she had sunk at once.

Strange tales were circulated of how she had been run into by unscrupulous fellows who had thought Byron was on board with a box full of gold. But there is no evidence except the alleged deathbed confession made by an ignorant sailor many years later and repeated at third and fourth hand. And there is another, more plausible, report of the *Ariel's* last moments.

The crew of a vessel on its way to Leghorn had seen her

after she had left the port and, fearing for the safety of so frail a bark in the storm, bore down upon her to take the passengers on board. A *shrill* voice was heard to say, "No!" The captain, not knowing what to make of such daring, watched the men through his telescope as the boat contended with the furious sea. "For God's sake," a sailor shouted to them through a speaking trumpet, "reef your sails or you are lost!" One of the men, Williams, from the report, made an effort to lower the sails, — it was at this point that Captain Roberts, watching from the lighthouse, had seen the mainsail being lowered, — when his companion seized him roughly by the arm, as if to restrain him. [1]

Had Shelley willfully sought death? There were those sorrowful poems of the last year; the lines to Gisborne complaining of Mary's imperfect sympathy. There was the request for prussic acid, and the visit to the notary at Leghorn for the will. There was that letter to Jane with its foreboding, and the parting remark to Marianne Hunt: "If I die to-morrow, I have lived to be older than my father." But the sea, though it gave up its wrecks, kept the secret of that death.

In the shadow of the pyramid of Cestius, near the graves of little William and Keats, Shelley's ashes were buried — but not his heart. As Orpheus's body was torn to pieces by the frenzy of the Bacchantes, so would Shelley's have been by the love of his friends, had not Trelawny prevented it. Byron had demanded the skull, but the faithful pirate had let it burn, knowing what use had been made of one at Newstead. A piece of the jawbone, however, was taken away; and Shelley's heart, that had remained entire, he entrusted to Hunt, who begged for it as Shelley's "dearest" friend. Mary, grieved that anyone but her should possess so dear a relic, demanded it of him, but Hunt would not give it up. Mary, he was convinced, had made Shelley unhappy. He had seen with his own eyes the pain even her letters had caused him in Pisa; and Shelley had told him of her lack of understanding. "In *his* case, above all other human beings, no ordinary appearance

[1] This record was obtained by Clarissa Trant from Taafe, a member of the Pisa group, when she spoke with him in 1826. *Journal of Clarissa Trant, 1800–1832.*

of rights, even yours, can affect me," he wrote roundly to Mary. He surrendered the heart to her, however, on Jane's representing to him how grievous it was that Shelley's remains should divide those who should more than ever be united by friendship.

In London, when the notice of Shelley's death appeared in the *Examiner*, two men took up their pens to comment upon it, on the selfsame day. Sir Timothy Shelley's letter to Whitton began with a pious platitude, showing relief, rather than sorrow, as he plunged at once into a discussion of his son John's altered status. William Godwin's to Mary fairly exulted under its grim condolences. She was his own again, leveled to his unhappy state by the hand of death. "I looked on you as one of the daughters of prosperity . . . and I thought it was criminal to intrude upon you for ever the sorrows of an unfortunate old man and a beggar. You are now fallen to my own level; you are surrounded with adversity and with difficulty; and I no longer hold it sacrilege to trouble you with my adversities. . . . This sorrowful event is, perhaps, calculated to draw us nearer to each other." Three days later he wrote again. "I should think, however, that now that you have lost your closest friend your mind would naturally turn homeward, and to your earliest friend. . . . We have no battle to fight, — no contention to maintain, — that is over now."

But for Mary, though she had still many years to live, life, too, was over. She saw, however, Shelley's star rising from the clouds of prejudice and misunderstanding to the zenith of fame. She saw at last Sir Timothy, who had never acknowledged her, soften toward her son Percy, after Harriet's Charles, a boy as gentle and as sensitive as Shelley, had died in the old man's arms. She lived to see the baronet in his grave and Percy the heir to the fortune on which Shelley had built so many hopes for the world's improvement. But she lived also to behold in Shelley's son what Sir Timothy had wished his own son to be.

With Shelley gone, his little circle scattered. Clare set out for Vienna to escape the fascination of Trelawny, who had

offered to marry her.   And Jane with her babies returned to
her people in England.   She was early reconciled to her double
loss.   Four months after the anguished days of waiting at
Casa Magni, Godwin, who saw her, could say that she appeared in better health and spirits than he had expected; that
she dropped not a tear, and that occasionally she smiled.
"She is a picturesque little woman," he summed up.   Thomas
Jefferson Hogg felt the power of that picturesqueness over his
bachelor heart, which he lost the more readily on hearing of
Shelley's part in her life.   In 1827 they were married.

The Hunts, a flock of cuckoos in the Byron eyrie, drove
him insane with loathing.   He hated Marianne; he abhorred
her six little Yahoos.   Out of respect to Shelley's memory
he kept them on their floor of the Lanfranchi Palace, with his
dog Moretto on guard to prevent their trespassing.   But when,
thanks to the Tuscan authorities, the peregrinating Gambas
were again exiled, he found a pretext to be rid of his burden.
Marianne, in revenge, exercised her sharp wit at his lordship's expense and her yet sharper scissors in a silhouette,
representing him sneering — and with one foot smaller than
the other.

The *Liberal* proved a dismal failure.   From its appearance
in October, it showed plainly that its days were numbered.
It had no unity of purpose, no animating spirit, and with the
fourth issue it yielded up what ghost it had, to the relief of
Murray and his synod.   Byron was no less relieved.   Hunt,
of course, still depended on his lordship for maintainance;
but under a separate roof in Genoa the cuckoo and his young
could be more decently ignored.

In England Byron's popularity waned in proportion as he
produced his finest poetry.   The many-faceted diamond of
Don Juan dazzled but did not warm a generation accustomed
to the brilliant cynicism of disillusioned genius, yet too weak-
visioned to perceive the inmost fire of his sincerity.   It had
prized him when the dross of the mine clouded him; the jewel,
cut and brightened by life, was above their valuation.   Tastes
changed.   And when they changed they left no quarter.
With the appearance of *Werner* — one of the poorest of his
dramas, it is true — the reviews, without exception, decried

BYRON

MRS. HUNT'S SILHOUETTE

the poet.   But already he was preparing for the last phase of the Byron drama.

The Greeks had revolted from Turkish dominion, and all over Europe bands of sympathizers were uniting for the cause. In London the Greek Committee, composed of Englishmen, elected Byron to membership, and in July 1823, squired by Trelawny, Dr. Bruno, another Polidori, Count Pietro Gamba, Fletcher, the Venetian Tita, and a number of servants, and fortified by firearms and two small cannon, he embarked on the *Hercules,* chartered for the expedition to Greece.   In England Hobhouse smiled indulgently at this new emprise of the Childe. The day was a Friday, next to Sunday one of Byronic ill-omen; the date, the thirteenth.   He was nearing the birth-day designated by Mrs. Williams, the fortune-teller, as one of his most dangerous.   In spite of such ill auguries, he went on.

La Guiccioli, whom both the papal court and the papal count besought to return to her wifely duty, mourned broken-hearted for the lover who, after five years of fidelity, could find the uncertain liberation of a foreign country a stronger lure than her proved charms.   How little in those five years had she learned to know him!   And how little did she know herself!   Yet how could she have imagined that, with one of those hands that she was so prettily wringing in grief like a heroine of tragedy, she was to write to one cognizant of her dealings with Byron's autographs: "I wish that Ravenna be not mentioned, for I would not have it known that I am the seller of those MSS., and that town always calls up at once the thought of me.[1]

Fate did her best to forewarn her devotee.   First the *Hercules* was becalmed in a dead sea; then storms drove it to harbor.   "Where shall we be this day year?" he asked Gamba. Had he been answered, "In England," he would not have believed.   The *Hercules* finally arrived at its destination.   For a time Byron waited in a Greek island for directions from the Committee, and then proceeded to Missolonghi.

January 24.   A month of anniversaries.   Nine years ago that month he had made his fatal marriage.   He did not think

---

[1] Unpublished letter at the Pierpont Morgan Library, dated Feb. 2, 1835.   Translation by the author.

back upon it as in other days, with cynicism and bitterness. He had lost his rancor against Annabella, and could now imagine without horror a return to England, perhaps to home and child. He had heard that Annabella appeared more forgiving. . . . On the twenty-second he passed his thirty-sixth birthday, in the fever hole of Missolonghi where, years ago, he had nearly lost his life.

The Greek cause was none too prosperous. Quarrels among the factions imperiled the common aim; murder and mutiny were not unknown. With the inexperienced Count Pietro as one of his marshals, there was incompetence, with waste of men and money. Trelawny, after the disembarking, went his own way, joined the chieftain Odysseus on a mountain fastness, and, provided with a colorful Suliote costume and a harem, found the new allegiance more to his liking.

Byron, in spite of the odds against him, somehow kept the flame of revolution alive, until his health failed. Rain, rain, rain, in the infested swamp of Missolonghi, the meagre provisions to which he subjected himself, and his own carelessness of his health, brought on an attack that neither Bruno, nor any of the doctors whom Fletcher called, could diagnose. While he was lying helpless in his bed, his Suliote troops revolted for more pay. Staggering to their midst, he succeeded in quelling them when his aides had failed. By the middle of April he was confined to his room, subjected to bleedings and treatments whose efficacy the doctors themselves were not sure of. The fever kept him in constant delirium, when he fancied himself a Jew, a Mohammedan, a Christian of all denominations. The old doubts were having their revenge.

On a chair beside his bed lay his two pistols and a pocket Bible, Augusta's last gift. He could no longer see to read. On Easter Sunday when, through the muddy lanes of Missolonghi, the holy processions passed, Byron, knowing the end had come, called Fletcher to him. "My dear Ada! My God! Could I but have seen her! Give her my blessing. And my sister Augusta, and her children — and you will go to Lady Byron, and say — " The rattle of death obscured the final words. Fletcher understood nothing of that last message.

On the nineteenth of April, Leigh Hunt, walking with some friends in Italy, saw an enormous butterfly of an unknown variety poise near by and remain a long time. Their talk, as they studied it, turned to the Greek idea of the psyche. What spirit had taken that form? That day Byron had died. Thunder rumbled through the land of Greece, recently sounding with the Easter chants, and lightning flared over the body that knew peace at last.

Greece offered her noblest temple as its final resting place. But Fletcher knew that at the end Byron had looked toward home. The body was embalmed. Greek chieftains bore it on their shoulders to the church for the last obsequies before it was sent to England. Thousands of soldiers, unashamed of their tears, lined the way through which it passed, and Byron, dead, inspired them even more than he had in life.

"O Daughter!" the funeral orator apostrophized over the solemn corpse ". . . your arms will receive him. Your tears will bathe the tomb which shall contain his body; — and the tears of the orphans of Greece will be shed over the urn containing his precious heart, and over all the land of Greece, for all the land of Greece is his tomb."

Many years were to pass before Ada wept over her father's grave, and then it was to turn accuser against Lady Byron. A dangerous mingling of her father's wildness and Annabella's mathematical mind made for her destruction, after a mad career of gambling induced by her confidence in some unfailing law.

On the fifth of July, almost to the day of Byron's questioning of fate, a ship in mourning, — black with a wide blue band, — and carrying on the mainsail at half mast a pennant marked with a coronet, drew into the London docks. A barge pulled up alongside, and a coffin wrapped in a black pall was lowered into it. Byron's body had returned to England. As it was being carried north by road to the village church of Hucknall Torkard, near Newstead, — after Westminster had denied it burial space, — the procession passed the waiting carriage of Lady Caroline Lamb, recovering from a recent nervous collapse. She was not told whose *cortège* it was. "Remember me!" she had written on the flyleaf of Byron's copy of *Vathek*, at the height of her infatuation. His relentless hate answered her, even after death, when Medwin made haste to publish his conversations with Lord Byron.

> Remember thee!   Remember thee!
>   Till Lethe quench life's burning stream
> Reproach and shame shall cling to thee,
>   And haunt thee like a feverish dream!
>
> Remember thee!   Ay, doubt it not.
>   Thy husband, too, shall think of thee:
> By neither shalt thou be forgot,
>   Thou *false* to him, thou *fiend* to me!

Strange that of the women who had loved him, the two he had most despised, Clare, from a lodging house in Kentish Town, and Lady Caroline, should have crossed him on his last journey.

Augusta looked upon him before the coffin lid was sealed, and drew back at the calm impassibility of a face that she had seen in its tenderness — and also in its passions. All tumults were now at rest. She grieved for him as deeply as she was able to grieve, and to the end remained devoted to his memory. Newstead Abbey became for her the shrine of her love for her brother, and when, years later, she saw it again, through the kindness of Colonel Wildman, she wept with emotion. "You will believe that I value the very *feathers* of a Newstead bird," [1] she told him gratefully. And then she made a strange request. "I have *often, often* thought, and more particularly of late, that if you would allow me to be *your tenant* for two or three rooms in any lodge or cottage within the domain, I *might* for some few hours of my life enjoy peace. . . . If I could make my escape for a week or two . . . and wander about that dearly beloved place and be within reach of *Hucknall* I think it would give me the only comfort and happiness I ever *can* know in this world of sorrow." [2]   Augusta was no oak, unshaken by the storms she had still to experience. Nor was she steadfast in her courage for Byron's repute. Indeed, she

---

[1] Autograph letter by Augusta to Colonel Wildman, dated Sept. 12, 1829, in the Pierpont Morgan Library.
[2] Autograph letter of Augusta to Colonel Wildman, dated April 21, 1831, in the Pierpont Morgan Library.

had no sooner heard of his death than with Hobhouse and Moore she hastened the destruction of his Memoirs — for Lady Byron's sake, as she said, and led herself to believe. Rather was she the willow, weak and bending, the companion of the dead, waving "with fond fidelity, its boughs above a monument."

And Lady Byron? Throughout her long, lonely life she was shadowed by that fallen angel who had come in the spring of her life and turned it to endless winter. She lived under his terrible incantation: —

> There are shades which will not vanish,
> There are thoughts thou canst not banish;
> By a power to thee unknown,
> Thou canst never be alone;
> Thou are wrapt as with a shroud,
> Thou art gather'd in a cloud. . . .

In the places where they had been together, she sought him. She found him in those of his blood — in Augusta, in Ada, in Medora. All of them disappointed or betrayed her at the last. Circumscribed by the circle of his magic, she lived her secret life apart from the phantoms of the real world, and, to the end, she loved him.

The whole world felt Byron's loss. In England, Alfred Tennyson, a young lad who had begun to make verses, hid himself in the woods and on a moss-covered rock scratched the words: "Byron is dead."

It was an epitaph and a commencement.

BIBLIOGRAPHY

AIRLIE, MABELL, COUNTESS, *In Whig Society*. London, 1921.
ANGELI, HELEN ROSSETTI, *Shelley and His Friends in Italy*. London, 1911.
Athenæum, London, August 31, 1917, "Shelley's Indian Serenade," by H. Buxton Forman.
AUSTIN, ALFRED, *A Vindication of Lord Byron*. London, 1869.

BARBER, THOMAS G., *Hucknall Torkard Church*. Hucknall, 1925.
BECKFORD, WILLIAM, *Vathek*. London, 1905.
BIAGI, GUIDO, *Gli ultimi giorni di P. B. Shelley, con nuovi documenti*. Firenze, *La Voce*, 1922.
Blackwood's Magazine, October 1817, November 1817, January 1818, August 1818, December 1821, March 1822.
BLESSINGTON, MARGUERITE, COUNTESS, *Journal of Correspondence and Conversations with Lord Byron, etc.* Cincinnati, 1851.
BLUNDEN, EDMUND, *Leigh Hunt's "Examiner" Examined*. London, 1928.
BORN, STEPHAN, *Lord Byron*. Basel, 1883.
BRAILSFORD, HENRY NOEL, *Shelley, Godwin and Their Circle*. London, 1913.
BRAMSTON, MRS. CLARISSA SANDFORD TRANT, *The Journal of Clarissa Trant*. London, 1925.
BRIDGES, ROBERT, *John Keats, a Critical Essay*. Privately printed, 1895.
BRINTON, CRANE, *The Political Ideas of the English Romanticists*. London, 1926.
BRISCOE, WALTER A., Ed., *Byron the Poet — A Collection of Addresses and Essays* (Centenary volume). London, 1924.

Brucà, Renzo, "L'ultima dimora di Shelley: Villa Magni," in *Emporium*. Bergamo, August 1908.

Bulletin of Keats-Shelley Memorial. Edited by Sir Rennell Rodd and H. Nelson Gay. London and New York, 1910–1913.

Burch, R. A., "The Case of Shelley v. Westbrooke," in *Case and Comment*. Vol. 23. New York, 1916.

Byron, Lady Anna Isabella, *Remarks Occasioned by Moore's Notices of Lord Byron's Life*. London, 1830.

Byron, Lord, *The Works of*, 13 vols.: *Letters and Journals*, edited by R. E. P. Ernle, Vols. 1–6; *Poetry*, edited by E. H. Coleridge, Vols. 1–7.

———— *The Works of* with his *Letters and Journals* and his *Life*, by Thomas Moore. 17 vols. London, 1832–1833.

Caclamanos, D., "Lord Byron et la Grèce," in *Græcia*, April 1912.

Campbell, Olwen Ward, *Shelley and the Unromantics*. London, 1924.

Censor, "Singular Anecdote of Lord Byron." September 6, 1828.

Charpentier, J., *Coleridge*. New York, 1929.

Chew, Samuel C., *Byron in England*. London, 1924.

Clarke, Charles Cowden, and Mary, *Recollections of Writers*. London, 1878.

Clarke, Isabel C., *Shelley and Byron*. London, 1934.

Clutton-Brock, *Shelley, the Man and the Poet*. London, 1909.

Colvin, Sidney, *John Keats*. New York, 1817, also ed. of 1887.

Cornhill Magazine, "Shelley's First Wife," by W. Courthope Forman. January 1922.

Dallas, Robert C., *Recollections of Lord Byron*. London, 1824.

Dobell, Bertram, *Sidelights of Charles Lamb*. London and New York, 1903.

Dowden, Edward, *The French Revolution and English Literature*. New York, 1908.

—— *Life of Percy Bysshe Shelley.* 2 vols. London, 1886.
—— *Southey.* London, 1884.
DRINKWATER, JOHN, *The Pilgrim of Eternity.* London, 1925.
DU BOS, CHARLES, *Byron et le besoin de la fatalité.* Paris, 1929.

EDGCUMBE, RICHARD, *Byron, the Last Phase.* London, 1910.
EIMER, MANFRED, *Die persönlichen Beziehungen zwischen Byron und den Shelleys.* Heidelberg, 1910.
ELZE, KARL, *Lord Byron.* Strassburg, 1886.

FORMAN, H. BUXTON, Ed., *The Elopement of P. B. Shelley and Mary W. Godwin, As Narrated by William Godwin.* Privately printed for William K. Bixby. 1911.
FOX, SIR JOHN C., *The Byron Mystery.* London, 1924.
FREEMAN, A. MARTIN, *Thomas Love Peacock.* London, 1911.

GALT, JOHN, *The Life of Lord Byron.* London, 1830.
GAMBA, PIETRO, COUNT, *A Narrative of Lord Byron's Last Journey to Greece.* London, 1825.
GARNETT, RICHARD S., Ed., *Letters about Shelley.* London, 1916.
GARROD, H. W., *Keats.* Oxford, 1926.
GEEST, SIBYLLA, *Der Sensualismus bei John Keats.* Heidelberg, 1908.
GODWIN, WILLIAM, *An Enquiry Concerning Political Justice, etc.* London, 1793.
GRAHAM, WILLIAM, *Last Links with Byron, Shelley and Keats.* London, 1898.
GRIBBLE, F. H., *The Romantic Life of Shelley and the Sequel.* London, 1911.
GRIERSON, H. J. C., "Lord Byron," *British Acad. Proc.* London, 1920.
GUICCIOLI, TERESA, COUNTESS, *My Recollections of Lord Byron, etc.* Philadelphia, 1869.

HAYDON, BENJAMIN ROBERT, *Autobiography and Memoirs.* Edited by Alexander Penrose. New York, 1929.
HAZLITT, WILLIAM, *The Spirit of the Age.* London, 1825.

HITCHENER, ELIZABETH, *Letters of, to Percy Bysshe Shelley.* New York, 1926. Also in British Museum, Add. MSS. 37496.

HOBHOUSE, JOHN CAM, 1st BARON BROUGHTON, Historical illustrations of the Fourth Canto of *Childe Harold,* etc. New York, 1818.

—— *Recollections of a Long Life,* 2 vols. London, 1909–1910.

HODGSON, JAMES THOMAS, *Memoir.* 2 vols. London, 1878.

HOGG, THOMAS JEFFERSON, *Life of P. B. Shelley,* in 4 vols. (only two of which appeared). London, 1858.

HOTSON, LESLIE, *Shelley's Lost Letters to Harriet.* London, 1930.

HUNT, LEIGH, *Autobiography.* A new edition revised by the author. London, 1860.

—— *Lord Byron and Some of His Contemporaries.* London, 1828.

—— *Shelley–Leigh Hunt.* Edited by R. Brimley Johnson. London, 1928.

INGPEN, ROGER, *Shelley in England.* 2 vols. Boston and New York, 1917.

JEAFFRESON, J. C., *The Real Lord Byron.* 2 vols. London, 1883.

—— *The Real Shelley.* London, 1885.

KEATS, JOHN, Keats letters, papers, and other relics forming the Dilke bequest, reproduced in collotype facsimile. London, 1914.

—— *Letters.* Edited by Maurice Buxton Forman. 2 vols. Oxford, 1931.

—— *Poetical Works.* Edited with an introduction and notes by H. Buxton Forman. Oxford, 1929.

—— *Poetical Works.* Edited by E. de Sélincourt. 5th edition, 1926.

KOEPPEL, EMIL, "Lord Byron's Astarte," in *Englische Studien.* Vol. 30, pp. 193–204.

KOSZUL, ANDRÉ, *La Jeunesse de Shelley.* Paris, 1910.

LAMB, LADY C., *Fugitive Pieces and Reminiscences of Lord Byron*. London, 1829.
—— *Glenarvon*. London, 1816.
La Tribuna Illustrata, "Due documenti su Shelley." Roma, 9 agosto 1908.
LEWIS, M. G., *The Monk*. Reprint of first edition. 3 vols. London, 1906.
Liberal, The, Verse and Prose from the South. Printed for John Hunt, 1822–1823.
London Mercury, "Keats and Joseph Severn," by B. Ifor Evans. Vol. 30.
LOWELL, AMY, *John Keats*. 2 vols. Boston and New York, 1925.

MACCARTHY, DENIS F., *Shelley's Early Life, from Original Sources*. London, 1872.
MACKAY, CHARLES, *Medora Leigh; a History and an Autobiography*. London, 1869.
Macmillan's Magazine, "Shelley at Tremadoc." Vol. LXXV. December 1896.
MARSHALL, MRS. JULIAN, *Life and Letters of Mary W. Shelley*. 2 vols. London, 1889.
MASSINGHAM, H. J., *The Friend of Shelley* (Trelawny). London, 1930.
MATHIESON, WILLIAM LAW, *England in Transition, 1789–1832*. London, 1920.
MAUROIS, ANDRÉ, *Byron*. New York, 1930.
MAYNE, ETHEL COLBURN, *Byron*. Revised edition. New York, 1924.
—— *Life and Letters of A. I., Lady Noël Byron*, with introduction and epilogue by Mary, Countess of Lovelace. New York, 1929.
MEDWIN, THOMAS, *Journal of the Conversations of Lord Byron*. Second edition. London, 1824.
—— *Life of Percy Bysshe Shelley*, with introduction and commentary by H. Buxton Forman. Oxford, 1913.
MILBANKE, RALPH, EARL OF LOVELACE, *Astarte, A Fragment of Truth Concerning George Gordon, Lord Byron*. New

edition with many additional letters edited by Mary, Countess of Lovelace. London, 1921.

MILLER, BARNETTE, *Leigh Hunt's Relations with Byron, Shelley and Keats.* Columbia University Press, New York, 1910.

MILNES, RICHARD MONCKTON, Ed., *Life, Letters and Literary Remains of John Keats.* New York, 1848.

MONKHOUSE, COSMO, *Life of Leigh Hunt.* London, 1893.

MURRAY, JOHN (1778–1843), *Notes on Captain Medwin's Conversations of Lord Byron.* London, 1824.

MURRAY, JOHN, *Lord Byron and His Detractors.* Privately printed. London, 1906.

—— *Lord Byron's Correspondence,* chiefly with Lady Melbourne, etc. 2 vols. London, 1922.

MURRY, JOHN MIDDLETON, *Keats and Shakespeare.* Oxford, 1925.

—— *Studies in Keats.* Oxford, 1930.

NICOLSON, HAROLD, *Byron: the Last Journey.* Boston, 1924.

Nineteenth Century, "The Story of Gifford and Keats," by David Masson. Vol. XXXI. April 1892.

Notes and Queries, "Two Letters of John Keats." Vol. 163. London, 1932.

PARRY, WILLIAM, *The Last Days of Lord Byron.* London, 1825.

PAUL, KEGAN, *W. Godwin, His Friends and Contemporaries.* London, 1876.

PEACOCK, T. L., *Headlong Hall; Nightmare Abbey.* London and New York, 1908.

—— *Letters to Edward Hookham and P. B. Shelley.* Edited by Richard Garnett. Boston Bibliophile Society, 1910.

—— *Memoirs of Shelley.* Edited by H. F. B. Brett-Smith. London, 1909.

PECK, WALTER EDWIN, *Shelley, His Life and Work.* 2 vols. Boston and New York, 1927.

Pierpont Morgan Library. Manuscripts relative to Byron, Shelley, and Keats; also holograph letters, etc., by Byron, Shelley, and Keats.

P.M.L.A., "The Biographical Element in the Novels of Mary Wollstonecraft Shelley," by Walter Edwin Peck. Vol. 38. 1933.

POLIDORI, JOHN, *Diary of*, Edited by William Michael Rossetti. London, 1911.

——— *The Vampyre.* London, 1819.

PRAZ, MARIO, *La fortuna di Byron in Inghilterra.* Firenze, 1925.

PRIESTLEY, J. B., *Thomas Love Peacock.* New York, 1927.

RICHTER, HELENE, *Lord Byron, Persönlichkeit und Werk.* M. Niemeyer, 1929.

RIDLEY, M. R., *Keats' Craftsmanship.* Oxford, 1933.

ROSSETTI, WILLIAM MICHAEL, *Life of John Keats.* London, 1887.

SAINTSBURY, GEORGE, *Essays in English Literature.* London, 1891.

SHARP, WILLIAM, *Life and Letters of Joseph Severn.* New York, 1892.

SHELLEY, FRANCES, LADY, *Diary.* Edited by Richard Edgcumbe. 1913.

SHELLEY, JANE G., LADY, Ed., *Shelley Memorials.* Boston, 1859.

SHELLEY, MARY W., *History of a Six Weeks' Tour, etc.* London, 1817.

——— *Frankenstein.* London, 1818.

——— *Letters of Mary W. Shelley,* with introduction and notes by H. H. Harper. Boston Bibliophile Society, 1918.

SHELLEY, PERCY BYSSHE, *Complete Works.* Edited by Roger Ingpen and W. E. Peck. Limited edition. 10 vols. London, 1926–1930.

——— *Complete Poetical Works,* with notes and a memoir by W. M. Rossetti. London, 1878.

——— *Letters of.* Collected and edited by Roger Ingpen. 2 vols. London, 1909.

——— *Letters from P. B. Shelley to Elizabeth Hitchener.* London, 1908.

——— *Note Books of P. B. Shelley.* From originals in the

library of W. K. Bixby, edited by H. Buxton Forman.
3 vols.   Boston Bibliophile Society, 1911.
────── *Prose Works*.   Edited by H. Buxton Forman.   4 vols.
London, 1880.
────── *Verse and Prose from the MSS. of P. B. Shelley*.   Ed-
ited by Sir John C. E. Shelley-Rolls, and Roger Ingpen.
Privately printed.   London, 1934.
────── *Works*.   Edited with notes by Mrs. Shelley.   London,
1847.
SOUTHEY, ROBERT, *Poetical Works, Collected by Himself*.
10 vols.   London, 1837–1838.
SPENDER, HAROLD, *Byron and Greece*.   London, 1924.
STOWE, HARRIET BEECHER, *Lady Byron Vindicated*.   Boston,
1870.
SWANN, ELSIE, *Christopher North* (John Wilson).   Edin-
burgh, London, 1934.

TRELAWNY, EDWARD JOHN, *Adventures of a Younger Son,* with
introduction by R. Garnett.   London, 1890.
────── *Records of Shelley, Byron and the Author*.   2 vols.
London, 1878.
────── Also original version, *Last Days of Shelley and Byron*.
Boston, 1858.

VAN DOREN, CARL, *Life of Thomas Love Peacock*.   London
and New York, 1911.

WILLIAMS, EDWARD ELLEKER, *Journal of,* with an introduction
by R. Garnett.   London, 1902.
WISE, THOMAS J., *A Bibliography of Byron*.   2 vols.   Pri-
vately printed.
────── *A Shelley Library*.   Printed for private circulation.
London, 1924.
────── *Letters of Harriet Shelley to Catherine Nugent*.   1889.

INDEX